Teaching and Researching Writing

APPLIED LINGUISTICS IN ACTION

General Editors:
Christopher N. Candlin and David R. Hall

Teaching and Researching Writing

Second Edition

Ken Hyland

Longman
is an imprint of

Harlow, England • London • New York • Boston • San Francisco • Toronto
Sydney • Tokyo • Singapore • Hong Kong • Seoul • Taipei • New Delhi
Cape Town • Madrid • Mexico City • Amsterdam • Munich • Paris • Milan

PEARSON EDUCATION LIMITED

Edinburgh Gate
Harlow CM20 2JE
United Kingdom
Tel: +44 (0)1279 623623
Fax: +44 (0)1279 431059
Website: www.pearsoned.co.uk

First edition published in Great Britain in 2002
Second edition published in 2009

© Pearson Education Limited 2002, 2009

The right of Ken Hyland to be identified as author
of this work has been asserted by him in accordance
with the Copyright, Designs and Patents Act 1988.

ISBN: 978-1-4082-0505-1

British Library Cataloguing in Publication Data
A CIP catalogue record for this book can be obtained from the British Library

Library of Congress Cataloging in Publication Data
A CIP catalog record for this book can be obtained from the Library of Congress

10   9   8   7   6   5   4   3   2   1
13   12   11   10   09

Set in 11/13pt Janson by 35
Printed in Malaysia (CTP-VVP)

The Publisher's policy is to use paper manufactured from sustainable forests.

Contents

General editors' preface

Applied Linguistics *in Action*, as its name suggests, is a Series which focuses on the issues and challenge to teachers and researchers in a range of fields in Applied Linguistics and provides readers and users with the tools they need to carry out their own practice-related research.

The books in the Series provide the reader with clear, up-to-date, accessible and authoritative accounts of their chosen field within Applied Linguistics. Starting from a map of the landscape of the field, each book provides information on its main ideas and concepts, competing issues and unsolved questions. From there, readers can explore a range of practical applications of research into those issues and questions, and then take up the challenge of undertaking their own research, guided by the detailed and explicit research guides provided. Finally, each book has a section which is concurrently on the Series *website* (www.pearsoned.co.uk/alia) and which provides a rich array of resources, information sources and further reading, as well as a key to the principal concepts of the field.

Questions the books in this innovative Series ask are those familiar to all teachers and researchers, whether very experienced, or new to the fields of Applied Linguistics.

1. What does research tell us, what doesn't it tell us and what should it tell us about the field? How is the field mapped and landscaped? What is its geography?
2. How has research been applied and what interesting research possibilities does practice raise? What are the issues we need to explore and explain?

3. What are the key researchable topics that practitioners can undertake? How can the research be turned into practical action?

4. Where are the important resources that teachers and researchers need? Who has the information? How can it be accessed?

Each book in the Series has been carefully designed to be as accessible as possible, with built-in features to enable readers to find what they want quickly and to home in on the key issues and themes that concern them. The structure is to move from practice to theory and back to practice in a cycle of development of understanding of the field in question.

Each of the authors of books in the Series is an acknowledged authority, able to bring broad knowledge and experience to engage teachers and researchers in following up their own ideas, working with them to build further on *their* own experience.

Applied Linguistics *in Action* is an **in action** Series. Its website will keep you updated and regularly re-informed about the topics, fields and themes in which you are involved.

The first editions of books in this series have attracted widespread praise for their authorship, their design, and their content, and have been widely used to support practice and research. The success of the series, and the realization that it needs to stay relevant in a world where new research is being conducted and published at a rapid rate, have prompted the commissioning of this second edition. This new edition has been thoroughly updated, with accounts of research that has appeared since the first edition and with the addition of other relevant additional material. We trust that students, teachers and researchers will continue to discover inspiration in these pages to underpin their own investigations.

Chris Candlin & David Hall
General Editors

Acknowledgements

First of all I would like to acknowledge the editors of the *Teaching and Researching* series, Chris Candlin and David Hall, for asking me to revise this book. I admit that I thought the process would be much easier than it turned out to be, but I was helped considerably by their distinctive format for the series, their encouragement and their good advice.

The book also owes a great debt to the colleagues and friends who have shared their research and materials with me. Here I would particularly like to thank John Swales and Chris Feak for extracts from *English in Today's Research World*; Janet Holst for her writing course *Writ 101*; John Milton for his programs *WordPilot*, *Check My Words* and *Mark My Words*; Stephen Hill for his teaching materials for a Foundation Degree course; and Polly Tse for her collaboration with me on the research which informs the section on the *Academic Word List*. I would also like to thank the Institute of Education, University of London, for the space to write this edition during a period of study-leave, my students and colleagues involved in the MATESOL at the IOE, and everyone in CAPLITS for their support, constant enthusiasm for writing and their teaching ideas.

Finally, for her encouragement, inspiration, and many thought-provoking conversations about writing, I thank Fiona Hyland.

Introduction

In some ways it is harder to rewrite than to write; one is constrained by the frame of the original yet there are things which need changing, others to delete, and more to discuss. But while the subject of writing has advanced through research and debate in the seven years since the first edition of this book, much of what we know about it, and about studying it, have remained more or less intact. Analysts have widened the scope of what they study to recognise the role of writing in areas such as conveying expertise and structuring identity, and have acknowledged its importance in fields such as forensic linguistics and rapidly changing internet communications such as blogs, wikis and twittering. Teachers too have moved on, making greater use of genre approaches to writing instruction and bringing computer communication more centrally into their work. Essentially, however, we are still concerned with writers, with readers, and with texts, although these may interact now in very different ways.

Those who know the first edition will recognise that I have retained the distinctive organisation of the series and also much of the content. All chapters have been extensively rewritten, but Chapters 2 and 4 are new. The intention behind the book also remains the same: to introduce readers to current thinking about writing: what we know of it, how we study it and how we teach it. My aim, then, is to provide a clear and critical introduction to the field of writing research and teaching.

Writing remains, of course, a central topic in applied linguistics and continues to be an area of lively intellectual research and debate in a range of disciplines. Its complex, multifaceted nature constantly evades adequate description and explanation, and many forms of enquiry have been summoned to help clarify both how writing works and how it should best be taught. One factor, which both drives this interest and complicates its study, is the overarching significance it has in our lives, not only in our professional and social activities, but in determining our life chances. Writing is central to our personal experience and social identities, and we are often evaluated by our control of it. The various purposes of writing, its myriad contexts of use and the diverse backgrounds and needs of those wishing to learn it, all push the study of writing into wider frameworks of analysis and understanding.

This book seeks to identify and survey these frameworks, setting out the dominant paradigms, exploring their key concepts, elaborating some applications of writing research, raising some important researchable issues, and providing a compendium of resources on writing.

Like other books in this series, *Teaching and Researching Writing* is divided into four main sections. In Section I I provide a brief historical and conceptual overview of the field and examine some of the key issues that occupy writing researchers. My purpose here is to map the terrain. Chapter 1 explores the main approaches to the study of writing, examining their strengths and shortcomings, and describes their theoretical orientations, methods and contributions, while Chapter 2 looks more closely at some of the key issues raised by these research paradigms.

In Section II I turn to some of the ways that writing theory and research currently inform practice, drawing on examples from Australia, Hong Kong, Papua New Guinea, New Zealand, England and North America, and which cover a range of age, proficiency and first-language contexts. Chapter 3 focuses on writing courses and Chapter 4 on pedagogic tools and methods, each case illustrating an element of the current debates on writing.

In Section III I discuss research issues and suggest some important areas which teachers, students or other practitioners can pursue through action research. Once again I present this section as a series of case-studies both to illustrate principal issues and to offer practical strategies for undertaking research in these areas. Chapter 5 discusses the nature of practitioner research, Chapter 6 presents research cases which involve methods of observation and reporting, and Chapter 7 examines examples of research into texts and contexts.

Finally, Section IV is a compendium of resources, indicating the major areas of writing research and practice and providing information on the key sources and contacts. In Chapter 8 I outline some of the main fields which contribute to our understanding of writing, and suggest a selection of key texts in these areas. In Chapter 9 I provide a directory of the most important sources of information, professional associations and conferences relevant to teachers and researchers of writing. Finally, there is a glossary of selected terms.

In this way I hope to cover the main theories, issues, research methodologies and teaching applications in a way which reveals the strong cycle of practice–theory–practice inherent in the field of writing. I also hope that the book will encourage readers to engage with the issues discussed and explore some of the issues the book raises.

Concepts and issues

Chapter 1

An overview of writing

This chapter will...

- explore approaches to teaching and research based on the main dimensions of writing: the code, the encoder, and the decoder;
- examine their principal ideas, key figures, significant findings and major weaknesses;
- consider how these approaches have influenced writing instruction.

In this chapter I discuss three broad approaches to researching and teaching writing, focusing in turn on theories that are mainly concerned with texts, with writers and with readers. I admit that this classification takes certain liberties, but I imply no rigid divisions, and in fact the approaches are only coherent to the extent that they respond to and critique each other. By focusing on writing in this way, however, I hope to highlight something of what we know about writing and what each offers to our understanding of this complex area.

Concept 1.1 **Approaches to writing**

- The first approach focuses on the products of writing by examining *texts*, either through their formal surface elements or their discourse structure.
- The second approach, divided into Expressivist, Cognitivist and Situated strands, focuses on the writer and describes writing in terms of the *processes* used to create texts.

> • The third approach emphasises the role that *readers* play in writing, adding a social dimension to writing research by elaborating how writers engage with an audience in creating texts.

1.1 Text-oriented research and teaching

The first category focuses on the tangible, analysable aspects of writing by viewing it as a textual product. By looking at surface forms, these theories have in common an interest in the linguistic or rhetorical resources available to writers for producing texts, and so reduce the intricacies of human communication to the manageable and concrete. Text-focused theories have taken a variety of forms, but I will describe two broad approaches here, together with the beliefs about the teaching and learning of writing that they imply.

1.1.1 Texts as objects

The dominant model for many years saw writing as a textual product, a coherent arrangement of elements structured according to a system of rules.

Concept 1.2   **Texts as objects**

Based on ideas inherited from structuralism and implicit in the Transformational Grammar of Noam Chomsky, a basic premise of this approach is that texts are autonomous objects which can be analysed and described independently of particular contexts, writers, or readers. Texts have a structure, they are orderly arrangements of words, clauses and sentences, and by following grammatical rules writers can encode a full semantic representation of their intended meanings.

The idea that texts can function independently of a context carries important ideological implications, and one of the most serious is the mechanistic view that human communication works by transferring ideas from one mind to another via language (Shannon and Weaver, 1963). Writing is disembodied. It is removed from context and the personal experiences of writers and readers because meanings can be encoded in texts and recovered by anyone who speaks the same language as the writer. Writers and readers conform to homogeneous practices so writing is treated like an object, and its rules imposed on passive users. This view of writing is still alive and kicking in a great deal of teaching of business writing and, indeed, is implicit in some notions of learning in western education systems. In many schools students are asked to write simply to demonstrate their knowledge of decontextualised facts with little awareness of a reader beyond the teacher–examiner. In these situations grammatical accuracy and clear exposition are often the main criteria of good writing.

Such a focus on form has led to considerable research into the regularities we find in texts. In recent years, for example, computer analyses of large corpora have been used to identify how functions such as stance (Biber, 2006) and negation (Tottie, 1991) are commonly expressed in writing. An orientation to formal features of texts has also underpinned a great deal of research into students' writing development. From this perspective, writing improvement can be measured by counting increases in features such as relative clauses, modality and passives through successive pieces of writing. White (2007), for instance, sought to assess language improvement in student writing by measuring increases in the number of morphemes, words and clauses in student essays. Shaw and Liu (1998), on the other hand, looked at features of academic writing such as impersonality, hedging and formality, and discovered 'a general move from a spoken to a written style' in essays in a three-month EAP presessional course.

From a perspective that regards texts as autonomous objects, then, learners' compositions are seen as *langue*, that is, a demonstration of the writer's knowledge of forms and his or her awareness of the system of rules to create texts. The goal of writing instruction therefore becomes training in accuracy, and for many years writing was essentially an extension of grammar teaching. Informed by a behavioural, habit-formation theory of learning, guided composition and substitution exercises became the main teaching methods, and these needed no context but the classroom and only the skill of avoiding errors. The teacher was an expert passing on knowledge to novices and there was a prescribed view of texts. This approach can still be found in classes around the world and survives in style guides, 'how to write effectively' books, and some textbooks.

But while this has been a major classroom approach for many years, the claim that good writing is context-free, that it is fully explicit and takes nothing for granted, draws on the rather old-fashioned and discredited belief that meaning is contained in the message. This lies behind the familiar *conduit metaphor* of language: that we have thoughts which we form into words to send to others which they receive and find the same thoughts – so meanings correspond with words and writing is transparent in reflecting meanings rather than constructing them. So we transfer ideas from one mind to another through language and meanings can be written down and understood by anyone with the right encoding and decoding skills. A text says everything that needs to be said – so there are no conflicts of interpretations, no reader positions, no different understandings, because we all see things in the same way. Clearly this fails to take account of the beliefs and knowledge writers assume readers will draw on in reading their texts.

Quote 1.1   On 'explicitness'

A text is explicit not because it says everything all by itself but rather because it strikes a careful balance between what needs to be said and what may be assumed. The writer's problem is not just being explicit; the writer's problem is knowing what to be explicit about.

Nystrand, Doyle and Himley (1986: 81)

Even academic articles, the most seemingly explicit of genres, draw on readers' assumed understandings. Through features such as references to prior research, technical lexis and familiarity with particular argument forms, writers work to establish a coherent context and enrich propositional meanings (e.g. Bazerman, 1988; Hyland, 2004a). Equally, this is how lawyers justify their fees, by disputing the exact meaning of even the most precisely written contracts and other legal documents. In sum, inferences are always involved in recovering meanings: no text can be both coherent and context-free.

Teacher responses to writing in this perspective tend to focus on error correction and identifying problems in students' control of language rather than how meanings are being conveyed. Moreover, we can see an autonomous view of writing reflected in the design of many large international exams. Indirect assessments, typically multiple choice, cloze or error recognition tasks, are widely used in evaluating writing. But while they are sometimes said to be reliable measures of writing skill (e.g. DeMauro, 1992) and facilitate reliability, they have little to do with the fact that communication, and not accuracy, is the purpose of writing. Moreover, even direct writing tasks, which require students to write one or two timed essays of a few hundred words, may lack 'authenticity' and provide little information about students' abilities to produce a sustained piece of writing for different audiences or purposes.

In fact, focusing on accuracy is exactly the wrong place to look for writing improvement as there is little evidence to show that either syntactic complexity or grammatical accuracy are the best measures of good writing. Many students can construct syntactically accurate sentences and yet are unable to produce appropriate written texts. Moreover, while fewer errors might be seen as an index of progress, this may equally indicate the writer's reluctance to take risks and reach beyond a current level of competence. To put this more directly, focusing exclusively on formal features of texts as a measure of writing competence ignores how texts are the writer's response to a particular communicative setting. Written texts cannot be autonomous precisely because they participate in a particular situation and reflect that situation in their pages.

> **Quote 1.2** Brandt on autonomous texts
>
> Identifying the mode of a text or enumerating its T-unit length or the density and range of its cohesive devices may lend insights into the structure of written texts, however, it can describe only one or another static outcome of the writer's dynamic and complex effort to make meaning. Yet the finished text need not be abandoned in our pursuit to understand the composing act – not, that is, if we shift our focus from the formal features of an isolated text toward the whole text as an instance of language functioning in a context of human activity.
>
> Brandt (1986: 93)

What this means for teaching is that no particular feature can be said to be a marker of good writing because what is 'good' varies across contexts. We can't just list the features needed to produce a successful text without considering appropriate purpose, audience, tone, formality, and so on. Simply, students don't just need to know how to write a grammatically correct text, but how to apply this knowledge for particular purposes and genres.

1.1.2   Texts as discourse

While an autonomous model views texts as forms which can be analysed independently of any real-life uses, another way of seeing writing as a material artefact looks beyond surface structures to see texts as *discourse* – the way we use language to communicate, to achieve purposes in particular situations. Here the writer is seen as having certain goals and intentions and the ways we write are resources to accomplish these. So instead of forms being disembodied and independent of contexts, a discourse approach sees them as located in social actions. Teachers following this line aim to identify the ways that texts actually work as communication by linking language forms to purposes and contexts.

Concept 1.3   Discourse

Discourse refers to language in action, and to the purposes and functions linguistic forms serve in communication. Here the linguistic patterns of texts point to contexts beyond the page, implying a range of social constraints and choices which operate on writers in any situation. The writer has certain goals and intentions, certain relationships to his or her readers, and certain information to convey, and the forms of a text are resources used to accomplish these. These factors draw the analyst into a wider perspective which locates texts in a world of communicative purposes and social action, identifying the ways that texts actually work as communication.

A variety of approaches has considered texts as discourse, but all have tried to discover how writers organise language to produce coherent, purposeful prose. An early contribution was the 'functional sentence perspective' of the Prague School which sought to describe how we structure text to represent our assumptions about what is known (*given*) or *new* to the reader (e.g. Firbas, 1986). This was taken up and elaborated in the work of Halliday (Halliday and Matthiessen, 2004) in the concept of *theme–rheme* structure. Roughly, theme is what the writer is talking about and rheme what he or she is saying about it: the part of the message that the writer considers important. Theme and rheme help writers organise clauses into information units that push the communication forward through a text and make it easy for readers to follow. This is because we expect old information to come first as a context for new, but breaking this pattern can be confusing. In (1), for example, the writer establishes a pattern in which the rheme of the first sentence becomes the themes of the next three, clearly signposting the progression. The theme of the final sentence, however, breaks the sequence, surprising the reader and disturbing processability.

(1) <u>Non-verbal communication</u> is traditionally divided into paralanguage, proxemics, body language and haptics. <u>Paralanguage</u> refers to the non-verbal vocal signs that accompany speech. <u>Proxemics</u> concerns physical distance and orientation. <u>Body language</u> describes expression, posture and gesture. The study of touch is called <u>haptics</u>.

A different strand of research has tried to identify the rhetorical functions of particular discourse units, examining what pieces of text are trying to do and how they fit into a larger structure. Winter (1977) and Hoey (1983), for example, distinguish several patterns which they label *problem-solution*, *hypothetical-real* and *general-particular*. They show that even with no explicit signalling, readers are able to draw on their knowledge of recognisable text patterns to infer the connections between clauses, sentences or groups of sentences. For example, we all have a strong expectation of how a problem–solution pattern will progress, so that we look for a positive evaluation of at least one possible solution to complete the pattern. This pattern is illustrated in Concept 1.4 below.

Concept 1.4   Problem–solution pattern

1. *Situation*: We now accept that grammar is not restricted to writing but is present in speech.
2. *Problem*: This can lead to assumptions that there is one kind of grammar for writing and one for speech.
3. *Response*: A large-scale corpus survey of English has been undertaken.
4. *Evaluation of response*: Results show the same system is valid for both writing and speech.

(Example based on a conference abstract.)

These kinds of descriptions lead us to the idea that we must draw on some notion of shared assumptions to account for what we recognise as connected text. That is to say, part of what makes writing coherent lies in the reader's background knowledge and interpretive abilities rather than in the text. One model of how this is done suggests that readers call on their conventionalised knowledge to impose a coherent frame on a message. They interpret discourse by analogy with their earlier experiences which are organised in their heads as *scripts* or *schemata* (e.g. Schank and Abelson, 1977). Thus we carry around stereotypical understandings which we use as 'scaffolding' to interpret the texts we encounter every day, allowing us to read texts as diverse as detective thrillers and postcards.

A second approach, more pragmatic than this cognitive model, proposes that writers try to create texts which are as relevant to readers as possible, and that readers anticipate this when recovering meaning. This approach originates with Grice's (1975) principles of conversational inference, which try to explain successful communication in terms of interactants' mutual assumptions of rationality and cooperation. Building on this idea, Sperber and Wilson (1986) argue that readers construct meanings by comparing the information they find in a text with what they already know about the context to establish meanings that are relevant. In other words, when we interpret a text, we assume that the writer is being cooperative by thinking of what it is we need to know to fully understand what is going on, and so we look for ways of interpreting what we read as relevant to the ongoing discourse in some way.

In these theories, interpretation depends on the ability of readers to supply needed assumptions from memory, but the text itself also plays an important part in this process. Kramsch argues that the construction of meaning from texts is a rhetorical and not just a cognitive process, and proposes seven principles of text interpretation which draw on current theories of discourse analysis.

Quote 1.3 **Principles of a rhetorical approach to text interpretation**

1. Texts both refer to a reality beyond themselves and a relationship to their readers.
2. The meaning of texts is inseparable from surrounding texts, whether footnotes, diagrams or conversations. Intertextuality refers to the extent our texts echo other texts.
3. Texts attempt to position readers in specific ways by evoking assumed shared schemata.
4. Schemata are created by relating one text or fact to another through logical links.
5. Schemata reflect the ways of thinking of particular communities or cultures.

6. Schemata are co-constructed by the writer in dialogue with others.
7. Schemata are rhetorical constructions, representing the choices from other potential meanings.

Kramsch (1997: 51–2)

The idea that forms express functions and that they vary according to context is a central notion of discourse analysis and underpins the key notion of *genre*.

Concept 1.5   **Genre**

Genre is a term for grouping texts together, representing how writers typically use language to respond to recurring situations. Every genre has a number of features which make it different to other genres: each has a specific purpose, an overall structure, specific linguistic features, and is shared by members of the culture. For many people it is an intuitively attractive concept which helps to organise the common-sense labels we use to categorise texts and the situations in which they occur.

The concept of genre is based on the idea that members of a community usually have little difficulty in recognising similarities in the texts they use frequently and are able to draw on their repeated experiences with such texts to read, understand and perhaps write them relatively easily. This is, in part, because writing is a practice based on expectations: the reader's chances of interpreting the writer's purpose are increased if the writer takes the trouble to anticipate what the reader might be expecting based on previous texts they have read of the same kind. We know immediately, for example, whether a text is a recipe, a joke or a love letter and can respond to it and write a similar one if we need to. We all have a repertoire of these responses we can call on to communicate in familiar situations, and we learn new ones as we need them. Genres encourage us to look for organisational patterns, or the ways that texts are rhetorically structured to achieve a social purpose.

We find such structures in even the most apparently personal and expressive kind of writing, such as the acknowledgements in the opening pages of a student thesis or dissertation. In an analysis of the acknowledgements in 240 dissertations written by Hong Kong Ph.D.

and M.A. students, for example, I found a three-move structure consisting of a main Thanking Move sandwiched between optional Reflecting and Announcing Moves (Hyland, 2004b).

As Concept 1.6 shows the writer begins with a brief introspection on his or her research experience. Then there is the main Thanking Move where credit is given to individuals and institutions for help with the dissertation, and this can consist of up to four steps. First, a sentence introducing those to be thanked, followed by thanks for academic help. This was the only step that occurred in every single text, supervisors were always mentioned, and always before anyone else. Next there is thanks for providing resources such as clerical, technical and financial help, and then thanks for moral support from family and friends for encouragement, friendship, etc. The final Announcing Move was uncommon, but here writers accept responsibility to show that the thesis is theirs and not the work of those they have thanked.

Concept 1.6   Dissertation acknowledgements

Move	Example
1. Reflecting Move	The most rewarding achievement in my life, as I approach middle age, is the completion of my doctoral dissertation.
2. Thanking Move	
2.1 Presenting participants	During the time of writing I received support and help from many people.
2.2 Thanks for academic help	I am profoundly indebted to my supervisor, Dr. Robert Chau who assisted me in each step to complete the thesis.
2.3 Thanks for resources	I am grateful to The Epsom Foundation whose research travel grant made the field work possible and to the library staff who tracked down elusive texts for me.
2.4 Thanks for moral support	Finally, thanks go to my wife who has been an important source of emotional support.
3. Announcing Move	However, despite all this help, I am the only person responsible for errors in the thesis.

The analysis showed this structure was common in almost all the acknowledgements and that where steps occurred they did so in this sequence. It also showed the ways thanks are typically expressed in this genre. So, of all the ways of expressing thanks (*I am grateful to, I appreciate, I want to thank*, etc.) the noun *thanks* was used in over half of all cases and this was modified by only three adjectives: *special, sincere*, and *deep*, with *special* comprising over two-thirds of all cases. When analysing these texts I also found that virtually all thanks included the reason for acknowledging the person, as in these examples:

(2) First of all, special thanks to my supervisor, Dr. Angel Lin, for her consistent and never-failing encouragement, support and help.

My special gratitude goes to my family who made it possible for me to embark on writing a Ph.D. thesis at all.

I should also thank my wife, Su Meng, who spent days and nights alone with our daughter taking care of all the tasks that should have been shared by me as a father and a husband.

This suggests that writers were not only addressing the people they acknowledged, who presumably knew what help they had given, but a much wider audience, representing themselves as good researchers and sympathetic human beings who are deserving of the degree. Examining specific genres by studying patterns and recurring features therefore tells us a lot about what writers are trying to achieve and the language they are using to do it.

In the classroom teachers build models based on such analyses of texts and adopt a highly interventionist role, acting as a guide leading students through the typical rhetorical patterns of the genres they need to produce (Hyland, 2004c).

Concept 1.7	**Advantages of genre-based writing instruction**
Explicit	Makes clear what is to be learnt to facilitate the acquisition of writing skills.
Systematic	Provides a coherent framework for focusing on both language and contexts.
Needs-based	Ensures that course objectives and content are derived from students' needs.
Supportive	Gives teachers a central role in scaffolding students' learning and creativity.

Empowering	Provides access to the patterns and possibilities of variation in valued texts.
Critical	Gives students the resources to understand and challenge valued discourses.
Consciousness Raising	Increases teachers' awareness of texts to advise students on writing.

Like the earlier views of writing as texts, there is an emphasis on writing as an outcome of activity rather than as activity itself. But while the focus has shifted from autonomous meanings to discourse, and from isolated sentences to the ways in which language creates texts, writing largely remains the logical construction and arrangement of forms.

1.2 Writer-oriented research and teaching

The second broad approach takes the writer, rather than the text, as the point of departure. The theories in this section address the general issue of what it is that good writers do when confronted with a composing task, and seek to formulate the methods that will best help learners acquire these skills. Here I want to sketch the main contours of three positions which together have contributed to the hugely influential process writing movement:

- the first focuses on the personal creativity of the individual writer
- the second on the cognitive processes of writing
- the third on the writer's immediate context.

1.2.1 Writing as personal expression

Concept 1.8   **Expressivist view of writing**

Originating with the work of Elbow (1998), Murray (1985) and others, this view encourages writers to find their own voices to produce writing that is fresh and spontaneous. There is an underlying assumption that thinking precedes writing and that the free expression of ideas can

encourage self-discovery and cognitive maturation. Writing development and personal development are seen as symbiotically interwoven to
the extent that 'good therapy and composition aim at clear thinking,
effective relating, and satisfying self-expression' (Moffett, 1982: 235).

The Expressivist view strongly resists a narrow definition of writing
based on notions of correct grammar and usage. Instead it sees writing
as a creative act of discovery in which the process is as important as the
product to the writer. Writing is learnt, not taught, and the teacher's
role is to be non-directive and facilitating, providing writers with the
space to make their own meanings through an encouraging, positive,
and cooperative environment with minimal interference. Because
writing is a developmental process, teachers are encouraged not to
impose their views, give models, or suggest responses to topics beforehand. On the contrary, they are urged to stimulate the writer's thinking
through pre-writing tasks, such as journal-writing and analogies
(Elbow, 1998), and to respond to the ideas that the writer produces.
This, then, is writing as self-discovery.

Quote 1.4 Rohman on 'good writing'

'Good writing' is that discovered combination of words which allows a
person the integrity to dominate his subject with a pattern both fresh
and original. 'Bad writing', then, is an echo of someone else's combination
which we have merely taken over for the occasion of our writing... 'Good
writing' must be the discovery by a responsible person of his uniqueness
within his subject.

Rohman (1965: 107–8)

Unfortunately, as North (1987) points out, this approach offers no
clear theoretical principles from which to evaluate 'good writing', nor
does it furnish advice that can help accomplish it. This is because good
writing, for Expressivists, does not reflect the application of rules but
that of the writer's free imagination.

The Expressivist manifesto, as Faigley (1986) observes, is essentially
a romantic one. It promotes vague goals of 'self-actualisation' and even
vaguer definitions of good writing which depend on subjective, hazy

and culturally variable concepts such as *originality, integrity* and *spontaneity*. This, then, is the extreme learner-centred stance. The writer is the centre of attention, and his or her creative expression the principal goal. Unfortunately the basic assumption that all writers have similar innate intellectual and creative potential and simply require the right conditions to express this, now seems rather naïve. Essentially the approach is seriously under-theorised and leans heavily on an asocial view of the writer, operating in a context where there are no cultural differences in the value of 'self-expression', no variations in personal inhibition, few distinctions in the writing processes of mature and novice writers, and no social consequences of writing.

While Expressivism has helped to move writing teaching and research away from a restricted attention to form, it ignores communication in the real-world contexts where writing matters. But despite its limitations, the Expressivist approach is still influential in many US first-language classrooms, underpins courses in creative writing, and has helped inspire research to support a cognitive view of writing.

1.2.2   Writing as a cognitive process

Interest in writers' composing processes has been extended beyond notions of creativity and self expression to focus on the cognitive aspects of writing. This is a very different view of process as it draws on the techniques and theories of cognitive psychology and not literary creativity. Essentially it sees writing as a problem-solving activity: how writers approach a writing task as a problem and bring intellectual resources to solving it. This view of writing has developed a range of sophisticated investigative methods, generated an enormous body of research, and was, until recently, the dominant approach to teaching writing.

Concept 1.9   **The writing process**

At the heart of this model is the view that writing is a 'non-linear, exploratory and generative process whereby writers discover and reformulate their ideas as they attempt to approximate meaning' (Zamel, 1983: 165). Following Emig's (1983) description of composing as 're-cursive', rather than as an uninterrupted, *Pre-writing->Writing->Post-writing* activity, a great deal of research has revealed the complexity of planning and editing activities, the influence of different writing tasks and the value of examining what writers do through a series of writing drafts. Case-studies and think-aloud protocols, rather than just texts themselves, have been widely used as research methods to get at these processes.

Flower and Hayes' (1981) model was decisive here. It suggested that the process of writing is influenced by the task and the writer's long-term memory. Its main features are that

- writers have goals
- they plan extensively
- planning involves defining a rhetorical problem, placing it in a context, then exploring its parts, arriving at solutions and finally translating ideas on to the page
- all work can be reviewed, evaluated and revised, even before any text has been produced
- planning, drafting, revising and editing are recursive, interactive and potentially simultaneous
- plans and text are constantly evaluated in a feedback loop
- the whole process is overseen by an executive control called a monitor.

This, then, is a computer model typical of theorising in cognitive psychology and Artificial Intelligence, giving priority to mechanisms such as *memory, Central Processing Unit, problem-solving programs* and *flow-charts*.

Faigley (1986) points out that the Flower and Hayes model helped to promote a 'science-consciousness' among writing teachers which promised a 'deep-structure' theory of how writing could be taught. The beauty of the model is its simplicity as the wide range of mental activities which can occur during composing can be explained by a fairly small number of sub-processes. The model also purports to account for individual differences in writing strategies, so immature writers can be represented as using a composing model that is a reduced version of that used by experts and so guided towards greater competence by instruction in expert strategies.

The process approach to teaching writing was also assisted by the increasing availability and affordability of personal computers in the early 1980s. Word processing was not just a new form of typing, but a different way of manipulating texts, making it easier to re-draft, revise and edit. Teachers were quick to see the pedagogical possibilities of this and specialist programs emerged such as Daedalus (www.daedalus.com) which contained modules to support the stages of the writing process: questions for generating material, multi-screens for editing, and connectivity for peer review and discussion. As Bloch (2008: 52) observes: 'The ease with which one could make changes or incorporate new ideas made it clear how all of these aspects of the writing process were now integrated.'

The impact on research and teaching has been enormous and we now know much more about composing processes. Process approaches also extended research techniques beyond experimental methods and text analyses to the qualitative methods of the social sciences, often seeking to describe writing from an *emic* perspective by taking account of the views of writers and readers themselves. In particular, these studies have made considerable use of writers' verbal reports while composing (Van Den Bergh and Rijlaarsdam, 2001), task observation (Bosher, 1998), and retrospective interviews (Nelson and Carson, 1998). Often research is longitudinal, following a few students over an extended period of their writing development (F. Hyland, 1998) and uses multiple techniques which may include recall protocols and product analyses of several drafts.

The extension of this research into studies of L2 writers, however, has been disappointing. Many teachers will find little that is surprising in the findings of process writing studies summarised in Concept 1.10, and the research generally supports our intuitions about the practices of skilled and unskilled writers. Even less encouraging for teachers is the fact that different studies often produce contradictory findings, often because they are limited to small samples of writers in a particular context and so lack generalisability to wider populations of writers. Moreover, despite the massive output of this research serious doubts have been raised about the methods used to explore cognitive models of writing.

Concept 1.10   **Process findings of L2 writing**

Silva (1993) summarises the main results of research into composing practices as:

- general composing process patterns seem to be similar in L1 and L2
- skilled writers compose differently from novices

- skilled writers use more effective planning and revising strategies
- L1 strategies may or may not be transferred to L2 contexts
- L2 writers tend to plan less than L1 writers
- L2 writers have more difficulty setting goals and generating material
- L2 writers revise more but reflect less on their writing
- L2 writers are less fluent, and produce less accurate and effective texts

One serious problem is that these results often rely heavily on *think-aloud protocols*, a method where researchers ask writers to report their thoughts and actions while involved in a writing task. These have been criticised as offering an incomplete picture of the complex cognitive activities involved, not least because many cognitive processes are routine and internalised operations performed without any conscious recognition and therefore not available to verbal description. In addition, asking subjects to simultaneously verbalise and carry out complex operations is likely to overload short-term memory due to 'a crowding of the cognitive workbench' (Afflerbach and Johnson, 1984: 311). As a result, such reports may only provide a partial record of processes. Worse, the act of reporting itself may merely be a narrative that participants construct to explain, rather than reflect, what they do, potentially distorting the thought processes being reported on.

Reservations have also been expressed about the status of the models themselves. Scardamalia and Bereiter (1986), for example, argue that such models do not represent fully worked-out theories and fail to either explain or generate writing behaviour. The models do not tell us *why* writers make certain choices and therefore cannot help us to advise students on their writing practices. In fact, Flower and Hayes' original model was too imprecise to predict the behaviour of real writers or to carry the weight of the research claims based on it and they have subsequently emphasised the importance of appropriate goal-setting and rhetorical strategies far more (Flower *et al.*, 1990). But such refinements cannot obscure the weaknesses of a model which seeks to describe cognitive processes common to all writers, both novice and expert and all learners in between these poles.

Bereiter and Scardamalia (1987) suggest that because skilled and novice practices differ so radically, two models account for the research findings better than one (see Concept 1.11).

Concept 1.11   **Knowledge-telling and knowledge-transforming**

A knowledge-telling model addresses the fact that novice writers plan less often than experts, revise less often and less extensively, and are primarily concerned with generating content from their internal resources. Their main goal is simply to tell what they can remember based on the assignment, the topic, or the genre.

A knowledge-transforming model suggests how skilled writers use the writing task to analyse problems and set goals. These writers are able to reflect on the complexities of the task and resolve problems of content, form, audience, style, organisation, and so on within a content space and a rhetorical space, so that there is continuous interaction between developing knowledge and text. Knowledge transforming thus involves actively reworking thoughts so that in the process not only text, but also ideas, may be changed (Bereiter and Scardamalia, 1987).

Bereiter and Scardamalia's model certainly adds psychological insight to writing activity and helps explain the difficulties often experienced by unskilled writers because of the complexity of the writing task and their lack of topic knowledge. It also helps account for reflective thought in writing, and therefore suggests that students should participate in a variety of challenging writing tasks and genres to develop their skills. It also draws attention to the importance of feedback and revision in the process of developing both content and expression. It remains unclear, however, how writers actually make the cognitive transition to a *knowledge-transforming* model, nor is it spelt out what occurs in the intervening stages and whether the process is the same for all learners. Many students, for example, continue to have considerable difficulty with their writing despite intensive teaching in expert strategies.

It is, however, difficult to exaggerate the impact of process ideas on both L1 and L2 writing classrooms. There are few teachers who do not set pre-writing activities to generate ideas about content and structure, encourage brainstorming and outlining, require multiple drafts, give extensive feedback, facilitate peer responses, delay surface corrections until the final editing, and display finished work (Reid, 1993). Process research has meant that cooperative writing, teacher conferences, problem-based tasks, journal-writing, group discussions, and mixed portfolio assessments are now all commonplace practices in our methodological repertoire (e.g. Casanave, 2004; Kroll, 2003).

However, while there is a great deal of case-study (e.g. Graves, 1984) and anecdotal support for this model, there is actually little hard evidence that process-writing techniques lead to significantly better writing. This is not really surprising as 'the approach' is actually many different approaches applied unevenly and in different ways. In addition, there are serious reservations about whether the underlying individualistic emphasis of the methods, which say little about social aspects of either language use or language learning, may handicap ESL students from more collectivist cultures (Ramanathan and Atkinson, 1999a). But we should not expect any method automatically to produce good writers. The process of writing is a rich mix of elements which, together with cognition, include the writer's experiences and background, as well as a sense of self, of others, of situation and of purpose. Writers, situations and tasks differ, and no single description can capture all writing contexts or be applied universally with the same results.

Concept 1.12   **Pros and cons of process teaching approaches**

Pros

- Major impact on the theory and methodology of teaching writing to L1 and L2 students
- A useful corrective to preoccupations with 'product' and student accuracy
- Important in raising teachers' awareness of what writing involves – contributing to a professionalisation of writing teaching
- Gave greater respect for individual differences among student writers
- Raises many new research questions which remain to be answered

Cons

- Overemphasises psychological factors in writing
- Focuses on the writer as a solitary individual and fails to recognise social aspects of writing
- Based on individualistic ideologies which may hamper the development of ESL students
- Ignores important influences of context, especially differences of class, gender and ethnicity
- Downplays the varied conventions of professional and academic communities
- Uncertain whether this approach greatly improves student writing

---

In sum, the process-writing perspective allows us to understand writing in a way that was not possible when it was seen only as finished products. It does, however, overemphasise psychological factors and fails to consider the forces outside the individual which help guide problem-definition, frame solutions and ultimately shape writing.

1.2.3   Writing as a situated act

A third writer-oriented perspective goes some way to addressing the criticisms levelled at cognitive modelling by giving greater emphasis to the actual *performance* of writing. Less a single theory than several lines of enquiry, this research incorporates the writer's prior experiences and the impact of the immediate, local context on writing and has had an important influence on both the ways we see writing and how it might be studied.

Concept 1.13   **Writing as a situated act**

Writing is a social act that can occur within particular situations. It is therefore influenced both by the personal attitudes and prior experiences that the writer brings to writing and the impact of the specific political and institutional contexts in which it takes place. By using detailed observations of acts of writing, participant interviews, analyses of surrounding practices and other techniques, researchers have developed interesting accounts of local writing contexts. These descriptions give significant attention to the experiences of writers and to their understandings of the demands of the immediate context as they write.

This perspective takes us beyond the possible workings of writers' minds and into the physical and experiential contexts in which writing occurs to describe how 'context cues cognition' (Flower, 1989). Of crucial importance is the emphasis placed on a notion of context as the 'situation of expression' (Nystrand, 1987). Flower (1989: 288) elaborates this as the effects of prior knowledge, assumptions and expectations together with features of the writing environment which selectively tap knowledge and trigger specific processes. The goal is to describe the influence of this context on the ways writers represent their purposes in the kind of writing that is produced. As Prior (1998: xi) observes:

> Actually writing happens in moments that are richly equipped with tools (material and semiotic) and populated with others (past, present and

future). When seen as situated activity, writing does not stand alone as the discrete act of a writer, but emerges as a confluence of many streams of activity: reading, talking, observing, acting, making, thinking and feeling as well as transcribing words on paper.

Studies therefore seek to analyse, often in considerable detail, how writing is constituted as a feature of local situations.

To accomplish such exhaustive or 'thick' descriptions (Geertz, 1973) of writing contexts, researchers have relied heavily on *ethnographic studies*. The term 'ethnographic' remains somewhat fuzzy and contested, but essentially it refers to research which is highly situated and minutely detailed, attempting to give an holistic explanation of behaviour using a variety of methods and drawing on the understandings of insiders themselves to avoid any prior assumptions of the researcher (Watson-Gegeo, 1988; Cicourel, 2007).

Concept 1.14   **Ethnographic research**

Ethnography is a type of research which undertakes to give, insider-oriented description of individuals' cultural practices (Ramanathan and Atkinson, 1999b: 49). It relies on the view that collecting and analysing a variety of different kinds of data makes possible a more valid description of complex social realities than any single kind of data alone. Applying this method to an understanding of how and why people write means gathering naturally occurring data under normal conditions from numerous sources, typically over a period of time, without interfering with either writers or the writing context.

Ethnographic methods typically include detailed, longitudinal, observations of a setting and the writing that occurs within it, interviews with participants on their writing and relevant autobiographical issues, recursive analyses of students' process logs and diaries, questionnaires and close examination of classroom interactions (e.g. Jarratt *et al.*, 2006; F. Hyland, 1998). Texts such as coursebooks, manuals and course outlines are also often studied, as is student writing itself and teacher responses to this. Sometimes the researcher participates in the class and follows students around to observe their daily activities and gain insights into the contexts and practices which might illuminate the writing process (Weissberg, 2006).

Ethnography, however, is not a term that everyone feels comfortable with. Its origins in anthropology mean it carries connotations of the researcher's total immersion in another culture rather than simply an attitude to research and use of varied methods. Because of this, John Swales' (1998) coining of the term *textography* in his case studies of particular departments and academics and their discipline specific texts in a university building, has offered a more manageable way of exploring the richness of the working contexts while avoiding a full cultural description.

Quote 1.5 Swales on textography

As textographer of the second floor I have tried to do justice to a number of themes that have emerged over a three-year involvement with its practices, rhythms, texts and personalities. One is a sense of locale, a sense of autonomous *place* . . . Juxtaposed to that, I have tried to capture a feeling of the academic personalities, and especially the scriptural personalities, of those I have chosen for inclusion . . . And juxtaposed to the partial accounts of careers that a textography engenders, the use of close, but nontechnical, analysis of particular stretches of text, illuminated on occasion by text-based interview data, shows how the language of normal science can . . . reveal the individual humanities of the authors.

Swales (1998: 141–2)

The features of local setting that have particularly interested 'situated' researchers have been the roles individual writers perform and how writers' interactions with local participants feed into the writing task, especially in collaborative contexts. Contexts are sites for interactions where relationships, and the rules which order them, can both facilitate and constrain composing. The social routines surrounding acts of writing have therefore been studied in detail (e.g. Willett, 1995; Storch, 2005) and attention given to certain tangible features of the local environment which have meaning for writers. Thus Chin (1994) has shown how students on a journalism course saw the use of physical space in their department as barriers which excluded them and restricted access to the material resources they needed for writing. Similarly, Canagarajah (1996) has revealed how the absence of resources like libraries and computers can serve to exclude Third World scholars from publishing their writing.

There is little doubt that this research has produced rich, detailed descriptions of particular contexts of writing, expanding greatly our understanding of the personal, social and institutional factors which can impinge on writing. One problem, of course, is that while these methods might illuminate what goes on in a particular act of writing, they cannot describe everything in either the writer's consciousness or the context which might influence composition, so we can never be certain that all critical factors have been accounted for. More importantly, this approach runs the risk of emphasising writers' perceptions and the possible impact of the local situation to the detriment of the rhetorical problems to which writing responds. In other words, by focusing on the context of production, we might be neglecting the effects of the wider social and institutional orders of discourse which influence writers' intentions and plans for writing.

One potential impact of such wider social worlds is the experiences writers might bring to the classroom as a consequence of prior negative evaluation of their writing. Social inequalities of power, educational and home backgrounds, and so on can result in what has been called *writing apprehension* (Faigley *et al.*, 1981) where individual's experience high degrees of anxiety when asked to write. These anxious feelings, about oneself as a writer, one's writing situation, or one's writing task can seriously disrupt the writing process and educational success. The term is used to describe writers who are intellectually capable of the task at hand, but who nevertheless have difficulty with it (e.g. McLeod, 1987), feeling their writing isn't sufficiently creative, interesting, sophisticated, or well expressed. This can result in students avoiding courses or careers which involve writing, low self-esteem and confidence, or the production of poor texts.

Overall, then, a focus on writers lacks a developed theory of the ways experience is constituted and interpreted in *social communities* and underplays the workings of wider factors. As a result, it fails to move beyond the local context to take full account of how an evolving text might be a writer's response to a reader's expectations. This neglect of the social dimension of writing has eventually led research away from internally directed process models to more socially situated approaches.

1.3 Reader-oriented research and teaching

A final broad approach expands the notion of *context* beyond features of the composing situation to the purposes, goals and uses that the completed text may eventually fulfill. The perspectives discussed in this section share the view that writers select their words to engage with others and to present their ideas in ways that make most sense to their readers. This involves what Halliday refers to as the *interpersonal function* of language, and it is encoded in every sentence we write. Readers must be drawn in, influenced and often persuaded by a text that sees the world in similar ways to them. In other words, writing is an interactive, as well as cognitive, activity which employs accepted resources for the purpose of sharing meanings in that context. I will discuss this social view under three headings:

- writing as social interaction
- writing as social construction
- writing as power and ideology.

1.3.1   Writing as social interaction

The idea that writing is an interaction between writers and readers adds a communicative dimension to writing. It moves away from our stereotype of an isolated writer hunched over a keyboard to explain composing decisions in terms of the writer's projection of the interests, understandings, and needs of a potential audience. This view has been developed by Martin Nystrand, who argues that the success of any text is the writer's ability to satisfy the rhetorical demands of readers: we have to embed our writing in a non-local discourse world.

> **Quote 1.6** Nystrand on writing as social interaction
>
> The process of writing is a matter of elaborating text in accord with what the writer can reasonably assume that the reader knows and expects, and the process of reading is a matter of predicting text in accord with what the reader assumes about the writer's purpose. More fundamentally, each presupposes the sense-making capabilities of the other. As a result, written communication is predicated on what the writer/reader each assumes the other will do/has done.
>
> M. Nystrand (1989: 75)

In a social interactive model, meaning is created via 'a unique configuration and interaction of what both reader and writer bring to the text' (Nystrand *et al.*, 1993: 299). A discourse is shaped by writers attempting to balance their purposes with the expectations of readers through a process of negotiation. For Nystrand, a text has 'semantic potential', or a variety of possible meanings, all but a few of which are closed down by a combination of the writer's intention, the reader's cognition and the objective properties of the text itself. Meaning, in other words, is not transmitted from mind to mind as in the model of autonomous texts, nor does it reside in the writer's cognition as in process models. Instead it is created between the participants themselves.

Essentially the process of writing involves creating a text that we assume the reader will recognise and expect and the process of reading involves drawing on assumptions about what the writer is trying to do. Hoey (2001) likens this to dancers following each other's steps, each building sense from a text by anticipating what the other is likely to do. Skilled writers are able to create a mutual frame of reference and anticipate when their purposes will be retrieved by their audiences, providing greater elaboration where they expect that there may be misunderstanding. The recursiveness of the drafting process thus becomes a way of responding to an inner dialogue with readers, part of how the writer monitors the evolving text for potential trouble-spots. Writing, then, is not an act of an isolated individual but a joint endeavour between writers and readers, co-constructed through the active understanding of rhetorical situations and the likely responses of readers.

Audience can be a difficult concept for teachers. Clearly, a writer who understands something of the needs and interests of his/her audience possesses important rhetorical knowledge about appropriate genre, content, stance and style. The ability to analyse an audience, however, obviously becomes more problematic the larger and less immediately familiar it gets. Texts are often addressed to a plurality of audiences. As I write this book I am picturing you, the reader, as someone with more than a passing interest in writing, but I cannot predict your cultural background, your knowledge of the subject, or what you want from this book. Perhaps you are a teacher, a student, a trainer; maybe a casual bookshop-browser, or someone supervising a thesis on writing. In other words, I am aware that my book could be read by specialists, novices, practitioners and lay people, and while I try to make the subject as explicit as I can, I know that not all readers will recover every intended meaning.

The notion of audience is a contentious area of debate in literary studies (e.g. Lecercle, 2000), has been much discussed in rhetoric (Park, 1982), and has become more complex in the era of electronic writing (e.g. Bloch, 2008). Audience is, in fact, rarely a concrete reality, particularly in academic and professional contexts, and must be seen as essentially representing a construction of the writer which may shift during the composing process.

Concept 1.15   **Audience**

Two models of audience have dominated much of the writing literature. Ede and Lunsford (1984) refer to these as ***audience addressed***, the actual or intended readers who exist independently of the text, and ***audience invoked***, a created fiction of the writer rhetorically implied in the text which can be persuaded to respond to it in certain ways. Park's more sophisticated conception focuses less on people and more on the writer's awareness of the external circumstances which define a rhetorical context and requires the text to have certain characteristics in response. Audience therefore exists in the writer's mind and shapes a text as 'a complex set of conventions, estimations, implied responses and attitudes' (Park, 1982: 251).

Issues of audience have encouraged a growing interest in the use of peer and teacher feedback among teachers so that students get an idea of how others understand their texts (e.g. Ferris, 2003; 2006). Equally, however, teachers recognise that they can promote a sense of audience among students by exposing them to examples of texts in target genres. This is because an understanding of audience largely involves exploiting readers' abilities to recognise intertextuality between texts. This idea originates in Bakhtin's (1986) view that language is dialogic: a conversation between writer and reader in an ongoing activity. Writing reflects traces of its social uses because it is linked and aligned with other texts upon which it builds and which it anticipates. 'Each utterance refutes, affirms, supplements, and relies on the others, presupposes them to be known and somehow takes them into account' (ibid.: 91). Here written genres are regarded as parts of repeated and typified social situations, rather than particular forms, with writers exercising judgement and creativity in responding to similar circumstances.

Concept 1.16   Intertextuality

Bakhtin's notion of intertextuality suggests that discourses are always related to other discourses, both as they change over time and in their similarities at any point in time. This connects text-users into a network of prior texts and so provides a system of options for making meanings which can be recognised by other texts-users. Because they help create the meanings available in a culture, the conventions developed in this way close out certain interpretations and make others more likely, and this helps explain how writers make particular rhetorical choices when composing. Fairclough (1992: 117) distinguishes two kinds of intertextuality:

Manifest intertextuality refers to various ways of incorporating or responding to other texts through quotation, paraphrase, irony, and so on.

Interdiscursivity concerns the writer's use of sets of conventions drawn from a recognisable text type or genre. Texts here then are associated with some institutional and social meanings.

A major pedagogical implication of an interactionist approach is obviously that a cultivated sense of audience is crucial to the development of effective writing strategies, and that this can only be accomplished through a sense of social context. This means teachers have tried to employ contexts for writing which reflect real life uses as far as possible, with a clear purpose and a specified external audience. Johns (1997), for example, advocates that students should engage in writing tasks that involve researching potential readers for their written arguments and Storch (2005) shows how collaborative tasks can improve essays by helping writers predict readers' problems with a text. The central importance of the social-interactionist orientation to teachers is therefore to encourage a focus on context as a set of recognisable conventions through which a piece of writing achieves its force. The text, in sum, is the place where readers and writers meet.

1.3.2   Writing as social construction

Another way of thinking about readers is to step back and see inter-action as a collection of rhetorical choices rather than as specific encounters. Here the writer is neither a *creator* working through a set of cognitive processes nor an *interactant* engaging with a reader, but a member of a *community*. The communicating dyad is replaced by the discourses of socially and rhetorically constituted groups of readers and writers.

Concept 1.17   **Social construction**

Social construction is based on the idea that the ways we think, and the categories and concepts we use to understand the world, are 'all language constructs generated by knowledge communities and used by them to maintain coherence' (Bruffee, 1986: 777). The everyday interactions that occur between people produce the world that we take for granted. Language is not just a means of self-expression then, it is how we construct and sustain reality, and we do this as members of communities, using the language of those communities. The features of a text are therefore influenced by the community for which it was written and so best understood, and taught, through the specific genres of communities.

Originating in sociology and postmodern philosophy, this approach takes the view that what we know and do is relative to a collectively organised conceptual schema. Writing is a social act, and to understand it fully we must go beyond the decisions of individual writers to explore the regular features of texts as the preferences of particular communities. A text carries certain meanings and gains its communicative force only by displaying the patterns and conventions of the community for which it is written. Essays produced by biology students, for example, draw on very different forms of argument, interpersonal conventions and ways of presenting facts and theories than those written by business students. So, whereas interactionists work from individuals to groups, constructionists proceed from social group to individuals: writing is a form of cultural practice tied to forms of social organisation.

Another way of putting this is that writers always have to demonstrate their credibility, that their text has something worthwhile to say, by positioning themselves and their ideas in relation to other ideas and texts in their communities. The notion of *discourse community* draws attention to the idea that we do not use language to communicate with the world at large, but with other members of our social groups, each with its own norms, categorisations, sets of conventions, and ways of doing things (Bartholomae, 1986). The value of the term lies in the fact that it offers a way of bringing writers, readers and texts together into a common rhetorical space, foregrounding the conceptual frames that individuals use to organise their experience and get things done using language.

More than this, however, through notions of community we can see writing as a means by which organisations actually constitute themselves and individuals signal their memberships of them. By engaging with others through writing we enter into a culture of shared belief or value concerning what is worth discussing and how things should be discussed. Through our language choices we align ourselves with, challenge, or extend what has been said before. In institutional contexts then, community is a means of accounting for how communication succeeds through the individual's projection of a shared professional context. Such language choices help us see that institutional practices are not just conventional regularities of a particular style. Instead they evoke a social environment where the writer activates specific recognisable and routine responses to recurring tasks. In a real sense, therefore, through these repeated practices, we 'construct' the institutions we participate in. Texts are created in terms of how their authors understand reality and, in turn, these understandings are influenced by their membership of social groups. Discourse is therefore a reservoir of meanings that give identity to a culture.

Concept 1.18   **Discourse community**

The term discourse community is perhaps one of the most indeterminate in the writing literature. It is possible to see communities as real, relatively stable groups whose members subscribe, at least to some extent, to a consensus on certain ways of doing things and using language. On the other hand, community can be regarded as a more metaphorical term for collecting together certain practices and attitudes. Swales (1990), for instance, sets out criteria for using language to achieve collective goals or purposes, while other writers have suggested a weaker connection. Barton (2007: 75–6), for example, defines it as a loose association of individuals engaged in either the reception or production of texts, or both:

'A discourse community is a group of people who have texts and practices in common, whether it is a group of academics, or the readers of teenage magazines. In fact, discourse community can refer to the people the text is aimed at; it can be the people who read a text; or it can refer to the people who participate in a set of discourse practices both by reading and writing.'

As Bazerman (1994: 128) notes, 'most definitions of discourse community get ragged around the edges rapidly'. To see discourse communities as determinate and codifiable runs the risk of framing them as closed, self-sufficient and predictable arenas of shared and agreed-upon values and conventions. On the other hand, reducing them to mere collections of competing voices reduces the idea's explanatory authority. Clearly we have to avoid the strong structuralist position of a single deterministic consensus which separates a community from its moments of creation in writing, but at the same time we need to acknowledge the obvious effects of groups on the ways individual communicative practices are realised.

The fuzziness of the term means that it is often unclear where to locate a discourse community. Can it, for example, refer to all academics, a university, a discipline, or just a specialism? We also have to account for the ways these groupings come into being, how they admit variable degrees of membership, exercise power over participants, accommodate differences, resolve conflict, and how they develop and change. Clearly the term is only useful if it is seen as connected to real individuals and the cultural frames that carry meaning for them. As a result, some writers have sought to 'localise' the concept into *place discourse communities* (Swales, 1998) or *communities of practice* (Lave and Wenger, 1991), defining a community in terms of the literacy practices and relations which emerge in some mutual endeavour over time.

Despite the term's imprecision, there is a core meaning of like-mindedness or *membership*, and this concept has proved central to research on writing. It has contributed to how we understand writing in business settings (Bargiela-Chiappini and Nickerson, 1999), the law (Candlin *et al.*, 2002), health care (Barrett, 1996), technology (Killingsworth and Gilbertson, 1992), and other professional contexts (Blyler and Thralls, 1993). Constructionism has been most influential, however, in describing academic writing.

Concept 1.19   **Social construction and EAP**

Academic disciplines use language in different ways (Hyland, 2004a) and might therefore be seen as academic tribes (Becher and Trowler, 2001) with their own particular norms and practices. Through the use of these disciplinary conventions and practices, members construct academic knowledge, as they galvanise support, express collegiality, resolve difficulties, and negotiate disagreement through patterns of rhetorical choices which connect their texts with their disciplinary cultures. Persuasion, then, is accomplished with language. But it is language that demonstrates legitimacy. Writers must recognise and make choices from the rhetorical options available in their fields to appeal to readers from within the boundaries of their disciplines.

This approach tells us that essays, reports, memos, dissertations, and so on, are not the same in all fields and disciplines and that the ability to produce them does not involve generic writing skills. Only when we use a language to create genres in specific contexts does our competence in writing cease to be a display of control of a linguistic code and take on significance as discourse. Expert writers are obviously better able than novices to imagine how readers will respond to a text because they are familiar with the ways experience is typically constructed in their communities. The role of the writing teacher is therefore to help students discover how valued text forms and practices are socially constructed in response to the common purposes of target communities. Ann Johns (1997) calls this a 'socioliterate' approach to teaching.

Quote 1.7 Johns on 'socioliterate' approaches to teaching

In socioliterate views, literacies are acquired principally through exposure to discourses from a variety of social contexts. Through this exposure, individuals gradually develop theories of genre. Those who can successfully produce and process texts within certain genres are members of communities, for academic learning does not take place independent of these communities...What I am advocating, then, is an approach in which literacy classes become laboratories for the study of texts, roles, and contexts, for research into evolving student literacies and developing awareness and critique of communities and their textual contracts.

Johns (1997: 14–19)

Rather than modelling the practices of experts, this approach offers students a guiding framework for producing texts by raising their awareness of the connections between forms, purposes and roles in specific social contexts. Teaching methods vary, but generally seek to give students experience of authentic, purposeful writing related to the kinds of writing they will need to do in their target communities. Johns (1997), for example, stresses the value of students researching both texts and community informants and of compiling mixed-skills portfolios. Myers (1988) points out the advantages of examining changes in pre-publication drafts, and Swales and Feak (2004) underline the benefits of student text analyses.

The danger of a constructionist perspective, of course, is that practitioners may represent, in their teaching or research, particular conventions as normative, static and natural. There is a risk that particular forms and practices will not only be seen as somehow fixed and 'correct', but uncritically regarded as naturally superior forms of communication, blessed with the prestige of the social groups which routinely employ them. This can only make the learning task harder for novice writers since they may view the indigenous literacies that they bring with them to the classroom as a deficit which has to be rectified and replaced. This brings us to the final perspective in this chapter.

1.3.3   Writing as power and ideology

A third reader-oriented view of writing also emphasises the importance of social context to writing but stresses that the key dimension of context is the relations of power that exist in it and the ideologies that maintain these relations. The importance of power as a force which mediates discourse and social groups has most extensively been explored by researchers working in *Critical Discourse Analysis* (CDA). This views 'language as a form of social practice' (Fairclough, 1989: 20) and attempts 'to unpack the ideological underpinnings of discourse that have become so naturalized over time that we begin to treat them as common, acceptable and natural features of discourse' (Teo, 2000). In other words, CDA links language to the activities which surround it, focusing on how social relations, identity, knowledge and power are constructed through written and spoken texts in communities, schools and classrooms. Discourse is thus a mediator of social life: simultaneously both constructing social and political reality and conditioned by it.

> **Quote 1.8** Fairclough on critical discourse analysis
>
> By 'critical' discourse analysis I mean analysis which aims to systematic-ally explore often opaque relationships of causality and determination between (a) discursive practices, events and texts, and (b) wider social and cultural structures, relations and processes; to investigate how such practices, events and texts arise out of and are ideologically shaped by relations of power and struggles over power; and to explore how the opacity of these relationships between discourse and society is itself a factor securing power and hegemony.
>
> Fairclough (1992: 135)

A central aspect of this view is that the interests, values, and power relations in any institutional and sociohistorical context are found in the ways that people use language.

Concept 1.20   **Principles of Critical Discourse Analysis**

- CDA addresses social problems and not simply language use by itself
- power relations are discursive
- discourse constitutes society and culture, and every instance of language use contributes to reproducing or changing them
- discourse does ideological work, representing and constructing society in particular ways
- discourse is historical, and must be related to other discourses
- the link between texts and society is mediated by 'orders of discourse'
- discourse analysis is interpretive and explanatory, requiring systematic methods
- discourse is a form of social action, and CDA is a socially committed paradigm.

(Wodak, 1996: 17–20)

The notion of *ideology* is important because it is concerned with how individuals experience the world and how these experiences are, in turn, reproduced through their writing. Fairclough (borrowing from Foucault) uses the term *'orders of discourse'* to refer to the relatively stable configurations of discourse practices found in particular domains or institutions. These are frames for interaction such as patient case-notes, lab reports, newspaper editorials, student records, academic articles, and so on, which have prestige value in different institutions and which are ideologically shaped by its dominant groups. They provide writers with templates for appropriate ways of writing and this means that any act of writing, or of teaching writing, is embedded in ideological assumptions.

But while these frameworks help enforce the authority of particular forms of discourse in any community, they do not exclude possibilities for change. This is because when we write we not only take up socially ratified social roles and relationships, but also draw on our personal and social experiences which cross-cut what we write.

Of importance in this perspective is the view that writing is both texts and contexts, the work of both individuals and institutions. This requires us to consider not only texts but also their relationship to the wider social environment and the part they play for individuals within specific situations. CDA is, therefore, analysis with attitude. It proclaims an interest and sets an agenda, as Fairclough and Wodak (1997: 259) make clear: 'What is distinctive about CDA is both that it intervenes on the side of the dominated and oppressed groups and against dominating groups, and that it openly declares the emancipatory interests that motivate it.'

While CDA does not subscribe to any single method, Fairclough (1992; 2003) and Wodak (Wodak and Chilton, 2007) draw on Systemic Functional Linguistics. This is useful as the model sees language as systems of linguistic features offering choices to users, but these choices are considerably circumscribed in situations of unequal power. Young and Harrison (2004: 1) claim that SFL and CDA share three main features:

1. a view of language as a social construct, or how society fashions language,
2. a dialectical view in which 'particular discursive events influence the contexts in which they occur and the contexts are, in turn, influenced by these discursive events',
3. a view which emphasises cultural and historical aspects of meaning.

SFL thus offers CDA a sophisticated way of analysing the relations between language and social contexts, making it possible to ground concerns of power and ideology in the details of discourse.

In practice CDA typically examines features of writing such as:

- vocabulary – particularly how metaphor and connotative meanings encode ideologies;
- transitivity – which can show, for instance, who is presented as having agency and who is acted upon;
- nominalisation and passivisation – how processes and actors can be repackaged as nouns or agency otherwise obscured;
- mood and modality – which indicate relationships such as roles, attitudes, commitments and obligations;
- theme – how the first element of a clause can be used to foreground particular aspects of information or presuppose reader beliefs;
- text structure – how text episodes are marked;
- intertextuality and interdiscursivity – the effects of other texts and styles on texts – leading to *hybridisation*, such as where commercial discourses colonise those in other spheres.

Unfortunately much CDA analysis has relied exclusively on the researcher's interpretations of texts, cherry-picking both the texts it studies and the features it chooses to discuss. This has the effect of simply confirming the analyst's prejudices while reducing pragmatics to semantics in assuming just one possible reading of the text (Widdowson, 2000). Moreover, as Blommaert (2005) observes, this privileging of the analyst's viewpoint is often reinforced by appeal to an explanatory level of social theory which lies above any analysis of the text itself. In other words, there is little dialogue with real readers; interpretation becomes a black box rather than a product of analysis. The plausibility of any interpretation of a text ultimately depends on our willingness to accept it, and this is best enhanced by obtaining the intentions and interpretations of participants. So, although it might be acknowledged that no analysis can be neutral, and that a clear political agenda helps to redress the invisible ideological presuppositions in much writing research, we need to go beyond good intentions. It is essential that any theory of writing is thoroughly grounded in the contextual understandings of the users that give it significance.

From a pedagogical perspective, a major task of CDA is to help students to an awareness of how writing practices are grounded in social (and especially institutional) structures. This means that teachers must build on the perceptions and practices of writing that students bring with them to the classroom to expose the authority of the prestige discourses that they seek to acquire. By the close study of texts and their contexts, students might become more aware of the ideological assumptions which underlie texts and the forms of persuasion found in an array of current discourses they encounter in their everyday lives. More directly, CDA helps to reveal writing as relative to particular groups and contexts, and so encourages teachers to assist students in unpacking the requirements of their target communities. What appear as dominant and superior forms of writing can then be seen as simply another practice, one among many, and thus open like others to scrutiny and contestation.

1.4 Conclusion

In this overview I have been concerned not only to cover the major frameworks used to look at writing but also to question the widely held views that writing is either simply words on a page or an activity of solitary individuals. Rather, modern conceptions see writing as a social practice, embedded in the cultural and institutional contexts in which it is produced and the particular uses that are made of it. When we pick up a pen or sit at a word-processor we adopt and reproduce certain roles, identities and relationships to engage in particular socially approved ways of communicating: to write an essay, make an insurance claim, or complain about a supermarket delivery. So while every act of writing is in a sense both personal and individual, it is also interactional and social, expressing a culturally recognised purpose, reflecting a particular kind of relationship and acknowledging an engagement in a given community. In the next chapter we look more closely at some of the issues that this raises.

Further reading

Fairclough, N. (2004). *Analyzing discourse* (London: Routledge). A mix of introductory SFL and social theory – a good primer for CDA in the social sciences.
Grabbe, W. and Kaplan, R. (1996) *Theory and practice of writing* (Harlow: Longman). An overview of key issues and frameworks.

Hyland, K. (2005). *Metadiscourse* (London: Continuum). A framework for studying how writing works as interaction.

Kroll, B. (ed.) (2002) *Exploring the dynamics of second language writing* (Cambridge: Cambridge University Press). An accessible introduction to second-language writing research and teaching.

Silva, T. and Matsuda, P. (eds) (2001) *Landmark essays on ESL writing* (Mahwah, NJ: Lawrence Earlbaum). Just what the title says.

Swales, J. (2004) *Research genres* (Cambridge: Cambridge University Press). A current overview of conceptions of genre in academic contexts.

Chapter 2

Key issues in writing

This chapter will...

- address some key topics in current writing research and teaching;
- examine what these topics tell us about writing and elaborate the questions that they raise about the analysis, teaching and use of written texts;
- discuss the main views currently held on these topics and point to some of the important thinkers, theories, and studies in these areas.

In this chapter I build on the conceptual overview of Chapter 1 to explore a number of key issues which dominate current understandings of writing. These issues, which I have selected from a much wider range of candidates, are *context, literacy, culture, technology, genre* and *identity*. Together they tell us something of the current state of play in writing research and teaching and, I hope, provide a basis for thinking, reflecting and reading further on the subject.

2.1 Writing and context

As we have seen in Chapter 1, the ways we understand writing have developed through increasingly sophisticated understandings of context. We recognise that meaning is not something that resides in the words we write and send to someone else, but is created in the interaction between a writer and reader as they make sense of these words in different ways, each trying to guess the intentions of the other. As a result, analysts and teachers now try to take account of the personal, institutional, and social factors which influence acts of writing.

Traditionally, contextual factors were largely seen as 'objective' variables such as class, gender or race, but now tend to be viewed as what the participants see as relevant. So, a personal letter, for example, might mean something different to the writer and addressee than a casual reader.

Quote 2.1 Van Dijk on context

It is not the social situation that influences (or is influenced by) discourse, but the way the participants **define** such a situation. Contexts thus are not some kind of 'objective' condition or direct cause, but rather (inter)subjective constructs designed and ongoingly updated in interaction by participants as members of groups and communities. If they were, all people in the same social situation would speak in the same way. Contexts are participant constructs.

Van Dijk (2008: viii)

So instead of seeing context as a cluster of static variables that surround language use, we have to see it as socially constituted, interactively sustained and time bound (Duranti and Goodwin, 1992). It has to be admitted, however, that context is rarely analysed in its own right and is usually taken for granted or defined rather impressionistically. After all, given all the situations in which we can read or write, context might intuitively include everything. Cutting (2002: 3) suggests that there are three main aspects of this interpretive context:

- the *situational context*: what people 'know about what they can see around them';
- the *background knowledge context*: what people 'know about the world, what they know about aspects of life, and what they know about each other';
- the *co-textual context*: what people 'know about what they have been saying'.

These aspects of interpretation have come to be rolled into the idea of *community*. As discussed in Chapter 1, this is something of a troubled concept, but it offers a principled way of understanding how meaning is produced *in interaction*. This means that all uses of written language can be seen as located in particular times and places: in the home, school, workplace, or university, and in particular communities who recognise particular combinations of genres, interpretive shortcuts, and communicative conventions.

More linguistically oriented analysts understand context in a different way and begin with texts, seeing the properties of a social situation as systematically encoded in a discourse. More than other approaches to language, Systemic Functional Linguistics has attempted to show how contexts leave their traces in (or are expressed in) patterns of language use. Halliday developed an analysis of context based on the idea that any text is the result of the writer's language choices in a particular *context of situation* (Malinowski, 1949). That is, language varies according to the situation in which it is used, so that if we examine a text we can make guesses about the situation, or if we are in a particular situation we make certain linguistic choices based on that situation. The context of situation, or register, is the immediate situation in which language use occurs and language varies in such contexts varies with the configuration of *field*, *tenor* and *mode*.

Concept 2.1   **Halliday's dimensions of context**

- *Field*: Refers to what is happening, the type of social action, or what the text is about (the topic together with the socially expected forms and patterns typically used to express it).

- *Tenor*: Refers to who is taking part, the roles and relationships of participants (their status and power, for instance, which influences involvement, formality and politeness).

- *Mode*: Refers to what part the language is playing, what the participants are expecting it to do for them (whether it is spoken or written, how information is structured, and so on).

Halliday (1985)

In other words, the language we use needs to be appropriate to the situation in which we use it, and register is an attempt to characterise configurations of writing (or speech) which limit the choices a writer will make in a situation. So, some registers contain fairly predictable features which allow us to identify a close correspondence between text and context. Legal documents and computer manuals, for example, are likely to conform to conventions of lexis and grammar rarely found elsewhere, while more open registers, such as letters and editorials, contain a less restricted range of meanings and forms.

The context of situation operates within a wider and more abstract context Halliday calls the *context of culture*. This refers to the ways social structures, hierarchies, and institutional and disciplinary ideologies influence the language used in particular circumstances. Russell's (1997) investigation into a university cell biology course, for example, shows that students' writing in the course was situated both in the micro-level context (e.g., the professor's research lab, the course, the university administration, and related disciplines) as well as in the macro-level social and political structures (e.g., drug companies, families, government research agencies).

So, unlike contexts of situations the influence of the context of culture on language use is more diffuse and indirect, operating at a more abstract level. Halliday sees the context of culture as expressed in or ('through') more specific contexts of situation, so that we describe social situations as part of a broader culture. What is not clear, however, is how this broader culture actually impinges on our local experiences. How do language users understand these instantiations in their everyday acts of writing and speaking? Presumably there is some level of cognition through which writers construct their social worlds and which influences the production or comprehension of discourse, but while SFG theorists attempt to track this through system networks, this is not satisfactorily developed in SFL notions of context.

But while it is difficult to see how the global relates to the local in actual acts of writing in this model, the issue has been picked up by writers in CDA. Fairclough (1992) sees *discourse* as the link between the local *context of situation* and the overarching institutional *context of culture*. This is because it is in discourse where 'orders of discourse', or approved institutional practices such as university assignments, seminars, essays, and so on, operate to maintain existing relations of power and authority. The practices which operate in education, for example, regulate what is worth knowing and who can know it, thus confirming status of those who have knowledge and the position to exercise it. So, for instance, by providing students with socially authorised ways of communicating, critical theorists argue that the genres we teach promote the values of powerful social groups by reinforcing particular social roles and relationships between writers and readers.

These various perspectives allude to the richness and complexity of context in writing and the necessity for a more comprehensive approach to studying context.

2.2   Literacy and expertise

Writing, together with reading, is an act of literacy: how we actually use language in our everyday lives. Modern conceptions of literacy encourage us to see writing as a social practice rather than as an abstract skill separable from people and the places where they use texts. As Scribner and Cole (1981: 236) put it: 'literacy is not simply knowing how to read and write a particular script but applying this knowledge for specific purposes in specific contexts of use.' It is worth considering the role of literacy as it helps us to understand how people make sense of their lives through their routine practices of writing and reading.

Traditional school-based views regard literacy as a learnt ability which facilitates logical thinking, access to information, and participation in the roles of modern society. This view sees literacy as psychological and textual, something which can be measured and assessed. Literacy is seen as a set of discrete, value-free technical skills which include decoding and encoding meanings, manipulating writing tools, perceiving shape–sound correspondences, etc., which are learnt through formal education. Writing is personal empowerment, but it is also defined in terms of its opposite: the personal stigma attached to illiteracy. You either have it or you don't. 'Literacy' is therefore a loaded term, a deficit label which carries with it the social power to define, categorise and ultimately exclude people from many aspects of life.

A social literacies view (note the plural form) contrasts markedly with this, as can be seen in Concept 2.2. Here writing (and reading) are means of connecting people with each other in ways that carry particular social meanings, so writing varies with context and cannot be distilled down to a set of cognitive or technical abilities. The idea of 'functional literacy', the ability of individuals to fit in and succeed within their societies by using writing and reading skills for particular purposes, is married to the notion of 'critical literacy', the refusal to take such purposes for granted. This approach sees literacy as a relative term, so there is no single literacy but a wide variety of different 'practices' relevant to and appropriate for particular times, places, participants and purposes. Moreover, these practices are not something that we simply pick up and put down, but are integral to our individual identities, social relationships and community memberships (Barton *et al.*, 2007; Street, 1995; Street and Lefstein, 2008).

Concept 2.2   **A social view of literacy**

1. Literacy is a social activity and is best described in terms of people's literacy practices.
2. People have different literacies which are associated with different domains of life.
3. People's literacy practices are situated in broader social relations, making it necessary to describe the settings of literacy events.
4. Literacy practices are patterned by social institutions and power relationships, and some literacies are more dominant, visible and influential than others.
5. Literacy is based on a system of symbols as a way of representing the world to others and to ourselves.
6. Our attitudes and values with respect to literacy guide our actions to communication.
7. Our life histories contain many literacy events from which we learn and which contribute to the present.
8. A literacy event also has a social history which help create current practices.

Barton (2007: 34–5)

Barton and Hamilton (1998: 6) define literacy *practices* as 'the general cultural ways of utilizing written language which people draw on in their lives'. It therefore stresses the centrality of context, as discussed in the previous section, and suggests how the activities of reading and writing are related to the social structures in which they are embedded and which they help shape. But while these practices are 'what people do with literacy', they are rather abstract as they refer to not only reading and writing but also the values, feelings and cultural conceptions that give meaning to these uses (Street, 1995: 2). In other words they include shared understandings, ideologies and social identities as well as the social rules that regulate the access and distribution of texts. More concretely, these practices cluster into what Heath (1983) calls 'literacy events'.

> **Quote 2.2** Literacy events
>
> Literacy events are observable episodes where literacy has a role. Usually there is a written text, or texts, central to the activity and there may be talk around the text. Events are observable episodes which arise from practices or are shaped by them. The notion of events stresses the situated nature of literacies, that it always exists in a social context.
>
> Barton and Hamilton (1998: 7)

How texts are produced and used in different events is a key aspect of studying literacy. The assumption that writing is always associated with particular domains of cultural activity means we need to study literacy in a new way, using detailed ethnographic accounts of how writing is put to use by real people in their schools, homes, neighbourhoods and workplaces.

> **Quote 2.3** Baynham on researching literacy
>
> Investigating literacy as practice involves investigating literacy as 'concrete human activity', not just what people do with literacy, but also what they make of what they do, the values they place on it and the ideologies that surround it.
>
> Baynham (1995: 1)

Some studies have focused on the situated nature of routine literacy events, such as letter-writing, and the cultural beliefs and values attached to this in different contexts (e.g. Barton and Hall, 1999). More often, however, research has sought to describe literacy practices as events in people's everyday lives. Thus, Jones (2000) describes the practices of agriculture officials translating bureaucratic English into vernacular Welsh when interacting with farmers at a Welsh cattle auction. More recently, Barton *et al.* (2007) have explored the complex relationships between learning and adults lives through a series of case studies of individuals at various learning sites such as a drug support centre, a homeless shelter and a domestic violence refuge. Studies such as these show that writing is located in the interactions between people, and that texts are inextricable from the local and institutional contexts in which they are created and interpreted.

When we look beyond words to the social aspects of the activity in which they are embedded, we find that writing is typically secondary to some other purpose. Writing a letter may be a means of keeping in touch with a distant friend, for example, while completing a form can be incidental to applying for a loan. Social literacy research also shows us how far talk is often closely related to texts in such settings. This is illustrated in multilingual communities where relatives, friends, or professional 'literacy-brokers' often help people cope with the demands of bureaucratic literacy. Shuman (1993), for instance, describes how Puerto Rican teenage girls in the United States often take responsibility for translating government forms in English into spoken Spanish. In British Gujarati homes it may be the mother who takes on the main literacy role when writing to family members in India, translating verbal messages into Gujarati for her non-Gujarati speaking children (Barton and Hamilton, 1998: 183).

These studies not only reveal something of the many varied ways that people use texts in their everyday lives, but also how literacy may reflect unequal social relationships of generation or gender within the home or community. In turn, this points to the unequal access people have to particular texts and discourses in society. Socially powerful institutions, such as education, the law, the academy and other professions, tend to support dominant literacy practices while vernacular and home literacies are less visible and less valued.

Concept 2.3   **Literacy and power**

Not all literacy practices are equal. The state has enormous power to define literacy, label illiterates, regulate entry into particular groups, and restrict access to knowledge. The question of access to, and production of, valued texts is central to the notions of power and control in modern society. The meanings of dominant literacy practices are constructed in contexts which have considerable power in our society, such as education and law. These controlling institutions erect and support particular prestigious practices and then maintain social inequalities through exclusion from them. Other, more everyday, acts of writing, in contrast, are less supported and are less influential.

The fact that the conventions of particular literacies become endowed with authority and prestige means that they serve as effective mechanisms for legitimising particular views of the world. Once again this leads us back to the position that language is not simply a neutral carrier of ideas but is fundamental to constructing our relationships with others and for understanding our experience of the world. As such it is central to how we negotiate and change our understanding of our societies and ourselves.

By looking at different literacy events it becomes clear that there is not one single literacy but different *literacies*. That is, there are different configurations of practices which are recognisable, named and associated with different aspects of cultural life, such as *academic literacy*, *legal literacy* and *workplace literacy*. The increased literacy demands of the modern world mean that people must constantly move beyond the familiarity of their vernacular practices to engage with those of dominant institutions. One example is access to higher education. In acquiring disciplinary knowledge and skills students simultaneously encounter a new and dominant literacy with its own norms, jargon, sets of conventions and modes of expression which constitute a separate culture (Bartholomae, 1986).

Quote 2.4   Bartholomae on academic literacy

Every time a student sits down to write for us, he has to invent the university for the occasion – invent the university, that is, or a branch of it, like History or Anthropology or Economics or English. He has to learn to speak our language, to speak as we do, to try on the peculiar ways of knowing, selecting, evaluating, reporting, concluding, and arguing that defines the discourse of our community.

Bartholomae (1986: 4)

Because academic ability is frequently evaluated in terms of competence in a specialist written register, students often find their own vernacular writing practices regarded as failed attempts to approximate these standard forms. But institutional views of literacy disguise variability and misrepresent academic literacy as a self-evident way of participating in academic communities (Candlin and Plum, 1998). This in turn encourages the idea that there is one general 'academic English' and one set of strategies for approaching reading and writing tasks that can be applied across disciplines and courses. All this means, of course, that writing instruction often becomes an exercise in 'fixing up' language problems. EAP is largely a response to this, finding ways to undermine a 'single literacy' view and to replace 'remedial' views of teaching with approaches that address students' own writing practices.

This view of literacy, then, has implications for notions of expertise and writing competence. We can no longer regard a 'good writer' as someone who has control over the mechanics of grammar, syntax and punctuation, as in the autonomous view of writing. Nor is it someone who is able to mimic expert composing and 'knowledge-transforming' practices by reworking their ideas during writing, as in process models. Instead, modern conceptions of literacy define an expert writer as 'one who has attained the local knowledge that enables her to write as a member of a discourse community' (Carter, 1990: 226).

Concept 2.4   **The nature of expertise**

Research in educational psychology sees the shift from novice to expert as a gradual acquisition of experiences which provide templates for competent behaviour in particular situations. Novices develop more sophisticated schemata or procedural knowledge as they gradually learn how to work in a specific domain. The novice begins with general strategies, and while the need for these diminishes as he or she gains familiarity with a situation, they are not entirely eliminated. Expertise is therefore a continuum rather than an end state, as general knowledge is increasingly applied in a specific context. When applied to writing, Carter (1990) characterises the development of expertise through five stages of increasingly more context-specific strategies, culminating in fluid, unreflective practice. Experts react intuitively to familiar situations, not relying on rules or strategies but simply doing what works based on the understanding that comes from experience.

Writing competence is now signalled as a marker of expertise in a wide range of professional activities where it refers to the writer's orientations to specific features of the institution. Candlin (1999) identifies a number of macro features which characterise expertise, including the ability to tailor both information and interpersonal aspects of messages to recipient needs and knowledge, and micro discursive acts such as negotiating, formulating and mediating. This is not to say that there are no transferable strategies, as both general and local knowledge seem necessary to account for writing expertise. However, the more learners become familiar with the genres and expectations of their target communities, the greater the accumulated store of experiences they can draw on to meet those expectations. These local competencies remain to be explored and specified for many domains.

2.3 Writing and culture

The idea that writers' experiences of the literacy practices of different communities will influence their linguistic choices suggests that teachers should consider the part that culture plays in student writing. Culture is generally understood as an historically transmitted and systematic network of meanings which allow us to understand, develop and communicate our knowledge and beliefs about the world (Lantolf, 1999). As a result, language and learning are inextricably bound up with culture (Kramsch, 1993). This is partly because our cultural values are reflected in and carried through language, but also because cultures make available to us certain taken-for-granted ways of organising our perceptions and expectations, including those we use to learn and communicate in writing. In writing research and teaching, this is the territory of contrastive rhetoric.

> **Quote 2.5** Connor on contrastive rhetoric
>
> Contrastive rhetoric is an area of research in second-language acquisition that identifies problems in composition encountered by second-language writers and, by referring to the rhetorical strategies of the first language, attempts to explain them ... contrastive rhetoric maintains that language and writing are cultural phenomena. As a direct consequence, each language has rhetorical conventions unique to it.
>
> Connor (1996: 5)

The field of contrastive rhetoric raises interesting questions for teachers about language and rhetorical choices in writing: it asks how features of discourse differ among language users and how these might influence writing in a second language. The basic idea is that students have certain preconceptions about writing which they have learned in their own cultures and which may be inappropriate in native English-speaking settings, acting to hinder effective communication. Drawing mainly on text-analyses and focusing on university contexts, studies have documented contrasting patterns in English and other languages.

> **Quote 2.6** Research on L2 vs L1 students' writing
>
> - different organisational preferences and approaches to argument-structuring
> - different approaches to incorporating material into their writing (para-phrasing, etc.)
> - different perspectives on reader-orientation, on attention-getting devices and on estimates of reader knowledge
> - different uses of cohesion markers, in particular markers which create weaker lexical ties
> - differences in use of overt linguistic features (such as less subordina-tion, more conjunction, less passivisation, fewer free modifiers, less noun-modification, less specific words, less lexical variety, predictable variation and a simpler style).
>
> Grabe and Kaplan (1996: 239)

However, CR has been fiercely attacked in recent years. For one thing, it is not entirely clear exactly what 'cultural patterns of rhetoric' are, where they reside, and how they are learnt. Nor has the strong link between cognition and writing suggested in early versions of contrastive rhetoric (Kaplan, 1966) weathered well, being criticised for ignoring 'the diversity, change and heteroglossia that are normal in any group of speakers or writers' (Cassanave, 2004: 39). More specifically, the approach has been criticized for being over-dependent on text analytic methods and for making broad generalisations about linguistic, cognitive or cultural norms in whole nations on the basis of one or two genres (Kubota, 1998; Leki, 1997). Theoretically, critics point out that because contrastive rhetoric starts from an assumption of difference, it has 'tended to look at L2 writing . . . mainly as a problem of negative transfer of L1 rhetorical patterns to L2 writing' (Casanave, 2004: 41). This not only sees L2 writing as a deficit, but runs the risk of ignoring the rich and complex histories of such students' literacies and what they bring to the L2 classroom (e.g. Horner and Trimbur, 2002).

CR has also been criticised for operating with a rather crude and un-nuanced view of culture as a relatively stable, homogeneous, and all encompassing system of norms that largely determines personal behaviour (Atkinson, 1999a; 2004). Cultures have been conflated with national entities; consensuality *within* cultures have been assumed and contrasted with differences *across* them; and CR practitioners have neglected the place of unequal power relations and the role of conflict in describing cultural influences. A 'received view' of culture therefore makes it easy to see writing preferences as the outcome of fixed traits so that individuals can be lumped together and culture read off from written texts.

Quote 2.7 Canagarajah on Contrastive Rhetoric

Though CR is a rare research and pedagogical tradition indigenous to ESL with considerable value for teachers, it must develop more complex types of explanation for textual difference if the school is to enjoy continued usefulness. Though difference is always going to be there in writing, and though much of it may derive from culture, the ways in which this influence takes place can be positive or negative, enabling as well as limiting, and teachers have to be aware of all these possibilities when they teach student writing. More importantly, teachers must keep in mind that no one needs to be held hostage by language and culture; students can be taught to negotiate conflicting rhetorical structures to their advantage.

Canagarajah (2002: 68)

The fact is that novice writers from different language backgrounds (including L1 English) write in ways that contradict the stereotypes. Research, however, has consistently shown differences in how L1 and L2 writers organise their texts and achieve different rhetorical purposes. Because of this, CR continues to be of considerable interest to teachers of writing, showing us that particular writing preferences may be the result of prior learning rather than deficit. Equally, however, students have individual identities beyond the language and culture they were born into and we should avoid the tendency to stereotype individuals according to crude cultural dichotomies. Cultures are fluid, diverse and non-determining and people may resist or ignore cultural patterns. But equally, prior experiences help shape schema knowledge, and are likely to impact on how students write and their responses to classroom contexts. As we have seen, this is particularly true if we look at communities as 'mini-cultures' which have methods of socialisation; norms and social practices, and well-defined roles and hierarchies.

The approach therefore offers insights into writing practices and opportunities to understand students' literacy experiences. Casanave (2004: 53–54), for example, suggests that teachers might use CR to generate questions for students, encouraging them to think about their educational backgrounds and writing experiences, about the sources of their writing preferences, and their beliefs, about good writing. We also find that teaching approaches in EAP based on 'consciousness raising' draw on CR research to help learners benefit from their bilingual experiences in the new context of academic writing (e.g. Swales and Feak, 2000).

For skilled writers then, what they write, how they write it, the examples they use, and the forms of argument they employ are options which may be influenced by their prior writing experiences, and possibly their culture. One explanation given for these differences is that they are related to writer expectations concerning the extent of reader involvement. Hinds (1987: 143) suggests that in languages such as English the 'person primarily responsible for effective communication is the writer', but in Japanese it is the reader. Similarly, Clyne (1987) argues that while English language cultures charge the writer with clarity, German texts put the onus on the reader to dig out meaning. This may help explain why English contains more metadiscourse signals to label text segments (*to conclude, in summary*), to preview text (*here we will discuss*) and to explicitly structure discussions (*I will make three points*). These features help the reader through a text (Hyland, 2005), but their significance may not always be obvious to L2 writers from more reader-responsible cultures (Crismore *et al.*, 1993).

A comparative perspective also helps us to see that our own writing practices are the product of historical and cultural factors rather than as a norm from which other patterns are merely deviations. The goal of L2 writing instruction can never, in other words, be to change the behaviour of second-language writers by encouraging them to adopt the rhetorical patterns of native speakers. A point made forcefully in the idea of *linguistic imperialism*.

Concept 2.5   **English linguistic imperialism**

The pedagogic response to contrastive rhetoric has largely been to bend the ways of thinking and writing of second language speakers to those of Anglo-American conventions, a practice criticised in Phillipson's (1992) notion of 'linguistic imperialism'. However, Yamuna Kachru (1999: 84) points out the impossibility of training the world's entire English-using population in the norms of one variety. Instead she suggests that it is readers, and particularly English educators, who need to become aware of different rhetorical conventions and to accept them in their work of learners. In addition to being a more plausible enterprise, she argues that this will prevent the continued exclusion of a vast majority from contributing to the world's knowledge simply on the basis of writing conventions.

2.4   Writing and technology

To be a literate person today means having control over a range of print and electronic media. Many of the latter have had a major impact on the ways we write, the genres we create, the authorial identities we assume, the forms of our finished products, and the ways we engage with readers. Some of the most significant of these are listed in Concept 2.6 below.

Concept 2.6   **Effects of electronic technologies on writing**

- Change creating, editing, proofreading and formatting processes
- Combine written texts with visual and audio media more easily
- Encourage non-linear writing and reading processes through hyper-text links
- Challenge traditional notions of authorship, authority and intellectual property
- Allow writers access to more information and to connect that information in new ways
- Change the relationships between writers and readers as readers can often 'write back'
- Expand the range of genres and opportunities to reach wider audiences
- Blur traditional oral and written channel distinctions
- Introduce possibilities for constructing and projecting new social identities

- Facilitate entry to new on-line discourse communities
- Increase the marginalisation of writers who are isolated from new writing technologies
- Offer writing teachers new challenges and opportunities for classroom practice

Perhaps the most immediately obvious, and by now very familiar, feature of computer-based writing is the way that electronic text facilitates composing, dramatically changing our writing habits. Commonplace word processing features which allow us to cut and paste, delete and copy, check spelling and grammar, import images and change every aspect of formatting mean that our texts are now longer, prettier and more heavily revised.

Equally significant changes result from the way electronic media allow us to integrate images with other modes of meaning relatively easily. Electronic technologies, in fact, are accelerating a growing preference for image over text in many domains so that the ability to both understand and even produce multimodal texts is increasingly a requirement of literacy practices in scientific, educational, business, media and other settings. Writing now means 'assembling text and images' in new visual designs, and writers often need to understand the specific ways of configuring the world which different modes offer. For Kress (2003), different modes have different affordances, or potentials and limitations for meaning.

Quote 2.8 Kress on 'affordances'

The two modes of writing and of image are each governed by distinct logics, and have distinctly different affordances. The organization of writing is governed by the logic of time, and by the logic of sequence of its elements in time, in temporally governed arrangements. The organization of the image, by contrast, is governed by the logic of space, and by the logic of simultaneity of its visual/depicted elements in spatially organized arrangements. To say this simply: in speaking I have to say one thing after another... meaning is attached to 'being first' and to 'being last', and so on. In a visual representation the placement of elements in the space of

> representation – the page, the canvas, the screen, the wall – will similarly have meaning. Placing something centrally means that other things will be marginal. Placing something at the top means that something else will likely be below. Both these places can be used to make meaning: being central can mean being the 'centre', in whatever way; being above can mean being superior, and being below can mean 'inferior'.
>
> Kress (2003: 2)

Images therefore have a structure similar to writing, and can be analysed as a visual grammar (e.g. Kress and van Leeuwen, 2006). For example, 'given' and 'new' information are often represented spatially, so that advertisements will tend to situate visual elements of what is known on the left, usually a problem, and what is new on the right, the solution. Think of teeth whitening or weight loss ads, for example. Clearly, contemporary electronic texts such as web-pages and CD ROM screens, are more often like images in their organisation and ask the reader to perform different semiotic work, offering different entry points to the 'page' and different reading paths from the order of words in a sentence, so providing opportunities for readers to design the order of the text for themselves. As a result, Kress and van Leeuwen (2006) draw attention to consequent shifts in authority, in changes in the ways we read, and shifts in forms of engagement with the world.

Given cultural differences in visual design, the use of multimedia in writing classrooms is therefore not just an aid for improving student writing, but for teaching new forms of writing which involve both how texts and images are arranged on a screen and how links are made to others.

This linking is *hypertext*: the glue that holds the Internet together, where active connections are provided to different parts of the current text and beyond it. This allows writers to provide links to digitised graphics, video, sounds, animation and other prose sources, enabling readers to construct different pathways through the text that reflect their own interests and decisions. This web of interconnected textual elements has important implications, as it transforms the familiar writing space of print and gives the reader greater freedom in how he or she can approach the text. A major effect of hypertext, then, is to actualise intertextuality, transforming the potential connections between texts into real ones by allowing readers immediate access to associated texts. While much of the promise of hypertext has been sub-verted by the aggressive commercialism of the Internet, it nevertheless offers great advantages to writers who want to express their arguments in more reflexive and relativistic ways by exploiting the explicit pres-ence of other voices and interpretations.

Perhaps more radically, the shift from print to screen undermines the immutability of an author's text. The ease with which we can collect large numbers of texts and paste them together in ways their writers never conceived of means that original writing is no longer inviolate and that plagiarism becomes harder to police. Any text becomes a temporary structure in a fluid maze of other texts from other times and contexts. In addition, it becomes harder to identify when a piece of writing is actually finished, since not only can readers alter it but it is constantly changing before it reaches the reader. This is most obvious in the architecture of wikis which not only allow individuals to post ideas but others to modify them (most famously in the on-line encyclo-pedia *Wikipedia* that anyone can edit). But virtually all electronic texts exist in multiple versions which the author may not always succeed in controlling. Electronic writing, in other words, heralds not only the death of the author but the death of the canon.

Quote 2.9 Douglas on hypertext argument

The beauty of hypertext is...that it propels us from the straightened 'either/or' world that print has come to represent and into a universe where the 'and/and/and' is always possible. It is an environment more conducive to relativistic philosophy and analysis, where no single account is privileged over any others, yet, because it is written in code, writers can ensure that readers traverse some bits of the argumentative landscape more easily and more frequently than others, or that readers are left to make their own connections between one bit of text and another.

Douglas (1998: 155)

Clearly there are new literacy skills involved here. The ability to read and write hypertext texts are not merely extensions of those required for linear texts but draw on very different competencies. This gains additional importance as there are no established gatekeepers to screen what is published so the ability to critically evaluate websites can be crucial composing and reading skills. Teachers often find a massive range of variation in both the quality and genres students cite in their academic term papers (Stapleton, 2003), for example, and are increasingly finding they must introduce these competencies into their writing classes.

But while technological innovations present challenges to writers, they also open up new identities, genres and communities to them. The emergence and huge popularity of blogs, chatrooms and listserves, for example, produce a sense of immediacy and speed of transmission which radically alter textual practices by encouraging a simulated conversational style in writing. Additionally, the ability of writers to link blogs together on a single page, to create blogrolls (lists of blogs alongside the main text), and to create specific wikis and listserve groups, all offer opportunities to build new communities around writing and texts.

Much has also been made of the absence of physical co-presence in Computer Mediated Communication (CMC) as this has had a tremendous impact on the ways writers see themselves and interact with others on-line (Beatty, 2010). Bloch (2008), for instance recalls a *New Yorker* cartoon of a dog sitting in front of a computer saying 'on the internet, nobody knows you are a dog'. Indeed, an on-line poll by *Read Write Web* in 2007[1] found that 55 per cent of respondents admitted to routinely fashioning fictional personalities. Turkle (1995) argues that the Internet allows people to 'try out' different aspects of their identity, and while this can range from the playful to the scary, it may actually benefit reticent or self conscious language users who may be more inclined to express themselves on-line (Bloch and Crosby, 2006).

Clearly these new genres and technologies not only demand new kinds of writing but also a response from writing teachers. We have moved beyond looking for the best ways to support student word-processing (Hyland, 1993) to exploit the wider opportunities that technology offers (e.g. Snyder, 1998; Tyner, 1998).

Concept 2.7   **Computer-mediated-writing instruction**

Many teachers today use commercial course management systems such as Blackboard or WebCT to display all course materials and messages in one place and to encourage students to post on-line. Increasingly, however, teachers are recognising the value of supporting students to develop and publish their own websites so they can practice new on-line literacy skills. Perhaps the most common use of technology in the writing class in the last few years have been listserves, or electronic mailing lists which exploit students familiarity with email in a restricted and supportive community, assisting teachers in L2 classes in particular to create new relationships and texts. Class blogs have also been used by teachers to foster the expression of students' opinions in writing creating both a sense of authorship and community (Bloch, 2008). Synchronous modes of CMC, such as MOOS and chatrooms, have also been exploited by teachers as this type of communication may encourage more participation which can be beneficial to students' processing of ideas (Herring, 1999). These modes can be confusing or irritating for newcomers as the posts fly by at a rapid rate, but some allow the teacher to archive sessions as a transcript for later study. Additional research and experience is needed to fully understand how best to use these opportunities in different contexts.

2.5 Writing and genre

Genres, as discussed in Chapter 1, are recognised types of communicative actions, which means that to participate in any social event, individuals must be familiar with the genres they encounter there. Because of this, genre is now one of the most important concepts in language education today. It is customary, however, to identify three approaches to genre (Hyon, 1996; Johns, 2002):

(a) the Australian work in the tradition of Systemic Functional Linguistics

(b) the teaching of English for Specific Purposes

(c) the New Rhetoric studies developed in North American composition contexts

  (a) *Systemic Functional views*: In the Systemic Functional model genre is seen as 'a staged, goal oriented social process' (Martin, 1992: 505), emphasising the purposeful and sequential character of different genres and reflecting Halliday's concern with the ways language is systematically linked to context. Genres are social processes because members of a culture interact to achieve them; goal-oriented because they have evolved to achieve things; and staged because meanings are made in steps and it usually takes writers more than one step to reach their goals. When a set of texts share the same purpose, they will often share the same structure, and thus they belong to the same genre. Concept 2.7 shows the structure, purpose and features of two key school genres.

Concept 2.8   **Two school genres**

Explanations

Explanations are written to explain the processes involved in phenomena or how something works.

Explanations usually consist of:

a general statement to introduce the topic,
a series of logical steps explaining how or why something occurs

Explanations are usually written:

in the simple present tense
using chronological and/or causal conjunctions
using mainly 'action' verbs

Explanations are usually found in science, geography, history and social science textbooks

Instructions

Instructions are written to describe how something should be done.

Instructions usually consist of:

a statement of what is to be achieved,
a list of materials/equipment needed to achieve the goal
a series of sequenced steps to achieve the goal

Instructions are usually written:

in the simple present tense
or imperative tense,
in chronological order,
focusing on generalised human groups rather than individuals,
using mainly doing/action verbs

Instructions are commonly found in instruction manuals, payment information and recipe books

Skills for life network (2008)

This approach is perhaps the most developed pedagogically of the three orientations, having had an enormous impact on first language and migrant writing in Australia (see part 3.2). It reminds us that successful writing demands an awareness of both rhetorical structure and control of grammar. This, however, is not the old disembodied grammar of the writing as object approach but one linked to the specific purposes of a genre (Hyland, 2004b).

Quote 2.10 On genre-based grammar in teaching

Grammar is a name for the resource available to users of a language system for producing texts. A knowledge of grammar by a speaker or a writer shifts language use from the implicit and unconscious to a conscious manipulation of language and choice of appropriate texts. A genre-based grammar focuses on the manner through which different language processes or genres in writing are codified in distinct and recognisable ways. It first considers how a text is structured and organised at the level of the whole text in relation to its purpose, audience and message. It then considers how all parts of the text, such as paragraphs and sentences, are structured, organised and coded so as to make the text effective as written communication.

Knapp and Watkins (1994: 8)

(b) *English for Specific Purposes (ESP)*: This orientation follows SFL in the emphasis it gives to the formal properties and communicative purposes of genres, but it differs in adopting a much narrower concept of genre. Instead of seeing genres as the resources available in the wider culture, it regards them as the property of specific discourse communities.

Quote 2.11 Swales on discourse communities and genres

Discourse communities evolve their own conventions and traditions for such diverse verbal activities as running meetings, producing reports, and publicizing their activities. These recurrent classes of communicative events are the genres that orchestrate verbal life. These genres link the past and the present, and so balance forces for tradition and innovation. They structure the roles of individuals within wider frameworks, and further assist those individuals with the actualisation of their communicative plans and purposes.

Swales (1998: 20)

The idea that people acquire, use, and modify the language of written texts in the course of acting as members of occupational groups is central to ESP as its goal is to describe the constraints and group practices of writing in academic and professional contexts. Genre here, then, comprises a class of communicative events employed by specific discourse communities whose members share broad communicative purposes (Swales, 1990: 45–7). These purposes are the rationale of a genre and help to shape the ways it is structured and the choices of content and style it makes available. It is a view of language motivated by pedagogical applications and descriptions of different genres have been widely used in methods and materials for university students and professionals (e.g. Hyland, 2003; Johns, 1997; Swales and Feak, 2004).

Perhaps the best-known ESP genre model is Swales' (1990: 141–8) description of research article introductions where writers Create A Research Space (CARS) to justify their work.

Quote 2.12 Swales' cars model for academic introductions

Move 1 Establishing a territory
         Step 1 Claiming centrality and/or
         Step 2 Making generalisation and/or
         Step 3 Reviewing previous research
Move 2 Establishing a niche
         By counter-claiming, indicating a gap, question-raising, or continuing a tradition
Move 3 Occupying the niche
         Step 1 Outlining purposes or announcing present research
         Step 2 Announcing principal findings
         Step 3 Indicating structure of the article

Swales (1990: 141)

Like plants competing for light and nutrients, the research article competes for a research slot and an audience. For Swales, this encourages writers to produce introductions which potentially consist of three main moves, each of which can be expressed in a number of different ways. It first attracts readers by foregrounding what is already known, then establishes an opening for the current work by showing that this prior knowledge is somehow incomplete, as in this example from Mechanical Engineering, where the second sentence sets up the basis from which the novelty of the writer's work can be understood:

(2) Stiffened planes are commonly used in many engineering structures (e.g. bridge decks, ship superstructures, aerospace structures, etc). Despite their wide application, little is known about their behaviour.

The writer then goes on to 'Occupy the Niche' by stating the precise contribution of the current paper.

Analysing schematic structures has proved invaluable to understanding writing, but there is a danger of oversimplifying if we assume blocks of texts to be monofunctional. Bhatia (1999; 2004) has pointed out that indirect purposes, or 'private intentions', may be expressed simultaneously with more 'socially recognised' ones. There is also the problem that the suggested structures may simply reflect the analyst's intuitions about the text. This highlights the need for moves to be carefully validated in terms of both the linguistic features they contain and the commentaries of users of those texts (Crookes, 1986). Increasingly then, analysts have moved beyond generic staging to identify clusters of features which seem to characterise particular texts or parts of texts. Thus research shows the importance of hedging and imperatives in academic texts and how the presence of extended collocations like *as a result of*, *it should be noted that*, and *as can be seen* help identify a text as belonging to an academic genre while *with regard to*, *in pursuance of*, and *in accordance with* are likely to mark out a legal text (Hyland, 2008).

Research into the features of genres, however, has provided valuable information about how language works which has replaced intuitive understandings and informed classroom practices. Teaching methods in ESP are more varied than those in SFL and tend to be specific to particular target groups, there is, however, a strong emphasis on offering students a variety of genres and requiring them to reflect on their genre practices. Methods therefore stress rhetorical consciousness-raising through classroom analyses of the genres students need to write, often by comparing texts and producing mixed-genre portfolios (e.g. Johns, 1997; Swales & Feak, 2000).

(c) *The 'New Rhetoric'*: This approach diverges from the previous two in seeing genres as more flexible and less straightforward to teach. Greater emphasis is given to the ways that genres evolve and exhibit variation, and this leads to a far more provisional understanding of the concept (Freedman and Medway, 1994). New rhetoric focuses less on genre forms than the actions these forms are used to accomplish, and so tends to use qualitative research tools which explore connections between texts and their contexts rather than those which describe their rhetorical conventions (Miller, 1984).

> **Quote 2.13** Coe on New Rhetoric genre
>
> Genres are a motivated, functional relationship between text type and rhetorical situation. That is to say, a genre is neither a text type nor a situation, but rather the functional relationship between a type of text and a type of situation. Text types survive because they work, because they respond effectively to recurring situations.
>
> Coe (2002)

As a result of this focus, research has examined issues such as the historical evolution of genres (Atkinson, 1999b); the processes of revising and responding to reviewers in writing scientific articles (Berkenkotter and Huckin, 1995); the social impact of transferring genres into new contexts with different purposes (Freedman and Adam, 2000); and the study of genres in the workplace (Pare, 2000; Dias *et al.*, 1999).

New Rhetoric also has a distinctive view on genre pedagogies. It criticises ESP and SFL approaches for abstracting genres from their complex, dynamic contexts (Freedman 1994); for locating the study of genres outside their authentic situations of use (Bleich, 2001); and for limiting the understanding of genres to features that writers already recognise (Bazerman, 2004). Genres are said to be too unstable and the classroom context too artificial to teach genre forms, and instead students should be given opportunities to observe genres in their actual situations of use. Students should therefore learn at least one genre in each course actively, by investigating it themselves through the use of 'mini-ethnographies', or focused studies that explore a particular event in a community (e.g. Devit *et al.*, 2004). Writing classes which link observation and interviews with analyses of genres can therefore be used to give students access to authentic contexts for language use.

> **Quote 2.14** Mary Jo Reiff on teaching genres in the New Rhetoric
>
> As a first assignment, I have students research a field site and observe and describe the participants and their interactions. The following assignment asks students to analyze the language patterns and genre use within that site. For the third assignment, students interview members of the community, culminating in a final ethnographic project that synthesizes the previous research...Making genre analysis the focal point

of ethnographic inquiry – having students examine an organization's newsletter or the employee manual at a business – ties communicative actions to their contexts and can illustrate to students how patterns of rhetorical behavior are inextricably linked to patterns of social behavior.

Johns *et al.* (2006)

In other words, emphasis is given to raising students' awareness of contextual features of genres and of the communities who use them (Bazerman, 1988: 323). It is knowledge of the social contexts which give life to texts and this is more important than their formal patterns.

It is important, however, not to overestimate genre flexibility. Genres are supported by powerful interests and so change only slowly, and the extent individuals, particularly students, are able to manipulate established forms is limited. New rhetoric advocates are correct though in cautioning us to be aware of the degree of genre differentiation. Often analyses show that moves overlap or occur out of sequence, and there is frequently less uniformity than might be expected. This is partly because writers make different choices from optional elements and partly because local communities may have specific uses that override common structures.

More serious variations are the result of interdiscursivity (or the use of conventions from other genres), particularly the increasing intrusion of promotional elements into genres often considered non-promotional (such as institutional advertisement in job announcements) and the growing 'synthetic personalisation' of formal public genres (such as letters from local government offices) (Fairclough, 1995). Mixing genres in this way blurs clear distinctions, sometimes to the extent that new genres become recognised in a community (e.g. *Infotainment*, *advertorial* and *docudrama*). Ultimately, however, genres are the ways that we engage in, and make sense of, our social worlds and our competence to use them does not lie in our ability to identify monolithic uses of language, but to modify our choices according to the contexts in which we write.

2.6 Writing and identity

Recent research has emphasised the close connections between writing and an author's identity. In its broadest sense, *identity* refers to 'the ways that people display who they are to each other' (Benwell and Stokoe, 2006: 6): a social performance achieved by drawing on appropriate linguistic resources. Identity is therefore seen as constructed by both the texts we engage in and the linguistic choices we make, thus moving identity from the private to the public sphere, and from hidden processes of cognition to its social and dynamic construction in discourse. In other words, this view questions whether there is an absolute, unchanging self lurking behind discourse and suggests that identity is a *performance*. We perform *identity work* by constructing ourselves as credible members of a particular social group, so that identity is something we *do*; not something we *have*. Almost everything we say or write, in fact, says something about us and the kind of relationship we want to establish with others.

As Bloemmaert (2005) observes, however, our identities are only successful to the extent that they are recognised by others, and this means employing, appropriating and transforming the existing discourses that we encounter (Bakhtin, 1986). Clearly, writers do not create a representation of themselves from an infinite range of possibilities but make choices from culturally available resources. The ways we perform an identity therefore involve interactions between the conventional practices of the literacy event and the values, beliefs and prior cultural experiences of the participants.

Concept 2.9   Writing and identity

Current notions of identity see it as a plural concept, socially defined and negotiated through the choices writers make in their discourses. These choices are partly constrained by the dominant ideologies of privileged literacies in particular communities, and partly open to writers' interpretations as a result of their personal and sociocultural experiences. Identity thus refers to the various 'selves' writers employ in different contexts, the processes of their connection to particular communities, and their responses to the power relations institutionally inscribed in them.

Identity therefore needs to be distinguished from the notion of *voice* in the Expressivist literature. Voice is a complex idea with various meanings and connotations, but essentially refers to the writer's distinctive signature, the individual stamp that he or she leaves on a text (Elbow, 1994). Writing teachers value this assertion of personal authority and often exhort student writers to 'discover their own unique voice' and achieve self-expression in their writing. In other words, this view sees identity as the manifestation of a private self, a highly individualistic concept deeply rooted in mainstream western culture and often antithetical to the communicative norms of ESL students from more collectivist cultures (Ramanathan and Atkinson, 1999a).

In contrast, instead of looking for textual evidence of the writer's private self, identity is located in the public, institutionally defined roles people create in writing as community members, including 'their representation of audience, subject matter, and other elements of context' (Cherry, 1988: 269). This social view sees identity as rhetorical traces of *membership*: the commitment to particular ways of seeing the world and representing it to others as an insider. In our public lives we play out professional roles and claim professional identities, writing as storekeepers, company executives, or cognitive psychologists, using the discourses of our trade. Identity here then concerns how writing takes on the discursive and epistemological features of a particular culture: how writers project an insider ethos and signal their right to be heard as competent members of a group.

Concept 2.10   **On membership**

Membership refers to a writer's ability to recognise, replicate and, within limits, innovate, a community's organisational structures, current interests, and rhetorical practices. It involves following certain conventions of impression management to project an insider status, the shared awareness of these conventions providing the defining feature of a community. We claim the competence to address colleagues by drawing on intertextual knowledge which includes typical ways of selecting and exploiting topics, referring to shared knowledge, interacting with our content and readers, and using specialised terminology. So, writing as an accountant, a magnetic physicist, or a production supervisor means positioning yourself within the apparently natural borders of your community through control of its legitimate forms of discourse.

In any context, then, one discourse is likely to be dominant and hence more visible, so that writers often consciously or unconsciously take up the identity options this privileged discourse makes available (Wertsch, 1991). Scollon and Scollon (1981) use the term 'essayist literacy' to refer to the specific literacy practices which are privileged in education. Students are typically required to adopt a style of writing at school on university which involves anonymising themselves and adopting the guise of a rational, disinterested, asocial seeker of truth. By stepping into an essayist literacy writers sacrifice concreteness, empathy with discussed entities, and ways of representing change as a dynamic process. On the other hand, they gain the ability to discuss abstract things and relations, and to categorise, quantify and evaluate according to the perspectives of their discipline. Such gains, of course, are only perceived as such if students value what this literacy allows them to do, and the kinds of people it allows them to be.

In fact, students often find that academic conventions do not allow them to represent themselves in their texts, suppressing the extent they can articulate personal a stance (Hyland, 2002). Ivanic (1998: 9) makes this clear in relation to mature students who often

> feel alienated and devalued within the institution of higher education. Their identities are threatened and they respond either by attempting to accommodate to the established values and practices of the context they are entering, or – more radically – by questioning and challenging the dominant values and practices.

In such situations students are often uncertain about who they are expected to be, and often feel more constructed by their texts than constructing them. We don't, then, blindly adopt such identities. Individuals do not define themselves only by one group membership but belong to different groups, so that their commitments and experiences often overlap and perhaps conflict. Socio-cultural factors such as gender, social class, age, religion, ethnicity, regional background, and so on are key aspects of our experiences and can help shape our projection of an authorial identity.

The ways that writers present themselves and find themselves positioned in constructing a discoursal identity have been extensively discussed by Ivanic (Ivanic, 1998; Ivanic and Weldon, 1999). She argues that writers' identities are socially constructed by the prototypical 'possibilities for self-hood' available in the context of writing. Interacting with this are three inseparable aspects of the identity of actual writers when creating a particular text.

Concept 2.11   Ivanic on writer identity

1. **The autobiographical self** is the self which writers bring to an act of writing, socially constrained and constructed by the writer's life-history. It includes their ideas, opinions, beliefs and commitments: their stance. An example might be how a writer evaluates the quotes he or she brings into a text, or the topics he or she chooses to address.

2. **The discoursal self** is the impression writers consciously or unconsciously convey of themselves in a text. This concerns the writers' voice in the sense of how they portray themselves. An example is the extent to which a writer takes on the practices of the community he or she is writing for, adopting its conventions to claim membership.

3. **The authorial self** shows itself in the degree of authoritativeness with which a writer writes. This is the extent to which a writer intrudes into a text and claims herself as the source of its content. This would include the use of personal pronouns and willingness to personally get behind arguments and claims.

(See Ivanic, 1998; Ivanic and Weldon, 1999.)

This is a dynamic view of identity which emphasises the tensions which exist when individual writers meet the discourses of the institutions in which they write. People are constrained, but not determined, by the dominant disciplinary, professional, gender and political identities which are set up by the conventions of specific genres and the practices which surround any act of writing. We all bring multiple possibilities to any act of writing which carry the potential to challenge the pressures to conform to dominant identities.

2.7 Conclusion

This chapter has examined some of the key issues in writing research and theory today. Because it has been necessarily selective, I have chosen to look at topics which have not only motivated much recent thinking in the field but which also best illustrate where contemporary research into text and composition is going, and which reflect our current understanding about writing. Once again I have been concerned to highlight ideas which present writing as social and interactive rather than simply cognitive and individual. A text is always inextricable from the processes of production and interpretation that create it and, as we shall see in the next sections, the ways we teach and research writing have come increasingly to reflect this.

Further reading

Clark, R. and Ivanic, R. (1997) *The politics of writing* (London: Routledge). An absorbing discussion of issues of writer identity and writer–reader relationships.

Barton, D. and Hamilton, M. (1998) *Local literacies: reading and writing in one community* (London: Routledge). An excellent study which clearly outlines and illustrates the major issues of a social literacy approach.

Block, D. (2007) *Second language identities* (London: Continuum). Examines how identity is an issue in different second-language-learning contexts.

Bloch, J. (2008) *Technologies in the second language composition classroom* (Ann Arbor, MI: University of Michigan Press). A comprehensive and accessible volume supporting teachers in adopting technologies in writing teaching.

Casanave, C. (2004). *Controversies in second language writing* (Ann Arbor, MI: University of Michigan Press). An intelligent and accessible discussion of some key issues in writing instruction.

Connor, U. (1996). *Contrastive rhetoric* (Cambridge: CUP).

Hyland, K. (2004). *Genre and Second Language Writers* (Ann Arbor, MI: University of Michigan Press). An overview of genre and how it can be used by teachers of EFL/ESL writing.

Kress, G. and van Leeuwen, T. (2006) *Reading images: the grammar of visual design, 2nd edn* (London: Routledge).

Johns, A.M. (ed.) (2002) *Genre and the classroom* (Mahwah, NJ: Erlbaum). An excellent collection covering a range of theoretical and practical issues of implementing genre approaches in the classroom.

Note

1 http://www.readwriteweb.com/archives/fake_web_identity_poll_results.php retrieved 28 July 2008.

Section

|| Applying writing research

Chapter 3

Research-based writing courses

This chapter will...

- show how research contributes to teaching in four English language courses;

- examine the methodologies, materials, and theoretical premises, of these courses;

- explore how each course draws on and reflects one of the major orientations sketched in Chapter 1.

3.1 Research and writing pedagogy

The previous two chapters have shown how writing instruction has been informed by a variety of research perspectives. From research on writers we are familiar with the idea that composing is non-linear and goal-driven, and that students can benefit from having a range of writing and revising strategies on which to draw. Equally, research on texts themselves shows the value of formal knowledge and the positive effects of language proficiency. This draws attention to the importance of encoding knowledge and relationships appropriately through lexical and grammatical choices and discourse structures. From research on audience we are aware of the importance of appropriate regard for reader perspective, interactional strategies and community-specific text conventions, and from critical approaches we recognise the need to see the often reified forms of target discourses as simply prestigious (and contestable) ways of making meanings.

Research, however, offers no universal solutions to the challenges of classroom practice, and implies no single method of teaching writing. There has probably never been a time when teachers have focused exclusively on just one of these elements of writing and blended approaches are common as a result of the diversity of teaching contexts and teacher beliefs. The diversity of students' prior experiences and future needs; the different resources, knowledge, preferences, and expertise of teachers; the climate of opinion and methodological fashion in the school; and the relationship of the writing course to its immediate social context will all differ from one situation to the next. But while we cannot simply apply some neat body of findings to ensure learning, classroom decisions are always informed by our theories and beliefs about what writing is and how people learn to write.

We need, of course, to always apply our theories to the real student writers in our classrooms and recognise that they are likely to have their own ideas of what 'good writing' consists of based on their prior cultural and social experiences. We also need to be aware that these expectations may emerge when confronted with writing in a foreign language or in an unfamiliar genre. This awareness means that we are more likely to see student writing difficulties as evidence of a struggle to control the conventions of a new target community rather than as the personal failings of individual writers. These considerations are particularly important when teaching EFL students.

Quote 3.1 Liebman on L2 student backgrounds

It is not enough to determine what will be expected of ESL students in the university and then give them models of what we want them to produce. We must also determine what these students' prior experiences are. Students from different backgrounds will require different approaches. When we seek to help ESL students use expressive writing more effectively, for example, we may find it necessary to use different techniques for Japanese and Arabic students in order to help these students achieve the goals reflected in the models we show them. Similarly, when we teach argument, we may need to approach it differently with Arabic and Japanese students.

Liebman (1992: 157–8)

Successful writing instruction requires an awareness of the importance of both cognitive and social factors, which teachers have understood to mean providing relevant topics, encouraging peer cooperation, and incorporating group activities of various kinds. Workshop environments have therefore been popular to provide peer support and opportunities for students to talk about their writing-in-progress. Many teachers offer students training in composition strategies which can be transferred across situations, helping them to brainstorm, draft, and revise, together with advice on how to structure their writing according to the demands and constraints of particular contexts and the needs of particular readers. In other words, while we learn to write through writing, what we write must be related to the genres and contexts we have to engage in. This means that attention to audience is vital, and that feedback from teachers and peers together with research on particular readers and appropriate reading can help students anticipate the expectations of particular readers (Grabe, 2003; Johns, 1997).

Theory and research therefore shape instructional practices in important ways, and reflecting on examples of how research can contribute to writing pedagogy can help improve our own practices. This chapter provides some extended examples of how different conceptions of writing and learning influence teaching practices in a number of real classrooms. This section begins with an overview of some issues raised by research and theory and then looks at four very different writing courses: from New Zealand, Australia, Papua New Guinea and England, to reveal the impact of research in very different contexts of teaching and learning.

3.2 Writ 101: process in practice

This first case is a successful application of process and rhetorical research to writing pedagogy[1] as discussed in part 1.2 above. Designed to develop the academic writing skills of New Zealand undergraduates, Writ 101 demonstrates an explicit appreciation of writing as personal, social and recursive as it progressively builds an awareness of genre and composing through a series of core assignments. The course resists a narrow focus on form and disciplinary genres to develop techniques for generating, drafting, revising and responding to a variety of texts, and develop recognition that writing involves a mediation between the writer and an audience. While it makes use of constructionist views of text structure and audience, its main sources are Flower's work on writing as problem-solving, Elbow's emphasis on prewriting, revision and peer response, and Murray's views on writing for learning (Holst, pc). The pedagogical implications of this are that basic writers can be guided, through invention strategies, multiple drafting and copious revision, to adopt the practices of experts.

Concept 3.1   **A process view of writing**

- **Writing is problem-solving**: writers use invention strategies and extensive planning to resolve the rhetorical problems that each writing task presents.

- **Writing is generative**: writers explore and discover ideas as they write.

- **Writing is recursive**: writers constantly review and modify their texts as they write and often produce several drafts to achieve a finished product.

- **Writing is collaborative**: writers benefit from focused feedback from a variety of sources.

- **Writing is developmental**: writers should not be evaluated only on their final products but on their improvement.

The approach

Writ 101 is an elective course which seeks to be both accessible and relevant to all majors, proficiencies and years, linking students' own writing experiences with the demands of academic study. To achieve this, the course moves from autobiographical writing, to topics within the writer's knowledge, and then to writing using multiple sources. This progressive abstraction of field and tenor is paralleled by a movement from writing for the teacher, to writing for peers, to writing for a public unknown audience.

Writ 101 seeks to 'give process a classroom presence' (Holst, pc) by engaging students in a recursive process of planning, drafting, reviewing, evaluating and revising, of providing a supportive environment, and of making use of various feedback sources (e.g. Raimes, 1987). Considerable emphasis is laid on helping students become aware of writing as a series of stages to help them compose free of the need to achieve correctness and completeness as they write. The emphasis on process-writing is clear from the foreword of the coursebook *Writ 101: Writing English* (Holst, 1995).

Quote 3.2 Janet Holst on Writ 101

Learning to write, like learning any other skill, is a matter of instruction, practice and critical feedback. Instruction in Writ 101 will be given in lectures, in workshops and in the Coursebook. The practice will come in the writing assignments and in the tasks you do in the workshops, and the critical feedback will come from your classmates in peer evaluations and from your tutor in marked assignments. You will quickly learn to become your own effective critic through editing your colleagues' work and revising your own. Most of all, you will learn by writing, in the struggles to find form for the meaning you want to convey.

Holst (1995: v)

The structure

The course comprises a one-hour lecture and three hours of workshops each week for a 14 week semester. It begins by focusing students on the writing process and their own practices as writers. Here students discuss commentaries by experienced writers such as Elbow and Murray on their composing strategies before moving on to practice invention, drafting and revising techniques. Tutors reinforce this exploratory and reflective approach by requiring students to keep a process journal in which they can examine their writing practices.

Concept 3.2   **Process stages in Writ 101**

Prewriting: brainstorming, free writing, clustering, topic analysis, organising, planning

Writing: drafting, unblocking techniques

Editing: cutting deadwood, strengthening sentences, improving style

Rewriting: identifying focus and structure, revising on different levels, peer feedback, adapting text for speaking

Publication: proofreading and polishing, evaluating the final product, publication.

After presenting students with an understanding of the writing process, the course then guides them through ways of responding to writing, looking at the features that contribute to good writing and equipping them with strategies of peer editing. Students concentrate on different aspects of sample texts, considering their content, purpose, possible audiences, degree of formality, sentence lengths, vocabulary choices, and so on, and discuss their evaluations in small groups. The purpose of this is not only to provide students with ways to approach their classmates' work with critical appreciation. It also helps them become more sensitive to issues of correctness, expression and organisation, and so encourages more awareness of their own readers when they write themselves.

Writ 101 is organised around four core assignments: a narrative, an exposition, an argument and a research paper based on one of these earlier assignments.

Quote 3.3 Writ 101 course work

Preliminary   An in-class piece about yourself as a writer, assessing your strengths and weaknesses and setting out your goals for the course.

Assignment 1   Narrative (700 words)

Assignment 2   Exposition (700–900 words)

Revision   Choose ONE of your first two assignments and revise your paper following the revision guidelines in this coursebook.

Assignment 3   Argument or critical review (800–900 words)

Assignment 4   Research essay (1000 words). You are advised to develop a topic you wrote for assignment 2 or 3 by referring to 3–4 sources and using correct documentation.

Talk   A 3–4-minute talk to group on a topic you are researching for this or another course

Essay test   A 2-hour in-class writing test

Portfolio   A minimum of FOUR assessable pieces, plus their earlier versions, and an introduction.

Holst (1995: 6)

Students work on each of these assignments with their peers in the workshops. Part of this involves discussion of sample essays and extracts in the relevant genre written by academics, novelists and students from earlier courses, including a narration by Orwell, an exposition by Thurber, and an argument by Amnesty International. These are treated not as models but as stimuli to produce reaction and discussion. Students may be asked to locate topic sentences, cohesive links, warrants, organisational patterns and so on before writing their own essays. All assignments begin with some kind of group discussion of texts, analysis of their typical contexts, freewriting, and practice, but develop in different ways, focusing on salient features of the genre and highlighting a particular aspect of the composing process.

The genres that drive the course are distinguished in terms of their different purposes and audience. The acronym RAFT (Role and Purpose, Audience, Focus, Tone) is strongly emphasised and students have to submit a statement detailing these with each assignment, together with a reflection on the writing. The weekly lectures emphasise the importance of these elements along with the features of each target genre. So, when working on narrative there is a focus on ways of generating ideas to write about, making sense to readers and strategies for revising. Work on expository writing then builds on this to develop more elaborate heuristics for pre-writing, lexical selection, topic sentences, and the importance of appropriate structure. Persuasion emphasises argument structure, use of evidence, logical sequencing and appropriate conventions. Finally, research writing focuses on problem identification, methods of enquiry, using documents and incorporating others' ideas.

Quote 3.4 Writing in different genres: RAFT

Before they begin to write, skilled writers in real life consider four important questions:

1. **What is the purpose of this piece of writing?** This has to do with the function of the writing and the role that the writer is adopting for this purpose. For example, is the purpose to explain carefully and clearly how something works? Is it to persuade readers and stimulate them to some action?

2. **Who am I writing this for?** By analysing our intended audience, we can clarify the content and focus on our writing task. Who are my readers? How much do they know already? What will be new to them? What is their attitude to my subject? Once we have a clear sense of purpose and audience, we can then think about more specific aspects of the writing task.

3. **What should this piece of writing look like?** This is related to audience and purpose and concerns the format of a piece. Is it a report, a memo, a research paper, a feature article? What conventions of organisation and layout should I follow?
4. **How should I sound? What tone should I adopt for this piece? Tone** has to do with formality and attitude.

Holst (1995: 111)

Feedback and assessment

Both tutor and peer feedback is a central element of the course. Each essay receives peer commentary based on a rubric which focuses the reader on specific aspects of the genre in question, thereby raising both participants' awareness of important issues. The response sheet for the expository writing assignment is shown in Concept 3.3. Writers redraft their essays on the basis of this peer commentary and submit the revised version to their tutor along with a response to the peer comments. This response focuses on what they learnt from the reader's comments and what they must do to improve the piece. Tutors comment on the strengths of the paper and suggest possible improvements. The final assignment, however, is edited and revised without written tutor feedback. While students are able to conference with their tutors and receive oral comments, they have to develop, edit and revise the research paper with only peer assistance.

Concept 3.3   **Peer response: expository writing assignment**

Reader: Read the writing and make a descriptive outline of each paragraph in the piece.

What was the writer saying in this paper? Did the writer show good understanding of the subject? Were the ideas interesting and worthwhile?

Was there any part where you wanted more information or clarification? Could it be expanded through detail, illustration or analogy?

How well did the lead work for you? Did it focus on the topic? Set the style and tone?

Was the language clear and concise? Did you notice:
- any unnecessary words that could be cut?
- a place where more concrete language, or verbs instead of nouns could be used?
- any ineffective transitions or a place where a transition was needed?

What struck you as the strongest feature in the paper?

What changes would you make if the piece was yours?

Holst (1995: 45)

Final assessment for the course is by the submission of a portfolio which reflects the course aims of developing students' abilities to research, write and respond to different texts. It consists of the four assignments completed during the course, accompanied by drafts and responses from peers and tutors, together with a reflective introduction and any other pieces written during the course which students feel display their proficiency. These assignments should show improvement and bear the influence of peer and tutor comments. The research paper, which is weighted more heavily in the portfolio, receives no tutor feedback and is submitted with two drafts responding to peer comments.

Conclusions

Overall, this is an extremely popular and successful course which gives a clear pedagogical focus to much process-writing research. It involves students in a great deal of writing practice as well as opportunities for reflection and feedback. As a result, students are given the opportunity to develop not only their writing skills but also a critical awareness of good writing and effective expression in several genres. The course places heavy burdens on tutors, however, as extensive feedback and conferencing are necessary if students are to benefit from the multiple redrafting the course requires, these efforts obviously pay off, however, as the course is consistently oversubscribed and receives glowing recommendations from students.

3.3   Genre in primary classrooms: the New South Wales (NSW) K-6 syllabus

Writing is central to children's intellectual, social and emotional development and plays a critical role in learning. It is therefore essential that the early teaching of writing should draw on research which describes the types of texts that students have to write at different stages. The

K-6 English syllabus (Board of Studies, 2007a; 2007b) in New South Wales, Australia, seeks to do exactly this through a genre approach. Informed by a Systemic Functional model of language (see Concept 3.4) and based on research into children writing in schools (e.g. Martin, 1993; Feez, 2001), the syllabus offers a clearly defined pedagogy founded on an explicit focus on the ways texts are organised and the language choices writers need to achieve their purposes.

Concept 3.4   A functional model of writing

- Language is a system for communicating meaning.
- Meanings are organised as texts and have distinctive characteristics depending on their purposes.
- Texts are never completely individual, they always relate to a social context and to other texts.
- Context is realised in texts through conventions of field (what), tenor (who) and mode (how).
- A knowledge of the resources for creating texts allows writers to write more effectively.
- All texts can be described in terms of both form and function, i.e. their organisation of elements for making meanings and the purposes that are being served with them.

The K-6 English syllabus[2]

The syllabus is based on research carried out at the University of Sydney (e.g. Rothery, 1986) to identify different genres by analysing the discourse and register features of samples of primary students' writing. The direct result of these analyses is a syllabus which emphasises language as a resource for making meanings and which places genre at the centre of writing development.

Syllabus genres

At the core of the syllabus is a range of genres seen as fundamental to the students' learning in the primary school curriculum and their effective participation in the world outside school. A basic distinction is made between literary genres, which explore and interpret human experience, and factual genres, which present information or ideas in order to enlighten or persuade. These text types lack the blending that one often finds in the real world, but they are regarded as starting points from which students can understand the grammatical features and patterns of organisation that allow them to write for different purposes.

Quote 3.5 Syllabus genres

Text Types

Literary texts		Factual texts	
Narrative	Literary description	Factual description	Factual recount
Literary recount	Personal response	Information report	Explanation
Observation	Review	Procedure	Exposition
		Procedural recount	Discussion

Board of Studies (2007b: 66)

Accompanying documents offer a description of the social purpose, structure and principal grammatical features for each of these target genres. The features of *Recounts*, for example, are described in Quote 3.6.

Quote 3.6 General features of *Recount*

Social Purpose
Recounts 'tell what happened'. The purpose of a factual recount is to document a series of events and evaluate their significance in some way. The purpose of the literary or story recount is to tell a sequence of events so that it entertains. The story recount has expressions of attitude and feeling, usually made by the narrator about the events.

Structure
Recounts are organised to include:

• an orientation providing information about 'who', 'where' and 'when';

• a record of events usually recounted in chronological order;

• personal comments and/or evaluative remarks, which are interspersed throughout the record of events;

• a reorientation, which 'rounds off' the sequence of events.

Grammar

Common grammatical patterns of a recount include:

- use of nouns and pronouns to identify people, animals or things involved;
- use of action verbs to refer to events;
- use of past tense to locate events in relation to speaker's or writer's time;
- use of conjunctions and time connectives to sequence the events;
- use of adverbs and adverbial phrases to indicate place and time;
- use of adjectives to describe nouns.

Board of Studies (2007b: 287)

Syllabus outcomes

For each genre the syllabus describes demonstrable learning outcomes which form the basis of planning and assessing students' writing at three stages of development, each of two years, through the primary school. These outcomes reflect two sub-strands of the syllabus: the ability to **use** language effectively and the ability to **talk about** the language being used. In general terms, the skills involved in learning to write include the ability to draft, revise, conference, edit, proofread and publish, to use computers, and to form well-structured, accurate sentences in legible handwriting. The second strand emphasises development of a shared language for talking about language, and using this to evaluate texts in terms of effectiveness, meaning and accuracy. An explicit focus on grammar is therefore central as it enables students not only to understand how sentences are structured so that they are meaningful, clear and syntactically accurate, but also to think about the relationship between a text and its context, how language changes over time, and how it changes in different situations.

> **Quote 3.7**   Writing outcomes for Stage 2 (years 3 and 4)
>
> **Learning to write**
> *Producing texts*: Drafts, revises, proofreads and publishes well-structured texts that are more demanding in terms of topic, audience and written language features

Grammar and Punctuation: Produces texts clearly, effectively and accurately, using the sentence structure, grammatical features and punctuation conventions of the text type

Spelling: Uses knowledge of letter–sound correspondences, common letter patterns and a range of strategies to spell familiar and unfamiliar words

Handwriting and computer use: Uses joined letters when writing in NSW Foundation Style and demonstrates basic desktop publishing skills on the computer

Learning about writing
Context and text: Discusses how own texts are adjusted to relate to different readers, how they develop the subject matter and how they serve a wide variety of purposes

Language structures and features: Discusses how own texts have been structured to achieve their purpose and the grammatical features characteristic of the various text types used.

Board of Studies (2007b: 19)

Classroom practices

A number of support documents accompany the syllabus which outline the structure and content of different genres, suggest relevant learning tasks, and specify the grammar and terminology appropriate for each stage. Beyond these, however, is the belief that learners' development of unfamiliar genres should be carefully supported through interaction with peers and teachers and clear modelling, as outlined in this quote from Martin *et al.* (1987).

Quote 3.8 **Genre modelling in schools**

1. *Introducing a genre* – modelling a genre implicitly through reading to or by the class
2. *Focusing on a genre* – modelling a genre explicitly by naming its stages
3. *Jointly negotiating a genre* – teacher and class jointly composing the genre under focus; the teacher guides the composition of the text through questions and comments that provide scaffolding for the stages of the genre

4. *Researching* – selecting material for reading; notemaking and summarising; assembling information before writing
5. *Drafting* – a first attempt at individually constructing the genre under focus
6. *Consultation* – teacher–pupil consultation, involving direct reference to the meanings of the text
7. *Publishing* – writing a final draft that may be published in class.

Martin *et al.* (1987: 68–9)

Research has also informed the materials developed to support the syllabus (e.g. Gibbons, 2002). A good example is a classroom practice suggested by Derewianka (1990) for introducing recounts to grade 2 children.

Quote 3.9 Constructing a Form 2 Recount

During the week some children from 4th class visited Alix's classroom and in small groups shared Recounts of what they had written of the school camp they had just been on. Over the next few days Alix read the children a number of different types of Recounts which she wrote out on butcher's paper and pinned around the room as models. She then suggested that they might like to write a Recount of the coming excursion.

On the day of the excursion, she took along the school's videocamera ...On their return to school, they shared their observations in the form of oral Recounts...The video served as a memory jogger reminding them of details which might otherwise have gone unrecorded. At various points Alix put the video on 'pause' and constructed a flowchart of the stages of the excursion...The flowchart gave the children a visual idea of the sequence, and served as a prompt for them when it came to constructing a class Recount of the excursion. Alix guided them in writing a text telling what happened during the outing and what they discovered at the various sites by asking questions like these:

Where did we go first?
What sort of plants did we find there?
What did they look like?

When they had finished, Alix suggested that they might start off by letting their readers know a bit of background information, like *who* took part in the excursion, *why*, *when* it happened. The session finished with a brief review of how the class had structured their Recount – an orientation followed by a series of events. The next day the children tried writing their own Recounts of the excursion for their families.

Derewianka (1990: 11–12)

Conclusions

When children begin their school lives they face a major shift in their language use from a familiar, spontaneous mode of face-to-face conversation to the more structured patterns of writing. This change means they need to learn how to guide readers through a text without immediate feedback from an interactional partner and to construct texts which are both cohesive and coherent for a particular purpose. By distinguishing learning to use language from learning about language, and by providing careful scaffolding, this syllabus provides a way for children both to develop the language they need to construct genres and to reflect on how language is used to accomplish this. Genres thus form the foundation of learning to write. Admittedly not all teachers are comfortable with this approach, but generally it has been welcomed, with similar syllabuses being adopted in other Australian states. The success of the model for teaching which underlies the K-6 Primary English syllabus undoubtedly derives from its solid research base.

3.4   Go for Gold – writing for a reason

Here I discuss a course that follows neither a process or genre path, but which employs writing as part of an overall communicative process in an experiential learning context. Here writing is a *social practice*, incidental to wider communicative goals in a chain of texts and interactions. It is produced to accomplish specific purposes with real audiences and is based on research which sees writing as interaction (Nystrand, 1989). Go for Gold (GfG) also draws on educational research emphasising the value of collaborative learning (e.g. Bruffee, 1984) by providing students with an environment of mutual support within their 'zone of proximal development' (Vygotsky, 1962), the difference between what a learner can do alone and through cooperation with capable peers.

This is then an English for Specific Purposes (ESP) course based on learning by doing, requiring learners to respond actively and engage purposefully in authentic communication with others (Hyland and Hyland, 1992).

Quote 3.10 Raymond Williams on learner engagement

There is no way to help a learner to be disciplined, active and thoroughly engaged unless he perceives a problem to be a problem or whatever it is to be learned as worth learning, and unless he plays an active role in determining the process of solution. That is the plain unvarnished truth, and if it sounds like warmed over 'progressive education', it is nonetheless true for it.

Williams (1962)

Williams' brief statement of pedagogical principles closely links learning with students' active involvement, a view echoed in language-learning by writers who advocate process syllabuses (e.g. Breen and Littlejohn, 2000) and learner control (e.g. Pierce, 1995). Rather than focusing exclusively on the outcomes of learning, process-oriented courses are based on the idea that learning derives from the kinds of interaction and negotiation which students engage in. Creating a simulated environment which encourages both speaking and writing, GfG establishes a balance between these two. It provides a structured framework of tasks, learning content, materials and broad outcomes, while allowing opportunities for learner reinterpretation and decision-making as they decide which methods and approaches they will use to achieve their goals. This potential for a variety of learner options means participants can reflect on the situations that confront them and respond strategically in writing to their audiences. Concept 3.5 summarises some advantages of this approach.

Concept 3.5   **Advantages of writing in a simulation**

- **Discoursal rehearsal**: helps learners establish ways of engaging in spoken and written interaction by simulating real-world events.

- **Learning to write**: provides opportunities to employ genres under realistic conditions.

- **Rhetorical consciousness raising**: promotes understanding of reader needs and of writing as a means of achieving social and persuasive purposes.

- **Motivated involvement**: provides students with reasons for writing based on their target needs and current interests.

- **Cooperative engagement**: requires students to work with others to collect data, exchange information and make decisions.

- **Learner control**: offers learners opportunities to determine their own routes and strategies to achieve the goals established by the simulation.

- **Real feedback**: requires students to respond immediately and authentically to peers' texts, helping writers to judge the effectiveness of their communication and develop reader sensitivity.

Background

Go for Gold is an ESP course for second-year business students at the English-medium Papua New Guinea University of Technology. The students come from a wide variety of language backgrounds and speak English as a second or third language at upper-intermediate or advanced levels. The course simulates the awarding of a contract to mine one of the world's richest gold reserves on a small island off the PNG coast. It runs for 56 hours over a 14-week semester and involves the students taking roles and engaging in a series of linked and roughly graded communication tasks to gather information, make decisions, cooperate in problem-solving and produce various written and spoken genres. The language is purposeful and authentic as it addresses issues of immediate interest to the participants and their future professional needs. Not only is the exploitation of PNG's natural resources by giant multinationals a highly charged political issue, but also these students are an educated élite who typically rise rapidly to influential positions after graduation where good English communication skills are vital.

Course structure

Concept 3.6   **Course description**

Input stage

Information input	**Language input**
Bid for Power video (BBC, 1983)	Bid for Power video
Public lecture	Focus on genres and language forms
Newspaper articles, reports, studies, etc.	Role-information cards

Activity stage

1. Preparations
arranging and holding meetings
intragroup and intergroup discussions
individual and group data collection – both from each other and source materials

2. Presentations
ministers' policy statements and local politicians' statements of interest
government's specification report
companies' bid proposal reports
oral presentations of reports
announcement of decisions
reactions to decisions

Feedback stage

Activity evaluation	**Language evaluation**
discussion of the tasks	discussion of language use
journal writing	assessment sheet
	corrected written work
	discussion of presentation
	video replays

Hyland and Hyland (1992: 228)

The **input** phase prepares students for the roles and activities they will meet in the project. Relevant concepts, identities, genres and language forms are introduced through the business English video 'Bid for Power' (BBC, 1983) which raises parallel issues to the GfG scenario and presents relevant aspects of language in a natural context. Students are also instructed in formal oral presentations, business writing, research skills and group work. Relevant written genres are introduced through study of authentic documents with reports, minutes and memos closely examined and their rhetorical structure discussed. While learning about these genres, students are gathering background information on the mining project through a public lecture from a mining company representative and a range of policy documents, newspaper articles, company reports, feasibility studies, maps, census data, and economic projections. Teachers are highly interventionist during this stage, particularly in modelling written genres and guiding writing practice, but once the activity is underway their main responsibility is to establish the conditions for communication, be available for consultation and monitor what goes on.

The **activities** require participants to select a role from a *political group*, consisting of ministers, local village representatives and a provincial premier, a *business group* made up of a number of competing consortia, and a small *consultant group* advising the government. These different roles involve different perceptions of the modelled reality and require different information and genres. Some relationships involve cooperation and sharing information while others entail competition and secrecy. Students gradually adopt their roles as they collect the information they need to meet activity objectives, interacting with others and collecting data from the library. Then the focus shifts to more cooperative approaches with meetings between consortia, politicians and consultants. This phase involves a considerable amount of writing in terms of notes, formal letters and memos, and minutes of meetings, much of which serves to facilitate interaction.

The role information also helps structure the syllabus in terms of text outcomes. Those in the political group write reports, summaries and press statements on the government's views on mining, finance, and environmental protection, the interests of the provincial government, and the demands for compensation and protection of the local community. Those in the business consortia write detailed bid proposals and the consultants write a project specification and a decision announcement. Writing depends on students resolving various problems concerning how best to develop the resource, raise capital, provide infrastructure and balance local, provincial and national interests. Thus written texts are not simply project goals but provide information essential to other participants and lead to the final decision regarding which consortium will win the contract.

Concept 3.7   **Writing in Go for Gold**

Input stage: Notes on public lecture, video, and original sources (reports, news cuttings, etc.)

Target lexis and structure practice

Practice of focus genres

Activity stage: Memos and letters to other groups

Notes and minutes of meetings and discussions

Various reports, press statements and written announcements.

Feedback is vital to the process of learning. Research shows it enables students to assess their performances, modify their behaviour and transfer their understandings (Brinko, 1993; Hyland and Hyland, 2006), and in GfG this occurs both during and after the activity. During the simulation learners receive constant peer feedback on the effectiveness of their communication as they respond in discussions, react to written material and question speakers after presentations. Because reports, memos and minutes contain important information for readers' own roles, they receive close scrutiny from an interested audience. Any vagueness or ambiguity is seized upon, and this encourages writers to present their ideas clearly. Following the activity teachers give feedback to review what was learned, helping students to interpret events and find connections which will make the experience transferable. Students also receive more conventional feedback in the form of detailed comments and conferencing on their writing.

Conclusions

Perhaps the main advantage of the course is that content reality and task variety encourage the use of language for genuine communicative and conceptual purposes and promote conditions of natural language use. In particular, the scale of the activity opens up enormous possibilities for interaction and avoids the potential artificiality of shorter activities which tend to concentrate on specific areas of language, content or function. The course materials are those of the real world and activities such as participating in discussions, reading documents and writing memos and reports all prepare students for work after graduation. Thus writing is not seen as a separate activity, artificially detached from actual communicative needs and interactions; it is a crucial aspect of what it means to engage with others in tackling real problems. Students are exposed to a wide range of different linguistic material and produce a variety of outputs, both within groups and individually, and in so doing learn a lot about what it means to write for real purposes and audiences.

Course evaluations by students and the client faculty have been positive and teachers have been impressed with the improvement of students' confidence and writing skills. On the negative side, teachers have expressed doubt about the limited opportunities the course offers to correct errors and provide students with feedback on written work during the simulation itself. Accuracy is sacrificed to fluency and teacher intervention through modelling or correction becomes intrusive and inappropriate. GfG also involves a number of esoteric genres, so while students will almost certainly need to write memos, minutes, letters and reports soon after they graduate, bid proposals and project specifications are unlikely to form part of their initial repertoire. But, in their struggle to construct them, writers both become conscious of the relationship between purpose and rhetorical function, and learn the importance of writing clear, appropriate and persuasive prose.

Overall, however, Go for Gold provides a rich learning environment which offers participants both a fruitful context for writing and an awareness of the relationships between purpose, audience and appropriate rhetorical structure. The course is an example of a successful working process syllabus, and represents one way that teachers can help motivate writing and raise students' awareness of important elements for its success.

3.5 Understanding professional and academic texts

My fourth case study looks at a credit-bearing writing support course offered by a writing centre as part of a UK Foundation degree programme: 'Understanding professional and academic texts'. It mainly draws on ideas discussed in Section 1.3 above. Foundation Degrees were introduced into the UK Higher Education award system in 2001 as part of a strategy to both help widen participation, making higher education accessible to students who have never traditionally considered it as an option, and to integrate academic and work-based learning.

Concept 3.8   **UK Foundation degrees**

These two-year qualifications provide alternative routes into higher education and allow students already employed to undertake a programme of study in order to get ahead in their chosen career, whilst continuing to work. Courses cover a diverse range of subject areas, although almost half of all students study education, business and art and design. Courses often involve flexible teaching arrangements including work based, online and distance learning modes, although most students study full time, juggling work, study and other responsibilities. There were 72,000 students registered on foundation degree programmes in 2007–08 with student numbers expected to rise to 97,000 before 2010.

Course aims

Understanding Professional and Academic Texts (UPAT)[3] is an innovative first-year course for those working in educational contexts. It is offered by the Centre for Professional and Academic Literacies (CAPLITS) at the Institute of Education in London. The students are typically working in teaching support roles such as teaching assistants, nursery and youth workers, and learning support assistants. They are taking the degree to gain relevant knowledge, understanding and skills which might help them to improve their performance in training and education roles. The students generally attend part time and have few formal qualifications or experience of higher education. The UPAT course is therefore a crucial component of students' initial experience of higher education and a key aspect of their ability to participate in it successfully. Essentially, it aims to facilitate their involvement in both their workplaces and the university through writing.

Quote 3.11   UPAT learning outcomes

As a result of participating in this module you will be able to:

(a) better understand the relationship between your work and academic contexts

(b) understand workplace texts in terms of how audience and purpose influence language

(c) construct appropriate frameworks in which to analyse and evaluate workplace texts

(d) conduct small-scale workplace investigations
(e) understand academic texts in terms of audience, purpose and language
(f) write academic essays of a standard required in your coursework

A key aspect of the course is the integration and comparison of workplace and academic genres. This allows academic literacy tutors to help students to see texts as socially situated and to understand the ways that writing is differently organised and expressed for different purposes and audiences. The course works through a series of mini-research projects and writing tasks which encourage students to reflect on the ways that language works in professional and academic contexts while at the same time developing the abilities to meet tutors' expectations of their assignments in other courses. These tasks are supported by regular readings by authors such as Bazerman on intertextuality, Crème and Lea on assignment writing, and Johns on academic literacy learning, as well as educational authors on the work of teaching assistants, reflective learning, and professional practice in education.

Course structure

The course is structured in five units each of two classes of two hours duration. The first class is given in the morning and normally involves input of various kinds, from discussion of readings or a teacher-led interactive lecture. The second class follows in the same afternoon and is based around activities and assignment tasks which arise from the input. It is ordered in this way:

A) *Sessions one and two – texts, observations and reflection.* These sessions provide students with the basic tools for looking at texts in an informed way, providing practice in the type of writing they will need for the work-based task later in the course. Issues include:
  • different methods associated with observation
  • ethics in the collection of qualitative workplace research
  • analysing work-based texts – e.g. policy documents, manuals instructions, etc.
B) *Sessions three and four – the essay plan and structuring academic writing* These sessions focus on the planning and presentation of academic writing, covering issues of formality, academic style, text organisation and the presentation of academic writing.

C) *Sessions five and six – criticality and argument*
These sessions explore the meaning of these key terms within the university and make explicit how students can incorporate them into their academic writing.

D) *Sessions seven and eight – using sources*
These sessions look at evaluating sources and how students can bring information into their academic writing from both academic texts and the research data they collect in their workplace projects. They involve referencing conventions, summary writing and creating a bibliography.

E) *Session nine and ten – proofreading and editing*
These last sessions focus on issues of clarity in academic writing, particularly grammar, spelling and punctuation, as well as how students can create editing and proof-reading sheets and make use of peer-editing groups.

The fact that these students have never studied in a college or university before, and less than a third stayed at school beyond the minimum required leaving age, means that they are at a disadvantage in academic environments. They are unfamiliar with the expectations of academic settings and generally lack confidence in their writing and communication skills. As a result, this course carefully scaffolds their learning, so that aspects of writing and knowing about writing unfold following a structured pattern of development.

Tasks and assessment

While the course is relatively short and involves what is often a considerable amount of new input for students, it nevertheless offers significant opportunities for learner collaboration within a teacher-scaffolded context. In particular, students are asked to discuss texts, plan activities, and carry out small projects either in groups or after dialogue with others. It therefore draws on educational theory (Vygotsky, 1962) and research (e.g. Gere, 1987) which suggest that learning is improved through collaboration. Such student-centred learning contexts offer opportunities for interaction and negotiation and are often said to promote language learning (Pica, 1987). It also employs cooperative peer response to writing which is seen to be important for exposing students to real readers (Caulk, 1994), for building their confidence as writers and for encouraging them to make active writing decisions rather than slipping into a passive kind of unthinking model-following.

In addition, the course seeks to be supportive through input and activities which draw on students' everyday situations, which increase difficulty only gradually, and which build assessment into classroom activities.

Assessment for the course consists of a work-based portfolio (50 per cent) and a 1500–2000 word academic essay (50 per cent). The portfolio requires three workplace observations that incorporate reflection (each reflection of about 800 words) and three work-based texts with a 400 word critical analysis of each. The tasks are based on the idea that writing is improved when students see the relevance of what they are asked to do. As a result, they begin with the kinds of texts students are familiar with in their workplace contexts and then move towards the more esoteric academic genre of the essay assignment expected by their other subject tutors. Some examples of the portfolio tasks are given in Quote 3.12.

Quote 3.12 Example tasks

Task one for Work-based Portfolio
Design an observation sheet to investigate your role in the workplace. You may want to contrast your role with someone else in your workplace. This observation sheet should be in the form of a table (example given). Include the headings – activity, your role, someone else's role, and other. Conduct your observation (checking the boxes) and then **reflect** on the observation sheet (incorporating your reading), what you found (choose a maximum of three activities) and yourself. The following is an example for a Teaching Assistant...

Task two for Work-based Portfolio
Observe people working together in an activity and describe in detail: the context, who is involved and what was generally said / what happened. Reflect on this activity (you could include commentary on whether you thought this activity was successful, typical, anything unusual etc.) and try to incorporate your reading into your reflection.

Task four for Work-based Portfolio
Collect three work-based texts for analysis (e.g. emails, reports, notices, etc.). Make sure that the texts are of a sufficient length and contain a sufficient amount of detail. These three texts should also be quite different from each other. In your analysis of the texts, comment on the intended audience, the language used, and the purpose (indirect and direct) of the text. Do not forget to give sufficient context for your analysis.

In addition to the portfolio material, students have to write a longer piece of work, selecting one from three essay topics which are constructed to dovetail with the work-based study tasks mentioned above. These are:

a) To what extent is academic text different from professional text?

b) Discuss what you view to be the main ethical concerns with observation in the workplace.

c) Discuss the implications of the differences between your role and the role of someone else close to you in your workplace.

Support for the essay task is provided not only in the classes, but in the analysis of exemplar essays by previous students on similar topics and by the suggestions included in essay advice packs. These include essay plans, useful phrases, suggested readings, and ideas for issues to address in the essay. So, for example, students choosing to write on topic b) concerning ethical observation, are advised that they might consider including information on children in the workplace, getting permission, anonymity and confidentiality, the observer's paradox, and the intrusiveness of different recording media.

Conclusion

While not linked explicitly to a particular theory of writing or body of research, UPAT nevertheless draws together a number of educational principles and research findings on academic writing. In particular, it recognises the value of 'starting where the students are' by considering their writing proficiencies, learning backgrounds, and workplace experiences, and of asking 'why are these students learning to write?', embedding instruction in their immediate and future writing needs as defined by academic and professional exigencies. As Johns (1997) points out, learners acquire a socioliterate competence through exposure to particular genres in specific contexts. They develop the skills to participate in particular communities by understanding how genres work in those communities, and the course discussed here helps scaffold such exposure through introduction, practice and discussion of the texts and writing practices they find in their workplaces and need in their studies.

Further reading

Carter, R., Goddard, A., Reah, A., Sanger, K., Bowring, M. (2001) *Working with texts*, 2nd edn (London: Routledge). A good introduction to language analysis to support students' understanding of language variety and purpose.
Derewianka, B. (1990) *Exploring how texts work* (Newtown, NSW: Primary English Teachers Association). Imaginative and teacher-friendly ideas for teaching primary school written genres.
Elbow, P. (1998) *Writing with power: techniques for mastering the writing process* (Oxford: Oxford University Press). Most recent edition of the process bible.
Hyland, K. (2004) *Disciplinary discourses: social interactions in academic writing* (Ann Arbor, MI: University of Michigan). Offers a framework for understanding the interactions between writers and readers in academic contexts.
Johns, A. (1997) *Text, role and context* (Cambridge: Cambridge University Press). Great ideas for teaching academic literacy at university level, encouraging learning through a 'socioliterate approach'.
Nunan, D. (2005) *Task based language teaching* (Cambridge: Cambridge University Press). A comprehensive and up-to-date appraisal of the field, including planning, designing and using tasks in language classes.

Notes

1 I am grateful to Janet Holst of Victoria University of Wellington for providing me with information and materials for Writ 101. The coursebook *Writing English* (Holst, 1995) is available from the Bookshop, Victoria University, Wellington, New Zealand.
2 The full syllabus is available at http://k6.boardofstudies.nsw.edu.au/files/english/k6_english_syl.pdf.
3 I would like to thank Stephen Hill of CAPLITS for making his materials and commentaries on them available to me.

Chapter 4

Research-based materials, methods and resources

This chapter will . . .

- discuss how teaching applications such as textbooks, computer software, classroom instruction, and assessment methods draw on writing research;
- examine how new technologies can contribute to teaching and learning writing;
- illustrate how current research on genre, concordancing, academic vocabulary and autonomy, have been applied in practice.

4.1 Research writing: an advanced EAP textbook

Swales and Feak's *English in Today's Research World* (2000), (*ETRW*),[1] is an advanced academic writing guide for graduate students and junior scholars who are non-native English speakers. The book is grounded in current conceptions of academic discourse analysis and draws on research which shows that students have specialised communicative needs defined by the practices of their disciplines. By basing pedagogical decisions on this research, ETRW effectively interprets how particular aspects of the real communicative world work and translates these understandings into classroom applications.

Concept 4.1   A genre orientation to EAP writing teaching

- Academic writing has to be acceptable to target communities and reflect variations in disciplinary traditions and conventions.
- Research genres reveal the influence of cross-cultural variation.
- Academic writing demands that writers respond to a range of rhetorical and strategic decisions.
- Student materials should be based on analyses of representative samples of the target discourse.
- Analyses and teaching are ideally descriptive and interpretive rather than prescriptive and didactic.
- Descriptions should offer a functional account of discourse features.
- Teaching should raise awareness of the rhetorical and linguistic constraints and opportunities involved in using different genres.

The approach

The approach is essentially task-based and seeks to develop in novice research writers both a sensitivity to the language used in different academic genres and insights into the conventions of their target disciplines. This is principally accomplished through consciousness raising as tasks encourage students to analyse the features of text extracts.

Quote 4.1   Swales on the approach of *ETRW*

There are several assumptions and principles that undergird the teaching materials. First, that there is value in a genre-based approach, especially one that sees academic communications as being comprised of a loose network of interlocking genres. Second, we take it as given that we are more concerned with producing better academic writers than with simply producing better academic texts. In other words we aim to provide our participants with skills and strategies that will generalize beyond the narrow temporal domains of our actual courses. This in turn means that we place considerable emphasis on rhetorical consciousness-raising and linguistic awareness. One activity that increases this level of linguistic meta-cognition is to have the participants themselves engage in their own discourse analysis.

Swales (1999)

The activities encourage students to harness their often considerable research and analytical skills to rhetorical practices to build on their existing skills and so develop an exploratory attitude towards texts. In addition, the book exploits the fact that advanced writing classes often contain students from different disciplines, using this heterogeneity to foster a comparative approach which emphasises the social, relativistic nature of academic writing discussed in part 1.3.2. Students can learn from each other and from the materials by discussing the published research findings provided in the text and sharing their own rhetorical experiences. The different rhetorical strategies and social practices of different communities thus become part of the teaching material. In terms of content, the book is largely organised around the features of key research genres and part genres, such as the conference poster, the literature review, and dissertation sections. Grammar and lexis are subordinated to the rhetorical features of these genres, so that tense and reporting verbs appear in the unit on literature reviews, for example, and bare participles in the discussion of Methods sections.

Some excerpts from the materials

The opening unit is distinctive in that it seeks to sensitise users to various sociorhetorical aspects of research writing rather than focus on a particular genre. It contains a series of tasks designed to heighten users' awareness of writing as a disciplinary practice, introducing some basic concepts of genre analysis and encouraging reflection on some of the ways that language is used to communicate research. A good example of how these tasks draw on the research literature is the task from Unit 1 shown in Quote 4.2 which summarises some of the cross-linguistic research.

Quote 4.2   Cross cultural differences in research writing (*ETRW*: 1: 5)

American academic English, in comparison to other research languages, has been said to:

1. be more explicit about its structure and purposes
2. be less tolerant of asides or digressions
3. use fairly short sentences with less complicated grammar
4. have stricter conventions for sub-sections and their titles

5. be more loaded with citations
6. rely more on recent citations
7. have longer paragraphs in terms of number of words
8. point more explicitly to 'gaps' or 'weaknesses' in the previous research
9. use more sentence connectors (words like *however*)
10. place the responsibility for clarity and understanding on the writer rather than the reader

Task Eight
Reflect upon your own first academic language. Place a checkmark before those points where academic writing in your L1 and American academic English differ. If you do not think the difference holds for your language, leave it blank.

Are there other differences that you think ought to be mentioned?

If you are writing for an American audience how much do you think you need to adapt to an American style? Do you think you need to fully 'Americanize' your writing, or can you preserve something of your own academic culture in your academic writing?

This kind of contrastive reflection is useful for both raising students' awareness of rhetorical features of academic writing in English and how these differ from practices students may be familiar with from their native language and culture. While the points appear to refer to surface features of academic writing, they raise wider issues of argument structure, reader awareness, the role of knowledge, appropriate interactions and cultural identity, each of which has attracted considerable attention in recent research.

Other tasks are devoted more explicitly to language itself and draw on research into text analysis. In each case, forms are clearly connected with the functions they perform in academic genres, such as this example from the section on Methods sections, where students are encouraged to reflect on the use of left-dislocation to express purpose (Quote 4.3).

Quote 4.3 Form and function of purpose statements (*ETRW*: 6: 3)

a) In order to assess the possibility that pleasant fragrances would mitigate the adverse effects of stress on task performance, participants in the present research performed...

b) In order to examine the related possibility that . . . participants also performed an additional task.

c) To counteract sensory adaptation to the fragrances, the study was conducted in two parts.

d) Because of the lingering quality of both fragrances employed, it was necessary to . . .

e) As an additional check on the effectiveness of the fragrance manipulation, participants were asked to . . .

Task Fourteen
Reflect upon the stylistic and discoursal effects of placing the purpose statements first. More specifically, what impressions do the left-dislocations create in the reader's mind?
   Consider the forms of the purpose statements. Do other ways of expressing them occur to you?

Conclusions

ETRW recognises that the communicative demands of research writing are both a major component of professional expertise and a serious challenge to students. Although biased towards an American tradition of writing and postgraduate study, it represents an excellent example of how research in a particular area of writing can be exploited for pedagogical purposes. Writing research forms the foundation of the book and is drawn upon both as a way of encouraging users to explore for themselves the conventions of their fields. This book, then, offers a particular view of academic writing founded on a major research orientation which places texts at the centre of pedagogic practice.

4.2   *WordPilot 2000*: corpora-assisted writing

In recent years there has been a movement from teaching as imparting knowledge to teaching as mediating learning, so that students can take a more active and reflective part in their learning. While technology has been slow to assist this move, attention has begun to shift from the computer in an *instructor* role to the application of computers as *informants*, drawing on their most obvious advantages of data storage and retrieval. *WordPilot 2000*[2] (Milton, 1999) is an excellent example of this as it encourages writers to develop their writing through exploration and use of corpus data.

Concept 4.2   **Corpus analysis**

A *corpus* is a collection of naturally occurring texts used for linguistic study. While a corpus does not contain any new theories about language, it can offer fresh insights on familiar, but perhaps unnoticed, features of language use, replacing intuition with evidence. This is because an electronic corpus can be accessed and studied using text retrieval and concordancing software. Because particular words and 'bundles' of word combinations can be isolated, counted and presented from large numbers of texts in this way, features which are typical of a particular genre or other sub-set of language can be identified. Corpora have therefore been extremely valuable in writing research as its findings have become important in ensuring that teaching is based on frequency of occurrence and typical collocational patterns (how words combine with other words).

Concordancing and instruction

While concordancing has only recently begun to influence teaching methodology (e.g. Hafner and Candlin, 2007; Partington, 1998; Wichmann *et al.*, 1997), its value lies in that it can both replace instruction with discovery and move the study of language away from ideas of what is correct, towards what is typical or frequent (Sinclair, 1991). Leech has set out some of the main advantages:

Quote 4.4 Leech on the advantages of concordancing for teaching

1. *Automatic searching, sorting, scoring.* The computer has immense speed and accuracy in carrying out certain low-level tasks, and can therefore deliver data in a form valuable to the human learner. Concordances and frequency lists are obvious examples.

2. *Promoting a learner-centred approach.* The computer brings flexibility of time and place, and adaptability to the student's need and motivation.

3. _Open-ended_ supply of language data. The computer thus encourages an exploratory or discovery approach to learning.

4. _Enabling the learning process to be tailored._ The computer can customize the learning task to the individual's needs and wishes, rather than simply providing a standard set of examples or data.

Leech (1997: 10–11)

While teachers can use corpora as a source for their own teaching materials, a more effective pedagogy is to train students to explore corpora themselves. This encourages inductive learning and raises students' consciousness of patterns in writing through the exploration of authentic texts. This direct learner access suggests two further approaches (Aston, 1997): corpora can be treated as _reference tools_ to be consulted for examples when problems arise while writing, or as _research tools_ to be investigated as a means of gaining greater awareness of language use. _WordPilot_ can be used in both ways. Incorporating a concordancer, dictionary, thesaurus, test-constructor, customisable word lists and a speech function which reads any highlighted text, _WordPilot_ facilitates both research and reference, allowing students to explore relevant authentic texts or draw on them while writing. The program is currently used in both secondary and university contexts in Europe, Australia, Hong Kong and the Middle East.

A research tool

Krishnamurthy and Kosem (2007) have recently criticised the complexity of corpus query tools and argued that simpler interfaces are required for classroom use. _WordPilot_, offers a relatively straightforward means for students to produce concordance lines and identify the most common patterns in a collection of texts. Typing in a search word or phrase produces KWIC (Key Word in Context) lines summoned from all the texts in a selected corpus with the search item at the centre of the screen. These lines give instances of language _use_ when read horizontally and evidence of _system_ when read vertically. This makes it possible for the user to see regularities in its use that might otherwise be missed. Users can see the immediate co-text of each example, and the wider context by double clicking on the line. In this way they can collect clues from patterns of use as to how the word is typically employed in that genre. Figure 4.1 shows concordanced lines for *besides*, for instance, and viewing real examples in this way can help students see where *besides* is used to add information and where it emphasises it.

To see which words the search item most commonly occurs with, students can click the 'collocations' button at the bottom of the screen. By focusing on such patterned regularities, learners can discover a great deal of information about the behaviour of common words, grammatical patterns, idiomatic expressions, and lexical bundles. How do relatively frequent lexemes such as *since* and *for* differ, for example? What are the connotations carried by *sheer* and *pure*? What words typically occur with *put*? (See Figure 4.2.)

Using the software for independent study in this way can help students become aware of the features which occur frequently in the kinds of texts they encounter and need to produce themselves. But while direct access to corpora can stimulate enquiry, promote independent learning and reveal unfamiliar or typical uses to students, the program will only display what is requested. Learners with restricted knowledge of forms are not always sure what they should look for nor are they always sufficiently interested in language to carry out research on it. This approach presupposes the necessary curiosity to drive learning, but for many writers language only becomes important

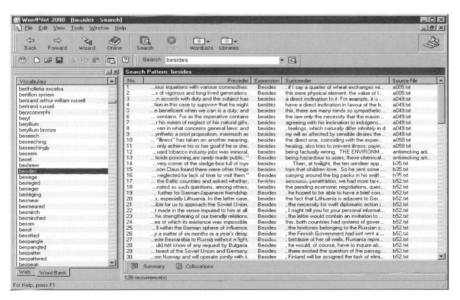

Figure 4.1 *WordPilot* concordance for *besides* in student essay corpus

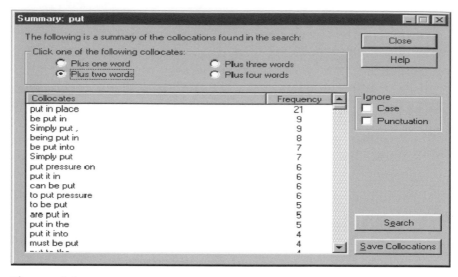

Figure 4.2   Concordance summary of *put*

when they need it to communicate. For these learners *WordPilot* may be more useful as a reference tool.

A reference tool

WordPilot functions as a reference tool by offering writers an effective way to search for words and phrases at the point when they need them most: when they are actually writing. By automatically installing a macro in their wordprocessor, *WordPilot* allows writers to call up a concordance by double-clicking a word or phrase while typing, giving them information about the frequency and use of expressions they need. Thus if a writer is unsure whether to use *possible for* or *possible that*, the concordance lines should provide sufficient examples to make the choice clear. Similarly, consulting *WordPilot* can help a writer decide whether *different to* is more acceptable than *different from* in a certain register. In other words, 'learning is more effective when students have direct access to information and timely advice on its use' (Milton, 1997: 239).

The program also provides rapid access to several online English and multilingual dictionaries, research sites and other corpora. This kind of immediate on-line assistance can be extremely useful in raising students' awareness of genre-specific conventions. In addition, *WordPilot* allows students to create customised word lists for private study and annotate these with concordance examples in a pop-up window. The program will also generate multiple-choice tests on target words by drawing on examples from a selected corpus, giving students a cumulative score when they have finished. Figure 4.3 shows part of a word-list of frequently confused words and a multiple-choice test question automatically generated from a corpus.

Conclusions

This software tool represents an interesting and useful application of writing research for novice writers which shows the insights that can be gained by providing writers with access to real texts. In this way, *WordPilot* overcomes the limitations both of current CALL programs, which are often autocratically didactic, and existing print materials, which cannot supply this kind of information. Its strength lies in its integration of various lexical databases, text corpora and hypertext links with an easy-to-use concordancer which enables students to query target-text uses from within their word-processor. The major limitation of the software is that it is based on a procedural model of learning rather than a more familiar declarative model, and so challenges common perceptions about how writing should be taught. But while the program may be daunting for students familiar with more directed learning,

Figure 4.3   Wordlist and test question with multiple-choice options

both the software and its innovative approach offer considerable advantages to the development of effective and independent writers.

4.3   A lexis for study? The Academic Word List

The idea of an academic vocabulary has a long history in university writing instruction. Variously known as 'sub-technical vocabulary' (Yang, 1986), 'semi-technical vocabulary' (Farrell, 1990), or 'specialized non-technical lexis' (Cohen *et al.*, 1988), the term refers to items which are reasonably frequent in a wide range of academic genres but are relatively uncommon in other kinds of texts (Coxhead and Nation, 2001). This vocabulary is seen as contributing an important element to an 'academic style' of writing and being 'more advanced' (Jordan, 1998) than the core 2,000 to 3,000 words that typically comprise around 80 per cent of the words students are likely to encounter in reading English at university (Carter, 1998).

Concept 4.3   **An academic vocabulary**

The notion that some words occur more frequently in academic texts than in other domains is generally accepted and corresponds with EAP's view that teaching should be based on the specific language features and communicative skills of target groups. This lexis is said to comprise a repertoire of specialised academic words which falls between an existing everyday general service vocabulary and a technical vocabulary which differs by subject area. However, whether it is useful for learners to possess a *general* academic vocabulary is more contentious, as it may involve considerable learning effort with little return.

Lists of academic vocabulary

A variety of vocabulary lists have been compiled from corpora of academic texts to describe the most frequently occurring words in different disciplines and genres (e.g. Coxhead, 2000; Farrell, 1990; Xue and Nation, 1984).[3] To avoid problems associated with specifying what counts as a word, these typically focus on word families, i.e. the base word plus its most frequent and regular prefixes and affixes (Bauer and Nation, 1993). This approach is also supported by the view that knowledge of a base word can assist the understanding of its forms and that members of the same word family are stored together in a 'mental lexicon' (Nation, 2001).

The most recent compilation is the Academic Word List (AWL) (Coxhead, 2000) which contains items considered essential for university students irrespective of their field of study.[4] Items were selected on the basis of their frequency and range across disciplines in an academic corpus of 3.5 million words of varied genres in 28 disciplines from arts, commerce, law and science (Coxhead, 2000: 221).

Quote 4.5 Coxhead on the AWL

The Academic Word List was compiled from a corpus of 3.5 million running words of written academic text by examining the range and frequency of words outside the first 2,000 most frequently occurring words of English. The AWL contains 570 word families that account for approximately 10.0% of the total words (tokens) in academic texts but only 1.4% of the total words in a fiction collection of the same size. This difference in coverage provides evidence that the list contains predominantly academic words.

Coxhead (2000: 213)

The AWL is an impressive undertaking and is based on the most extensive research into core academic vocabulary to date. But while it has contributed to published teaching materials (e.g. O'Regan, 2003; Schmitt and Schmitt, 2005) and is widely used by teachers, it remains unclear how far a single inventory can represent the vocabulary of 'academic discourse', and so be valuable to all students irrespective of their field of study.

Word distributions across fields

In a study designed to examine assumptions that there is a single core vocabulary for academic study, Hyland and Tse (2007) explored how far items in the AWL are equally useful for learners in disciplines as varied as biology, linguistics, business studies and electronic engineering. Using a corpus of 3.3 million words of student and research genres, we found that while the AWL provides an impressive overall coverage of 10.6 per cent of the corpus, individual items on the list occur and behave differently across disciplines in terms of range, frequency, collocation and meaning.

For one thing, only a third of the AWL items were actually frequent overall in our texts, with the research terms *process, analyse, research, data* and *method* being the most common. But more worrying was the fact that some items were only frequent overall because of their concentration in one or two fields, 15 of our top 50 items, for example, had over 70 per cent of their occurrences in just one field. In fact, almost all the AWL families have irregular distributions across science, social science and engineering fields and over 90 per cent of all cases of *participate, communicate, output, attitude, conflict, authority, perspective* and *simulate* occurred in just one field. This clustering suggests considerable discipline-specificity in their use, so the list seems most useful to students in computer sciences, where 16 per cent of the words are covered by the list, and least useful to biologists, with only 6.2 per cent coverage.

Word meanings and uses

Another problem with compiling a 'common core' vocabulary is that items not only have to be common across a range of fields, but they must also *behave* in roughly similar ways. This means a vocabulary list must either avoid items with clearly different meanings and dissimilar co-occurrence patterns, or these must be taught separately rather than as parts of families. Most words have more than one sense, however, and there were clear preferences for particular meanings and collocations in different disciplines in our corpus. In fact, when we look more closely at the meanings of words with potential homographs (unrelated meanings of the same written form such as *major* which can mean both *important* and a *military rank*), we find a great deal of difference across fields. Table 4.1 shows the main meanings for selected words with their ranking and frequencies in the AWL together with their distributions.

Clearly there are some wide variations in the ways writers use words, with social science students far more likely to meet *consist* as meaning 'to stay the same' and science students rarely finding *volume* as a book. With less frequent words the preferred meanings differ dramatically.

In addition to different semantic meanings, students are also likely to encounter different grammatical meanings. One example is the word *process*, which is frequent in all three fields but far more common as a noun in science and engineering. This is the result of nominalisation, or 'grammatical metaphor' (Halliday, 1998), whereby writers in the

Table 4.1   Distribution of meanings of selected AWL word families across fields (%)

FAMILY	MEANING	SCIENCE	ENGINEERING	SOCIAL SCIENCE
Consist	stay the same	34	15	55
(rank 41)	made up of	66	75	45
Issue	flow out	7	6	18
(46)	topic	93	94	82
Attribute	feature	83	35	60
(93)	ascribe to	17	65	40
Volume	book	1	7	50
(148)	quantity	99	93	50
Generation	growth stage	2	2	36
(245)	create	98	98	64
Credit	acknowledge	0	60	52
(320)	payment	100	40	48
Abstract	précis/extract	76	100	13
(461)	Theoretical	14	0	87
offset	counter	0	14	100
(547)	out of line	100	86	0

sciences regularly transform experiences into abstractions to create new conceptual objects. Embedding an item such as *process* into complex abstract nominal groups produces terms like:

• a constant volume combustion process . . .

• the trouble call handling process . . .

• processing dependent saturation junction factors . . .

• the graphical process configuration editor . . .

The AWL does not help students unpack the meanings this embedding creates and also obscures the fact that words take on extra meanings by regularly occurring with other items (e.g. Arnaud and Bejoint, 1992). The term *value* in computer science, for instance, is often found as *value stream* (21 per cent of all cases) and *multiple-value attribute mapping* (7 per cent of all cases). Even high frequency items such as *strategy* have preferred associations with *marketing strategy* forming 11 per cent of all cases in business, *learning strategy* making up 9 per cent of cases in applied linguistics, and *coping strategy* comprising 31 per cent of cases in sociology.

Conclusions

In sum, while the term 'academic vocabulary' may be a convenient shorthand for a variety, it conceals massive variability which misrepresents academic literacy as a uniform practice and can mislead learners into thinking that they just need to learn a single collection of words. Vocabulary lists, such as the AWL, may provide some guidelines for teaching, but because individual items occur and behave differently across disciplines we are forced to acknowledge the importance of disciplinary conventions. As we learn more about the different contexts of writing at university, we have begun to see that many language features, including vocabulary, are specific to particular disciplines. This suggests that the best way to prepare students for their studies is not to search for overarching, universally appropriate teaching items, but to help them understand the features of the discourses they will encounter in their particular courses.

4.4   Scaffolding literacy skills: writing frames

Instructional scaffolding means providing students with sufficient supports to promote learning, particularly when new concepts and skills are first being introduced. These supports are gradually removed as students develop familiarity with the task and acquire new cognitive, affective and psychomotor learning skills and knowledge. In writing instruction *scaffolding* is closely related to the idea that learners develop greater understanding by working with more knowledgeable others.

Concept 4.4   **Scaffolding**

Bruner's metaphorical term 'scaffolding' has come to be used for interactional support, often in the form of adult–child dialogue. Scaffolding refers to the gradual withdrawal of adult control and support as a function of children's increasing mastery of a given task. Bruner (1978) refers to it as 'the steps taken to reduce the degrees of freedom in carrying out some tasks so that the child can concentrate on the difficult skills he or she is acquiring'. It is thus a special form of help which moves learners towards new skills, concepts and understandings.

This model originates with Vygotsky (1978) who suggested that interaction with more skilled and experienced others assists learners to move through 'the zone of proximal development' from their existing level of performance to a level of 'potential performance', or what they are able to do without assistance. Children first experience a particular cognitive activity in collaboration with experts. The child is firstly a spectator as the majority of the cognitive work is done by the parent or teacher, then, as the child develops greater capabilities in the task, the expert passes ever greater responsibility to the learner while still acting as a guide and assisting at problematic points. Eventually, the child assumes full responsibility for the task and the expert takes the role of a supportive audience. Using this 'apprenticeship' approach to teaching, children participate at a little beyond their current level so that the task continually provides sufficient challenge to be interesting; they are constantly 'stretched' in their language development but never have to perform an unfamiliar task (Gibbons, 2002).

Writing frames

The degree of teacher intervention and the kinds of tasks selected for students to engage with play a key role in offering a cline of support from closely controlled activities to autonomous extended writing (see section 3.3). In writing instruction, the use of writing frames is one way that teachers have sought to scaffold children's early attempts at a new genre.

Concept 4.5   **Writing frames**

Writing frames consist of outlines, which can be used to scaffold learner's writing by setting out a sequence of cohesive ties to which the writer supplies the content. Each outline consists of different words or key phrases, depending on the particular genre which is being scaffolded. Writing frames guide learners through a writing activity by giving them a structure within which they can concentrate on communicating what they want to say, rather than getting lost in the form. They can be created for a range of genres and different stages of the writing process, such as planning or drafting.

Writing frames (Wray and Lewis, 1997; Lewis and Wray, 1997) are flexible and provisional forms of scaffolding to help young children develop a sense of genre when introducing them to non-fictional writing. Often children have considerable difficulty in recognising the appropriate genre they need for their purposes and fall back on familiar *narrative* and *recount* genres when they may need an *argument* or *report*. The tradition of getting learners to write about 'real experiences', clearly invites a personal telling, but does not provide learners with the rhetorical resources to deal with more formal and abstract genres which they will meet in other areas of the school curriculum.

A frame is simply a skeletal outline to scaffold and prompt students' writing, providing a genre template which enables them to start, connect and develop their texts appropriately while concentrating on what they want to say. Frames provide a structure for writing which can be revised to suit different circumstances, taking different forms depending on the genre, the purpose of the writing, and the proficiency of the students. Essentially, however, they mirror the kinds of supportive oral guidance that teachers frequently offer children, providing the prompting missing between a writer and blank sheet of paper.

Concept 4.6   **Advantages to students of frames**

- Provide a varied vocabulary of connectives and sentence beginnings to extend learners experience beyond 'and then'.

- Offer students a structure through the cohesive ties of the text and so helps them maintain the sense of what they are writing.

- Challenge children by involving them in a close examination of the features of text.

- Model a wide range of techniques for responding to literature or their experience.

- Require learners to review and revise their responses after a guided reading of a text.

- Encourage learners to think about what they have learnt by reordering information rather than just copying out text.

- Improve self-esteem and motivation by helping learners achieve some success at writing.

- Avoid the discouragement of starting with a blank sheet of paper.

Using frames

Normally, frames are introduced only after extensive reading, teacher modelling, and explicit discussion of the forms needed for a particular kind of text. They are also seen as more effective if located in meaningful experiences and used to help learners produce writing they want to produce, rather than in de-contextualised skills-centred lessons. The best use of a writing frame is therefore when learners have a purpose for undertaking some writing, like needing a new genre, or when they are stuck in a particular mode of writing, such as the repeated use of 'and then' when writing an account. Wray and Lewis (1997) show how frames can be useful for planning to write a discussion genre (Figure 4.4).

Frames are, however, perhaps more usually employed in drafting (Figure 4.5), providing students with both a skeletal outline of the genre and the connectives needed to achieve a logical development of their ideas.

The frame therefore encourages students to think before they write, provides appropriate connectives, supports their efforts to achieve coherence and scaffolds the generic form. Wray and Lewis suggest that following drafting, the students' frames can provide the basis for teacher–pupil conferencing or peer editing before the final version is written out.

Conclusions

Writing frames are useful to writing teachers in primary and secondary schools who can devise their own frames by drawing on their knowledge of the genres they are teaching and the particular abilities and

The issue we are discussing is	*School uniform*

Arguments For	Arguments Against
1. *it is smart*	1. *school uniform can be expensive*
2. *represents the college*	2. *make you feel the same as everyone else*
3. *parents because of washing*	3. *people without much money can wear*
4. *people might turn up to school in*	*whatever they want*
hundreds of kinds of clothes	4. *we won't get into so much trouble if we*
5. *expensive jewelry may get stolen*	*aren't wearing a jumper or something*
6. *rich children could end up in fancy clothes*	*like that*

My Conclusion

I think we should wear whatever we want but not being too outrageous and it is suitable to wear!

Figure 4.4   **A writing frame for planning a discussion (Wray and Lewis, 1997: 126)**

There is a lot of discussion about whether *smoking should be allowed in public buildings*

The people who agree with this idea claim that *people have rights and should be allowed to enjoy themselves*

They also argue that *there are too many laws stopping people to do what they like*

A further point they make is *smoking is an addiction and people cannot stop easily*

However there are also strong arguments against this point of view. *Most of our class* **believe that** *people shouldn't be allowed to smoke anywhere they like.*

They say that *smoking is dangerous even for people who do not smoke*

Furthermore they claim that *it is a bad influence to children and creates pollution and litter.*

After looking at the different points of view and the evidence for them I think *smoking should be banned in public* **because** *it is dangerous and dirty.*

Figure 4.5   A writing frame for first draft of a discussion (from Wray and Lewis, 1997: 128–9)

needs of their students. Using these kinds of templates, writers can become increasingly familiar with a new text type and experience ways of using language to express their purposes effectively. Students will need to use them less and less as their confidence in writing and their competence in writing target genres grows.

4.5   *Check My Words*: technology and autonomy

Learning technologies have a long association with autonomy, particularly in the area of computers in self-access, as they provide learners with opportunities to self-direct their own learning (e.g. Benson, 2001). Less celebrated, however, are automated feedback tools which encourage student writers to look up words and language patterns as they write and so become less dependent on their teachers' support. But while researchers now recognise that acquisition is optimised when learners are attending to both meaning and form (Ellis, 2002), teachers often feel demoralised by what seem ineffective efforts to correct sentence level errors (Tsui, 1996). In response to these issues, John Milton (2006) has developed a suite of resources – *Check My Words*[5] and *Mark My Words*[6] – to provide students and tutors with the means to improve writing by referring to advice and resources during the writing process.

Driven both by the rapid advance of educational technologies and growth of distance courses, students now often find themselves reading feedback on their electronically submitted essays which has been produced by an unseen tutor or by the computer itself. Sophisticated software capable of scanning student texts and generating immediate evaluative comments on them are beginning to emerge which target grammatical errors, content and organisation (e.g. Ware and Warschauer, 2006). The *Criterion e-rater* developed by the Educational Testing Services (Burstein, 2003), for example, scans a student text and provides real-time feedback on grammar, usage, style and organisation. But while these automatic feedback programs may eventually assist teachers with the burdens of growing class sizes and expectations for personal support, they have been criticised for being unreliable (Krishnamurthy, 2005) and realising poor pedagogic principles (Chapelle, 2001). Equally, such programs only deliver formative assessment and so contribute to students' continuing dependence on expert response. A very different approach is *Check My Words* which offers a discovery-based approach, supporting novice writers while they are writing.

Check My Words

> **Quote 4.6** Milton on *Check My Words*
>
> The approach provides students with the means to check and improve their language by referring to copious, authentic, and comprehensible resources during the writing process. This access, combined with resource-rich feedback from their teachers, can greatly increase the amount of positive and negative evidence available to students. Many researchers believe such evidence promotes acquisition, and if this approach can help students become more confident, responsible, and independent in selecting forms and patterns that are accurate and appropriate, it can also help relieve teachers of the need to act as proofreading slaves.
>
> Milton (2006: 125)

Check My Words is an add-on toolbar for *Microsoft Word* that helps learners of English to write more accurately and fluently (Figure 4.6). The bar links writers to various online resources such as *Word Neighbors*, which brings up collocations of the target word, dictionaries, example sentences, word family information, grammar information, and a 'My Words' list of personal or assigned words to use together

Figure 4.6   *Check My Words* toolbar

with a list of lexical bundles common in academic writing. Additionally, students can get comments on the grammar of any word in their text by clicking the mouse on it.

Two of these tools are illustrated in Figure 4.7. Here a student has activated the 'highlight' button on the toolbar which has searched for, and highlighted, potential errors in the text, marking these in blue and common errors in red. The two pop-up screens overlaying the essay are in response to clicking the 'similar meanings' and 'check' buttons on the word 'facilitate'. This has thrown up a list of synonyms and antonyms and an information box on grammatical usage which allows the writer to review other members of the word family to see if he or she is using the correct form and to look up common grammatical errors.

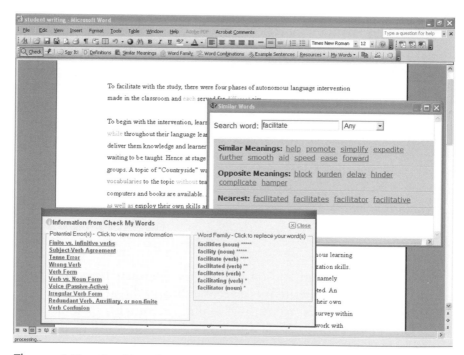

Figure 4.7   Checking the word 'facilitate' in *Check My Words*

The potential errors list hyperlinks students to the *English Grammar Guide* where they can find explanations for the most common grammatical errors made by second language writers of English. Figure 4.8 shows the EGG main screen together with information called up by clicking on *which* in an essay, giving advice on its use and common difficulties for learners.

Other buttons in the toolbar allow writers to get definitions and translations of words, to hear stretches of text spoken aloud, and to get example sentences which can help them select the appropriate phrasing. The *resources* button pulls down a list of potentially useful websites, and gives access to *Word Neighbors*, which displays the words that are most frequently used before or after a target word in a selected genre. *Check My Words* can access about 50 million words in 20 different genres and makes such searches easy via a dialogue box which allows users to display up to four words either side of the target word, choose whether to include all forms of the word, get a summary of collocations, and, if needed, see all sentences containing the target expression. Figure 4.9 is a screen showing the frequency of immediate right collocates of 'carry' clustered by word class. This assists the writer to

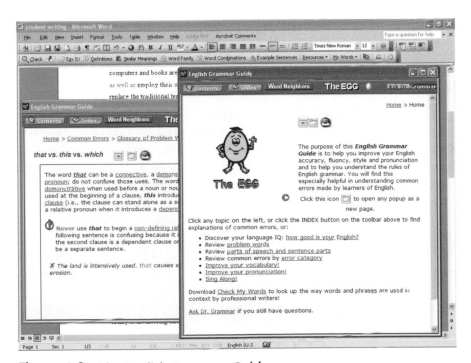

Figure 4.8   **The English Grammar Guide**

Word·Neighbors

Show 0 ▾ word(s) before	carry ☐ Show all word forms The phrase may span 1 ▾ word(s)	Show 1 ▾ word(s) after

Search in:
⊞ ☐ All available texts (141,000,000 words)

☐ Link to Cambridge Dictionary ▾
(Audio/Video Examples NEW)

[Find it!!]

Patterns/Words			Frequency
VERB ☖ + ADV ☖:	e.g. "carry out"	[Show results]	4725
VERB ☖ + DET ☖:	e.g. "carry the"	[Show results]	2197
VERB ☖ + NOUN ☖:	e.g. "carry ons"	[Show results]	814
VERB ☖ + PRON ☖:	e.g. "carry it"	[Show results]	616
VERB ☖ + ADJ ☖:	e.g. "carry large"	[Show results]	392
VERB ☖ + PREP ☖:	e.g. "carry with"	[Show results]	342
VERB ☖ + VERB ☖:	e.g. "carry is"	[Show results]	50
VERB ☖ + CONJ ☖:	e.g. "carry and"	[Show results]	44

Total Expressions: 9180

Figure 4.9 Word Neighbors concordance examples for *facilitate*

see the appropriate phrasal verb combination 'carry out', with the option to view real examples.

Mark My Words

Mark My Words is the companion program to *Check My Words*, allowing tutors to provide detailed feedback on student texts by using the same online resources. This not only enables the tutor to give detailed feedback without correcting the student's language, but also encourages students to use CMW itself.

Again, this program installs as a word processor toolbar (Figure 4.10) so that the teacher simply highlights a word or structure in a student text and clicks the 'mark' button to indicate the lexical or grammatical error indicated. Teachers are aided here by the 'comments' button which allows them to insert brief pre-written (and customisable)

Figure 4.10 *Mark My Words* toolbar in MS Word

comments linked to detailed web-based explanations, interactive tutor-ials, concordancers, references, and so on. In addition, the software automatically identifies and inserts comments on a subset of common grammatical and lexical errors.

Quote 4.7 Milton on *Mark My Words*

I designed *Mark My Words* to help teachers insert customizable com-ments in any language in a student's electronic document and to link the comments to the same online resources that are available to stu-dents. The commenting toolbar lists approximately 200 recurrent lexico-grammatical and style errors common in the writings of Chinese speakers, with suggested links to resources. Crucially, teachers who must respond to a wide range of sentence-level errors do not need to scroll through this long list. The programme can identify word classes and lexical patterns and automatically shortlist suggested comments.

Milton (2006: 130)

Figure 4.11 is a screen shot of a student essay with drop down options from the 'comment' button and a number of comment bubbles created by the program and posted by the tutor into the text. These include links to relevant resources, such as *Word Neighbors*.

After comments have been inserted in a student's assignment, the teacher can generate a summary for each student or assignment, including running totals for the semester, by clicking the 'grid' button. This log provides a record of comments given to particular students and groups of students from one assignment, semester, course and instructor to another. In this way instructors can maintain a database of frequent errors, track student progress, identify learnability problems, and remind individual students of previous comments.

Conclusions

The My Words programs build on current research on feedback and autonomy and on automated grammar-checking software which facil-itates writing through point-of-need assistance and specific teacher response. This combination seems to overcome some of the limitations of existing error-flagging mechanisms by making the writer responsible for judgements of correctness with the aid of advice and authentic data.

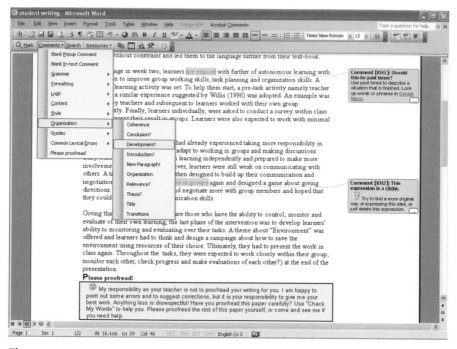

Figure 4.11   Drop down comments menu and tutor posted comments from choices available.

To be successful, however, such an approach has to be integrated into the curriculum and potential resistance overcome. Students are not always comfortable revising without explicit reformulation of their errors and teachers may be uneasy about using new methods and correcting online. Server logs tracking student revisions and surveys of teachers using the program, however, suggest that students eventually use the resources effectively and that rates of successful revisions increase (Milton, 2006). Such resources may therefore be a step towards the development of autonomous writing skills.

4.6   Writing portfolios: pedagogy and assessment

In this final illustration I focus on the evaluation of writing performance through the use of portfolios, looking at some examples and highlighting central issues.

Concept 4.7   **Writing portfolios**

Portfolios are multiple-writing samples, written over time, purposefully selected from various genres to best represent a student's abilities, progress and most successful texts in a particular context. They can include drafts, reflections, readings and teacher or peer responses as well as a variety of finished texts. Most are assembled by students in a folder and comprise four to six core items in categories determined by curriculum designers to reflect the goals of their programme. There are two types of portfolio. *Showcase portfolios* contain only the student's best work while *process types* include both drafts and final products. In both the act of assembling texts over time encourages students to observe changes and discover something about the entries and their learning.

Some advantages

The use of writing portfolios is a response to the problems of traditional multiple-choice tests and, later, of holistically scored single-essay tests (Brown and Hudson, 1998). Yancey (1999) points out that the first approach stressed *reliability* by consistently measuring writing through standardisation and rater-proofing statistical correlations. The use of essay tests, by contrast, addressed the importance of *validity*, stressing the need to base judgements on actual writing. Behind portfolios is the idea that multiple samples will increase validity and at the same time make evaluation more congruent with teaching programmes (Bailey, 1998). Some of the main advantages discussed in the literature are summarised in Concept 4.8.

Concept 4.8   **Potential pros of writing portfolios**

- **Integrative**: combines curriculum and assessment to make evaluation developmental, continuous and fairer by reflecting writing progress over time, genres and contexts.
- **Valid**: closely related to what is taught and what students can do.
- **Meaningful**: students often see their portfolio as a record of work and progress.
- **Motivating**: students have a range of challenging writing experiences in a range of genres and can see similarities and differences between these.

- **Process-oriented**: focuses learners on multi-drafting, feedback, collaboration, revision, etc.
- **Coherent**: assignments build on each other rather than being an unrelated set of texts.
- **Flexible**: teachers can adopt different selection criteria, evaluation methods and response practices over time, targeting their responses to different features of writing.
- **Reflexive**: students can evaluate their improvement and critically consider their weaknesses, so encouraging greater responsibility and independence in writing.
- **Formative**: by delaying grading until the end of the course, teachers can provide constructive feedback without the need for early, potentially discouraging, evaluation.

Portfolios therefore help integrate instruction with assessment, representing a coherent model of organising writing processes and products for ongoing reflection, dialogue and evaluation. A growing literature advocates the use of portfolios as a way of strengthening learning by exposing students to a variety of genres, encouraging them to reflect on their writing processes and promoting greater responsibility for writing (Purves *et al.*, 1995). They are said to enhance learning by increasing teacher and student involvement in the writing-testing process and by engaging students in a variety of tasks. Finally, they can potentially give teachers a more central coaching role by providing more data on individual progress (Brown and Hudson, 1998).

An example

A good example is a portfolio designed by a group of English teachers in Singapore for a class of advanced EFL students studying for a public school-leaving examination. The portfolio includes five core entries and reflection questions (Concept 4.9).

Concept 4.9   **A portfolio for a GCE class in Singapore**

1. **A timed essay.** Students select one timed essay (argumentative, expository, or reflective). Reflection questions include: What was your interpretation of the question? How did you decide when dividing your paragraphs? What was your main problem and how did you solve it?

2. **A research-based library project.** Students submit all materials leading to the final paper. What timing and other goals did you set? What difficulties did you find? What did you learn?

3. **A summary.** Students select one summary of a reading for inclusion. Why did you select this particular summary? How is it organised? Why is it organised like this? What are the basic elements of all the summaries you have written?

4. **A writer's choice.** A 'wild card' in the L1 or L2 that has been important to the student. What is this? When and where did you write it? Why did you choose it? What does it say about you as a literate person?

5. **An overall reflection of the portfolio.** A general reflection integrating the entries. What were the goals of this class? Describe each entry and why it was important for achieving these goals.

Johns (1997: 140–41)

This structure is obviously highly flexible, and shows that portfolios can have value even in a curriculum constrained by a public exam. Student reflections are encouraged to create a metacognitive awareness of their strategies, attitudes, writing experiences and the texts themselves. Such reflections are often seen as a major strength of portfolios as they make visible a great deal of what students see in their work, in their development, and what they value about writing. This information can therefore both guide instruction and enhance learning through students' self-awareness of what they have done and what they can do. This emphasis on the portfolio as a teaching tool, providing opportunities for feedback, conferencing and awareness-raising, can also be achieved by publishing portfolios on the Web. This not only allows students to include a variety of multimedia formats in the portfolio but also enables peers to respond electronically and anonymously to their classmates' essays.

Some problems

While Elbow and Belanoff (1991) question whether it is appropriate to grade portfolios, this is often a necessary evil for teachers. Although portfolios provide more evidence for assessment, its multiple entries complicate the process because of the need to ensure reliability across raters and rating occasions, and because of the heterogeneous nature of what is assessed. Standardising a single score to express a student's ability from a variety of genres, tasks, drafts and different disciplines can be extremely difficult. Concept 4.10 lists some of the assessment problems this raises.

Concept 4.10   **Potential cons of writing portfolios**

- **Logistic**: Can produce a daunting amount of work for teachers.
- **Design**: Needs to ensure grading criteria are clearly understood by all teachers.
- **Reliability**: Needs to ensure raters are trained and standardised grading processes adhered to across raters, genres, portfolios and courses.
- **Product variation**: Problem of fairly assigning a single grade to a mixed text collection.
- **Task variation**: Some tasks may be more interesting, and therefore elicit better writing, so teachers may be evaluating the task rather than students' performance on it.
- **Authenticity**: Lack of close teacher supervision may mean some students plagiarise or get considerable external help.

Hamp-Lyons and Condon (2000) point out that for a portfolio programme to be fully accountable it must have explicable, shared and consistent criteria which teachers fully understand and regularly review. In practice, portfolios are often scored holistically, requiring raters to respond to a sample as a whole, rather than focusing on a single dimension. The rubric below (Quote 4.8) is used by the State of Kentucky for assessing the portfolios of grade 12 students (Callahan, 1997). Callahan, however, points to the problems of inadequate rater training and the inconsistent identification of categories as major problems.

Quote 4.8 Holistic scoring guide for Grade 12 portfolio

Novice	Apprentice	Proficient	Distinguished
Limited awareness of audience and/or purpose	An attempt to establish and maintain purpose and communication with audience	Focused on a purpose; evidence of voice and/or suitable tone	Establishes and maintains clear focus; evidence of distinctive voice and/or tone
Minimal idea development; limited details	Unelaborated idea development; unelaborated and/or repetitious details	Depth of idea development supported by elaborated details	Depth and complexity of ideas supported by rich details; insight analysis, reflection
Random and/or weak organisation	Lapses in focus and/or coherence	Logical organisation	Careful and/or subtle organisation
Incorrect and/or ineffective sentence structure	Simplistic and/or awkward sentence construction	Controlled and varied sentence structure	Variety in sentence structure and length
Incorrect and/or ineffective wording	Simplistic and/or imprecise language	Acceptable, effective language	Precise and/or rich language
Surface errors are disproportioate to length and complexity	Some errors in surface features that do not interfere with communication	Few errors in surface features relative to length and complexity	Control of surface features

Abbreviated from Callahan (1997: 330)

Scoring criteria are a crucial part of the pedagogic context as they can be fed into the course as principles of good writing. This guide, however, provides no basis for using assessment information in instruction, making it difficult to support process pedagogies. More critically, it is doubtful whether a single holistic score can be reliably assigned to a complex collection of materials as raters are likely to weigh one text against another rather than get an impression of the whole (Hamp-Lyons and Condon, 1993).

Conclusions

While there are clear advantages to using portfolios for both teachers and students, the approach may not actually be a better assessment tool than, say, a timed essay. Portfolios do not necessarily bring greater accuracy to assessment, but they do promote a greater awareness of what good writing might be and how it might be best achieved. The advantages lie principally in that the validity, and value, of assessment is increased if it is situated in teaching and learning practices. By basing assessment on a clearer understanding of what it is we value in writing, we enhance learning by firmly creating a link between research and teaching as an ongoing, integrated and reflective practice.

Further reading

Ferris, D. and Hedgcock, J. (2005) *Teaching ESL composition: purpose, process, practice*, 2nd edn (Mahwah, NJ: Lawrence Erlbaum). Presents practical applications of research for L2 writing teachers, including portfolios.

Hamp-Lyons, L. and Condon, W. (2000) *Assessing the portfolio: principles for practice, theory, and research* (Cresskill, NJ: Hampton Press). Clear and informative discussion of writing portfolios in a variety of contexts.

Hyland, K. (2003) *Second language writing* (New York: Cambridge University Press). An introduction based on current research to teaching writing to EFL/ESL students.

Lewis, M. and Wray, D. (1997) *Writing frames* (Reading: NCLL). Offers theoretical support for using writing frames together with photo-copiable frames and planning grids to support pupils in writing a range of genres.

Warshaver, M. and Kern, R. (eds) (2000) *Network-based language teaching: concepts and practice* (Cambridge: Cambridge University Press). A collection discussing the research and practice of CMC.

Wichmann, A. *et al.* (eds) (1997) *Teaching and language corpora* (Harlow: Longman). A useful text that deals with all aspects of using corpora in classrooms.

Notes

1 I am grateful to John Swales and Chris Feak for making these materials available to me.
2 *WordPilot* is available from the developer's website (http://home.usi.hk~aviolang) which also contains hints, worksheets and links to other useful internet sites. I am grateful to John Milton for his help and permission to reproduce the screen shots of the program.
3 The 6.5 million word British Academic Written English (BAWE) corpus is now available to researchers. BAWE was developed at the Universities of Warwick, Reading and Oxford Brookes to investigate genres of assessed writing in British higher education. See Chapter 9 for details.
4 The headwords of families in the Academic Word List together with the items grouped by sublist are available from the Massey University website at: http://language.massey.ac.nz/staff/awl/headwords.shtml
5 The toolbar for *Check My Words* can be downloaded free from http://mws.ust.hk/cmw/ There is also a tutorial screen at the site and information about the suite of programs.
6 *Mark My Words* can be downloaded free of charge from http://mywords.ust.hk/mmw/

||| Researching writing

Chapter 5

Research practices and research issues

This chapter will . . .

- outline some major areas of writing which are amenable to small-scale research;

- provide an overview of the main methodological approaches typically used in writing research;

- discuss how research can be conducted into texts, writers and readers.

In previous chapters I have focused on areas of theoretical and practical concern, outlining what we know about writing and how we have used this knowledge for teaching. I have tried to show that theory, research and pedagogy interact in important ways and that knowledge invariably informs action. I have said little, however, about how teachers, students and researchers go about actually studying writing. Teachers, in fact, often see teaching and research as entirely separate things, one practical and the other rather esoteric, so that research is regarded as an activity unrelated to their everyday lives and they may even feel apprehensive at the prospect of it. Research, however, is a practical activity which, by revealing how effective texts are constructed and work, is central to what we do as teachers.

In other words, as Stake (1995: 97) observes, 'research is not just the domain of scientists, it is the domain of craftspersons and artists as well, all who would study and interpret'. Because it stimulates curiosity, validates classroom observations, and helps develop a critical perspective on practice, research is at the heart of professional development since it helps to transform a personal understanding into an informed awareness. This section therefore turns to look at research in more detail, providing something of a practical guide to some key researchable areas. In this chapter I provide an overview of different ways in which research on writing might be conducted, and in the next two I present some example cases.

5.1   Practitioner research

Small-scale practitioner studies have always been important in writing research. Often these originate in the desire of individual teachers or materials designers to understand something of the texts they present in their classes, the writing processes of their students, or the textual practices of target communities. The systematic study of practice therefore provides a basis for theoretical reflection and modelling which in turn feeds back into, and improves, that practice. This kind of enquiry is often called *action research*.

Concept 5.1   **Action research**

Action research, the process of progressive problem solving led by individuals, often working in teams, by collecting and analysing data to improve some original action (Wallace, 1998: 4). Unlike classic controlled experimental models of research, which are based on objectivity and control, action research is often more pragmatic, employing methods which address issues of concern most effectively. This is not only a very accessible type of research for practitioners and students but is also often regarded as an essential form of professional development as it encourages us to address problems in our own professional lives.

Cohen *et al.* (2000) provide some clear guidelines for those embarking on this kind of research:

1. Identify, evaluate and formulate a problem that is viewed as important in their everyday workplace. This might involve a particular class or curriculum changes.

2. Consult with other interested groups (co-workers, administrators, parents, etc.) to focus the issue and clarify objectives and assumptions.

3. Review the relevant academic literature to discover what can be learnt from other studies on the topic.

4. Use the readings to redefine the initial statement of the problem as an hypothesis or research questions to be answered by the study.

5. Specify the research design in terms of participants, methods and data sources.

6. Clarify how the project will be evaluated.

7. Implement the project and collect the data.

8. Analyse the data, draw inferences, and evaluate the results.

This procedure is useful in any research undertaking, but in identifying possible projects and methodologies I want to cast my net a little wider than traditional conceptions of action research. Writing research aims to help us understand writing more clearly or to teach writing more effectively and this is an enormous field with many unresolved issues and potential areas of enquiry. This diversity encourages numerous lines of investigation and can involve methodologies which go beyond those traditionally regarded as action research, including quantitative as well as qualitative methods and approaches which may involve the researcher as an 'anthropological' outsider rather than a participant in the context. Moreover, projects may just as obviously emerge from something we read as something we confront in our classrooms or workplaces. It may begin with the researcher's curiosity, interest and intuition rather than a practical problem to solve.

Here, then, I include not only problem-driven studies which have an immediate pay-off for the researcher, but also studies motivated by simple curiosity about particular texts or practices. My frame for this section therefore goes beyond practitioner research as it is traditionally understood to consider a wider range of issues and a broader set of methods.

In addition, it is important to recognise that writing research does not simply involve fitting suitable methods to particular questions. Methods are inseparable from theories and how we understand writing itself. As I sketched out in Chapter 1, for some people, writing is a product, an artefact of activity which can be studied independently of users by counting features and inferring rules. For others, it is a pattern of choices influenced by experience, purposes and contexts. Others see it is a kind of cognitive performance which can be modelled by analogy with computer processing through observation and writers' on-task verbal reports. Yet others understand writing as the ways we connect with others to construct our social worlds while others see it as the carrier of ideologies and control. In other words, while different methods will tell us different things about writing, they always start with our preconceptions.

Concept 5.2   **Writing research**

All research originates where theory and practice intersect, arising from a need to clarify what people do in certain situations and why. The ways individuals write, the issues they consider when composing, the texts they produce, the influence of contexts, purposes, and creativity on style, and the strategies writers use to understand writing and improve their practices are all major areas of research. Our ability to answer these questions, and the bigger issues about expertise, literacy, community, pedagogy, and genre which underlie them, is always going to be contingent on the context that is studied. This is the law of 'it depends', and it informs all research. To be answerable, our questions must relate to specific students, writers, texts, users, or practices, and this makes small-scale research as valuable to the accumulation of our understanding of writing as much larger government-funded projects. So in conducting small-scale research which focuses on the specific issues that concern us, we are also nibbling away at the larger questions which occupy our profession.

This chapter turns to address research more directly, to offer something of a practical guide and overview on writing research. First I outline the main ways that writing research is conducted and then go on to suggest some research topics.

5.2   Research issues

Research often begins by isolating something that interests or worries us and then asking questions about it. We then go on to make those reflections concrete by collecting and analysing data about the issue, what is often seen as the core of research. But while this is a common enough picture, there is no 'one-size-fits-all' formula to carrying out research on writing or on anything else. It is not only researcher preferences and preconceptions which influence research decisions, but also the topic studied, the context, the access one has to data, and the time and resources which are available to us. In fact, research has to be carefully planned so that it stands a good chance of success without alienating participants, mishandling data, or corrupting results. Essentially, this involves three broad aspects:

1. *Viability*: **Setting up a realistic way of carrying out the research.**
   Clearly, the research needs to be feasible with issues of access and management uppermost. Gaining access to texts and institutions, securing the cooperation of participants, managing record-keeping and tracking progress all involve resources of time, effort, and perhaps, money while enough space needs to be found to engage intellectually with the data and to reflect periodically on the changing shape of the project.

2. *Ethicality*: **Establishing procedures to protect the participants in the research.**
   Ethical considerations are also a crucial dimension of research and care needs to be taken to guard against exploiting colleagues or students through lack of negotiation or confidentiality. Participants should have the right to know the aims of the project, what information is sought, how it will be used and who will have access to it. They should also know that they have the right to anonymity, to withdraw, or to veto the release of data (Cohen *et al.*, 2000; Hitchcock and Hughes, 1995).

3. *Validity*: **Ensuring that the research will answer the questions it has set itself.**
   This mainly involves decisions about 'objectivity' and how far the researcher will intervene to collect and analyse data, boiling down to the familiar opposites of *qualitative* and *quantitative* research. Common in the hard sciences, quantitative methods aim at securing objectivity by testing hypotheses through structured and controlled procedures. The researcher approaches an issue from the outside, working to discover facts about a situation that can be measured and compared. Qualitative researchers, in contrast, argue that it is important to explore a situation from the participants' perspective and is more inductive and exploratory. There is no attempt to control the context because behaviour is seen as subjective and relating closely to its context, which means that the researcher focuses on

instances and does not seek to generalise to other situations (Denzin and Lincoln, 1998).

But while certain methods suit some questions better than others and are associated with particular ways of understanding writing, it is also true to say that much writing research combines several methods to gain a more complete picture of a complex reality. In fact, the concept of triangulation, or the use of multiple data sources, investigators, theories, or methods (Patton, 1990), can bring greater plausibility to the interpretation of results. The qualitative–quantitative distinction, however, does raise the important contrast between *elicited* and *naturalistic* data: that is, whether data is to be gathered in controlled conditions or in circumstances not specifically set up for the research.

Concept 5.3   **Naturalistic research**

Writing research tends to favour data gathered in naturalistic rather than controlled conditions. As a result, it differs from positivistic, more quantitative research in terms of how it views reality, the relationship of the researcher to the research subject, issues of generalisability, and causality. While methods that elicit data through questionnaires, structured interviews or experiments can provide interesting and useful insights into writing, data collected via observations or analyses of authentic texts are more common.

While no data can ever be free of the effects of the researcher collecting it, more interventionist research methods risk producing data that is simply the product of an artificially contrived situation. Ethnographically-oriented methods have been used to prevent this and to collect data from real-life situations which are as far as possible undistorted by the researcher and which are faithful to the reality experienced by participants.

Quote 5.1   Flowerdew on ethnography

Ethnography can be defined briefly as the study of a social group or individuals representative of that group, based on direct recording of the behaviour and voices of the participants by the researcher over a period.

> An important dimension of any ethnographic study is the part played by language, but language is considered within the context of its production and reception, rather than in isolation, simply as text.
>
> Flowerdew (2002: 235)

Ethnographic and naturalistic approaches therefore take a broader and more contextual view of writing than many other approaches and tend to presuppose a more prolonged engagement with the research site (see Pole and Morrison, 2003). They also use different methods, favouring descriptive observation, reflective and in-depth interviews, focus group discussions, narrative diaries, and the analyses of documents and texts. The fact that research often originates with solving a problem or resolving a question originating with practice, means that the transferability of results to other groups is not a major issue. In fact, a strength of this kind of research is that it allows for a detailed explanation and understanding of what is specific to a particular group. This also encourages us to take research out of the classroom and into the community, investigating people's everyday writing practices.

5.3   Research methods

The main methods for researching writing are summarised in Concept 5.4 (from Hyland, 2003: 253) and discussed briefly below.

Concept 5.4   **Methods for investigating writing**

Questionnaires: Focused elicitations of respondents' self reports about actions and attitudes

Interviews: Adaptable and interactive elicitations of respondent self reports

Focus Groups: Questions discussed by participants in an interactive group setting

Verbal reports: Retrospective accounts and think aloud reports of thoughts while composing

Written reports: Diary or log accounts of personal writing or learning experiences

---

Observation:	Direct or recorded data of 'live' interactions or writing behaviour
Texts:	Study of authentic examples of writing used in a natural context
Experiments:	Manipulation of a context to study a single feature under controlled conditions
Case studies:	Multiple techniques capturing the experiences of participants in a situation

(i) Elicitation: questionnaires, interviews and focus groups

These are the main methods for eliciting information and attitudes from informants.

Questionnaires are widely used for collecting large amounts of structured, often numerical, easily analysable self-report data, while interviews offer more flexibility and greater potential for elaboration and detail. Both allow researchers to tap people's views and experiences of writing, but interviews tend to be more qualitative and heuristic and questionnaires more quantitative and conclusive. Questionnaires are particularly useful for exploratory studies into writing attitudes and behaviours and for identifying issues that can be followed-up later by more in-depth methods. One major use of questionnaires in writing research has been to discover the kinds of writing target communities require. Evans and Green (2007), for example, used a questionnaire to survey 5,000 Hong Kong students about the difficulties they experience when studying through the medium of English, identifying problems of style, grammar and cohesion.

Interviews offer more interactive and less predetermined modes of eliciting information. Although sometimes little more than oral questionnaires, interviews generally represent a very different way of understanding human experience, regarding knowledge as generated between people rather than as objectified and external to them. Participants are able to discuss their interpretations and perspectives, sharing what writing means to them rather than responding to pre-conceived categories. This flexibility and responsiveness means that interviews are used widely in writing research to learn more about writing practices, such as what people do in approaching a writing task, about teaching and learning writing, and about text choices, to discover how text users see and respond to particular features of writing.

Interviews are particularly valuable as they can reveal issues that might be difficult to predict, such as the kinds of problems that students might have in understanding teacher feedback (Hyland and Hyland, 2006), and can be used to feed into questionnaire design.

Focus groups are groups of people with some similar characteristics who are brought together to discuss an issue in depth. They are more interactive than interviews as participants are free to talk with other group members, and are generally seen as less threatening contexts for gathering information about group perspectives and practices. So while they take some control away from the interviewer, they can produce richer data. Usually conducted face to-face, these may be held as synchronous computer-mediated sessions where transcripts can be saved and considered later. Groups have been used to discover students' academic writing needs (Zhu and Flaitz, 2005) and both students' and teachers' perspectives on a new programme in Hong Kong that tries to draw on learners' relevant experiences and concerns (Lo and Hyland, 2007).

(ii) Introspection: verbal and written reports

The use of verbal reports as data reflects the idea that the process of writing requires conscious attention and that at least some of the thought process involved can be recovered, either by talking aloud while writing or as retrospective recalls.

Simultaneous *think aloud protocols* (TAPs) involve participants writing in their normal way but instructed to verbalise what he or she is doing at the same time so that information can be collected on their decisions, strategies and perceptions as they work. Think aloud data have been criticised as offering an artificial and incomplete picture of the complex cognitive activities involved in writing (see part 1.2.2). For one thing many cognitive processes are routine and internalised operations and therefore not available to verbal description while, more seriously, the act of verbal reporting may distort the process being reported on. But despite these criticisms the method has been widely used, partly because the alternative, deducing cognitive processes from observations of behaviour, is less reliable. The technique has been productive in revealing the strategies writers use when composing, particularly what students do when planning and revising texts, so that de Larios *et al.* (1999), for instance, used it to examine what students did when they were blocked by a language problem. Stimulated recalls, on the other hand, involve videotaping the writer while writing then discussing the writer's thought processes while watching the video together immediately afterwards (e.g. Bosher, 1998).

Diaries offer anther way of gaining introspective data. These are first-person accounts of a writing experience, documented through regular entries in a journal and then analysed for recurring patterns or significant events. Diarists can be asked to produce 'narrative' entries which freely introspect on their learning or writing experiences, or follow guidelines to restrict the issues addressed. These can be detailed points to note ('what do you think your readers know about this topic?') or a loose framework for response ('note all the work you did to complete this task'). Alternatively, researchers may ask diarists to concentrate only on 'critical incidents' of personal significance or to simply record dates and times of writing. While some diarists may resent the time and intrusion this involves, diaries provide a rich source of reflective data which can reveal social and psychological processes difficult to collect in other ways. Thus Marefat (2002) used diaries to discover how her 80 Farsi speaking undergraduates reacted to class events, materials and the instructor herself in an EFL writing course. The approach provided a rich account of students' reflections on particular areas of difficulty and interest, thus leading her to revise the syllabus and materials.

(iii) Observations

While elicitation and introspective methods provide reports of what people *say* they think and do, observation methods offer actual *evidence* of it by systematic documentation of participants engaged in writing. They are based on conscious noticing and precise recording of actions as a way of seeing these actions in a new light. Once again there are degrees of structure the researcher can impose on the data, from simply checking pre-defined boxes at fixed intervals or every time a type of behaviour occurs, to writing a full narrative of events. The most highly structured observations employ a prior coding scheme to highlight significant events from the mass of data that taped or live observation can produce (see Hyland, 2003 for examples). All observation will necessarily privilege some behaviours and neglect others, as we only record what we think is important, but while a clear structure is easier to apply and yields more manageable data, such pre-selection may ignore relevant behaviour that wasn't predicted.

Observation is often combined with other methods, as in Louhiala-Salminen's (2002) observation study of a Business Manager's discourse activities through one day. Oral encounters were tape-recorded, and copies were taken of the written materials. The data were supplemented with interviews and particular attention paid to the decisive role of e-mail.

(iv) Text data

A major source of data for writing research is writing itself: the use of texts as objects of study. While we have seen in previous chapters that texts can be approached in a variety of ways, notably to see how they operate as systems of functional choices, how they embody and realise institutional power and ideologies (Chapter 1), how they differ across languages and the first language of their authors, how they express group memberships and social identities, and how they combine and link to other texts (Chapter 2).

Quote 5.2 **Connor on text analysis**

Text analysis describes texts and evaluates their quality, both from the viewpoint of texts that learners produce as well as the kinds of texts they need to learn to produce. Text analysis can help ESL researchers, teachers, and language learners identify rules and principles of written or spoken texts at a variety of levels: sentences, sentence relations, and complete texts. This research orientation differs from traditional linguistic analysis in two major ways: (a) It extends analysis beyond the level of sentence grammars, and (b) it considers the multidimensional, communicative constraints of the situation.

Connor (1994: 682)

Text analysis embraces a number of different tools and attitudes to texts. Sometimes researchers work with a single text, either because it is inherently interesting or because it seems to represent a particular genre. A major policy speech, a newspaper editorial or an essay can offer insights into forms of persuasion, particular syntactic or lexical choices, or students' uses of particular forms. Bhatia (1993) suggests some basic steps for conducting a genre analysis in this way, emphasising the importance of locating texts in their contexts.

> **Quote 5.3** Bhatia on doing genre analysis
>
> 1. Select a text which seems to represent the genre you want to study.
> 2. Use your background knowledge and text clues to put the text in a context, guessing where the genre is used, by whom, and why it is written the way it is.
> 3. Compare the text with similar texts to ensure that it represents the genre.
> 4. Study the institutional context in which the genre is used (visit sites, interview participants, study manuals, etc.) to understand its conventions.
> 5. Decide what you want to study (moves, lexis, cohesion, etc.) and analyse the text.
> 6. Check your analysis with a specialist informant to confirm your findings and insights.
>
> (Bhatia, 1993: 22–34)

While analysis of a single text can reveal important features, it also raises questions about how it can represent a genre or a writer's opus. Representativeness is strengthened if evidence can be secured from several texts, and corpus analysis is the main way to achieve this as it represents a speaker's experience of language in some restricted domain, thereby providing a more solid basis for text descriptions. A corpus provides an alternative to intuition by offering both a resource against which intuitions can be tested and a mechanism for generating them. As we saw in the previous chapter, the key starting points are *frequency* and *association*. *Frequency* is the idea that if a word or pattern occurs regularly in a genre, then we can assume it is significant in that genre. *Association* refers to the ways features associate with each other in collocational patterns, pointing to common usage in the genre.

(v) Experimental data

Experimental methods are used to discover if one variable influences another in a situation by holding other factors constant and varying the treatment given to two groups. Statistical tests are then carried out on the data to find if differences between the control and the experimental groups are significant. While experiments have largely been rejected in writing research in favour of more qualitative, natural, and 'thicker' data collection techniques, there are contexts in which they may be appropriate. A recent example is Truscott and Hsu's (2008) study of the influence of corrective feedback on learning. In this study learners wrote an in-class narrative which they revised during the next class. Half the students had their errors underlined and used this feedback in the revision task while the other half did the same task without feedback. Results matched those of previous studies in that the underline group was significantly more successful than the control group. One week later, all students wrote a new narrative as a measure of short-term learning, but the two groups were virtually identical in the change in error rate from the first narrative to the second. This suggests that improvements made during revision are not evidence of learning.

While this is a good example of how experimental research can apply to writing and so feed back into teaching, results of experimental studies should be treated cautiously. Classrooms are not laboratories and there are serious difficulties of holding variables constant in two contexts. Differences in teaching styles, learner preferences, teacher attitudes, peer relationships, and so on can all influence results and experimental methods are best combined with other forms of data if used at all.

(vi) Case studies

Case studies are not an actual method but the investigation of a single instance, usually a writer, a context, or set of texts, explored as a totality using a range of methods. They attempt to provide a rich and vivid description of real people acting in real situations, blending description and analysis to understand actors' perceptions and experiences. Their strength lies in their potential for revealing the complexity and interactions in a context, and although this often means they are of limited generalisability, others may recognise them as representing aspects of their own experience. On the minus side, the very richness and variety of the data collected can mean that cases are difficult to organise and keep track of (Cohen *et al.*, 2000: 182). Case studies can comprise various methods, and are often closely associated with ethnographic approaches, although they do not always carry the re-searchers commitment to research which 'will convey the subjective reality of the lived experience of those who inhabit' the research site (Pole and Morrison, 2003: 16).

A recent example of a case study is Youngjoo Yi's (2007) examination of one Korean high school student's composing practices outside of school. The findings revealed the diversity and richness of her involvement with multiple literacies and genres in her voluntary composing practices. In presenting the student's story as a case study, the research helps to build an understanding of out-of-school writing as experienced by students with immigrant backgrounds.

5.4   Research topics

While research on writing can be done in a variety of ways and for different purposes, it essentially seeks to discover what texts are like and how people write and use them in specific contexts. Clearly some research topics will be more relevant in first-language contexts and others in L2, but all research in writing addresses, and has implications for, our understanding of questions in one or more of the three areas of the framework of text, writer and reader outlined in Chapter 1. While there are obvious overlaps, and research in one area can clearly illuminate another, this is once again a useful way of exploring potential research topics.

Researching texts

Perhaps most research on writing looks at texts, largely because studies are often conducted with the aim of improving students ability to produce texts. Texts can be explored in various ways: for the frequency and use of specific features such as tense, lexis, or cohesion; they can be examined for particular discourse features such as interpersonal marking, hedging or move structure; and they can be measured for the quality of student writing or its improvement over time. We can examine a text in isolation or as a sample from a single genre, a single discipline, or a single writer, and we can compare the work of writers of different proficiencies, genres, time periods, first-language backgrounds, or social contexts. Some of these issues are very tricky to operationalise in a study: how do we ensure that the genres we are examining from different cultures are comparable (Casanave, 2004)? How do we identify moves in a text (Hyland, 2004b)? How can we measure linguistic accuracy (Polio, 1997) or writing improvement (Shaw and Liu, 1998)?

Researchers examine students' writing for various reasons, but a common one is to study the effect of some intervention, such as the impact of different essay prompts on linguistic performance (Kuiken and

Vedder, 2008), the type of feedback given (Ferris and Roberts, 2001), the instruction (Tsang, 1996), or as mentioned above, the impact of peer response training (Berg, 1999). Many such studies are *experimental* in design as the researcher manipulates the independent variable such as the instruction or the feedback, on the dependent variable, such as some feature of the text. Other research of this type is *correlational* in that the researcher seeks to measure the relationship, or co-variation, between two or more dependent variables, such as students' ability to speak French and their ability to write it. An example is Helms-Park and Stapleton's (2003) study which found little evidence of a relationship between features of L1 'voice' and the quality of L2 academic writing as rated by three raters.

Text research, however, draws mainly on genre and corpus analyses, examining either individual or sets of texts by looking at salient patterns or formal or rhetorical features. Again, in educational contexts, such studies are often undertaken to describe the features of texts which students need to write, either in their current studies or future workplaces. The literature provides numerous models and examples of text researcher projects which can assist teachers and students to investigate how texts are organised and the ways they can be improved or better understood. Current topics of interest in studying texts include focusing on features such as 'lexical bundles', or regularly occurring phrases such as *as can be seen* in academic texts and *in the event of* in legal texts (e.g. Biber, 2006; Hyland, 2008) and of intertextuality and textual borrowing in students' texts (Abasi and Akbari, 2008; Pecorari, 2008). Finally, there is enormous scope for new researchers to usefully replicate studies they find in the literature with other writers, texts and contexts.

Concept 5.5   **Some researchable questions on texts**

- What writing tasks are typical in a particular context (e.g. a workplace or classroom)?
- How are the genres linked together in a context and how do they relate to speech and reading?
- What are these texts like in terms of their typical lexical, grammatical or discoursal features?
- How are particular meanings typically expressed in this genre?
- What is the purpose of a given genre (persuasion, description, explanation, entertainment, information) and how is this achieved through its structure and language?

- Does a genre in one context, such as a course or discipline, differ from the same genre in another?
- What can specific text features tell us about the assumptions or identities of the writer?
- What can text features tell us about the contexts in which the text is used?
- Do the target text(s) exhibit intertextuality and what is the source of this?
- What features are typical of a particular group of writers?
- Do these features differ from those in texts produced by other writers?
- Can these differences be explained by reference to language proficiency or L1 conventions?
- What teaching interventions might best assist learners towards producing better texts in a given context?

Researching writers

In addition to knowing *what* written texts are like, research also addresses *what writers do* when they write, and often too, *how* they can be helped to do it better. This involves focusing research more on the writers themselves, and so on some part of the writing process, rather than on the outcomes of writing and this obviously requires different questions and methods. Generally, most of these studies focus either on what writers do when they write or how various kinds of feedback are used in the process and so methods involve observation of writers at work and analysing their perceptions of what they are doing. Added to this are intervention studies which examine the effects of instructional treatments on writing behaviour.

Many of the research methods used to investigate writers originated in psychology and aimed to uncover writers' mental strategies (see Chapter 1). Now, however, most are widely used to explore how contextual factors shape writing decisions and practices. Semi and unstructured interviews, think-aloud protocols, stimulated recalls, reflective diaries, observations, and analyses of peer or teacher–student interactions now represent standard practices in writing research. These qualitative methods allow researchers to explore the context-dependent nature of writing events as they occur, or soon after they are completed, examining what is regular and what is idiosyncratic about them.

Quote 5.4 Erikson on qualitative research

What qualitative research does best and most essentially is to describe key incidents in functionally relevant descriptive terms and place them in some relation to the wider social context, using the key incident as a concrete instance of the workings of the abstract principles of social organisation.

Erikson (1981: 22)

A great deal of research has been conducted on writers, but because each situation is different and because contextual factors play a large part in both writing and its development, there are considerable opportunities to say more. In particular, there is still much to learn about what writers do in different situations, the influence of proficiency, cultural background, and first language on writing processes. Even in the classroom there are opportunities to discover aspects of the writing process. For example, Bosher's (1998) stimulated recall study compared the writing processes of two writers while de Larios *et al.* (2008) used protocol data to investigate whether the writer's proficiency level influences the time devoted to writing. Interviews are popular in process research and have been used to explore issues such as how L2 writers use dictionaries (Christianson, 1997) and choose topics during a writing exam (Polio and Glew, 1996).

Technology has also been employed to explore the writing process, with keystroke recording during composing software such as JEdit used to register all key-strokes, including all pauses and revisions, during a writing session so that the entire text can later be replayed exactly as it was created to give insights into thinking and revision (e.g. Sullivan and Lindgren, 2006). The more we learn about writers in the contexts in which we work, the fuller our understanding of writing becomes more generally.

Concept 5.6   **Researching the writing process**

- What strategies does a group of writers employ in accomplishing a given writing task?
- How do they interpret prompts, plan, draft, edit, etc?

- What use do writers make of written sources, notes, and other students when writing?
- Do the strategies of experts differ from novices and in what ways?
- Do L2 learners transfer composing strategies from their L1?
- What role does talk about and around writing play in the writing process?
- What role does reading play in the writing process?
- Are the processes of writing on computers different to writing on paper?
- What strategies do these writers use when revising their texts?
- What is the focus of their revisions (sentence level, meaning, formal conventions, organisation)?
- Does writing on computers make a difference to revising quantity/quality?
- What use is made of feedback, in what areas, and from what sources?
- Are there differences in L2 students' revising strategies in their L1 and in their L2?

In addition to research on writing and revision practices, writer-oriented research also addresses the impact of particular teaching methods on the writing process and the use that different writers make of various kinds of feedback. Experimental techniques have been used in this regard, particularly when seeking to evaluate the relative claims of different teaching practices on learners' writing. This is often done by randomly assigning students to two groups and providing different instruction to each group then testing to determine which method was more effective. This was the approach adopted by Song and Suh (2008), for example, in determining the relative effectiveness of two types of writing tasks in noticing and learning of the past counter-factual conditional.

Experiments have also been popular in feedback studies. The study by Truscott and Hsu (2008), mentioned earlier is one example, as is that by Lundstrom and Baker (2009) on whether giving or receiving peer feedback is more beneficial. Here the *givers* reviewed anonymous papers but received no peer feedback over the course of the semester, while the *receivers* received feedback but did not review other students' writing. An analysis of writing samples collected at the beginning and end of the semester indicated that the givers made more significant gains in their own writing over the semester than did the receivers and that lower proficiency givers made the most gains.

Generally, more qualitative research has dominated intervention studies, particularly into the effects of teacher and peer feedback. Lee and Schallert (2008), for instance, used interviews, class observations, and writing samples with teacher written comments to understand the influence of the teacher–student relationship on a teacher's written feedback and in how students responded to this feedback in their revisions. Jones *et al.* (2006) used transcripts of face-to-face tutoring sessions and logs of online sessions conducted by the same peer-tutors to compare the interactions of face-to-face and online peer-tutoring, finding more hierarchical relations in the former and less emphasis on 'global' writing concerns. Needless to say, this kind of qualitative, interpretive research confronts the researcher with an enormous quantity of unpredictable data which has to be organised, analysed and categorised in some way. Moreover, researchers often have to face the need to reconsider procedures mid-study, and the challenge of the idiosyncratic nature of each project they undertake. Studying writing processes therefore requires a necessarily provisional approach to draw inferences from observations and reports.

Concept 5.7   **Researching instruction effects on writers**

How is teacher feedback given and responded to?

- What are the effects of teacher written and/or oral feedback on writers' behaviours?
- What kinds of response styles do teachers use and how do these influence revision?
- What do teachers focus their feedback on?
- What kinds of feedback are most effective in a given context?
- What interactions occur in teacher–student conferences and how do these influence revision?
- How does mitigation and direction influence revision?
- What individual/cultural/proficiency differences influence feedback?
- What kinds of feedback do particular learners prefer and why?

- Is oral conferencing more effective than written feedback in improving student texts?
- What impact does online feedback have on writers and how does it differ from face-to-face feedback?

How is peer feedback given and responded to?

- What are the effects of peer written and/or oral feedback on writing?
- What does peer feedback focus on and what do revisions address?
- What kind of response sheets are most effective in encouraging peer comments?
- Does proficiency make a difference in peer interactions and uptake on comments?
- What differences does training make on peer comments and revision practices?
- Is oral or written feedback more effective in changing revising behaviour?
- Are there cultural differences in giving and responding to peer feedback?
- What interactions take place in peer conferences and how do these influence revision?
- Do learners prefer teacher or peer feedback and why?
- Is teacher or peer feedback more effective in improving writing processes and texts?

Finally, writer-oriented research has also explored how people write and participate in literacy events in going about their everyday lives. This social literacies approach (discussed in part 2.2) links writing with local contexts and examines how the activities of reading and writing are located in particular times and places. Research methods here take considerable pains to capture an understanding of the participants, the setting, the materials involved, and the activities participants perform. This 'visible evidence' helps the researcher infer the knowledge, feelings, purposes, values, and so on which lie beneath the surface and inform the context. Ethnographic methods are therefore widely used in studying social literacies in order to understand the meaning in participants' activities from their own perspectives. Interviews, photographs, case studies, observation and the study of texts are familiar techniques in this research.

Concept 5.8   **Researching social literacies**

- How are texts produced and used in a particular social context?
- How do the writing practices of specific writers connect people with each other?
- What languages do people use for different writing activities?
- How are complex writing tasks organised?
- How is writing related to other events and goals in the writers' domains of activity?
- How is writing related to reading and speech in specific contexts?
- What are writers' attitudes to writing and its role in their lives?
- How do writers express their individual identity and group membership in a context?
- How do writers feel about the institutional genres in which they participate?
- Which writing practices are privileged (and which ones less so) in different contexts?

Some studies have already been mentioned in part 2.2, but people participate in literacy practices in many ways which can be investigated as small scale projects. Hamilton (2000), for example discusses how photographs can provide evidence of a range of everyday uses of literacy, from words on clothing and tattoos to people interacting around texts. Barton mentions numerous studies conducted by students (Barton, 2000: 171) and posts more on the Lancaster University website for the Literacy Studies course.[1] Some students investigated their own lives, such as breakfast time around the kitchen table reading and discussing the morning papers, others studied everyday activities, such as buying a Mother's Day card or a lottery ticket, and yet others started from specific places and the practices in the places such as pubs, churches, libraries, bookshops and a video store. The methods involve trying to observe the event as an outsider, collecting texts, then interviewing participants about their activities and trying to make sense of how they see them. Barton summarises these steps in Quote 5.5.

> **Quote 5.5** Barton on researching literacy practices
>
> 1. Identify domain or domains
> 2. Observe visual environment
> 3. Identify particular literacy events and document them
> 4. Identify texts and analyse practices around texts
> 5. Interview people about practices, sense making.
>
> Barton (2000: 170)

Researching readers

Issues regarding audience, or readers' expectations, have formed the least-explored area of writing research. This is despite the fact that developing an ability to address a particular audience is essential to communicative success in writing, and that student writers often have problems shaping their ideas for readers. People read texts with different needs and make different judgements of their merit. Research is therefore needed to determine what these needs and evaluations are in given contexts and how to help novice writers accommodate them in their writing. Research in this area has mainly focused on the task requirements and perceptions of student writing by university faculty, the reading practices of professional academics and others, and the evaluation of teaching practices designed to raise student awareness of audience.

Once again the specific research method adopted will largely depend on the questions asked and the orientation of the researcher. Document surveys and questionnaires have been widely used to collect data on what genres teachers require their students to write, for example. So Horrowitz (1986), for instance, looked at writing assignment handouts and exam questions while Jenkins *et al.* (1993) distributed questionnaires to faculty members to determine the role of writing in graduate engineering schools. Protocols and interviews have been used to explore writers' mental representations of their intended audience as they write (Wong, 2005) and the ways experts read (Berkenkotter and Huckin, 1995). Researchers have also used case-study approaches and protocol analyses to determine writers' awareness of audience when composing, and have analysed reader comments to compare L1 and L2 evaluations of student writing (Hinkel, 1994).

Experimental or *quasi*-experimental methods have also been used to study writers' awareness of readers. Roen and Willey (1988), for example, used an experimental study to see if focusing on audience before or during revising influenced writing quality, while Schriver (1992) conducted an experiment to assess the effects of reader protocols on the ability of L2 writers to anticipate readers' comprehension problems. As noted earlier, there are serious problems with holding variables constant and eliminating extraneous factors to isolate a single feature from all those which may influence writing. Classrooms and offices are complex places, with many activities that can potentially affect research outcomes and so many writing experiments have been conducted in specifically created artificial contexts. Because of this, researchers conducting classroom experiments may need to draw on several data collection methods to get a complete picture of the phenomena they are studying.

In fact, it is probably a good rule of thumb for researchers to collect as much contextual information as possible, including the views of the participants they have studied, in any research. Researchers must manage the complex task of controlling multiple methods. Different methods have different affordances and tell us different things about texts and the ways they are used in real life. So, by analysing texts, by conducting interviews or focus groups, by distributing questionnaires, by observing actors writing or learning to write, by studying photographs or artefacts, and by asking writers to tell us what they are doing as they write, we can build a finely nuanced understanding of writing or learning to write.

Concept 5.9   **Some researchable issues on readers**

- Who are the target audiences for a particular group of writers?
- What do these readers typically look for in a text and how do they read it?
- What do writers need to know about the target audience to write successful texts?
- What interactional features are important to engage a particular audience?
- How is the discourse community represented in a particular genre?
- How do considerations of audience influence writing?
- How do these considerations differ between experienced and novice writers?

- What do readers see as an effective text in a particular context?
- Are there general principles of audience that writers can transfer across contexts?
- What help can we give students to accommodate audiences in their writing?

To summarise some of this discussion: there is a need for research that tells us about the features of specific text-types, the practices of specific writers, and the relationships between instructional practices and writing effectiveness. Research conducted by teachers and students can illuminate each of these areas, contributing to what we know about writing by exploring and validating existing practices and analyses and grounding them in specific contexts. More immediately it can also have great practical pay-offs for individual practitioners, both for our understanding of the kinds of writing that we encounter, and the contribution this understanding can make to our professional practices.

Further reading

Burns, A. (1999) *Collaborative action research for English language teachers* (Cambridge: Cambridge University Press). A practical teacher's guide to classroom research techniques.

Cohen, L., Manion, L. and Morrison, K. (2000) *Research methods in education*, 5th edn (London: Routledge). Clearly written, authoritative and wide-ranging discussion of major issues and approaches.

Edge, J. (2001) *Action research* (Alexandria, VA: TESOL). Contains plenty of ideas based on reports of different action research studies.

Lofland, J. and Lofland, L. (1995) *Analyzing social settings: a guide to qualitative observation and analysis* (Belmont, CA: Wadsworth). The classic qualitative social research text with full discussion of gathering, focusing and analysing data.

Pole, C. and Morrison, M. (2003) *Ethnography for education* (Maidenhead: Open University Press). A clear overview of the theory and methods of ethnography and its potential for educational research.

Note

1 The Lancaster literacy page is at http://www.literacy.lancs.ac.uk/resources/studentprojects.htm

Chapter 6

Research cases: observing and reporting

This chapter will . . .

- present and evaluate examples of five small published research projects based on data collected through observation and self-report methods;

- use these cases to examine some central themes and good practices of recent writing research;

- suggest how researchers might develop the methods and results of these cases for projects of their own.

In the previous chapter I suggested some issues that can usefully be tackled by small-scale research and sketched the ways such issues have typically been addressed. Here, and in the following chapter, I try to flesh out these methods and topics by presenting a number of cases which have the potential for further research. I have selected these to represent a range of different research areas and methodologies, taking in research on writers, texts and readers. Like action research projects generally, these examples centre on local, concrete issues of relevance to practitioners and generally occur in natural settings (Burns, 1999: 2). They are all initiated by a question, supported by data and interpretation, and conducted by researchers, teachers, or students. In this chapter I focus on research methods which might be more familiar to teachers: those which involve observing what people do and recording what they say.

6.1 Questionnaire research on faculty beliefs and practices

Summary

Leonora, J., Wilhelm, M. and Parkinson, J. (2005). A study of the writing tasks and reading assigned to undergraduate science students at a South African University. *English for Specific Purposes*, 25: 260–81.

This study surveyed faculty members in 14 science disciplines at three campuses of a large South African university to discover the reading and writing tasks assigned to undergraduate students. Questionnaire results provided data on teachers' views on academic literacy and the main genres that students were required to read and write.

Surveys of academic writing can play an important role in understanding readers' needs and in developing appropriate course material for both L1 and L2 writers in university settings. Jackson *et al.* became interested in this issue through teaching academic literacy on a year-long Science Foundation Programme designed to prepare students who do not qualify to enter first-year tertiary studies. These are largely Black African students from disadvantaged backgrounds and poor schools who are required to study courses in Mathematics, Chemistry, Physics, Biology and Communication to develop their knowledge and skills so they are ready for first-year studies. This study is part of the preparation for redesigning the academic literacy courses so the information gained would ensure that their course would be grounded in a solid research base.

Aims

The main goal was to determine the kinds of writing and reading expected and the literacy expectations of science lecturers and to this end the questionnaire addressed three main areas:

1. the amounts of reading and writing science students were expected to do;
2. the nature of this reading and writing and the difficulties for students as seen by the lecturers;

3. the lecturers' personal perceptions of students academic literacy problems.

Methodology

The questionnaire covered the three issues above in just six questions. The first asked respondents how much guidance and feedback they gave students on different aspects of writing, with the option to indicate whether they corrected, gave brief or extensive written comments, verbal feedback or no comments at all. The same language features of organisation, grammatical accuracy, referencing and plagiarism, and tone and style also appeared in the next question which asked lecturers to indicate, on a four-point scale, the extent to which poor performance affected students' marks. The remaining questions concerned the frequency and type of writing tasks the lecturer had set the previous semester, the frequency of reading tasks, and their perception of how well students generally performed the written tasks.

The categorisation of the writing tasks was based on those used by Braine (1995) and Horrowitz (1986). These were: summary of/reaction to readings, experimental (laboratory) report, experimental report (design), case study (knowledge of a theory to solve a problem) and research paper (combines information from a number of sources). To which they added the essay genre which is often used in the science faculty. The questionnaires were sent to lecturers from the science faculties at three campuses of a large South African university. A total of 47 questionnaires were returned (25 per cent of those distributed), representing 14 disciplines from the three campuses. Most responses concerned first-year courses, but some referred to second- or third-year teaching. The responses were analysed only descriptively and no tests of statistical significance were calculated.

Results

The results showed that lecturers set between three and four pieces of writing on average per semester and that the nature of these assignments depended on the discipline. *Report* is the most common genre in science, comprising 66 per cent of assignments, followed by summaries of readings (16 per cent) with essays being relatively rare (10 per cent). Academics in the experimental sciences expected a lot of writing, largely in the form of laboratory reports, while staff in maths and physics set very little and awarded grades based on mathematical accuracy rather than writing.

In terms of awarding grades, the lecturers appeared to value the organisation of written assignments above other aspects, followed by attention to referencing conventions and avoidance of plagiarism. Grammatical accuracy influenced students' marks to a lesser extent and tone and style only marginally. Feedback on student writing mainly took the form of brief written comments, with corrections to the grammar also being common. The final question concerned reading tasks and revealed that the textbook was the most common source of reading material for science students closely followed by photocopied readings of chapters from other textbooks. Students were almost never assigned journal articles to read.

Concept 6.1   Questionnaire research

Questionnaires can be useful for collecting self-report data on writing and reading practices and have been used extensively in research on reader preferences, attitudes and judgements. They have the advantage of being easier and quicker to administer than interviews and the responses of far more informants can be gathered. Data is more amenable to analysis and quantification, and because the information is controlled by the questions, they allow considerable precision and clarity. We need to remember, however, that questionnaires only provide reports of what people say they think or do and not direct evidence of it, and they may need to be validated with other methods, typically by following up with in-depth interviews with a sample of respondents. In any case, questionnaires need to be carefully constructed and piloted to ensure reliability, avoid ambiguity, and to achieve a balance between having sufficient data and not overburdening respondents.

Statistical tests are often used to establish the significance of results and Brown (1988), and Hatch and Lazaraton (1991) are straightforward and accessible sources of information on different kinds of statistical tests in applied linguistics research. In small-scale studies, however, researchers often simply use descriptive measures such as means and percentages to identify general features.

Commentary

This study is a good example of both the strengths and weaknesses of questionnaire research. The information gathered provided the researchers with valuable information about the writing needs of their students and the expectations of their immediate audience. From their results they learnt that the lab report is the main way that students learnt about scientific writing and that there was a serious discrepancy between this writing assignment and the kinds of reading the students did. Textbooks prove very poor models for writing lab reports, as these are far more similar to a research article in terms of audience interactions and stance (Hyland, 2004a). On the other hand, the absence of any follow-up interviews and lack of provision for open-ended comments on all but one question meant that respondents were straitjacketed into the initial perceptions of the research. Several interesting issues, such as the fact the form and content of the laboratory reports differed across disciplines, were not followed up and the specific characteristics of particular writing assignments were not clarified or explored.

Further research

Jackson *et al.* give a clear account of their research, and their questionnaire is appended to their paper for use by others. The study could therefore be replicated in other contexts to provide information about the views and practices of those working with students outside the writing classroom. Students in different disciplinary areas and at different levels of education need different kinds of help with writing, but the writing requirements and problems of many student groups remain unknown. This is a very fruitful area for further research, and similar studies would be useful to determine the tasks, evaluation criteria and audience expectations in other contexts.

Such studies are not only likely to show us what the important writing issues for our students might be, but also raise the awareness of subject lecturers' concerning the importance of writing and their own practices, perhaps leading to greater cooperation between subject tutors and academic literacy tutors in providing students with authentic writing experiences. More generally, surveys of this kind are very valuable in building up a picture of discipline-specific writing practices and how these might vary in different institutions. This kind of information can contribute to what we know about variations in disciplinary writing, faculty attitudes and practices, and the need for specifically tailored writing programmes.

Equally, survey studies can also help target more specific reader-oriented features of context. It would be useful, for example, to know what it is our students actually have to write, so we can go beyond generic labels to the specific tasks required. This means exploring audience perceptions of exactly what constitutes a '*term-paper*', an '*essay*', or a '*laboratory report*', in different fields, the differences they perceive in the writing of L1 and L2 students, and the relative importance they assign to different features of student writing. While surveys alone cannot give us all the information we need, researchers can complement questionnaires with more qualitative procedures to reveal the demands and complexities of specific writing practices. Interviews with selected respondents, the study of departmental documents and style sheets, and analyses of target discourses, could also be used with questionnaires to tell us a great deal more about the relationship between what we teach, what writers do and what real audiences want.

6.2   Experimental research on peer-response training

Summary

Berg, E.C. (1999). The effects of trained peer response on ESL students' revision types and writing quality. *Journal of Second Language Writing*, 8(3): 215–37.

Catherine Berg's study examined whether the feedback given by ESL students trained in peer response improved the type and quality of text revisions in the writing of their peers. She used an experimental methodology which compared a trained with a non-trained group by holistically rating first and revised drafts and examining meaning and form changes. The results indicated that trained peer response positively affected students' revision types and quality of texts.

Peer response is part of the process approach to teaching and is widely used in both L1 and L2 contexts as a means to improve writers' drafts and raise awareness of readers' needs (see part 1.2). The benefits of peer response have been hard to confirm empirically, however, particularly in ESL classrooms, and many studies have reported that students themselves doubt its value, overwhelmingly preferring teacher feedback. L1 studies have shown that peer conferencing needs careful planning by the teacher and that students have to be taught how to respond to texts. Peer response training is likely to have beneficial effects in L2 contexts because students often see revision as error correction and may feel culturally uncomfortable with criticising peers' work. This second study of readers thus sought to determine the impact of trained peer response on written texts in an L2 writing context, both in terms of the overall quality of texts and the types of revisions made.

Aims

The main issue addressed in this study was whether responses by trained peers shape revision types and writing outcomes of ESL student texts. More specifically Berg addressed three questions:

1. Does trained peer response generate a greater number of meaning changes in revised drafts?
2. Does trained peer response produce higher quality scores in revised drafts?
3. Are the relative effects of trained peer response on writing outcomes influenced by proficiency?

Methodology

Berg studied her own students in two intermediate and two advanced level groups in a university intensive English course. One group from each level, with 12 students in each, was trained to participate in peer response to writing. These students received instruction in the language needed (e.g. asking questions, using specific words, giving opinions, etc.), and the foci of discussions (rhetorical aspects of meaning). Both the trained and the untrained classes received similar writing instruction, used the same course text, and participated in similar composing and revising activities. Both groups received peer feedback. The intermediate students wrote on the topic of a memorable personal experience and the advanced group on a personal opinion. They received no teacher comments on their first drafts.

Concept 6.2   **Experimental research methods**

Experimental methods are often used to investigate the language behaviour of sample groups under controlled conditions. While experiments have largely fallen from grace in writing research in favour of more qualitative, natural, and 'thicker' data-collection techniques, there are contexts in which they may be appropriate. Experimental techniques explore the strength of a relationship between two variable features of a situation such as test scores, proficiency, instruction, and so on. The idea is that the researcher seeks to discover if one variable influences another by holding other factors constant and varying the treatment given to two groups. The experiment is set up so that data is collected to minimise threats to the reliability and validity of the research. Statistical tests are then carried out on the data to find out if differences between the control and the experimental groups are significant.

Pre-peer first drafts and post-peer second drafts were collected and examined for revisions. Two procedures were used. First, to determine the number of changes, each student's first and second drafts were placed side by side and all meaning changes, i.e. revisions that involved new content or the deletion of content, were marked and counted as units. A second rater marked a sample to ensure validity. Second, to find if training influenced writing quality, each essay was graded holistically on a 19-point scale by two trained raters. They focused not on minor grammatical alterations but on the quality of the writing as a unit of discourse. The quality of the revisions of each student was measured by the degree of difference between the average score of the two raters for the first draft and the second draft.

Results

The study had three main findings. First Berg found that the students trained in peer response made significantly more meaning revisions than untrained students; second, trained students improved their writing over the two drafts more than untrained writers; and third that level of proficiency made little difference to the improvement of writing quality. Thus, taken together, the results suggest that appropriate training can lead to more meaning-type revisions and better-quality writing overall, confirming the advantages of training for successful peer response.

Commentary

This is a good example of how research can feed back into practice. Berg's study addresses an important classroom issue with clear relevance for teachers, suggesting both the value of peer conferencing in improving student writing and the advantages of peer training to make the most of this. However, while there is a clear pedagogical pay-off to this research, the finding that trained students were able to improve their writing suggests the possibility that we might simply instruct students in revision skills to get the same results, eliminating peer feedback entirely. Berg argues, however, that while this may help students to revise for meaning, they still need to know where to make such revisions. A peer who has not been involved in creating the text is better able to spot unclear aspects of the writing as someone who lacks access to the writer's additional knowledge. We should, however, be cautious in placing too much faith in the results of experimental studies due to the difficulties of holding variables constant in the two contexts. Classrooms are not laboratories, and differences in teaching styles, learner preferences, relationships, and so on can all influence results.

Further research

This study indicates a number of areas for further investigation. First, future research is needed to substantiate these results with other learners in other contexts and to reveal more precisely the relationship between the processes of training and revisions in these contexts. We might usefully look at the ways that writers from different language backgrounds respond to various instructional approaches, for example, or how individual aspects of training are picked up and used to change texts. It would also be helpful to learn which aspects of training are most useful for improving student revisions and how extensive this instruction needs to be. In addition, we know little about the benefits of training over longer time periods and whether these advantages fall away. The effects of training thus need to be monitored beyond a single essay. Each of these issues might profitably be addressed by using an experimental methodology similar to that employed by Berg.

It is also important to discover what occurs in peer negotiations, how these differ between trained and untrained students, how trained responders draw on their instruction in these discussions, and the effects these have on revisions. Obviously more qualitative approaches are needed to obtain this kind of data. Research here could employ observation techniques, perhaps using video recordings of peer-response sessions, interviews with participants focusing on the interactions which occurred, scrutiny of interview or conferencing transcripts, and close analysis of student drafts in the light of this spoken data.

6.3   Interview research on scientists' writing practices

Summary

Okamura, A. (2005). Two types of strategies used by Japanese scientists when writing research articles in English. *System*, 34(1): 68–79.

This study examined how some writers succeed in mastering scientific discourse in English, in a non-English speaking environment. Okamura interviewed 13 Japanese researchers of varying experience, focusing both on their difficulties and on their strategies to cope with them. The results showed that identification of their audience and their learning strategies distinguished established researchers from others. While all read academic texts in their field to learn typical writing patterns, only five sought to master English speakers' language use

English is now unquestionably the language of international scholarship and an important medium of research communication for non-native English speaking academics around the world. Non-English-speaking scientists often face enormous difficulties however, and interviews and questionnaires have been used with both experienced and novice researchers to discover what difficulties they have. However, most academic communities contain individuals who are successful in publishing in English, and have overcome these difficulties. This study examines differences among researchers in a linguistically less advantageous environment, Japan, where English is taught as a foreign language from secondary school. The study focuses on junior, middle-ranking researchers and established global players in the sciences to reveal something of how they survive and succeed when writing research articles, despite their linguistic handicap.

Aims

The study aimed to identify Japanese researchers' language difficulties in relation to experience, then compare the strategies that helped them to cope with these difficulties in writing research articles. It addressed two main questions:

1. What kinds of difficulties are non-English-speaking professional researchers aware of, when writing research papers?

2. What learning/writing strategies do they employ to cope with these difficulties?

Methodology

Concept 6.3 **Interview research**

Interviews enable participants to discuss their interpretations of the world and to express how they see situations. The method acknowledges that human interaction is central to understanding and emphasises the social situatedness of research data. Interviews have been widely used in writing research and have three main purposes: as the principal source of gathering data; as a means of testing hypotheses or generating new ones; and as one method with others to triangulate information or cross-check data. They can be characterised on a spectrum of formality. These include 1) A structured format where the researcher has an agenda and works through a set of predetermined questions; 2) A semi-structured pattern where the researcher knows where he or she wants the discussion to go but allows the respondent considerable freedom in getting there; 3) An unstructured format where the interview is guided by the responses of the interviewee rather than the agenda of the researcher, enabling unanticipated themes and topics to emerge.

Cohen *et al.* (2000: 267–72)

Okamura interviewed 13 Japanese researchers (2 lecturers, 3 associate professors and 8 professors) in science and engineering departments in major research universities. All were educated in Japan to Ph.D. level and were actively publishing in American, European and Japanese journals in English. Three professors had spent two to three years working outside Japan and been invited to international conferences as leading figures in their fields. He therefore categorised respondents into three groups: 5 junior researchers (the lecturers and associate professors), 5 mid-ranking researchers (5 professors) and 3 established researchers (3 professors). Participants provided copies of two of their published papers which were referred to in the semi-structured interviews. The interviews lasted 45–90 min. each, and were conducted in the researchers' offices, in Japanese. The use of the native tongue, the fact that the interviewer was not an English speaker, and the interviewer's obvious interest helped create rapport when talking about their difficulties in writing in English.

Results

All the writers mentioned their lack of vocabulary which created difficulties in describing their results and staking a claim. Two biologists believed this was likely to be more of a handicap in their discipline, which relied less on mathematical formulae than other sciences. They also recognised less tangible difficulties. Although all agreed that they had to consider the readers to be accepted by their target journal, the junior and middle-ranking researchers stated they did not have specific readers in mind, and that they were unable to think of subtle linguistic forms that would persuade readers. Two junior researchers, in fact, said they were so preoccupied with grammatical accuracy that they did not consider their readers when writing. The three established writers, in contrast, were able to talk about their target readers, and described strategies to draw their attention.

To improve their writing, all adopted 'subject knowledge-oriented strategies' such as reading and collecting useful phrases at an early career stage. After internalising set phrases, they tended to become ambivalent about the need to achieve native-like fluency in writing, recognisng that time pressures meant they could not spend extra time polishing their English. They also commented that, with experience they realised that the discourse community is tolerant of non-English speakers' writing. Seven of 13 therefore showed no interest in going beyond using short sentences and simple structures while the remainder continued to develop their writing skills, often by contacting English speakers about the use of English in research articles. In addition to learning strategies, the writers also differed in their use of writing strategies, with the junior and middle-ranking researchers reporting that they thought mainly in Japanese but wrote only in English and the established researchers both thinking and writing only in English.

Commentary

This is an uncomplicated but effective study of the writing practices of a specific group, identifying some of their difficulties and describing the coping strategies they use when writing scientific papers in English. The research shows that while the junior or middle-ranking researchers were aware of the need to convince their fellow researchers that their findings are worth publishing, they had difficulty in visualising readers. Established researchers, on the other hand, are not merely concerned with getting published, but being read by their target audience. These differences in experience seem to affect the learning and writing strategies used to overcome their difficulties with most writers happy to work within their limited English, because they see no reason to go beyond it. While it is not possible to conclude that success is related to English skills, the interviews suggest that adopting language-oriented strategies seems necessary for success in academic writing.

Further research

While this paper has identified some of the difficulties that Japanese researchers experience, and has described the coping strategies they use when writing scientific papers in English, it is essentially preliminary and exploratory. The idea that the writer's experience in the discourse community can play a part in perceiving language problems and adopting strategies is interesting, however, and worth further study. It might be worth exploring experiences and background with other groups of writers and to discover the strategies they use to overcome any disadvantage. The views of writers in other disciplines and language groups, for example, can offer interesting comparisons with the Japanese writers and also help teachers become aware of their learners' professional experience and the kinds of guidance different students might need, perhaps feeding into teaching of localised strategies for writers.

6.4   Protocol research on the writing process

Summary

Wong, A. (2005). Writers' mental representations of the intended audience and of the rhetorical purpose for writing and the strategies that they employed when they composed. *System*, 33(1): 29–47.

This paper studies the composing strategies employed by four advanced L2 writers as influenced by their mental representations of the intended audience and rhetorical purpose for writing. The writers were asked to verbalise all the thoughts that went through their minds when they wrote an assignment and the video protocols were transcribed, coded and analyzed in conjunction with the drafts they produced and their follow-up interviews. Wong found that while the writers used a similar range of composing strategies, they used them differently and to serve different purposes at different junctures of the composing process.

This study is in the tradition of cognitive research which has helped us to understand the strategies writers use in the writing process (see Section 1.2.2). This research has shown that writing is not simply a series of actions, but a series of decisions which involves setting goals and selecting strategies to achieve them. Wong was interested in understanding something of these strategies in the writing of L2 graduate students, looking in particular at whether there is a correspondence between how they compose and their perceptions of the rhetorical purpose for writing and of the intended audience.

Aims

The study sought to discover how far the writers' perceptions of writing purposes and target audience had an impact upon their composing strategies. Specifically, he wanted to answer the following questions:

- What strategies do advanced L2 writers employ when they write in an academic context?

- Do advanced L2 writers have different mental representations of the target audience and of the rhetorical purpose for performing the writing task? If so, in what ways are these representations different?

- Is there a correspondence between advanced L2 writers' mental representations of the target audience and the purpose for performing the writing task and the composing strategies they use?

Methodology

Four Chinese L1 English major student-teachers with similar academic backgrounds and near-native-speaker proficiency in English were given a writing task that required them to reflect upon their experience of teaching. They were given the topic only at the start of the writing sessions, but were told beforehand that the task would be on the teaching of grammar and that they should bring relevant reference materials with them. They were told that there was no time limit and the suggested length of 500 words could be taken flexibly. Data were collected by asking them to verbalise all the thoughts that ran through their minds while they composed. The think-aloud protocols were triangulated with data from the video-recording of the writing behaviour of the writers, follow-up interviews and analysis of the writing plans and drafts produced during the composing sessions.

Following some short training and warm-up tasks, the participants were given the following set of instructions:

1. Say whatever is on your mind. Don't hold back hunches, guesses, images and intentions.
2. Speak as continuously as possible. Say something at least once every five seconds, even if only, 'I am drawing a blank'.
3. Speak audibly. Watch out for your voice dropping as you become involved.
4. Speak as telegraphically as you please without worrying about complete sentences or eloquence.
5. Don't over explain or justify. Analyse no more than you would normally do.
6. Don't elaborate past events. Get into the pattern of saying what you are thinking now.
7. Verbalise in English, Cantonese, or mixed code as you prefer.

The sessions were video recorded with one camera focused upon the writer full front and the other capturing the writer's pen movement on paper. Following the composing session the observation notes were used as a basis for an interview to discover why they behaved in certain ways during composing, why they adopted certain composing strategies, what they saw as the purpose of the assignment, and the audience that they had in mind when they composed. The protocols themselves were coded using a scheme adapted from Raimes (1987) and were checked for *intra*-rater reliability and 10 per cent were selected and coded by another rater to ensure inter-rater reliability. (As we have seen in Section 1.2.2.) Protocols have been criticised for their artificiality, their incompleteness, their heavy reliance on inference and the fact that they may even distort writers' normal composing processes, but it is a method which produces extremely rich data.

> **Quote 6.1** Smagorinsky on protocol analysis
>
> Often represented as a mechanical procedure conducted by automatons on information-processing subjects, protocol analysis is in fact an essentially human experience, fraught with the potential for mishap through personal flaws and vagaries and the fragility of social interactions, and dogged throughout by agonizing decision making at every level. Researchers who understand the magnitude of their task and account for the potential perils to the greatest extent possible can provide a rich source of data that, when seen in the context of validating research, can provide a unique and important view of composing process.
>
> Smagorinsky (1994: 16)

Results

The results show that the four writers displayed a richly diverse repertoire of mental representations of audience. Typical of school-sponsored writing and knowledge display, two perceived their course lecturer as their audience, one trying out ideas to solicit feedback and the other relating to the teacher as an evaluator. Another saw his students as the primary audience and wrote with simpler English than his counterparts, focusing on grammar and seeking to help the reader learn more about auxiliary verbs. The final writer perceived the rhetorical purpose as reflecting on her own experience in order to improve her teaching and so wrote as the audience of her own text, finally sharing it with peers towards the end. This suggests that the mental representations of audience may have an influence on shaping writing decisions.

The protocols showed that writers used a range of common strategies such as reading and rereading, planning or goal setting, editing and revising, but in addition they also used questioning and self-assessment to facilitate their writing. Wong also discovered a correspondence between how the writers saw the context and their strategies, with the student writing for the lecturer-evaluator employing a narrower range of strategies with lower incidence of use to 'get it right the first time she put words on paper'. The writer addressing the lecturer as coach, saw the assignment as an opportunity to try out ideas to solicit feedback, and so produced a high incidence of major text revisions. The student who invoked his students as the intended audience attached great importance to planning at the rhetorical level when he constructed the plan of the assignment while the more reflective writer made use of the broadest range of composing strategies and with the highest frequencies.

Commentary

This study highlights some of the complex operations of composing, pointing to the multilayered considerations which occupy students as they write. In particular it suggests that perception of rhetorical purpose and audience influences particular composing strategies. For teachers this suggests that it may be important that the intended audience should be clarified and explained to students, replicating what happens in real life language use. Interestingly, the participants seemed to become far more aware of their composing strategies as a result of verbalising their thoughts while composing and reflecting on their composing behaviours. This may encourage teachers of writing to employ a limited amount of think-aloud activities in writing programmes. This kind of research is therefore valuable for increasing our understanding of what can occur when we write and why we do what we do. Protocol analysis, however, needs to be carefully handled, particularly in L2 contexts where reporting and writing simultaneously may overburden novice writers.

Further research

Many process research methodologies are easily adapted for the classroom. Through think-aloud protocols we can 'listen in' on students' writing processes to see how they handle the tasks we give them, the effects of different prompts, or the choices they make at given points in writing. Protocols are also useful for examining the ways that writers plan and revise their work, respond to feedback, integrate source material into an essay, select themes and arguments, or draw on prior rhetorical experiences. In addition to helping us learn more about writing processes, protocols can reveal the effects of our teaching on composing strategies or the particular social factors which influence writers' goals and strategies. These might include the rhetorical context, prior instruction, knowledge of academic conventions, earlier experiences with the genre, and so on. As we have seen here, the technique can be particularly useful when examining the importance of audience to writers, identifying the points where they anticipate the expectations of readers.

6.5   Diary research on the research process

Summary

Nelson, J. (1993). The library revisited: exploring students' research processes. In A. Penrose and B. Sitcoe (eds) *Hearing ourselves think: cognitive research in the college writing classroom* (New York: Oxford University Press).

This research examined how three L1 students interpreted and completed a research paper assignment in an introductory psychology class. Nelson asked the participants to keep a daily log of their research and writing activities for their assignment and to provide her with all their notes, outlines and drafts as they were produced. Her results show the important role that writers' goals and task definitions can play in influencing their writing.

As in the previous case, this study employs introspective research techniques to explore writing practices, attending to an earlier stage of the process by focusing on how students find and use sources for an undergraduate research project (see part 1.2.2). Despite the ubiquity of source-based research writing in university contexts, the ways that students gather, interpret, integrate and use research material in preparing a topic for writing are frequently overlooked by subject teachers and have largely been ignored by researchers. It appears, however, that while experiensced writers have a range of purposeful strategies for locating relevant sources, this is generally not the case with novices. Nelson chose to explore this issue using students' process logs in which participants recorded their activities in working on the paper.

Aims

The major aim was to discover how these students went about completing a research paper. The main questions were:

- When did each student begin to gather and read sources?
- How did they interpret the task?
- How did the drafts produced by the three students differ and how did they use the sources?
- What resources (assignment guidelines, prior experiences, friends, teachers) did they rely on?

- What goals did they set and what paths did they follow to achieve these goals?
- What kind of paper did each student produce, and how was it evaluated?

Method

Nelson used a case-study approach in which participants' diaries figured prominently. Focusing on three students, she collected data from their notes, plans and drafts, and from daily logs of all the work done on the assignment. Diary studies are not commonly used in writing research, which helps explain why I have chosen an older study here, but logs are important introspective tools in language research and can provide insights into language use that would otherwise be difficult to obtain. Unlike think aloud methods, they are retrospective and therefore offer the benefit of hindsight and reflection on writers' practices, suggesting why writers acted as they did and their perceptions of the contextual influences on them.

Nelson instructed her participants to make regular entries in their logs and even to record 'no work' days. She asked them to deliver the logs to her at least three times a week. She told them that the entries could include notes on their trail through the library, how they evaluated sources and took notes, the conversations they had with others, insights that occurred to them at any time, decisions about planning the paper, and so on. They understood that their objective was to explain in as much detail as possible how their research evolved, from the time they were given the assignment to the handing in of their paper.

Concept 6.4   **Diaries/process logs**

Bailey (1990: 215) defines diary studies as 'a first-person account of a language learning or teaching experience, documented through regular, candid entries in a personal journal and then analysed for recurring patterns or salient events'. Students are generally encouraged to enter all relevant activities on a regular basis. When a substantial amount of material has been produced, the researcher examines the log for patterns which are then interpreted and discussed with the writer. Logs can provide valuable insights into both social and psychological processes that might be difficult to collect in other ways.

Results

The diaries provided rich information about students' attitudes and concerns as well as data on their choices, actions and reasons for acting as they did. They showed that each student developed different ideas about what the assignment required, and that these task definitions influenced their strategies for completing the assignment. Most importantly, the logs revealed that students actively interpreted their writing assignments in different ways, creating their own research and writing goals and working out the ways they were going to achieve them. One relied wholly on the unexamined assumption that the task was simply to assemble and reproduce material, and created a last-minute pastiche of a few sources. The two others drew from a richer set of resources to define the task and took a more self-conscious and critical approach to interpreting and defining the assignment. The diaries showed that these two students evolved goals over time, examined sources carefully, got feedback from classmates and personalised the task far more, learning more from the experience and finding the task more satisfying.

Commentary

This is an interesting piece of process research which focuses on a largely unexamined aspect of student perceptions and writing. It provides a detailed behind-the-scenes look at the different assumptions and strategies that students employ when they research a writing topic, revealing the beliefs that students can hold, identifying the practices they might engage in, and distinguishing those strategies that work from those that don't. The results have obvious implications for classroom practice, suggesting that some L1 students may have inappropriate assumptions about the goals of research writing and poor strategies for producing successful texts. Teachers need to challenge these assumptions so that students may reconsider the ways they interpret such assignments, and to model the strategies of successful student research. This might involve sharing the logs of students whose strategies resulted in successful papers to encourage others to try their searching and note-taking practices. In these ways we can feed information from research into ways of providing practical, peer-based support for students to make critical and reflective choices when they write.

Further research

Research into the ways that students write or carry out particular writing tasks, the factors that influence their strategies, and the assumptions they hold about each of these are clearly important both for our understanding of writing and success in learning to write. There are clear possibilities for further research in this area with other students, other assignments and other types of writing. The influence of age, proficiency, prior learning, different cultural backgrounds, or various types of instruction on how students interpret and process writing tasks might be usefully explored in developing further research. In addition, longitudinal studies might be valuable to reveal how students' task interpretations evolve over time and how these affect the choices they make as researchers and writers.

While research into the ways that writers participate in decision-making and writing activities is important, Nelson's study points less to questions that need to be answered than to a particular style of research. Though not widely used to study writing, diaries and logs have become very popular means of conducting class-based and other forms of action research as they provide access to elements of writing and learning that are otherwise hidden. Through learner-process logs we can discover students' beliefs about the writing they do, the tasks they are set and the teaching they receive, while gaining insights into their composing strategies. It is, then, an instrument for conducting research on affect and practice, as well as cognition. Logs have also been used as introspective tools by teachers to record their own writing experiences or the effects of their classroom practices on students' writing improvement. Effective writing teaching cannot be based solely on the implementation of abstract theoretical principles but needs to be grounded in local knowledge of what works with particular students and logs help reveal something of this.

The information gathered from diaries therefore offers both a rich source of research data into the writing process and a means of privileging the writer's perspective when seeking to solve the problems of teaching and learning to write.

6.6 Conclusion

Throughout this book I have tried to emphasise the importance of research to both our understanding of writing and to the practices involved in teaching it. This research is often conducted on a small scale by teachers, students, trainers or other practitioners interested either in texts, composition, or the teaching and learning of writing. Because of this, I have focused here on how projects might be effectively carried out by novice researchers working in their own professional contexts and using cases which might be familiar to them. In the next chapter I turn to another group of methods which typically work by combining these and other approaches to gain a fuller picture of writing and writing practices.

Further reading

See also the recommended texts in Chapters 5 and 7.

Brown, J.D. (2001) *Using surveys in language programs* (Cambridge: Cambridge University Press). What it says on the cover – a guide to questionnaire research in language teaching.

Brown, J.D. and Rodgers, T.S. (2002) *Doing second language research* (Oxford: Oxford University Press). A comprehensive guide to conducting research on L2 students.

Dornyei, Z. (2007) *Research methods in applied linguistics: quantitative, qualitative, and mixed methodologies* (Oxford: Oxford University Press).

Gass, S., Sorace, A. and Selinker, L. (1999) *Second language learning data analysis*, 2nd edn (Mahwah, NJ: Lawrence Erlbaum).

Hatch, E. and Lazaraton, A. (1991) *The research manual: Design and statistics for applied linguists* (Boston, MA: Heinle & Heinle). Key text for quantitative applied linguistics and TESOL research.

Nunan, D. (1992) *Research methods in language teaching* (Cambridge: Cambridge University Press). Introductory overview of research techniques with clear, practical examples.

Chapter 7

Research cases: texts and contexts

This chapter will . . .

- present and evaluate examples of five research projects which draw on the analysis of texts and the contexts which surround them;
- examine some central themes and good practices of contemporary writing research;
- consider the extension of these studies to other topics of research.

In the previous chapter I presented some sample studies based on methods which principally involved collecting data through observation and self-report techniques. Here I turn to what may seem more esoteric approaches. Training teachers in how to compile corpora, analyse texts and investigate interaction have not typically figured in teacher education courses and perhaps are more demanding of the researcher. This is, in part, because they often combine several data collection methods in a single study. It is also, however, because they require reflection and the ability to step back to conduct a detailed interrogation of talk, text and communication. Again, each case begins with a brief context for the research and is followed by a summary of its aims, methodology and results, then a commentary on its design and contribution to our understanding of writing. I conclude each case with some brief suggestions for further research which, while not intended to restrict possible approaches and topics, might stimulate readers into extending and adding to what we know about writing.

7.1 Genre analysis research on scientific abstracts

Summary

Ayers, G. (2008) The evolutionary nature of genre: An investigation of the short texts accompanying research articles in the scientific journal *Nature*. *English for Specific Purposes*, 27(1): 22–41.

This study analysed the short texts accompanying research articles in the journal *Nature* from 1991 to 2005 focusing on their move structure and promotional elements and how these changed over the period. The findings showed that these texts differ from prescriptive models of abstracts, but that they changed following the introduction of the e-version of the journal in 1997 to become more standardised and concerned with the 'general reader', indicating a kind of 'democratisation' of the scientific community.

Abstracts are one of the most studied genres of the academy, their brevity and clear purpose making them ideal for genre studies. Several researchers have noted their value as a vehicle for projecting news value and promoting the accompanying article by encouraging the reader to continue into the main paper. This is typically done by a structure which foregrounds important information for easy access and grammatical features which highlight novelty and immediacy. This study was undertaken to trace any changes in the abstracts accompanying articles in *Nature*, the world's top multidisciplinary journal publishing research in all fields of science.

Aims

This genre study follows the tradition discussed in part 1.1.2. It was designed to provide a fuller understanding of the abstract in a single, highly prestigious journal and how it might have evolved over a period of 14 years which included the introduction of an e-version of the journal. In particular, the author was interested in the following questions:

1. How far do these texts vary from the traditional model of abstracts?
2. In what ways have they changed since the introduction of the e-version of the journal?

The study, then, was both descriptive, exploring *what* these texts were like, and *explanatory*, seeking to account for any changes in them over this period.

Methodology

The researcher collected two small corpora of texts to reflect pre- and post-1997 practices: 61 abstracts from copies of *Nature* published during 1991–92 and 1996 and 32 abstracts from internet copies of *Nature* from 1999–2005. Since abstracts after 1997 were double the length of the earlier ones, the two samples contained an equivalent amount of text. Analyses revealed that moves were generally signalled by the use of tense, voice and lexis and their relative brevity often meant that the introduction and methods were conflated into a single move in the earlier texts. The post-1997 abstracts were more complex and difficulties in identifying moves were often resolved by appealing to the accompanying text. Steps or sub moves were then identified, often following the directions in 'Guide to Authors'. The textual analyses were supplemented by advice in the journal's 'Guide to Authors' and interviews with the journal's executive editor and four scientists from different fields.

Concept 7.1   **Genre analysis**

Genre is understood in different ways and there are numerous ways of approaching *analysis*. Some of these focus exclusively on text structure, some give greater attention to sociocultural factors, some examine the practices of writers, and others explore the expectations of readers. Ultimately all approaches share the same goal of adding to a model of language use which is rich in social, cultural, and institutional explanation, which links language to contexts, and which may have practical relevance for teachers by suggesting ways of presenting conventionalised aspects of texts. Genre analysis seeks to:

- identify how texts are structured in terms of functional moves
- identify the features which characterise texts and help realise their purposes
- examine the understandings of those who write and read the genre
- discover how the genre relates to users' activities
- explain language choices in terms of social, cultural and psychological contexts
- provide insights for teaching language

Results

The study found that these texts deviated considerably from traditional models of abstracts and that they had undergone further recent changes. Up until 1997 the texts (called 'headings' in the journal) emphasised more news value than is generally recognised in abstracts through the manipulation of structure and tense, the use of persuasive language and the removal of hedging. Following the introduction of the e-version of the journal in 1997, texts became more traditional with the new label 'summary/abstract', the extension of the text from 50–80 words to 150–180, and a more self-contained, stand alone relationship to the main paper to summarise the paper explicitly for readers outside the field. The two versions remain similar in terms of tense, with the predominant use of the Present, and persuasive lexical items, such as the use of descriptive adjectives, which indicate a continued concern for the promotional content of the text.

However, the post-1997 abstracts displayed greater efforts to 'explain' by making clear to the reader the importance of a particular study, the greater standardisation of structure, the elimination of the methods move, the incorporation of the results into the conclusion move, a greater amount of commentary in the conclusion move, expanding discussion of the study's effect of the field, and the inclusion of definitions. Together these changes promote the aims of the journal by showing how a study 'moves the field forward'. Ayers suggests that this demonstrates a growing concern for the general reader and the multidisciplinary nature of the journal. Methods have become far more numerous and specific in the sciences making them too complex and specialised to be relevant to the average *Nature* reader. At the same time, the expansion of the results into the conclusion move, where they are interpreted for the non-specialist reader, and the growth of definitions in the introduction, all suggest a greater concern for the general reader.

Commentary

In many ways this paper is exploratory since the samples are small and the study is confined to a single journal. *Nature* is perhaps an unusual choice because it occupies a niche position among the top-ranked journals, being both multidisciplinary and retaining high prestige among scientists. This may largely explain these recent attempts to make it more reader-friendly and to promote its findings to a wider public, but while Ayers suggests this represents a 'democratisation' of the scientific community by extending the audience for research, it seems equally likely to be yet another promotional strategy by appealing to the press – to whom it looks to carry research as news to a wider audience. The study does raise interesting points which confirm observed tendencies in scientific publishing, revealing how writers use textual and rhetorical features to respond to the distributional impact brought about by e-publishing, to the greater specialisation of science, and to the need to include an ever wider readership. These changes underline and reflect social changes which mean the audience to whom information about methods is meaningful is shrinking and the academic and career pressures to reach ever wider audiences is growing.

Further research

While this looks a complex piece of research, it is a relatively straightforward study which could easily be replicated with other texts. Most obviously, it might be asked whether the features found by Ayers have found their way into more mainstream science journals, or into the abstracts of articles in other disciplines. With more time and resources it would be possible to collect comparative data to count the features Ayers identifies and track any changes that may occur between two dates. Perhaps more relevantly for our own students, we might want to investigate the texts they have to write, looking at company sales letters, internal emails, engineering reports, or other genres. Such research has a pedagogic pay-off by providing writers in different academic, workplace or professional contexts with the communicative resources they need to interact effectively in these genres.

7.2 Contrastive rhetoric research on hedging and boosting

Summary

Hyland, K. and Milton, J. (1997) Qualification and certainty in L1 and L2 students' writing. *Journal of Second Language Writing*, 6(2): 183–205.

This study examined a computer corpus to compare the expression of doubt and certainty in the examination scripts of Cantonese school-leavers writing in English with those of British learners of similar age and education level. The analysis found that the Cantonese learners uses a more restricted range of epistemic modifiers and have considerable difficulty conveying the appropriate degrees of qualification and confidence.

This study arose from the authors' concern about the difficulties their students seemed to have in expressing doubt and certainty appropriately when writing in English. Our impressions were that Hong Kong learners often overstate their claims and are generally unable to control features of 'hedging' and 'boosting' in academic writing. We were also concerned by the fact that L2 writers' efforts to master these forms are often measured against unrealistic standards: the requirements of an academic community to which they do not belong and of which they have little experience. We therefore decided to compare features in texts written by Hong Kong students with those of British students of comparable age and educational level in a similar context. This study therefore draws on principles of contrastive rhetoric, looking at the ways people write in a second language, and learner corpora, or authentic language data produced by learners of a foreign/second language, in English for academic purposes.

Aims

The study focuses on issues in both Discourse Analysis (part 1.2) and Contrastive Rhetoric (part 2.3) and addressed three principal questions:

1. What were the most frequent forms used by each group to express doubt and certainty?
2. To what extent did each group of students boost or hedge their statements?
3. Were there differences in how these two groups handled these meanings?

The purpose of the study was therefore to determine the ways the two groups presented their statements in academic English.

Method

One of the most significant innovations in writing research in recent years has been the ability to compile corpora of students' writing. L2 learners admittedly share a number of difficulties with novice native writers but they have also been proven to have their own distinctive problems, which a careful corpus-based investigation can help uncover. Corpora can provide insights into authentic learner language, telling us how particular groups of students typically express certain meanings or approach rhetorical problems. To do this, however, we need reliable comparative data of the ways analogous target groups write, then we can identify which features students typically over- or under-use in their writing or use in error or how they use various features. In other words we can compare particular learners' uses with native-speaker uses to identify potential difficulties or infelicities in their work.

This study consisted of two large corpora. The first was a collection of 900 essays written by Hong Kong students for the high-school matriculation General Certificate of Education (GCE) A level 'Use of English' examination consisting of 500,000 words in six ability bands. The second corpus, also of 500,000 words, was transcribed from GCE A level General Studies scripts written by British school-leavers of similar age and education level. A list of 75 of the most frequently occurring lexical expressions of doubt and certainty in native-speaker usage was compiled from the research and pedagogic literature. The corpora were then examined to determine the frequency of these words in each grade of the Use of English corpus and in the GCE data. Fifty sentences containing each of those items (if there were 50 occurrences) were randomly extracted from each grade and from the L1 sample using a text retrieval program. All target items were analysed in their sentence contexts by both researchers working independently to ensure they expressed the writer's certainty or doubt. Figures were then extrapolated for the entire sample.

> **Quote 7.1** Leech on learner corpora
>
> Let us suppose that higher-education teacher X in a non-English speaking country teaches English to her students every week, and every so often sets them essays to write, or other written tasks in English. Now

> instead of returning those essays to students with comments and a sigh of relief, she stores the essays in her computer, and is gradually building up, week by week, a larger and more representative collection of her students' work. Helped by computer tools such as a concordance package, she can extract data and frequency information from this 'corpus', and can analyse her students' progress as a group in some depth. More significant are the research questions which open up once the corpus is in existence.
>
> Leech (1998: xiv)

Results

Overall the results showed that both student groups depended heavily on a narrow range of items, principally modal verbs and adverbs, and that the use of these features was particularly problematic for the L2 students. The Hong Kong learners employed syntactically simpler constructions, relied on a more limited range of devices, and exhibited greater problems in conveying a precise degree of certainty. Most importantly, the results confirmed that the academic writing of these learners is characterised by firmer assertions, more authoritative tone and stronger commitments than the writing of native English speakers. The UK group used more markers of tentativeness and caution than the Hong Kong students, with about two-thirds of the modifiers serving to hedge, compared with only a third of the Hong Kong students' choices. Interestingly, the weaker Cantonese speaking students used fewer devices overall and their writing was characterised by far stronger statements, so the more proficient the writers, the more they approximated the writing of the native speakers in this regard, thereby suggesting that the main reason for these differences is proficiency rather than 'culture'.

Commentary

Through our analysis of the learner corpora, we discovered that a feature we had noticed in our own Hong Kong students' writing was common to this language group more generally, and that it differed considerably from comparable L1 usage. While both groups relied on a limited number of forms, the L2 writers were much less able to use hedges and boosters appropriately and displayed less awareness of relevant discourse conventions. One conclusion of this research is that in addition to needing a good understanding of L2 writing to help students effectively, teachers may also need an idea of how their novice writers differ from comparable L1 language groups. The literature suggests it is unlikely that Hong Kong students differ greatly from other L2 learners in the difficulties they experience in expressing doubt and certainty in English. English language teaching and research agendas, however, have largely overlooked the importance of epistemic language, and the kinds of difficulties revealed in this study are partly attributable to this neglect.

Further research

Contrastive rhetoric has had a great deal to offer to the study and teaching of English for academic purposes but has not always lived up to its potential, partly because of dubious text comparisons and unwarranted generalisations about learners' writing preferences (see Section 2.3). The use of learner corpora and comparisons of features in learner and target language forms, however, has the potential to overcome some limitations. Although rarely used in small-scale studies, this kind of analysis is likely to increase in significance and come to have a tremendous impact on the way we understand and teach writing. There are numerous ways in which learner corpora can be used. There are advantages, for instance, in compiling longitudinal corpora of the work of the same students at different stages of writing development, or of different individuals or, as above, of writing from comparable learner groups. In particular, such corpora studies can play an important part both in improving our teaching practices by concentrating remedial work where it is most needed and, more generally, by revealing the overuse, underuse and error in L2 target language behaviour peculiar to native speakers of any particular language.

Although the compilation of learner corpora, giving proper attention to quality, design, size, and so on, can be a painstaking and time-consuming business, researchers can alternatively download or examine corpora on the web. Chapter 8 gives some sources for this. There is great potential in this work for small-scale research. The analysis of both vocabulary frequencies and the expression of particular functions and meanings are likely to reveal interesting cross-linguistic differences and tell us more about the strengths and weaknesses of our students' writing.

7.3 Case-study research of workplace writing

Summary

Gollin, S. (1999) 'Why? I thought we'd talked about it before': Collaborative writing in a professional workplace setting. In C. Candlin and K. Hyland (eds) *Writing: texts, processes and practices* (Harlow: Longman), pp. 267–90.

This study investigated a collaborative writing project at a private consultancy company in Australia. Using a case-study approach, it focused on the written and spoken products generated by the writing team and the impact of their interactions with contributors and informants outside the team. The research not only reveals the complexity and interactivity of collaborative writing and the roles of personal and organisational power in the writing process but also highlights the distinct purposes of pedagogic and institutional collaborative writing.

In a workplace context, writing for or on behalf of an organisation is often done in teams for pragmatic reasons centred on the goals of the organisation. Typically this is to draw on a range of expertise which may be beyond the professional scope of one writer, to ensure that documents are completed within tight deadlines, or to persuade a diverse audience from a variety of perspectives that a single writer could not adequately represent. This kind of 'collaborative' writing often differs significantly from the writing of individuals modelled in traditional pedagogy, where the main purpose is to develop individuals' writing skills. Gollin's study seeks to reveal some of these differences by a close analysis of both the social processes in which the writing is embedded and the written and spoken texts generated by these processes.

Aims

The case-study exemplifies some of the kinds of collaborative writing activity in which professionals such as public servants, teachers and engineers regularly engage. It therefore treats writing as a situated act (part 1.2.3) by exploring two questions:

1. When texts are produced collaboratively in an institutional context, how does participation in the process by different categories of contributor affect the development of the written text?

2. How can the modelling of this process inform the teaching of professional writing?

Methodology

Concept 7.2   **Case-study research**

A case-study is 'an instance in action', a means of portraying what a
particular situation is like by capturing the close-up reality of participants' lived experiences and thoughts about a situation. It is concerned
with a rich description of events and blends this description with interpretive analysis that draws on participants' own perspectives. A key issue
is the selection of information, for while it may be useful to record
typical actions, infrequent but critical incidents or events crucial to
understanding the case may also be highlighted by the researcher. Case-
studies typically represent research in a more publicly accessible form
than other methods as they are often less dependent on specialised
interpretation.

Cohen *et al.* (2000: 181–5)

Gollin was granted considerable freedom to follow the progress of
a team working in a small private consultancy firm specialising
in environmental projects. She employed a single-case naturalistic
methodology which lasted three months and drew on several data
sources:

- observation and audio-taping of collaborative planning and writing
  sessions;
- interviews with writers including a focus on critical moments in the
  taped data;
- taping of two teleconferences between the writers and the steering
  committee;
- interviews with directors about the philosophy and management
  style of the company;
- collection of published information about the various stakeholders;
- analyses of draft documents including annotated comments from the
  steering committee;
- attendance at a public meeting to promote the scheme with the
  tourist industry.

Results

The study shows that the collaborative writing in the workplace not only involves various categories of participant, but also the subtle negotiation of interpersonal and organisational relationships in addition to those which occur in constructing the written text.

Thus Gollin identifies four categories of participant. The *inner circle*, the project manager and a consultant, who performed the core research and writing activity; the *outer circle*, comprising industry stakeholders and various interest groups, whose views were fed into the process; the *Steering Committee*, representing government agencies to which the inner circle had to report; and *the client*, who generated the project and provided funding. These categories interacted in various ways in contributing to the final product.

The research found that power, based on differential access to *status*, *prominence*, *authority* and *control*, was an important dimension of the negotiations between and within these groups. Different categories of contributor were able to exert influence on others by virtue of belonging to different levels, but contributors who were hierarchically differentiated in one collaborative circle acted as peers in another. So, for example, while the employee and consultant were of different status and negotiated power between themselves in their inner-circle meetings, they acted more as peers to jointly protect their power when meeting with the more powerful steering committee. These distinctions show that in different group contexts individuals may play different roles and may be able to exert more or less influence on the process of shaping the emerging text.

Commentary

This case-study highlights the interactivity and complexity of collaborative writing in an institutional context. It shows that team writing often involves a variety of more or less influential groups in addition to the core group of writers themselves, and that the negotiation of personal and organisational power can be a significant factor in completing a writing task. Negotiation between participants is a major strength of collaborative writing, and one reason why it is so often used in the workplace. Such negotiation, however, is often seen as either un-problematically cooperative or as adversarial, but this fails to capture the subtlety of the negotiations that occur around the writing. Gollin shows that disputes are often handled subtly, as open conflict is neither conducive to the goal of finishing the writing task on time nor to the working relationships of the participants beyond the life of the project. These findings have implications for the teaching of professional collaborative writing where the negotiation of personal and organisational power is often subsumed to the development of individuals as writers.

Further research

Questions of validity and reliability are often raised in relation to the findings of single-case research studies such as this, but Gollin's multifaceted approach helps overcome the deficiencies of any particular method as well as offering a way of cross-checking data. The study thus provides a clear model for achieving both internal consistency in further research and shows how sufficient information can be provided for readers to draw informed conclusions.

Collaborative writing is complex and very context-bound, and further research is needed to better understand what goes on when people work together to produce texts. The study highlights the ways in which the interactions of a collaborative writing project can extend beyond the text being produced to the participants themselves. Such interactions reflect wider social processes which create and maintain professional relationships among co-workers and are of vital importance to the company involved and the success of individual projects. The nature of these interactions and their effects could be usefully studied in other contexts. More cases are needed, for example, to identify the main components of organisational and personal relationships in different industries and companies, how these are negotiated, and how they influence composing processes and product outcomes. It would also be useful to know the relative importance of status, affect and power on the negotiations of writing teams and their interactions with other stakeholders. In this way we can build a more complete picture of the collaborative process and find ways to make it more effective.

7.4   Ethnographic research on teacher written feedback

Summary

Hyland, F. (1998) The impact of teacher written feedback on individual writers. *Journal of Second Language Writing*, 7(3): 255–86.

This research investigated six ESL writers' reactions to, and uses of, teacher written feedback in two courses at a New Zealand university. Hyland used a longitudinal case-study approach and a variety of data sources including observation notes, interview transcripts and written texts. Her results show not only the value students place on feedback, but also the ways that they respond to and use it in their subsequent writing.

Giving effective feedback is a major concern for writing teachers and an important area of both L1 and L2 writing research (part 1.2). However, this research has been equivocal about the effectiveness of such feedback in improving texts, particularly in L1 settings where it is often seen as being of poor quality and frequently misunderstood or ignored by students. Although the response of L2 students to teacher feedback has recently become a lively area of study, there is still a need for more research which examines the effects of feedback within the total context of teaching. Hyland's study addresses this need by providing in-depth information about the effects of feedback on individual L2 students over a 14-week course preparing them for academic study in English.

Aims

There were four main research questions:

1. What were the students' attitudes and expectations about the purpose and value of feedback and did these change over the course?
2. How did they interpret and use the written feedback on their writing?
3. Were there individual differences in the way students responded to feedback and what might have accounted for these?
4. What types of revisions were made and which revisions could be linked to a feedback source?

Methodology

Two classes were studied and six students participated as case-study subjects. All written teacher feedback and students' revisions were catalogued and analysed to investigate the relationship between feedback and revision. Measures taken to ensure reliability included triangulation and respondent validation or 'member checking' of interpretations. While Hyland would not claim the research represents a full ethnography of events, the study has clear ethnographic aspects and conforms to general characteristics of the approach.

Concept 7.3	**Ethnographic research**
Collaborative	The research entails the involvement of various participants, including the researcher, the teachers, and the students.
Contextual	The research is carried out in the context in which the subjects normally work.
Emic	Privileging the perspectives of participants.
Interpretive	The researcher carries out interpretation of the data.
Longitudinal	The research takes place over several weeks or months.
Organic	Generalisations and hypotheses emerge during data-collection and analyses rather than being predetermined.
Unobtrusive	The researcher avoids intruding on the subjects or manipulating the phenomena.

The research employed data from the following sources:

- researcher's participant knowledge as a teacher of earlier courses;
- pre- and post-course questionnaires to all students in the classes;
- collection of class documents and observations of writing workshops;
- pre- and post-course interviews with the case-study participants and the two teachers;
- think-aloud protocols given by teachers as they marked assignments;
- retrospective interviews with students immediately after they had revised the same assignment;
- analysis of all forms of feedback on drafts, from both teachers and peers;
- analysis of all students' written drafts and revised versions of these following feedback;
- all day observations of classes and participants' out of class activities.

Each instance of teacher feedback was categorised according to its purpose, the degree of intervention, its focus (meaning, form or academic issues), and its span over the text. All student revisions in second drafts were also identified and categorised according to focus, span and the extent to which they improved the quality of the text. The 'usable' feedback points were then cross-linked to the student revisions to see how feedback triggered revision and in what areas. Detailed information about the role of teacher feedback in each writer's development came from a longitudinal examination of all student writing and feedback over the complete course. The interviews, questionnaires and observations were used to refine and validate the analyses and to provide a detailed contextual description.

Results

The findings showed that students tried to incorporate most of the usable teacher feedback when revising their drafts, but that this varied greatly according to their individual needs, prior experiences and approaches to writing. Many revisions either closely followed the suggestions offered, acted as an initial stimulus which triggered changes beyond the point addressed, or simply prompted deletions. A considerable amount of the revisions, however, seemed not to be related to the written feedback at all, and originated from self-evaluation, peer or external sources. Interestingly, the data also revealed that despite different stances on feedback, both the teachers tended to concentrate on *form* and that this encouraged revision at the same level, but did not appear to have a long-term developmental effect. In contrast, a very small proportion of the feedback addressed academic issues, even though this kind of feedback was more extensively used in the revisions and the knowledge gained appeared to be transferred to later pieces of writing. The fact that the study revealed communication breakdowns partly due to basic differences in the value that teachers and students placed on written feedback suggests the need for an open dialogue concerning the kinds of feedback students want and what teachers will give.

Commentary

In the best traditions of practitioner research, Hyland's study is concerned with ways of improving writing teaching based on a specific classroom issue with both practical and theoretical implications. In practical terms the results indicate the need to be sensitive to individual students' perceptions on what constitutes useful feedback and the need to gain an understanding of their past experiences, expectations and requirements. More widely, the research underlines the importance of examining feedback as part of a whole teaching and learning context rather than simply as an isolated event in the writing–revising cycle. This research is useful for teachers of both L1 and L2 writers, as it encourages us to see feedback from the learner's perspective as part of a wider context of learning to write. It also urges teachers to help students develop their own sources of feedback and strategies for revising by monitoring their own revision practices.

Further research

This study could be usefully replicated in other contexts, but it also highlights several areas for further research in both feedback and revision practices. In terms of feedback, Hyland's work indicates that the teachers were aware of individual students and their possible responses to feedback when they gave comments and that they tailored their feedback according to this awareness. Researchers might wish to extend this to investigate the relationship between teachers' personal conceptions of students and the amount and type of feedback they offer. Another line of enquiry would be to begin with the students and to study their independently selected sources of feedback, such as friends or partners, and how these interact with teacher feedback. Neither of these areas has been considered in L2 feedback research yet both are highly significant factors in writing development and would be a valuable extension of this study.

An important conclusion of this study is that the relationship between teacher written feedback and the ways that students respond to it in their revisions is highly complex, and this opens up a number of interesting areas for small-scale research into the influence of different learner variables. The part played by prior experience, proficiency level, or various aspects of affect, for example, are clearly worth further study. Most importantly perhaps, research that looks at cross-cultural differences in attitudes to written feedback and its use are also needed. A greater understanding of what students bring with them to writing classes through comparative studies of the ways writing teachers in different cultures and settings provide feedback would be extremely useful for teachers working in EFL contexts. Smaller-scale studies than this one could therefore produce important results with a narrower focus. More research is also needed to establish what problems limited linguistic resources can cause outside EAP classes, and what areas feedback should target to have the greatest effect.

7.5 Literacy research among disadvantaged adults

Summary

Barton, D., Ivanic, R., Appleby, Y., Hodge, R. and Tusting, K. (2007) *Literacy, lives and learning* (London: Routledge).

This book reports a major research project which explored the literacies in people's lives and their engagement in learning at various adult education sites. Drawing on various qualitative methods in a series of case studies, the research takes a literacy practices view of writing and reading to understand the complexity of different contexts and the factors which impact on choices. In particular, the methodology sought to be collaborative, by engaging participants, and responsive to how they experience the context in order to explain the meanings it has for them.

One important way for us to increase our understanding of writing is to research the everyday literacy practices of those around us (see part 2.2). The study of how people use literacy in their everyday lives provides insights into how writing works and the situated meanings it has for them, underlining the fact that a study of language needs to be both a study of texts and those who use them. This last case study moves away from the small action-oriented projects discussed in other cases to present a major study into the connection between people's lives and their participation as adults in formal learning in a range of settings. While focusing on learning, the study offers important insights into both what writing means to people and how it might be studied.

Aims

Barton *et al.* were aiming to understand something of the meanings and connections that adults make between learning and their everyday lives, taking account of social and economic factors. This wider project focused on adults whose education had been interrupted and were attending classes in ESOL, literacy or numeracy, but also addressed people's everyday literacy practices, how they used literacy to manage and enjoy their lives, and the meanings these had for them. Consequently, they asked:

1. What is the significance of literacy for people in their everyday lives?
2. What range of literacy practices do they engage in?
3. How is literacy learned though participation in everyday activities?

Methodology

Quote 7.2 Barton *et al.* on researching literacy practices

To draw upon the richness and complexity of people's lives and social practices we used many tools common in qualitative research. These included participant observation with detailed field notes; in-depth and repeated interviews, both structured and unstructured; case studies which focused on particular issues in detail and over time; photography and video-recording people's practices and working with them to record their own; collecting images and documents, as well as examples of free-writing, poems and rap. This enabled us to gather different types of data and allowed us to see complexity, multiple values, different positions, opposing perceptions, and different identities in different contexts.

Barton *et al.* (2007: 39)

The research was conducted in adult literacy, numeracy and ESOL learning classrooms in colleges and community adult education venues such as a drug support and aftercare centre, a young homeless project, and a domestic violence project, all in the north of England. It involved collaboration with six teachers and over 30 learners who formed the longitudinal cohort of the study. The participants typically had unconventional educational experiences and felt excluded from or disaffected with mainstream culture and conventional educational discourses. One element of the literacy practices element of the research was to focus on five people and how they used literacy outside their classes. The research methods typically employed in literacy studies are a mixture of observing particular literacy events and asking people to reflect on their practices.

An important aspect of the methodology was its emphasis on situated practice, which entails explaining the meanings of what is involved for those engaging in the practice. As the authors of the study point out, this cannot be achieved without collaboration with the participants. It also involves a certain degree of responding to the situation as it evolves and making the results useful to those involved.

Results

Barton *et al.* found that these men and women of different ages and with diverse life circumstances and experiences used literacy in a variety of different ways, although for three broad purposes:

- *For finding out and learning about things*: All the subjects had hobbies or interests such as wrestling stars or model aircraft, which they discovered more about by reading books, magazines, adverts and the Internet. One participant followed-up her reading by writing applications for grants and voluntary work posts.

- *For life purposes*: This included everyday activities such as reading food labels and participating in chat rooms. While some participants read avidly and kept in touch with family and pen-friends through emails and letters, others read little apart from functional texts such as bus timetables and wrote only sms messages or shopping lists. One created hand-made greetings cards, another kept a diary, wrote poems and found it easier to communicate with peers through writing than speaking, and a third catalogued his CD collection on computer.

- *For literacy learning through everyday events*: Using reading and writing to get things done provides many opportunities to expand literacy and participants used a variety of strategies to do this. One struggled with formal spelling conventions and frequently used previous pages in record books to see how words had been spelt or asking for 'acceptably difficult words' like *diarrhoea* to be spelled. Another participant leant webpage creation from her grandfather and another learnt through routinely emailing a close friend.

Reading and writing therefore offered these individuals important options for self-expression and pleasure, interaction with others, and learning, while revealing how these vary from person to person. The book in which the study is reported goes on to document how a wider group of people use literacy for learning and life purposes as well as the practices they had to engage with when dealing with bureaucracy and employment demands.

Commentary

Through their observations and conversations with these adults about their writing and uses of literacy, the researchers came to understand the importance of writing in their lives: as personal statements, as tools for learning, as aspects of their work, and as intimate exchanges of friendship. More generally, these vignettes help reveal how literacies fit into a larger picture of people's interests, identities, sense of self and imagined futures. For these individuals their writing practices were vehicles for accomplishing personal goals and sustaining relationships; it shows, in other words, not only that literacy mediates social life in various ways, but that it is often a highly collaborative activity which draws us into relationships with others.

Future research

This research highlights both the academic and personal value of researching local literacies as it not only increases our understanding of literacy as a plural and social concept but can also help us to reflect both on our own ideas and the lives of those around us. The links between writing and its meaning in the regularities of cultural life offer a rich source of research, and detailed studies of various domains can yield important insights into literacy practices. Equally, however, is what it might bring to the researcher's awareness of the richness and value of the writing culture of students, perhaps forcing us to review unexamined beliefs, widely held in education, which see vernacular discourses as rebellious or inadequate. Taking literacy variations seriously shows such vernacular discourses to be more than simply deviations from legitimate forms and reveals the ideological underpinnings of dominant literacies.

   This kind of research, moreover, need not start with individuals in a particular context. Instead it might take a particular text such as a church notice, or type of text such as a betting slip or a benefit-claim form, and examine the practices associated with them, tracing the ways they are used, discussed and responded to. Alternatively, research can focus on the vernacular practices of particular groups, such as taxi drivers or canteen workers, or detail the writing that occurs in particular places, such as a pub, a job centre or video store. Another departure point might be to look at certain routine activities, such as buying a lottery ticket, celebrating Christmas or writing to a newspaper, breaking them down into sets of literacy practices. There is also enormous potential for research into bi-cultural communities and groups and the ways they use writing in their daily lives. Studies into any of these areas are likely to uncover many seen but unnoticed acts of reading and writing, and reveal a surprising degree of literacy.

When analysing data such as this, concepts from a social theory of literacy are crucial to interpreting what is going on. This might involve examining the particular roles participants take, looking at gender, class or age differences, studying how various media interact, or researching how a particular practice has developed over time or is acquired by users.

7.6   Conclusion

It should be clear that the topic of writing is enormous, embracing a huge range of issues and requiring a variety of research strategies. My aim here has simply been to suggest some topics which are representative of central themes in contemporary thinking on writing, and to illustrate how these can be tackled using current methodological approaches. I hope to have captured some of the variety and flavour of research in this field and perhaps to have encouraged others to contribute to our growing understanding of writing.

Further reading

See also the recommended texts in Chapter 5.

Barton, D., Hamilton, M. and Ivanic, R. (eds) (2000) *Situated literacies: reading and writing in context* (London: Routledge). An excellent collection of studies offering insights and guidelines for further literacy research.

Bhatia, V. (1993) *Analysing genre: language use in professional settings* (Harlow: Longman). Through a range of example genres, this comprehensive introduction gives clear procedures for the analysis of written data.

Hyland, K. (2004) *Genre and second language writing* (Ann Arbor, MI: University of Michigan Press). Includes ideas for research and discussion of methods for studying written genres

McKay, S. (2006) *Researching second language classrooms* (London: Routledge). Introduction to classroom research for teachers.

Swales, J. (1998) *Other floors, other voices. A textography of a small university building* (Mahwah, NJ: Lawrence Erlbaum). Excellent discourse-oriented ethnography of systems of texts in one setting. Clear methodological principles for further research.

IV References and resources

Chapter 8

Key areas and texts

This chapter will . . .

- offer a series of thumbnail sketches of fields which draw on and contribute to what we know about the theory, teaching and research of writing;
- briefly outline the ways that writing is understood in these areas;
- suggest a selection of key texts for further reading in these fields.

8.1 Literacy

The field of literacy studies is concerned with the use of writing as situated social practice, as discussed in Chapter 2. Work in the New Literacy Studies (NLS) has shown that writing is a complex human activity, always located in particular times and places and indicative of wider social forces and relationships. This perspective therefore draws on many of the same sources as contemporary writing research, such as critical theory and social constructionism, shares a similar interest in detailing the social practices that surround writing, and employs similar ethnographic approaches to research. However, contemporary literacy theory also complements writing research in applied linguistics and language teaching. The study of everyday practices has expanded both our understanding of literacy, by making connections between research data of literacy-in-use and social theory, and our understanding of writing, by showing how it is positioned in relation to social institutions and dominant ideologies.

In other words, by focusing on the study of writing in peoples' everyday lives, literacy studies have moved writing research away from academic, media, literary and other published texts to embrace what people do when they read and write, the contexts that surround these activities, and how they understand them.

Key readings: literacy

Barton, D. (2007) *Literacy*, 2nd edn. Oxford: Blackwell.
Barton, D. and Hamilton, M. (1998) *Local literacies: reading and writing in one community*. London: Routledge.
Barton, D., Hamilton, M. and Ivanic, R. (eds) (2000) *Situated literacies: reading and writing in context*. London: Routledge.
Barton, D., Ivanic, R., Appleby, Y., Hodge, R. and Tusting, K. (2007) *Literacy, lives and learning*. London: Routledge.
Baynham, M. (1995) *Literacy practices*. Harlow: Longman.
Blommaert, J. (2008) *Grassroots literacy: writing, identity and voice in Central Africa*. London: Routledge.
Grainger, T. (ed) (2004) *The Routledge Falmer reader in language and literacy*. London: Routledge.
Street, B. (1995) *Social literacies: critical approaches to literacy in development, ethnography and education*. Harlow: Longman.
Street, B. and Lefstein, A. (2008) *Literacy: an advanced resource book*. London: Routledge.

8.2 Rhetoric

Rhetoric is essentially the role of discourse toward some end: how language can be used to persuade, convince or elicit support. In the west it originated with Aristotle, Cicero and Quintilian, and describes the ways that writers (and speakers) attempt to engage their audiences, gain assent for their views, or establish the credibility of a reported event through the organisation and style of their discourses. While other rhetorical traditions, particularly African and Indian, have influenced the features of political and religious spoken rhetoric in English, many of the analytic and presentation skills of traditional rhetoric are still taught and extensively used in writing in a range of fields.

Classical rhetoric was organised into a series of categories which describe the composition and delivery of a text: *invention, arrangement, style, memory* and *delivery*, with each further subdivided to elaborate the different strategies that can be used. Modern rhetorical analysis has largely tended to focus on the subdivision of *invention* and particularly the appeals of non-evidential, or 'artificial', proof. These are *logos*, the appeal to reason, *pathos*, the appeal to the passions or emotions, and *ethos*, the appeal to the character and authority of the writer. The rhetorical study of written discourse today flourishes in a range of analytical approaches, particularly critical linguistics, sociolinguistics and genre studies, and seeks to elucidate the interaction of a text with its context to see how it responds to, reinforces or alters the understanding of an audience. It also reaches beyond politics and advertising into genres which were not previously considered rhetorical such as academic, technical and business texts. The rhetorical appeals underlying newspaper, fund-raising, and commercial discourses, for example, have been explored using discourse and corpus research.

Key readings: rhetoric

Bizzell, P. (2005) *Rhetorical agendas: political, ethical, spiritual.* London: Routledge.

Dillon, G.L. (1991) *Contending rhetorics: writing in academic disciplines.* Bloomington, IN: Indiana University Press.

Freedman, A. and Medway, P. (eds) (1994) *Genre and the new rhetoric.* London: Taylor & Francis.

Foss, K., Foss, S. and Trapp, R. (2002) *Readings in contemporary rhetoric.* Prospect Heights, IL: Waveland Press.

Foss, K. (2004) *Rhetorical criticism: exploration and practice*, 3rd edn. Prospect Heights, IL: Waveland.

McGroskey, J.C. (2005) *Introduction to rhetorical communication.* Boston, MA: Allyn & Bacon.

Roberts, R. and Good, J. (eds) (1993) *The recovery of rhetoric.* Charlottesville, VA: University of Virginia Press.

8.3   Scientific and technical writing

Resources in this area comprise both practical primers to assist students and novice researchers to produce technical papers and reports, and academic studies which seek to illuminate the features of these discourses. While the former mainly confine themselves to prescriptive advice about the nature of scientific writing, the latter recognise the importance of writing for a community and that successful writing depends on the writer's projection of a shared context. Writers write for communities of peers existing at a particular time and place, and texts embody the ways that knowledge is constructed, negotiated and made persuasive for those communities. In other words, they tend to take a social constructivist view which sees language choices as helping to create a view of the world, constructing what we can know.

Research has, for instance, examined the practices of a particular lab or research programme, the negotiations involved in the referee process, the regularity of patterns in academic texts, and the ways these features have changed over time in response to changes in the social context of science. These research issues and methods closely overlap and intersect with the interests of applied linguistics, particularly in the areas of ESP and critical discourse analysis.

Key readings: scientific and technical writing

Atkinson, D. (1999) *Scientific discourse in sociohistorical context: the philosophical transactions of the Royal Society of London. 1675–1975.* Mahwah, NJ: Erlbaum.

Gross, A. (2006) *Starring the text: the place of rhetoric in science studies.* Carbondale, IL: Southern Illinois University Press.

Hyland, K. (2004) *Disciplinary discourses: social interactions in academic writing.* Ann Arbor, MI: University of Michigan Press.

Latour, B. and Woolgar, S. (1986) *Laboratory life: the construction of scientific facts.* Princeton, NJ: Princeton University Press.

Martin, J. and Halliday, M.A.K. (1993) *Writing science: literacy and discursive power.* London: Routledge.

Myers, G. (1990) *Writing biology: texts in the social construction of scientific knowledge.* Madison, WI: University of Wisconsin Press.

8.4 Professional and business communication

Training courses which focus on the specialised communication needs of engineers, business people, lawyers, therapists, technicians, and other professional groups have burgeoned in recent years. Language is now recognised as one of the most important tools of the workplace and a marker of professional expertise, particularly in English as it becomes the accepted medium for cross-linguistic transactions. The value of effective writing to these professionals is obviously crucial, and courses, textbooks and reference materials have addressed both writing skills and the components of texts such as manuals, technical reports, memos, proposals and a variety of report genres. Only recently, however, have these materials come to be informed by writing research.

This applied research has drawn on a range of approaches, including text linguistics, discourse analysis, corpus studies, social constructionism and critical linguistics, and has played an important part in developing both linguistic theories and methods for analysing writing more generally. Studies of professional texts have been important, for example, in sharpening our understanding of genre analysis and the ways social interactions are negotiated in writing, as well as providing insights into bureaucratic obfuscation, promotional discourses and the connections between texts and graphics. There is every reason to believe that research into professional communication will continue to deepen our knowledge of many aspects of written communication in the future.

Key readings: professional communication

Bamford, J. and Bondi, M. (eds) (2006) *Managing interaction in professional discourse*. Rome: Officina Edizioni.

Bargiela-Chiappini, F. and Nickerson, G. (eds) (1999) *Writing business: genres, media and discourses*. Harlow: Longman.

Barron, C., Bruce, N. and Nunan, D. (eds) (2002) *Knowledge and discourse: language ecology in theory and practice*. Harlow: Pearson Education.

Bhatia, V.K. (2004) *Worlds of written discourse: a genre-based view*. London: Continuum.

Bhatia, V., Candlin, C. and Engberg, J. (eds) (2008) *Legal discourse across cultural systems*. Hong Kong: HKU Press.

Candlin, C. (ed.) (2002) *Research and practice in professional discourse*. Hong Kong: City University of Hong Kong Press.

Christie, F. and Martin, J.R. (eds) (1997) *Genre and institutions: social processes in the workplace and school*. London: Cassell.

Gunnarsson, B.-L. (2009) *Professional discourse*. London: Continuum.

Gunnarsson, B.-L., Linell, P. and Nordberg, B. (eds) (1997) *The construction of professional discourse*. Harlow: Longman.

Koester, A. (2010) *Workplace discourse*. London: Continuum.

Palmer-Silveira, J.-C., Ruiz-Garrido, M.F. and Fortanet-Gomez, I. (eds) (2006) *Intercultural and international business communication*. Bern: Peter Lang.

8.5   First-language writing

The field of first-language writing has informed much of what we know about texts and composition and has provided a theoretical basis for pedagogy and research. Research has followed a number of clear paths. Educational psychologists have sought to elaborate the stages which children pass through in learning to write, and to suggest some of the reasons why this can be problematic for some learners. This research has often employed case-studies to follow individual children or focused on the learning experiences of groups of learners. The most interesting lines of study have explored the educational contexts for learning and have drawn on Vygotskian theories of language development.

More sociolinguistically-oriented research has examined educational disadvantage and the ways that school expectations can conflict with the home environments of learners. These studies have adopted ethnographic approaches to identify the various cultural and social features which can place learners' writing development at risk, pointing to the crucial role of literacy experiences, positive attitudes and meaningful teaching in acquiring writing skills. Two other areas of research have also been central to L1 writing. These are the studies conducted by cognitive psychologists into writing processes and by functional linguists into the genres written by school children. I have discussed this research, and some of the materials and teaching programmes that have emerged from them, in Chapters 1 and 3.

The growth of composition studies as an area of professional emphasis has drawn on, extended and sharpened our methods and theoretical perspectives, and been responsible for a tremendous transformation of both writing teaching and research. It has changed the teaching of writing from an intuitive, trial-and-error process to a dynamic, inter-active and context-sensitive intellectual activity. As teachers we are now more aware of the value of a thorough theoretical, social and pedago-gical understanding of writing in our classrooms. We are also aware of the contribution that research can make to this understanding. The knowledge we have gained from these advances in L1 composition has had a considerable impact on virtually all the related fields sketched here.

Key readings: first-language writing

Cope, B. and Kalantzis, M. (1993) *The powers of literacy: a genre approach to teaching writing*. Pittsburgh, PA: University of Pittsburgh Press.

Candlin, C.N. and Hyland, K. (eds) (1999) *Writing: texts, processes and practices*. Harlow: Longman.

Delpit, L. (1995) *Other people's children: cultural conflict in the classroom*. New York: The New Press.

Gimenez, J. (2010) *Narrative discourse*. London: Continuum.

Grabbe, W. and Kaplan, R. (1996) *The theory and practice of writing*. Harlow: Longman.

Hasan, R. and Williams, G. (eds) (1996) *Literacy in society*. Harlow: Longman.

Kress, G. (1994) *Learning to write*, 2nd edn. London: Routledge.

Kress, G. (1997) *Before writing: rethinking paths to literacy*. London: Routledge.

Martin, J.R. (1989) *Factual writing: exploring and challenging social reality*. Oxford: Oxford University Press.

Schleppegrell, M. and Colombi, M. (eds) (2002) *Developing advanced liter-acy in first and second languages*. Mahwah, NJ: Earlbaum.

8.6 Journalism and print media

Research on written media texts has always interested linguists and has tended to have a generally applied or critical focus. Efforts have been mainly devoted either to teaching or to elaborating how these texts use language to shape and reflect political and sociocultural forms in society.

The considerable influence that print media exercises in contempor-ary society is a powerful driver of interest in the forms which news, entertainment and advertisements take. In addition, the easy accessibility of these texts has long made them popular with writing teachers as sources for topics and models for writing while the growth of courses specialising in writing for the media in recent years has increased the attention given to the rhetorical features of media texts. Research has identified a highly aggressive, audience-oriented style across a range of genres. Competing in a market crowded with information and stimulation, media writing is characterised by attention-getting and promotion devices, sometimes involving literary-like creativity, but almost always based on the inverted-triangle principle which draws the reader from a general statement or idea into the message of the text. Whether a headline and lead paragraph, an advertising graphic, or a sports report, media genres appear to rely heavily on a similar formula, often described as AIDCA (Attention, Interest, Desire, Conviction, Action).

The second broad area of linguistic research into media texts emphasises a concern with issues of power and ideology and the ways that (principally) news media work to construct particular representations of the world. This research has examined text structure, topic organisation, vocabulary, production practices and audience comprehension, and has largely been conducted under a CDA banner. A number of authors have noted the modified narrative structure of media texts and the ways that their 'news-driven' organisation may distort source information. Trends towards 'commodification' and 'conversationalisation' in news reporting (i.e. shifts to market models and linguistic informality) are examples of intertextuality seen in other forms of public discourse. This growing research not only helps us to understand what media language is like and what it reveals about the media, but also tells us a lot about writing more generally. In addition, the analytical methods employed in this research are increasingly, and usefully, applied to other texts.

Key readings: mass media

Bell, A. (1994) *The language of news media*. Oxford: Blackwell.

Bell, A. and Garrett, P. (eds) (1998) *Approaches to media discourse*. Oxford: Blackwell.

Conboy, M. (2006) *Tabloid Britain*. London: Routledge.

Fairclough, N. (1995) *Media discourse*. London: Edward Arnold.

Fairclough, N. (2000) *New Labour new language*. London: Routledge.

Fowler, R. (1991) *Language in the news.* London: Routledge.

Myers, G.A. (1994) *Words in ads.* London: Edward Arnold.

Reah, D. (2002) *The language of newspapers,* 2nd edn. London: Routledge.

Richardson, J. (2006) *Analysing newspapers: an approach from critical discourse analysis.* London: Palgrave Macmillan.

Scollon, R. (1998) *Mediated discourse as social interaction: a study of news discourse.* Harlow: Longman.

Stovall, G. (1994) *Writing for the media.* Englewood Cliffs, NJ: Prentice Hall.

van Dijk, T. (1991) *Racism and the press.* London: Routledge.

8.7 Second-language writing instruction

Second-language teaching has been both a significant driving force and a major consumer of writing research in recent years, ensuring that research contributes to practice. While a great deal has been learnt about writing from studying how native speakers acquire composing skills, the emergence of L2 writing as a sub-discipline has opened new theoretical perspectives, research methods and pedagogical strategies. Particularly instructive has been the work on the differences between L1 and L2 writing practices, the significance of cultural background to writing, and the nature of L2 texts.

This research has suggested broad similarities between L1 and L2 writers. It seems that while writers proficient in their L1 are able to transfer strategies across to the L2 and display skills similar to those of L1 writers, writers inexperienced in their L1 are likely to suffer similar problems to their native-speaker counterparts. These weaker writers often lack direction and tend to focus on mechanical accuracy to the detriment of organisation, ideas and audience. Research also suggests, however, that it is unwise to overemphasise these similarities. As discussed in Chapter 1, the contrastive rhetoric literature indicates that L2 writers are likely to operate with very different schemata to first-language writers and have very different conceptions of rhetorical patterns. In addition to alerting teachers to these possible difficulties, research has identified key features of target discourses and the problems L2 writers typically have in controlling these in their own texts.

esearch, based on the empirical findings from a range of dif-
heoretical standpoints and methodological approaches, has
antly influenced our assumptions and practices. It has fed into
ooms and greatly assisted composition teachers better to address
the specific, and highly distinct, rhetorical, linguistic and strategic
needs of L2 writing students.

Key readings: second-language writing instruction

Belcher, D. and Braine, G. (eds) (1994) *Academic writing in a second language: essays on research and pedagogy*. Norwood, NJ: Ablex.

Canagarajah, S. (2002) *Critical academic writing and multilingual students*. Ann Arbor, MI: University of Michigan Press.

Casanave, C. (2004) *Controversies in second language writing*. Ann Arbor, MI: University of Michigan Press.

Connor, U. (1996) *Contrastive rhetoric*. New York: Cambridge University Press.

Ferris, D. and Hedgecock, J.S. (2007) *Teaching ESL composition: purpose, process and practice*, 3rd edn. Mahwah, NJ: Lawrence Erlbaum.

Hyland, K. (2003) *Second language writing*. Cambridge: Cambridge University Press.

Hyland, K. (2004) *Genre and second language writing*. Ann Arbor, MI: University of Michigan Press.

Hyland, K. and Hyland, F. (eds) (2006) *Feedback in second language writing: contexts and issues*. New York: Cambridge University Press.

Kroll, B. (ed.) (2001) *Exploring the dynamics of second language writing*. Cambridge: Cambridge University Press.

Silva, T. and Matsuda, P.K. (eds) (2001) *On second language writing*. Mahwah, NJ: Lawrence Erlbaum.

8.8 Pragmatics

Pragmatics is a broad approach to discourse that studies the use of context to make inferences about meaning. In other words, the focus of pragmatics is on both the processes of communication and its products, including the situatedness of language and its consequences. Historically, pragmatics originated in the philosophy of language and concerned itself with isolated utterances, but its contemporary linguistic importance lies in its approach to the analysis of discourse, although unfortunately, this has mainly been restricted to conversation. The relevance of pragmatics to writing, however, lies in the ways particular text features can be seen as signalling contextual presuppositions, or shared meanings, which provide an interpretive framework for understanding written discourse.

While researchers in pragmatics have not generally been active in studying writing, many of its central concepts have been applied to written texts. The goal has been to understand better the ways that writers interact with readers by drawing on and manipulating common ground and cultural understandings. Pragmatic processes such as speech acts, relevance, cooperation, reference and politeness provide ways to analyse how writers seek to encode their messages for a particular audience, and how readers make inferences when seeking to recover a writer's intended meaning. Speech-act theory, for example, has contributed the idea that linguistic communication involves not only surface forms but the ways these forms work to gain the reader's recognition of the writer's intention in the context of the discourse. Thus in persuasive writing a writer not only wants his or her words to be understood (an illocutionary effect in speech-act terms), but also to be accepted (a perlocutionary effect, or reader action). This might be accomplished by various features such as hedges, boosters, attitudinal lexis, and so on, which can mark consideration for the reader or appeal to common cultural understandings based on a shared professional or personal relationship.

Pragmatics thus points to the possible analysis of recurring patterns of specific text features, supported by discourse-based interviews with users of these texts, to identify the ways that writers engage with their readers by constructing a shared reality. But while such a programme promises to reveal a great deal about the notions of context and inference in writing, much of this value remains largely potential and awaits further research.

Key readings: pragmatics

Blakemore, D. (1992) *Understanding utterances: an introduction to pragmatics*. Oxford: Blackwell.
Cutting, K. (2002) *Pragmatics and discourse*. London: Routledge.
Grundy, P. (2000) *Doing pragmatics*, 2nd edn. London: Hodder Arnold.
Horn, L.R and Ward, G. (eds) (2005) *The handbook of pragmatics*. Oxford: Blackwell.

Levinson, S. (1993) *Pragmatics*. Cambridge: Cambridge University Press.

Mey, J. (2001) *Pragmatics: an introduction*, 2nd edn. Oxford: Oxford University Press.

Thomas, J. (1995) *Meaning in interaction: an introduction to pragmatics*. Harlow: Longman.

Verschueren, J. (1999) *Understanding pragmatics*. London: Arnold.

Yule, G. and Widdowson, H.G. (1996) *Pragmatics*. Oxford: Oxford University Press.

8.9 Translation studies

Translation research concerns the problems involved in transferring meaning from one culture to another. Obviously not all cultures interpret situations in the same way; perceptions can differ enormously, and words carry connotations which do not have exact equivalence in another language. Translation scholars are therefore occupied with many of the same concerns which interest writing researchers in other areas. Despite this, however, translation is often an invisible practice, and has tended to exist on the periphery of intellectual activity in applied linguistics.

Translation is the rewriting of an original text, and as such raises issues of subjectivity, ideological manipulation, cultural distortion and the fossilisation of interpretation. More positively, however, this kind of writing can introduce new concepts, new genres, new meanings and new forms of expression, leading to innovation and change. Translation studies is therefore, like other areas of writing, a field in which both theory and reflection on cultural, methodological and social issues are vital. Because of this a number of questions central to writing more generally have emerged, including the nature of context and situationality, the role of interpretation in cross-cultural communication, the challenge of rendering idiomaticity and the part played by audience. Of particular importance has been the debate over 'equivalence' and the move away from absolute fidelity to a source text, to the production of a target text. This has increased the translator's role as a professional author and paved the way for greater creativity and interpretation.

Translation has also expanded beyond its established literary and technical areas. Both machine translation (MT) and computer-assisted translation (CAT), represent rapidly expanding domains of practice and flourishing research areas. Translators themselves have grown in importance in an ever widening variety of communities, workplaces and languages. So, while notions of accuracy and correctness remain as measures of quality in assessing translated texts, translation studies are nevertheless deeply involved in the debates about meaning and communication which consume researchers and teachers in other areas of writing practice.

Key readings: translation

Baker, M. and Saldanha, G. (2001) *Routledge encyclopedia of translation studies.* London: Routledge.

Bassnett, S. (2002) *Translation studies (new accents),* 3rd edn. London: Routledge.

Bell, R.T. (1991) *Translation and translating: theory and practice.* Harlow: Longman.

Gentzler, E. (1993) *Contemporary translation theories.* London: Routledge.

Hatim, B. (1997) *Communication across cultures: translation theory and contrastive text linguistics.* Exeter: University of Exeter Press.

Hatim, B. and Munday, J. (2004) *Translation: an advanced resource book.* London: Routledge.

Munday, J. (2008) *Introducing translation studies: theories and applications.* London: Routledge.

Ricoeur, P. (2006) *On translation.* London: Routledge.

Schiffner, C. (ed.) (1999) *Translation and norms.* Clevedon: Multilingual Matters.

Venuti, L. (2004) *The translation studies reader,* 2nd edn. London: Routledge.

8.10 Literary Studies

Literary Studies is an immensely important area of writing which covers a vast terrain. Studied as a product, literary texts are seen as aesthetic artefacts amenable to a range of critical theories or as models of writing to be emulated. Seen as a resource, they are valuable tools for the teaching of writing in both L1 and L2 contexts.

For the first 60 years of the twentieth century reading and analysis of literature were the main principles motivating writing instruction. Native speakers were required to read short stories, plays, poems and novels, understand them, and then write about them, with little explicit instruction of how to do this. Instruction focused on knowledge about the texts themselves and the fixed, pre-given meanings they contained. This notion that a body of authoritative literary texts can provide models for good writing remains alive today in courses and texts on creative writing. The best of these take the student through the composing process from creative imagination to fixing a text on paper. They deal with both the mind observing, recalling and searching for ways to vividly recount experience, and with the engagement of the reader with the text through conscious editing and the shaping of interpretation. The practice of writing about literature employs the theories and resources of a range of approaches from new criticism via feminism and cultural studies to deconstruction and are important to the work of discourse analysts and text linguists.

Literary texts have also been seen as a resource for focusing on language and developing both language and writing skills in L1 and L2 classrooms. Originally this mainly involved stylistic analyses, drawing on concepts such as 'foregrounding', the way that writers often use language which draws attention to itself in order to surprise the reader into a fresh appreciation of the topic. Stylistics draws heavily on linguistics, particularly pragmatics and discourse analysis, and provides a productive means of both raising learners' conscious awareness of how language is used and a foundation for interpretation based on the text itself which can be transferred to other contexts and genres. More generally, however, teaching has sought to integrate language and literature by encouraging learners to actively construct and interpret texts rather than simply respond to an existing canon. In these ways contemporary research and teaching practices have responded to current ideas and approaches in other areas of writing theory and pedagogy.

Key readings: Literary Studies

Carter, R. (1997) *Investigating English discourse: language, literacy and literature*. London: Routledge.

Carter, R. and Simpson, P. (eds) (1995) *Language, discourse and literature: an introductory reader in discourse stylistics*. London: Routledge.

Kirszner, L. and Mandell, S. (2009) *Literature: reading, reacting, writing*, 7th edn. Florence, KY: Wadsworth Publishing.

Lecercle, J.-J. (2000) *Interpretation as pragmatics*. London: Macmillan.

Lynn, S. (2007) *Texts and contexts: writing about literature with critical theory*, 5th edn. Harlow: Longman.

Nash, W. (1998) *Language and creative illusion: the writing game*. Harlow: Longman.

Roberts, E.V. (2006) *Literature: an introduction to reading and writing*, 8th edn. Upper Saddle River, NJ: Prentice Hall.

Short, M. (1996) *Exploring the language of poems, plays and prose*. Harlow: Longman.

Simpson, P. (1997) *Language through literature*. London: Routledge.

Simpson, P. (2004) *Stylistics: a resource book for students*. London: Routledge.

Verdonk, P. (2002) *Oxford introductions to language study: stylistics*. Oxford: Oxford University Press.

8.11   English for Academic Purposes (EAP)

EAP is usually defined as teaching English with the aim of assisting learners' study or research in that language. In this sense it is a broad term covering all areas of academic communication including administrative practice, pre-tertiary, undergraduate and post-graduate teaching and classroom interaction as well as the description of research genres, student writing, and writing for publication. The field has evolved rapidly over the past 20 years or so from a branch of English for Specific Purposes (ESP) in the early 1980s to a major force in English language teaching and research around the world. Drawing its strength from variety of theories and a commitment to research-based language education, EAP has expanded with the growth of university places, the increasing numbers of international students undertaking tertiary studies in English, and the emergence of English as the international language of scholarship and research. These developments mean that countless students and researchers must gain fluency in the conventions of academic discourses to understand their disciplines, establish their careers and to successfully navigate their learning.

While EAP often tends to be a practical affair driven by an understanding of local contexts and the needs of particular students, it is also a theoretically grounded and research informed enterprise. There is a growing awareness that students have to take on new roles and engage with knowledge in new ways when they enter university, and in particular this involves writing and reading unfamiliar genres. In diverse ways, EAP therefore seeks to understand and engage learners in a critical understanding of the increasingly varied contexts and practices of academic communication. More specifically, current EAP aims at capturing thicker descriptions of academic language use at all age and proficiency levels, incorporating and often going beyond immediate communicative contexts to understand the demands placed by academic contexts on communicative behaviours and the nature of disciplinary knowledge itself.

Key readings: English for Academic Purposes

Benesch, S. (2001) *Critical English for Academic Purposes*. Mahwah, NJ: Erlbaum.

Becher, T. and Trowler, P. (2001) *Academic tribes and territories*. Buckingham: Open University Press.

Coffin, C., Curry, M., Goodman, S., Hewings, A., Lillis, T. and Swann, J. (2003) *Teaching academic writing: a toolkit for higher education*. London: Routledge.

Dudley-Evans, T. and St John, M.J. (1998) *Developments in English for specific purposes*. Cambridge: Cambridge University Press.

Flowerdew, J. and Peacock, M. (eds) (2001) *Research perspectives on English for Academic Purposes*. Cambridge: Cambridge University Press.

Hyland, K. (2004) *Disciplinary discourses: social interactions in academic writing*. Ann Arbor, MI: University of Michigan Press.

Hyland, K. (2006) *English for Academic Purposes: an advanced coursebook*. London: Routledge.

Hyland, K. (2009) *Academic discourse*. London: Continuum.

Johns, A.M. (1997) *Text, role and context: developing academic literacies*. Cambridge: Cambridge University Press.

Lea, M. and Steirer, B. (eds) (2000) *Student writing in Higher Education: new contexts*. Buckingham: Open University Press.

Lillis, T. (2001) *Student writing: access, regulation, desire*. London: Routledge.

8.12   Blogs, wikis and webpages

While considerable emphasis has been devoted to the technological advances of these electronic channels, the language employed by writers of these genres have begun to attract the attention of linguists and writing teachers. This interest not only focuses on aspects of the language such as grammar, spelling, and innovative lexis, but also on discourse and the way language is used to accomplish interactions between people. A *blog* is essentially a frequently up-dated webpage with new entries placed on top of older ones. They are unlike personal home pages, because they are regularly updated, and they are unlike diaries, because they are built around links to other sites and blogs. They can contain text, pictures, sounds, and video. A *wiki*, on the other hand, involves many authors collaborating on one text on a webpage. Unlike a paper encyclopedia it is designed to enable anyone to contribute or modify its content, using a simplified markup language. In contrast to the personal stance of blogs, wikis are impersonal, prompting Myers to comment that: 'A wiki is a device for putting people together, and a blog is a device for setting them apart as individuals.'

The linguistic study of blogs, websites and wikis is, like the genres themselves, very recent, but it allows analysts to say something about the writing and not just the content. This is interesting because they have emerged as distinctive kinds of text with characteristic ways of commenting, arguing, interacting and making sense. Analysis of the language can therefore reveal something of how language helps users to interact and construct social identities and communities. Most blogs, for example, show a careful informality, strong stance, tolerance of views, and creative linking, while wikis display a creative construction of facts, multiply assembled, and sometimes vandalised, which offer immediate access to information for users. While the latter can be corrupted by the biases of its writers, it is the mix of cooperation, conflict and obstructiveness among writers and what they produce which provides interest to writing researchers.

Key readings: blogs, wikis and webpages

Bloch, J. (2008) *Technologies in the second language composition classroom.* Ann Arbor, MI: University of Michigan Press.

Blood, R. (2002) *The weblog handbook: practical advice on creating and maintaining your blog.* Cambridge, MA: Perseus.

Boardman, M. (2005) *The language of websites.* London: Routledge.

Bruns, A. (2008) *Blogs, wikipedia, second life, and beyond.* New York: Peter Lang.

Bruns, A. and Jacobs, J. (eds) (2006) *The uses of blogs.* New York: Peter Lang.

Keren, M. (2006) *Blogosphere: the new political arena.* Lanham, MD: Lexington Books.

Lankshear, C. and M. Knobel (2006) *New literacies: everyday practices and classroom learning*. Milton Keynes: Open University Press.

Myers, G. (2009) *The discourse of blogs and wikis*. London: Continuum.

Lamy, M.-N. and Hampel, R. (2007) *Online communication in language learning and teaching*. London: Palgrave.

Beatty, K. (2009) *Teaching and researching computer assisted language learning*, 2nd edn. London: Longman.

8.13 Multimodal discourses

For many linguists the analysis and teaching of writing cannot be restricted to linguistic forms of representation alone but must encompass all meaningful semiotic activity. While language plays a central role in written interaction, images are often a key aspect of many genres and are displacing writing in arenas such as advertising and screen-based genres. There has certainly been a shift in our systems of representation away from the purely verbal to the visual in a whole range of information, persuasive and entertainment genres in recent years. The trend has extended into textbooks and teaching materials and students are now often required to produce essays or reports which include visual elements such as graphs, photographs, and diagrams.

As I discussed briefly in Chapter 2, researchers are interested in this area because text and image configure the world in different ways, with consequent shifts in authority, in forms of meaning, and in forms of engagement with both content and readers. Most dramatically, this can require very different semiotic work from the 'reader' as contemporary electronic texts often offer a range of entry points to the 'page' and different reading paths through it when compared with print texts. At the same time, the reader is more actively involved in filling the relatively 'empty' words with meaning. Multimodal analyses seek to describe these differences in various contexts and discover the potentials and limitations (or 'affordances') for making meaning which attach to different modes. Kress, for example, suggests that writing and image are governed by different logics: writing by time and image by space. So in writing meaning is attached to 'being first' and 'being last' in a sentence, while in a visual centring and positioning something above gives it greater significance. The expansion of genres using new technologies hasten and intensify different potentials for communication, interaction and representation, and simultaneously encourages writing teachers to understand these changes and bring them into their classrooms.

Key readings: multimodal discourses

Kress, G. (2003) *Literacy in the new media age.* London: Routledge.

Kress, G., Jewitt, C., Osborn, J. and Tsatsarelis, C. (2001) *Multimodal teaching and learning: the rhetorics of the science classroom.* London: Continuum.

Kress, G. and van Leeuwen, T. (2001) *Multimodal discourse: the modes and media of contemporary communication.* London: Hodder Arnold.

Kress, G. and Van Leeuwan, T. (2006) *Reading images: the grammar of visual design*, 2nd edn. London: Routledge.

Norris, S. (2004) *Analysing multimodal interaction: a methodological framework.* New York: Routledge.

O'Halloran, K.L. (ed.) (2004/2006) *Multimodal discourse analysis.* London: Continuum.

O'Halloran, K.L. (2008) *Mathematical discourse: language, symbolism and visual images.* London: Continuum.

O'Halloran, K.L. (2009) *Multimodal approach to classroom discourse.* London: Equinox.

Royce, T. and Bowcher, W. (eds) (2006) *New directions in the analysis of multimodal discourse.* London: Routledge.

Selfe, C.L. (ed.) (2007) *Multimodal composition: resources for teachers.* Kresskill, NJ: Hampton Press.

Unsworth, L. (ed.) (2009). *Multimodal semiotics: functional analysis in contexts of education.* London: Continuum.

8.14   Forensic linguistics

Dealing with written and spoken texts implicated in legal or criminal contexts, forensic linguistics is one of the fastest growing branches of applied linguistics. Dealing with everything from high profile plagiarism cases, falsified confessions, hoaxes and ransom demands to suicide notes, hate mail and trademark copying, forensic linguistics has developed rapidly. Forensic linguistics is now of considerable use to law enforcement and criminal justice professionals in investigations and linguists are called to appear as expert witnesses in courtrooms.

Forensic linguistics has evolved from authorship studies and disputes over biblical and Shakespearian texts in the late eighteenth century. Statistical and computational linguistics, and then corpus linguistics, has helped support the idea that every text carries the 'linguistic fingerprint' or 'stylistic profile' of its writer, distinguishing it from the writing of others. Frequency and collocational differences, misspellings and preferences for particular forms of expression, grammar, lexis, punctuation, or formatting can indicate particular patterns of choices and help reveal the writer of a given text. One high profile example of the work of forensic linguistics was the overturning of Derek Bentley's conviction for murder in 1998. Malcolm Coulthard was able to show that Bentley's statement to police, allegedly transcribed verbatim from a spoken monologue, actually contained features which suggested question and answer interactions and so indicated police co-authorship. In particular, his analysis compared the frequency of the word 'then', which was far more common in the confession than in a corpus of witness statements, and the particularly high frequency of *I then* rather than *then I*, which is fairly rare in general English usage outside of police statements.

Analyses such as these go beyond the courtroom to questions of plagiarism in educational settings and can help students and researchers to see individual diversity in the common patterns of various written genres.

Key readings: forensic linguistics

Coulthard, M. and Johnson, A. (2007) *An introduction to forensic linguistics: language in evidence*. London: Routledge.

Gibbons, J. (2003) *Forensic linguistics: an introduction to language in the justice system*. Oxford: Blackwell.

Hanlein, H. (1998) *Studies in authorship recognition: a corpus-based approach*. Frankfurt: Peter Lang.

Olsson, J. (2004) *Forensic linguistics: an introduction to language, crime and the law*. London: Continuum.

Olsson, J. (2008) *Forensic linguistics*, 2nd edn. London: Continuum.

McMenamin, G.R. (2002) *Forensic linguistics: advances in forensic stylistics*. Boca Raton, FL: CRC Press.

Shuy, R.W. (2005) *Creating language crimes: how law enforcement uses (and misuses) language*. Oxford: Oxford University Press.

Shuy, R.W. (2006) *Linguistics in the courtroom: a practical guide*. Oxford: Oxford University Press.

8.15 Creative writing

Finally, I should briefly mention an area of writing which, while more closely associated with reading for most of us, nevertheless appeals to many people from all backgrounds and walks of life: creative writing. We can see this as any writing, fiction or non-fiction, that occurs outside of everyday professional, journalistic, academic and technical forms of writing. Most typically we think of novels, short stories and poems in this category, but it can also include screenwriting and play-writing, which are texts to be performed, and creative non-fiction such as personal and journalistic essays.

Creative writing is now seen as an independent academic discipline and taught both at undergraduate and postgraduate levels at some universities, leading to Bachelor or Masters of Fine Arts. Unlike its academic writing courses that teach students the rhetorical conventions and discourse expectations of disciplinary communities, creative writing attempts to focus on students' self-expression. Creative writing students typically decide to focus on either fiction or poetry, although screenwriting and playwriting courses are also available in some programmes. Input normally involves critical appraisal of literature and the development of writing techniques such as editing, idea generation and overcoming writer's block. Courses normally follow a workshop format where students develop skills through process techniques of drafting and rewriting and submitting their original work for peer critique. Students also work outside their classes by participating in writing-based activities such as publishing clubs, university literary magazines or newspapers, and writing contests. Because many of these courses are run in the US, texts available in the area of creative writing tend to be American and address the needs of students on these courses.

Key readings: creative writing

Amberg, J. and Larson, M. (1996) *Creative writing handbook*. Tucson, AZ: Good Year Books.

Bernays, A. and Painter, P. (1991) *What if? Writing exercises for fiction writers*. New York: Collins.

Kiteley, B. (2005) *3 a.m. epiphany*. Cincinnati, OH: Writer's Digest Books.

Mueller, L. and Reynolds, J. (1990) *Creative writing: forms and techniques*. Lincolnwood, IL: National Textbook Co.

New York Writers Workshop (2006) *Portable MFA in creative writing*. Cincinnati, OH: Writer's Digest Books.

Vogler, C. (2007) *The writers journey: mythic structure for writers*, 3rd edn. Studio City, CA: Michael Wiese.

Whiteley, C. (2002) *The everything creative writing book: all you need to know to write a novel, play, short story, screenplay, poem, or article*. Cincinnati, OH: Adams Media.

Williams, B.A. (2006) *Writing wide: exercises in creative writing*. Kandiyohi, MN: Filbert Publishing.

Chapter 9

Key sources

This chapter will . . .

- catalogue some of the main sources of information relevant to teachers and researchers of writing;
- list the main writing journals, conferences and professional associations;
- list a number of Internet writing sites, bulletin boards and email discussion groups.

The huge reach, scope and productivity of the field of writing, together with tight space constraints in this book, mean that I can offer only a very limited, and idiosyncratic, collection of resources. I hope, however, that this provides a starting point from which readers might explore some of these very rich areas in much greater detail. The list is organised by the type of source: books, journals, professional bodies, conferences, email lists and bulletin boards, Internet sites and databases.

9.1 Books

The main texts in specific areas of writing have been listed above or appended to the ends of chapters and a good overview of the field should include reference to them. There is no shortage of textbooks about writing. These range from collections of grammar tasks to those representing serious scholarship which increases our understanding of the subject. Box 9.1 suggests some books which together would represent a good library on writing and while new textbooks are regularly introduced, Box 9.2 lists a few of the better ones.

9.1   General books on writing

Casanave, C. (2004) *Controversies in second language writing*. Ann arbor, MI: University of Michigan Press.

Clark, R. and Ivanic, R. (1997) *The politics of writing*. London: Routledge.

Elbow, P. (1998) *Writing with power: techniques for mastering the writing process*. Oxford: Oxford University Press.

Fairclough, N. (2004) *Analyzing discourse*. London: Routledge.

Hyland, K. (2003) *Second language writing*. New York: Cambridge University Press.

Hyland, K. (2004) *Genre and second language writers*. Ann Arbor, MI: University of Michigan Press.

Johns, A.M. (ed.) (2002) *Genre and the classroom*. Mahwah, NJ: Erlbaum.

Kroll, B. (ed.) (2002) *Exploring the dynamics of second language writing*. Cambridge: Cambridge University Press.

Silva, T. and Matsuda, P. (eds) (2001) *Landmark essays on ESL writing*. Mahwah, NJ: Lawrence Earlbaum.

Weigle, S. (2002) *Assessing writing*. Cambridge: Cambridge University Press.

9.2   Some key textbooks

(Writing for publication) Swales, J. and Feak, C. (2000) *English in today's research world: a writing guide*. Ann Arbor, MI: University of Michigan Press.

(Post-graduate) Swales, J. and Feak, C. (2004) *Academic writing for graduate students: essential tasks and skills*, 2nd edn. Ann Arbor, MI: University of Michigan Press.

(Advanced) Leki, I. (1998) *Academic writing*, 2nd edn. New York: St Martin's Press.

(Advanced) Raimes, A. (2006) *Keys for Writers*, 4th edn. Boston MA: Houghton Mifflin.

(High-intermediate) Oshima, A. and Hogue, A. (2006) *Writing academic English*, 4th edn. Harlow: Pearson.

(High-intermediate) Mulvaney, M.K. and Jolliffe, D.A. (2004) *Academic writing: genres, samples, and resources*. Harlow: Pearson.

(Intermediate) Strauch, A. (1998) *Bridges to academic writing.* Cambridge: Cambridge University Press.

(Low-intermediate) Jordon, R. (1999) *Academic writing course*, 3rd edn. London: Collins.

(High beginners) Hogue, A. (2007) *First steps in academic writing*, 2nd edn. Harlow: Pearson.

9.2 Journals

This section lists the main writing periodicals, both print and on-line, together with journals in related areas that carry relevant articles. Website addresses often provide a description of the journal, submissions guides, names of editorial board members, contents, and so on, and I have supplied these where they exist. Be warned that the Internet is in constant flux and that sites regularly change, move or disappear entirely. A list of the website addresses of major educational publishers can be found at Acqweb's directory of publishers and vendors at: http://www.acqweb.org/pubr.html.

Core writing journals

Assessing Writing http://www.elsevier.com/locate/asw (interdisciplinary journal for writing teaching and assessment issues).

College Composition and Communication http://www1.ncte.org/store/journals/105392.htm (composition studies from a broadly humanistic perspective. For US college writing teachers).

Composition Studies http://www.compositionstudies.tcu.edu/ (all aspects of composition and rhetoric, particularly in relation to US universities).

Computers and Composition http://www.elsevier.com/locate/compcom (all aspects of computers in writing teaching: software, tagging, LANs, ethics, effects, etc.).

Journal of Advanced Composition http://www.jacweb.org/ (theoretical articles on topics related to rhetoric, writing, literacy and politics of education).

Journal of Basic Writing http://www.asu.edu/clas/english/composition/cbw/jbw.html (theory, research and teaching of basic writers).

Journal of Technical Writing and Communication http://www.baywood.com/journals/previewjournals.asp?id=0047-2816 (functional writing in a range of technical, scientific and professional environments).

Journal of Second Language Writing http://www.elsevier.com/locate/ jslw AND http://www.jslw.org/ (the leading journal of theoretically grounded research into L2 writing issues).

Pre-Text http://www.pre-text.com (journal of rhetorical theory).

Rhetoric Review (journal of rhetorical theory and practice with a philosophical orientation).

Text and Talk http://www.degruyter.de/journals/text/detail.cfm (interdisciplinary forum for discourse studies).

Written Communication http://wcx.sagepub.com/ (the leading journal in the field of research, theory and application of writing. Cutting-edge issues from linguistics, composition, sociology, psychology and cognitive sciences).

Written Language and Literacy http://www.benjamins.com/cgi-bin/ t_seriesview.cgi?series=WL%26L (journal of writing systems and the institutionalised use of written language).

Writing Lab Newsletter http://writinglabnewsletter.org/ (monthly journal on one-to-one writing teaching issues).

On-line writing journals

Academic Writing archive: http://wac.colostate.edu/atd/archives.cfm? showatdarchives=aw (refereed journal concerned with all aspects of writing across the curriculum published 2000 to 2003).

Across the Disciplines http://wac.colostate.edu/atd/ (refereed journal devoted to language, learning, and all aspects of academic writing).

The Internet Writing Journal http://www.internetwritingjournal.com/ (refereed journal which includes articles, interviews and reviews of creative writing in print).

Kairos http://kairos.technorhetoric.net/ (refereed electronic journal for teachers and researchers of all kinds of Internet-based writing and dealing with rhetoric, technology, and pedagogy).

Related journals (regularly carry papers on writing)

Applied Linguistics http://www3.oup.co.uk/applij/

English for Specific Purposes http://www.elsevier.com/locate/esp

Discourse and Society http://www.sagepub.co.uk/journalsProdDesc. nav?prodId=Journal200873

Discourse Studies http://dis.sagepub.com/

International Journal of Applied Linguistics http://www. blackwellpublishing.com/journal.asp?ref=0802-6106

International Review of Applied Linguistics in Language Teaching
http://www.degruyter.de/journals/iral/

Journal of Applied Linguistics http://www.equinoxjournals.com/ojs/
index.php/JAL

Journal of Business Communication http://job.sagepub.com/

Modern Language Journal http://mlj.miis.edu/

System http://www.elsevier.com/locate/system/

TESOL Quarterly http://www.tesol.org/tq

9.3 Professional associations

Associations specifically devoted to writing

Alliance for Computers and Writing (ACW) http://english.ttu.edu/
acw/ (a US based body committed to supporting teachers at all levels
of instruction in the use of computers in writing instruction by providing a forum for sharing ideas and information).

American Medical Writers' Association http://www.amwa.org/ (the
leading professional organisation for medical communicators).

Association of Writers and Writing Programs http://www.awpwriter.
org/ (seeks to foster literary talent and achievement, to advance
the art of writing as essential to a good education, and to serve the
makers, teachers, students and readers of contemporary writing).

European Association for the Teaching of Academic Writing (EATAW)
http://www.eataw.eu/ (a scholarly forum for all those involved in
academic writing in Universities).

European Society for Translation Studies (EST) http://www.est-
translationstudies.org/ (an international society of translation and
interpreting scholars devoted to translation studies).

National Association of Science Writers http://www.nasw.org/ (a body
which fosters the dissemination of accurate information regarding
science to the public. Members include science writers, editors and
science-writing educators and students).

Society for Technical Communication http://www.stc.org/ (an organisation dedicated to advancing the arts and sciences of technical
communication. It is the largest organisation of its type in the world
with 14,000 members which include technical writers and editors,
documentation specialists, technical illustrators, instructional
designers, academics, information architects, web designers and
developers, and translators).

Associations with an interest in writing issues

AAAL (American Association of Applied Linguistics) http://www.aaal.org/

Association for Business Communication (ABC) http://www.businesscommunication.org/ (an international organisation devoted to advancing business communication research and teaching).

AILA (Association Internationale de Linguistique Appliquée) http://www.aila.info/ (the International Association of Applied Linguistics has several interest groups or Research Networks (ReNs) focused on special topic areas, some of which concern writing).

BAAL (British Association of Applied Linguistics) http://www.baal.org.uk/

IATEFL (Int. Association for Teachers of English as a Foreign Language) http://www.iatefl.org

International Association of Business Communicators. http://www.iabc.com/

JALT (Japanese Association of Language Teachers) http://www.jalt.org/

TESOL (Teachers of English to Speakers of Other Languages) http://www.tesol.org/9.4

9.4   Writing conferences

There are only a handful of international conferences devoted to writing, but many language conferences include papers on writing. More details are available from the websites.

Association for Business Communication (ABC) http://www.business-communication.org/ (hosts an annual conference on business communication in the USA and lists others on its website).

Association of Writers and Writing Programs Annual conference http://www.awpwriter.org/conference/index.php (one of the biggest literary gatherings in North America with 5,000 attendees and 400 publishers).

College Composition and Communication http://www.ncte.org/ccc (the world's largest professional organisation for researching and teaching composition, from writing to new media).

BAAL Conference diary http://www.baal.org.uk/confs_diary.htm EATAW Conference bi-annual conference of the European Association for Teaching Academic Writing.

Internet TESL Journal's conference list http://iteslj.org/links/TESL/Conferences/

Linguists list conference list http://www.linguistlist.org/callconf/index.html (lists up to 500 current teaching and linguistics conferences and calls for papers).

Purdue L2 writing symposium http://sslw.asu.edu/ (an annual international conference for teachers and researchers who work with second- and foreign-language writers).

Right writing conference list http://www.right-writing.com/conferences.html (calendar of creative writing conferences and advice on the best ones).

Roy's resources http://www.royfc.com/confer.html (lists of conferences worldwide for linguistics, translators and teachers of languages).

TESOL conference list http://www.tesol.org/s_tesol/sec_document.asp?CID=23&DID=2145 (includes conferences for teachers of English to Speakers of Other Languages).

Wikipedia list of creative writing conferences http://en.wikipedia.org/wiki/List_of_writers'_conferences

9.5   Email lists and bulletin boards

These are on-line conferences, listserves and discussion groups. Those specifically concerned with writing are given first, the others occasionally address topics related to writing.

ACW-L (Alliance for Computers and Writing List) List: listproc@listserv.ttu.edu http://English.ttu.edu/acw

Newsgroups and mailing lists for translators http://www.iol.ie/~mazzoldi/lang/maillist.htm

WAC-L (Writing across the Curriculum List) http://www.lsoft.se/scripts/wl.exe?SL1=WAC-L&H=LISTSERV.UIUC.EDU

WPA-L (Writing Programme Administration List) http://www.wpacouncil.org/wpa-l (for those involved in writing program administration at universities, colleges, or community colleges).

Writing across boundaries http://groups.google.com/group/writing-across-boundaries

TESL-L http://www.hunter.cuny.edu/~tesl-l/ (teachers of English as a second language list).

TechRhet. http://www.interversity.org (a list that explores the intersections among teaching, learning, communication, community and the new literacies).

Critical writing group http://groups.yahoo.com/group/critical_writing/?v=1&t=search&ch=web&pub=groups&sec=group&slk=2 (for writers interested in getting and giving criticism/critiques on creative writing including short stories, cross-genre, romance, detective stories, etc.).

Mike's writing workshop http://groups.yahoo.com/group/ mikeswritingworkshop/?v=1&t=search&ch=web&pub=groups&sec= group&slk=6 (one of Writer's Digest's Best Web Sites for Writers, as well as the Best Writers Workshop in the 2007 Editors Readers Poll, this group offers all writers a place to post work, ask questions, and discuss ways to improve their writing).

WAC-L http://www.lsoft.se/scripts/wl.exe?SL1=WAC-L&H= LISTSERV.UIUC.EDU (the leading list for discussion of writing across the curriculum).

WAD: Writing Across the Disciplines http://www.fiu.edu/~wad/ (click on 'WAD Mailing List' in the Menu).

WCENTER: Writing Centers' Online Discussion Community lists. uwosh.edu/mailman/listinfo/wcenter

WPA-L: Writing Program Administration http://www.wpacouncil. org/wpa-l (sponsored by the Council of Writing Program Administrators).

List of language discussion lists (all languages) http://www.evertype. com/langlist.html

EST-L (English for Science and Technology) http://www.bio.net/ bionet/mm/bionews/1994-October/001523.html

9.6 Writing websites

The web is heaving with writing sites of all types and quality and I do not claim completeness. Most sites are US-based, but I have tried to include a variety of both source and focus. The list simply presents some of the best sites that I know and which I think represent key sources and starting points for further reading and exploration.

Corpora and concordancers

These sites provide information on corpus linguistics and often an on-line concordancer and (limited) access to a written text corpus.

British Academic Written English (BAWE). http://ota.ahds.ac.uk/ headers/2539.xml The corpus contains 2,761 student assignments, produced and assessed as part of university degree coursework, and fairly evenly distributed across 35 university disciplines and four levels of study (first year undergraduate to Masters level) (6.5 million words). About half the assignments were graded at a level equivalent to 'distinction' (70 per cent or above), and half at a level equivalent to 'merit' (between 60 per cent and 69 per cent). The majority were written by L1 speakers of English. The corpus is suitable for use with concordancing programs such as AntConc or WordSmith Tools Users must register with the Oxford Text Archive (free) and is listed as resource number 2539.

Cobuild corpus sampler http://www.collins.co.uk/Corpus/CorpusSearch. aspx

Corpus of Contemporary American English http://www.americancorpus. org (385 m words of various genres from 1990–2008. Easy to use interface).

Text corpora and corpus linguistics http://www.athel.com/corpus.html

Oxford text archive http://ota.ahds.ac.uk/ (collection of electronic literary and linguistic resources with searchable corpus of British novels).

Check My Words http://www.compulang.com/cmw/ (free student writing aid with word processor accessed concordance).

The web concordances http://www.dundee.ac.uk/english/wics/wics.htm (searchable corpora of poems by Shelley, Keats, Blake, Milton, etc.).

Monolonc Pro (concordancer and corpora) http://www.athel.com

Wordsmith Tools 5 (concordancer) http://www.lexically.net/wordsmith/ index.html

VLC Web concordancer http://vlc.polyu.edu.hk/concordance/ (at Polytechnic University of Hong Kong).

Specialist sites

Association of Writers and Writing Programs (AWP) http://www. awpwriter.org/ (website provides guide to US creative writing courses, conferences, retreats, workshops and other resources).

Writing Across the Curriculum Clearinghouse http://wac.colostate. edu/index.cfm (publishes journals, books, and other resources for teachers who use writing in their courses).

Inkspot http://inkspot.com/ (allows users to create an on-line portfolio to showcase their talents).

Daedalus Educational Software http://www.daedalus.com (for collaborative learning and the writing process).

Lancaster Literacy Research Centre http://www.literacy.lancs.ac.uk.

Rhetoric and composition http://eserver.org/rhetoric (a variety of resources useful to rhetoricians including links to works of classical rhetoric, articles on literacy and education, bibliographies, mailing lists and links to glossaries of rhetorical terms).

Literacy matters http://www.literacymatters.com/ (teaching materials and shop for school literacy).

On-line writing labs

National Writing Centres Association http://cyberlyber.com/ writing_centers_and_owls.htm (comprehensive list of some 200 OWLs or On-Line Writing Centres in the United States).

Purdue OWL http://owl.english.purdue.edu/ (one of the best sites devoted to the teaching of academic writing).

The Writing Machine http://ec.hku.hk/writingmachine/ (an Internet resource created at the Centre of Applied English Studies, the University of Hong Kong, designed to help students understand and master the process of writing academic essays).

CAPLITS Online writing centre http://www.ioe.ac.uk/caplits/ writingcentre/

Academic writing course (at Hong Kong PolyU Writing Centre) http:// vlc.polyu.edu.hk/academicwriter/Questions/writemodeintro.htm

Garbl's Fat-Free Writing Links http://garbl.home.comcast.net/ ~garbl/writing/concise.htm (an annotated directory of web sites that give advice on writing).

Style guides and writing mechanics

APA style resources http://www.psychwww.com/resource/apacrib.htm

Long Island University guide to citation style http://www.liu.edu/cwis/ cwp/library/workshop/citation.htm

Resources for writers http://webster.commnet.edu/writing/writing. htm (grammar guides, advice, links, style books, etc.).

Enhance my Writing.com http://www.enhancemywriting.com/ (more writing resources).

Way to Write http://www.ucalgary.ca/UofC/eduweb/writing/ (an interactive guide to writing).

The writing process

Steps in the Writing Process http://karn.ohiolink.edu/~sg-ysu/process.html

ABCs of the writing process http://www.angelfire.com/wi/writingprocess/

Research and Writing Step by Step http://www.ipl.org/div/aplus/ stepfirst.htm (research and writing for high school and college students).

The Writing Process http://www.suelebeau.com/writingprocess.htm (list of process-based websites for teachers).

Genre writing sites

The Writing Site http://www.thewritingsite.org/resources/genre/
default.asp (describes writing various genres with prompts and tips).
Blogs about genre http://wordpress.com/tag/genre-writing/
Purdue Owl page on writing genres http://owl.english.purdue.edu/
internet/resources/genre.html
World writer http://worldwriter.homestead.com/writerslinks.html
(links and resources for writers of various fiction genres).

Sites for specific text types

On-line technical writing http://www.free-ed.net/free-ed/MiscTech/
TechWriting01/default.asp (a course covering various business and
technical genres and aspects of the writing process).
PIZZAZ http://darkwing.uoregon.edu/~leslieob/pizzaz.html (creative
writing with poetry fiction and creative ideas for writing
teachers).
Ten steps to writing an essay http://www1.aucegypt.edu/academic/
writers/
Guide to writing an essay http://members.tripod.com/~lklivingsto n/
essay/
Science Research paper http://www.ruf.rice.edu/~bioslabs/tools/report/
reportform.html
Writing and presenting theses http://www.learnerassociates.net/
dissthes/
Business persuasion materials http://www.superwriter.com/persuasi.
htm
Business writing blog http://www.businesswritingblog.com/
Writing in arts and humanities http://www.dartmouth.edu/~writing/
materials/student/humanities/write.shtml
Writing humanities papers http://www.geneseo.edu/~easton/humanities/
convhumpap.html

9.7   Databases

This section refers to information on articles, theses, conference
papers, and so on. These are mainly of Australian, US or UK origin
and are available either on the web or in CD-ROM format. Obviously

not all the records in these sources relate to writing and further searches will need to be made in sub categories.

ERIC document reproduction service http://www.eric.ed.gov/ (ERIC provides unlimited access to more than 1.2 million bibliographic records of journal articles and other education-related materials, with hundreds of new records added twice weekly. If available, links to full text are included).

Dissertation Abstracts Online http://library.dialog.com/bluesheets/html/bl0035.html (a definitive subject, title, and author guide to virtually every American dissertation accepted at an accredited institution since 1861).

Dissertation Abstracts Online http://www.oclc.org/support/documentation/FirstSearch/databases/dbdetails/details/Dissertations. htm (selectively covers masters theses and dissertations including dissertations from Canada, Great Britain, and Europe – over 2.2 million records).

Linguist List dissertation abstracts http://www.linguistlist.org/pubs/diss/index.html About 1700 entries on language and linguistics.

Index to theses http://www.theses.com/ (a comprehensive listing of theses with abstracts accepted for higher degrees by universities in Great Britain and Ireland since 1716).

Linguistics and language behaviour abstracts http://www.csa.com/factsheets/llba-set-c.php (CSA Linguistics and Language Behavior Abstracts covers all aspects of the study of language in the international literature including phonetics, morphology, syntax, discourse, and semantics).

MLA international bibliography of books and articles on modern languages and literature http://journalseek.net/cgi-bin/journalseek/journalsearch.cgi?field=issn&query=0024-8215 (database with limited access to 45,000 citations, indexed from over 3,000 periodicals, series, books, conference proceedings, and dissertations on language, literature, linguistics, and folklore).

Scopus http://www.scopus.com/scopus/home.url (the largest abstract and citation database of research literature and web sources with smart tools to track, analyse and visualise research. Subscription required).

Science Direct http://www.sciencedirect.com/ (operated by the publisher Elsevier, this is the world's largest electronic collection of academic books and journals with free access to abstracts and subscription access to full text articles).

Glossary

These definitions are to help you understand how I use the terms in this book and offer a general resource for reading and talking about writing more generally. They are, however, brief and perhaps idiosyncratic so readers interested in more precise and extensive definitions should refer to specialist language encyclopaedias such as:

Long, M.H. and Doughty, C. (eds) (2009) *Handbook of language teaching*. Oxford: Blackwell.
Malmkjær, K. (ed.) (2009) *Routledge encyclopedia of linguistics*, 3rd edn. London: Routledge.
Brown, K. (ed.) (2006) *Encyclopedia of language and linguistics*, 2nd edn. Oxford: Elsevier.
Cummins, A. and Davison, C. (eds) (2006) *The international handbook of English language education*. Norwell, MA: Springer.

Alternatively, you might consult a good grammar such as Biber *et al.* (1999) for grammatical terms or *Wikipedia* for media and Internet terms.

affordance A term for the potentials and limitations of different modes of meaning making, especially written vs. visual modes.

audience The writer's construction of his or her readers, whose imagined beliefs, understandings and values are anticipated and appealed to in the conventional features and structure of a text.

coherence The ways a text makes sense to readers through the relevance and accessibility of its concepts, ideas and theories.

cohesion The grammatical and lexical relationships which tie a text together.

collocation The regular occurrence of a word with one or more others in a text. The term can also refer to the meanings associated with a word as a result of this association.

concordance A list of unconnected lines of text called up by a concordance program with the search word at the centre of each line. This list allows common patterns to be seen by reading down the lines.

context The relationship between linguistic and non-linguistic dimensions of communicative events. These dimensions are seen to stand in a mutually influential relationship, with text and the interpretive work it creates helping to shape context and context influencing the conventions, values and knowledge a text appeals to.

contrastive rhetoric The view that the rhetorical features of L2 texts may reflect different writing conventions learned in the L1 culture. It also refers to the cross-cultural study of these differences.

corpus A collection of texts, usually stored electronically, seen as representative of some subset of language and used for linguistic analysis.

critical discourse analysis (CDA) An approach which seeks to reveal the interests, values and power relations in any institutional and socio-historical context through the ways that people use language.

direct writing assessment Testing methods based on a communicative purpose of writing, emphasising validity, particularly the psychological reality of the task, rather than just statistical reliability.

discourse Language produced as an act of communication. This language use implies the constraints and choices which operate on writers in particular contexts and reflects their purposes, intentions, ideas and relationships with readers.

discourse community A rather fuzzy concept used in genre studies to refer to a group of writers (or speakers) who share a communicative purpose and use commonly agreed texts to achieve these purposes. The term carries a core meaning of like mindedness of membership which is widely used in research on writing to help explain discourse coherence.

discursive practices A CDA term which refers to the acts of production, distribution and interpretation which surround a text and which must be taken into account in text analysis. These practices are themselves embedded in wider social practices of power and authority.

drafting The recursive process of text creation, rewriting and polishing: it involves getting ideas on paper and responding to potential problems for readers.

editing Typically the final stage in the writing process where the writer attends to surface-level corrections of grammar and spelling.

ethnography A research approach which seeks to gather a variety of naturally occurring data to provide a highly situated, minutely detailed and holistic account of writers' behaviours.

Expressivist view The belief that the free expression of ideas leads to self-discovery and that teachers should help students to find their own voices to produce fresh and spontaneous prose.

feedback The response given to student writing. It can refer to either oral or written types provided by peers, teachers or computers. Widely regarded as central to writing development.

genre Broadly, a set of texts that share the same socially recognised purpose and which, as a result, often share similar rhetorical and structural elements to achieve this purpose.

hedging Linguistic devices used to indicate either the writer's lack of commitment to the truth of a statement or a desire not to express that commitment categorically for interpersonal reasons.

Identity Is now widely seen as the ways that people display who they are to each other, a social performance achieved by drawing on appropriate linguistic resources at particular times, rather than a universal *who you are*.

interaction Refers to the social routines and relationships which surround acts of writing or the ways that these are expressed in a text. The former have been studied to elaborate the influence of context on writing processes, and the latter to show how texts can reflect a writer's projection of the understandings, interests and needs of a potential audience.

intertextuality An element of one text that takes its meaning from a reference to another text, for instance by quoting, echoing or linking.

literacy practices The general ways of using written language within a cultural context which people draw on in their lives.

membership An ability to display credibility and competence through familiarity or exploitation of discourse conventions typically used in a community. This can identify one as an 'insider', belonging to that community and possessing the legitimacy to address it.

New rhetoric perspective An approach to text analysis that foregrounds the social and ideological realities that underlie the regularities of texts and which employs the use of ethnographic methods to unpack the relations between texts and contexts.

New Literacy Studies The view that written language is socially and historically situated and that literacy practices reflect broader social practices and political arrangements.

portfolio A collection of multiple writing samples selected either to showcase a student's most successful texts or to reveal a process of writing development. Used to structure writing courses, encourage reflection and provide more comprehensive and equitable assessment.

process approach A teaching approach to writing which emphasises the development of good practices by stressing that writing is done in stages of planning, drafting, revising and editing, which are recursive, interactive and potentially simultaneous.

protocol research A research technique widely employed in composition research as a means of getting at the processes which underlie writing by eliciting the verbalised thoughts of writers.

register A term from systemic linguistics which explains the relationship between texts and their contexts in terms of field (What the text is about), tenor (who the writer and reader are), and mode (what medium is used). Registers refer to broad fields of activity such as legal papers, technical instructions, advertisements and service exchanges.

schema A model of interpretation which suggests that readers make sense of a text by reference to a set of organised, culturally conventional understandings of similar prior experiences.

Systemic Functional Linguistics (SFL) The theory of language developed by Michael Halliday based on the idea that language is a system of choices used to express meanings in context.

text A piece of spoken or written language.

References

Abasi, A.R. and Akbari, N. (2008) Are we encouraging patchwriting? Reconsidering the role of the pedagogical context in ESL student writers' transgressive intertextuality. *English for Specific Purposes*, 27(3): 267–84.

Afflerbach, P. and Johnson, P. (1984) On the use of verbal reports in reading research. *Journal of Reading Behaviour*, 16(4): 307–22.

Arnaud, P. and Bejoint, H. (eds) (1992) *Vocabulary and applied linguistics*. London: Macmillan.

Aston, G. (1997) Involving learners in developing learning methods: exploiting text corpora in self-access. In P. Benson and P. Voller (eds), *Autonomy and independence in language learning* (pp. 204–14). Harlow: Longman.

Atkinson, D. (1999a) TESOL and culture. *TESOL Quarterly*, 33: 625–53.

Atkinson, D. (1999b) *Scientific discourse in sociohistorical context*. Mahwah, NJ: Lawrence Erlbaum.

Atkinson, D. (2004) Contrasting rhetorics/contrasting cultures: why contrastive rhetoric needs a better conceptualization of culture. *Journal of English for Academic Purposes*, 3(4): 277–89.

Bailey, K. (1990) The use of diary studies in teacher education programs. In J. Richards and D. Nunan (eds), *Second language teacher education*. Cambridge: Cambridge University Press.

Bailey, K. (1998) *Learning about language assessment: dilemmas, decisions, and directions*. Boston: Heinle & Heinle.

Bakhtin, M. (1986) *Speech genres and other late essays*. Austin, TX: University of Texas Press.

Bargiela-Chiappini, F. and Nickerson, G. (eds) (1999) *Writing business: genres, media and discourses*. Harlow: Longman.

Bartholomae, D. (1986) Inventing the university. *Journal of Basic Writing*, 5: 4–23.

Barton, D. (2000) Researching literacy practices: learning from activities with teachers and students. In D. Barton, M. Hamilton and R. Ivanic (eds), *Situated literacies: reading and writing in context* (pp. 167–79). London: Routledge.

Barton, D. (2007) *Literacy: an introduction to the ecology of written language*, 2nd edn. Oxford: Blackwell.

Barton, D. and Hall, N. (1999) *Letter-writing as a social practice*. Amsterdam: John Benjamins.

Barton, D. and Hamilton, M. (1998) *Local literacies*. London: Routledge.

Barton, D., Ivanic, R., Appleby, Y., Hodge, R. and Tusting, K. (2007) *Literacy, lives and learning*. London: Routledge.

Bauer, L. and Nation, P. (1993) Word families. *International Journal of Lexicography*, 6(4): 253–79.

Baynham, M. (1995) *Literacy practices*. Harlow: Longman.

Bazerman, C. (1988) *Shaping written knowledge*. Madison, WI: University of Wisconsin Press.

Bazerman, C. (1994) *Constructing experience*. Carbondale, IL: Southern Illinois University Press.

Bazerman, C. (2004) Speech acts, genres, and activity systems: how texts organize activity and people. In C. Bazerman and P. Prior (eds), *What writing does and how it does it: an introduction to analyzing texts and textual practices* (pp. 83–96). Hillsdale, NJ: Erlbaum.

BBC (1983) *Bid for power*. London: BBC English by Television.

Beatty, K. (2010) *Teaching and researching computer-assisted language learning*. Harlow: Pearson.

Becher, T. and Trowler, P. (2001) *Academic tribes and territories: intellectual inquiry and the cultures of disciplines*. Milton Keynes: SRHE and Open University Press.

Benson, P. (2001) *Teaching and researching autonomy*. Harlow: Longman.

Benwell, B. and Stokoe, E. (2006) *Discourse and identity*. Edinburgh: Edinburgh University Press.

Bereiter, C. and Scardamalia, M. (1987) *The psychology of written composition*. Hillsdale, NJ: Erlbaum.

Berg, E.C. (1999) The effects of trained peer response on ESL students' revision types and writing quality. *Journal of Second Language Writing*, 8: 215–41.

Berkenkotter, C. and Huckin, T. (1995) *Genre knowledge in disciplinary communication*. Hillsdale, NJ: Erlbaum.

Bhatia, V.K. (1993) *Analysing genre: language use in professional settings*. Harlow: Longman.

Bhatia, V.K. (1999) Integrating products, processes, and participants in professional writing. In C.N. Candlin and K. Hyland (eds), *Writing: texts, processes and practices* (pp. 21–39). Harlow: Longman.

Bhatia, V.K. (2004) *Worlds of written discourse*. London: Continuum.

Biber, D., Johansson, S., Leech, G., Conrad, S. and Finegan, E. (1999) *Longman grammar of spoken and written English*. London: Longman.

Biber, D. (2006) Stance in spoken and written university registers. *Journal of English for Academic Purposes*, 5(2): 97–116.

Bleich, D. (2001) The materiality of language and the pedagogy of exchange. *Pedagogy: Critical Approaches to Teaching Literature, Language, Composition, and Culture*, 1: 117–41.

Bloch, J. (2008) *Technology in the second language composition classroom*. Ann Arbor, MI: University of Michigan Press.

Bloch, J. and Crosby, C. (2006) Creating a space for virtual democracy. *The Essential Teacher*, 3: 38–41.

Blommaert, J. (2005) *Discourse*. Cambridge: Cambridge University Press.

Blyler, N. and Thralls, C. (eds) (1993) *Professional communication: the social perspective*. London: Longman.

Board of Studies (2007a) *K-6 English Syllabus*. Sydney, NSW: Board of Studies.

Board of Studies (2007b) *K-6 English Syllabus: Modules*. Sydney, NSW: Board of Studies.

Bosher, S. (1998) The composing processes of three southeast Asian writers at the post-secondary level: an exploratory study. *Journal of Second Language Writing*, 7(2): 205–33.

Braine, G. (1995) Writing in the natural sciences and engineering. In D. Belcher and G. Braine (eds), *Academic writing in a second language: essays on research and pedagogy* (pp. 113–34). Norwood, NJ: Ablex.

Brandt, D. (1986) Text and context: how writers come to mean. In B. Couture (ed.) *Functional approaches to writing: research perspectives* (pp. 93–107). Norwood, NJ: Ablex.

Breen, M. and Littlejohn, A. (eds) (2000) *Classroom decision-making: negotiation and process syllabuses in practice*. Cambridge: Cambridge University Press.

Brinko, K. (1993) The practice of giving feedback to improve teaching. *Journal of Higher Education*, 64: 574–93.

Brown, J.D. (1988) *Understanding research in second language learning*. Cambridge: Cambridge University Press.

Brown, J.D. and Hudson, T. (1998) The alternatives in language assessment. *TESOL Quarterly*, 32(4): 653–75.

Bruffee, K. (1984) Collaborative learning and the 'conversation of Mankind'. *College English*, 46: 635–52.

Bruffee, K. (1986) Social construction: language and the authority of knowledge. A bibliographical essay. *College English*, 48: 773–9.

Bruner, J. (1978) The role of dialogue in language acquisition. In A. Sinclair, R. Jarvelle and W. Levelt (eds), *The child's concept of language*. New York: Springer.

Burns, A. (1999) *Collaborative action research for English language teachers*. Cambridge: Cambridge University Press.

Burstein, J. (2003) The *e-rater* scoring engine: automated essay scoring with natural language processing. In M. Shermis and J. Burstein (eds), *Automated essay scoring: a cross-disciplinary perspective* (pp. 113–22). Hillsdale, NJ: Lawrence Erlbaum.

Callahan, S. (1997) Tests worth taking? Using portfolios for accountability in Kentucky. *Research in the Teaching of English*, 31(3): 295–336.

Canagarajah, A.S. (1996) 'Nondiscursive' requirements in academic publishing, material resources of periphery scholars, and the politics of knowledge production. *Written Communication*, 13(4): 435–72.

Canagarajah, A.S. (2002) *Critical academic writing and multilingual students*. Ann Arbor, MI: University of Michigan Press.

Candlin, C.N. (1999) How can discourse be a measure of expertise? *Paper presented at International Association for Dialogue Analysis*. Birmingham: University of Birmingham.

Candlin, C.N. and Hyland, K. (eds) (1999) *Writing: texts, processes and practices*. Harlow: Longman.

Candlin, C.N. and Plum, G. (eds) (1998) *Framing student literacy: cross cultural aspects of communication skills in Australian university settings*. Sydney: NCELTR, Macquarie University.

Candlin, C.N., Bhatia, V.K. and Jenson, C. (2002) Developing legal writing materials for English second language learners: problems and perspectives. *English for Specific Purposes*, 21(4): 299–320.

Carter, M. (1990) The idea of expertise: an exploration of cognitive and social dimensions of writing. *College Composition and Communication*, 41(3): 265–86.

Carter, R. (1998) *Vocabulary: applied linguistics perspectives*. London: Routledge.

Casanave, C. (2004) *Controversies in second language writing*. Ann Arbor, MI: University of Michigan Press.

Caulk, N. (1994) Comparing teacher and student responses to written work. *TESOL Quarterly*, 28(1): 181–7.

Chapelle, C. (2001) *Computer applications to second language acquisition: foundations for teaching, testing, and research*. Cambridge: Cambridge University Press.

Cherry, R. (1988) Ethos versus persona: self-representation in written discourse. *Written Communication*, 5: 251–76.

Chin, E. (1994) Redefining 'context' in research on writing. *Written Communication*, 11: 445–82.

Christianson, K. (1997) Dictionary use by EFL writers: what really happens? *Journal of Second Language Writing*, 6(1): 23–43.

Cicourel, A.V. (2007) A personal, retrospective view of ecological validity (Special issue: four decades of epistemological revolution: work inspired by Aaron V. Cicourel) *Text & Talk*, 27(5/6): 735–52.

Clyne, M. (1987) Cultural differences in the organisation of academic texts. *Journal of Pragmatics*, 11: 211–47.

Coe, R.M. (2002) The new rhetoric of genre: writing political briefs. In A.M. Johns (ed.) *Genre in the classroom* (pp. 195–205). Mahwah, NJ: Erlbaum.

Cohen, A., Glasman, H., Rosenbaum-Cohen, P.R., Ferrara, J. and Fine, J. (1988) Reading English for specialized purposes: discourse analysis and the use of standard informants. In P. Carrell, J. Devine and D. Eskey (eds), *Interactive approaches to second language reading* (pp. 152–67). Cambridge: Cambridge University Press.

Cohen, L., Manion, L. and Morrison, K. (2000) *Research methods in education*, 5th edn. London: Routledge.

Connor, U. (1994) Text analysis. *TESOL Quarterly*, 28(4): 673–703.

Connor, U. (1996) *Contrastive rhetoric*. Cambridge: Cambridge University Press.

Coxhead, A. (2000) A New Academic Word List. *TESOL Quarterly*, 34(2): 213–38.

Coxhead, A. and Nation, I.S.P. (2001) The specialized vocabulary of English for academic purposes. In J. Flowerdew and M. Peacock (eds), *Research perspectives on English for Academic Purposes* (pp. 252–67). Cambridge: Cambridge University Press.

Crismore, A., Markkanen, R. and Steffensen, M. (1993) Metadiscourse in persuasive writing: a study of texts written by American and Finnish university students. *Written Communication*, 10(1): 39–71.

Crookes, G. (1986) Towards a validated analysis of scientific text structure. *Applied Linguistics*, 7: 57–70.

Cutting, J. (2002) *Pragmatics and discourse. A resource book for students*. London: Routledge.

de Larios, J., Murphy, L. and Manchon, R. (1999) The use of restructuring strategies in EFL writing: a study of Spanish learners of English as a Foreign Language. *Journal of Second Language Writing*, 8(1): 13–44.

de Larios, J.R., Manchón, R., Murphy, L. and Marín, J. (2008) The foreign language writer's strategic behaviour in the allocation of time to writing processes. *Journal of Second Language Writing*, 17(1): 30–47.

DeMauro, G. (1992) *An investigation of the appropriateness of the TOEFL test as a matching variable to equate TWE topics*. Princeton, NJ: Educational Testing Service Report 37.

Denzin, N.K. and Lincoln, Y.S. (1998) *The landscape of qualitative research: theories and issues*. Thousand Oaks, CA: Sage.

Derewianka, B. (1990) *Exploring how texts work*. Newtown, NSW: Primary English Teaching Association.

Devitt, A., Reiff, M.J. and Bawarshi, A. (2004) *Scenes of writing: strategies for composing with genres*. New York: Longman.

Dias, P., Freedman, A., Medway, P. and Paré, A. (1999) *Worlds apart: acting and writing in academic and workplace contexts*. Mahwah, NJ: Lawrence Erlbaum.

Douglas, J.Y. (1998) Will the most reflexive relativist please stand up: hypertext, argument and relativism. In I. Snyder (ed.), *Page to screen: taking literacy into the electronic era* (pp. 144–62). London: Routledge.

Duranti, A. and Goodwin, C. (eds) (1992) *Rethinking context. Language as an interactive phenomenon*. Cambridge: Cambridge University Press.

Ede, L. and Lunsford, A. (1984) Audience addressed/audience invoked: the role of audience in composition theory and pedagogy. *College Composition and Communication*, 35: 155–71.

Elbow, P. (1994) *Voice and writing*. Davis, CA: Hermagoras Press.

Elbow, P. (1998) *Writing with power: techniques for mastering the writing process*. New York and Oxford: Oxford University Press.

Elbow, P. and Belanoff, P. (1991) SUNY Stony Brook portfolio-based evaluation program. In P. Belanoff and M. Dickson (eds), *Portfolios: process and product* (pp. 3–16). Portsmouth, NH: Boynton/Cook.

Ellis, R. (2002) The place of grammar instruction in the second/foreign language curriculum. In S. Fotos and E. Hinkel (eds), *New perspectives on grammar teaching in second language classrooms* (pp. 17–34). Mahwah, NJ: Erlbaum.

Emig, J. (1983) *The web of meaning*. Upper Montclair, NJ: Boynton/Cook.

Erikson, F. (1981) Some approaches to enquiry in school-community ethnography. In H. Trueba, G. Guthrie and K.H. Au (eds), *Culture and the bilingual classroom: studies in classroom ethnography* (pp. 17–35). Rowley, MA: Newbury House.

Evans, S. and Green, C. (2007) Why EAP is necessary: a survey of Hong Kong tertiary students. *Journal of English for Academic Purposes*, 6(1): 3–17.

Faigley, L. (1986) Competing theories of process: a critique and a proposal. *College English*, 48: 527–42.

Faigley, L., Daly, J. and Witte, S. (1981) The role of writing apprehension in writing performance and competence. *Journal of Educational Research*, 75: 16–20.

Fairclough, N. (1989) *Language and power*. London: Longman.

Fairclough, N. (1992) *Discourse and social change*. Cambridge: Polity Press.

Fairclough, N. (1995) *Critical discourse analysis*. Harlow: Longman.

Fairclough, N. (2003) *Analysing discourse: textual analysis for social research*. London: Routledge.

Fairclough, N. and Wodak, R. (1997) Critical discourse analysis. In T. Van Dijk (ed.), *Discourse as social interaction* (pp. 258–84). London: Sage.

Farrell, P. (1990) *Vocabulary in ESP: a lexical analysis of the English of electronics and a study of semi-technical vocabulary*. CLCS Occasional Paper No. 25. Dublin: Trinity College.

Feez, S. (2001) Heritage and innovation in second language education. In A.M. Johns (ed.), *Genre in the classroom* (pp. 47–68). Mahwah, NJ: Erlbaum.

Ferris, D. (2003) *Response to student writing*. Mahwah, NJ: Erlbaum.

Ferris, D. (2006) Does error feedback help student writers? New evidence on the short- and long-term effects of written error correction. In K. Hyland and F. Hyland (eds), *Feedback in second language writing* (pp. 81–104). Cambridge: Cambridge University Press.

Ferris, D. and Roberts, B. (2001) Error feedback . in L2 writing classes. How explicit does it need to be? *Journal of Second Language Writing* 10: 161–84.

Firbas, J. (1986) On the dynamics of written communication in light of the theory of functional sentence perspective. In C. Cooper and S. Greenbaum (eds), *Studying writing: linguistic approaches* (pp. 40–71). London: Sage.

Flower, L. (1989) Cognition, context and theory building. *College Composition and Communication*, 40: 282–311.

Flower, L. and Hayes, J. (1981) A cognitive process theory of writing. *College Composition and Communication*, 32: 365–87.

Flower, L., Stein, V., Ackerman, J., Kantz, M., McCormick, K. and Peck, W. (1990) *Reading-to-write: exploring a social and cognitive process.* Oxford: Oxford University Press.

Flowerdew, J. (2002) Ethnographically inspired approaches to the study of academic discourse. In J. Flowerdew (ed.), *Academic discourse* (pp. 235–52). London: Longman.

Freedman, A. (1994) Anyone for tennis? In A. Freedman and P. Medway (eds), *Genre and the new rhetoric* (pp. 43–66). London: Taylor & Francis.

Freedman, A. and Adam, C. (2000) Write where you are: situating learning to write in university and workplace settings. P. Dias and A. Pare (eds), *Transitions: writing in academic and workplace settings* (pp. 31–60). Creskill, NJ: Hampton Press.

Freedman, A. and Medway, P. (1994) *Genre and the new rhetoric.* London: Taylor & Francis.

Geertz, C. (1973) Thick description: toward an interpretive theory of culture. In C. Geertz (ed.), *The interpretation of cultures: selected essays* (pp. 3–30). New York: Basic Books.

Gere, A. (1987) *Writing groups: history, theory, and implications.* Carbondale, IL: Southern Illinois University Press.

Gibbons, P. (2002) *Scaffolding language; scaffolding learning.* Portsmouth, NH: Heinemann.

Grabe, W. (2003) Reading and writing relations: second language perspectives on research and practice. In B. Kroll (ed.), *Exploring the dynamics of second language writing* (pp. 242–62). Cambridge: Cambridge University Press.

Grabe, W. and Kaplan, R. (1996) *Theory and practice of writing.* Harlow: Longman.

Graves, D. (1984) *A researcher learns to write.* London: Heinemann.

Grice, H.P. (1975) Logic and conversation. In P. Cole and J. Morgan (eds), *Syntax and semantics*, vol. 3, *Speech acts* (pp. 41–58). New York: Academic Press.

Hafner, C.A. and Candlin, C.N. (2007) Corpus tools as an affordance to learning in professional legal education. *Journal of English for Academic Purposes*, 6(4): 303–18.

Halliday, M.A.K. (1985) *Spoken and written language.* Oxford: Oxford University Press.

Halliday, M.A.K. (1998) Things and relations: regrammaticising experience as technical knowledge. In J.R. Martin and R. Veel (eds), *Reading science* (pp. 185–235). London: Routledge.

Halliday, M.A.K. and Matthiessen, C. (2004) *An introduction to functional grammar*, 3rd edn. London: Edward Arnold.

Hamilton, M. (2000) Expanding the new literacy studies: using photographs to explore literacy as social practice. In D. Barton, M. Hamilton and R. Ivanic (eds), *Situated literacies: reading and writing in context* (pp. 16–34). London: Routledge.

Hamp-Lyons, L. and Condon, W. (1993) Questioning assumptions about portfolio-based assessment. *College Composition and Communication*, 44(2): 176–90.

Hamp-Lyons, L. and Condon, W. (2000) *Assessing the portfolio: principles for practice, theory and research*. Cresskill, NJ: Hampton Press.

Hatch, E. and Lazaraton, A. (1991) *The research manual*. Boston, MA: Heinle & Heinle.

Heath, S. (1983) *Ways with words: language life and work in communities and classrooms*. Cambridge: Cambridge University Press.

Helms-Park, R. and Stapleton, P. (2003) Questioning the importance of individualized voice in undergraduate L2 argumentative writing: an empirical study with pedagogical implications. *Journal of Second Language Writing*, 12(3): 245–65.

Herring, S. (1999) Interactional coherence in CMC. *Journal of Computer-Mediated Communication*, 4(4). http://jcmc.indiana.edu/vol4/issue4/herring.html

Hinds, J. (1987) Reader versus writer responsibility: a new typology. In U. Connor and R.B. Kaplan (eds), *Writing across languages: analysis of L2 text*. Reading, MA: Addison Wesley.

Hinkel, E. (1994) Native and nonnative speakers' pragmatic interpretations of English texts. *TESOL Quarterly*, 28(2): 353–76.

Hitchcock, G. and Hughes, D. (1995) *Research and the teacher*. London: Routledge.

Hoey, M. (1983) *On the surface of discourse*. London: Allen & Unwin.

Hoey, M. (2001) *Textual interaction: an introduction to written text analysis*. London: Routledge.

Holst, J.K. (1995) *Writ 101: Writing English*. Wellington, NZ: Victoria University Press.

Horner, B. and Trimbur, J. (2002) English only and college composition. *College Composition and Communication*, 53(4): 594–630.

Horrowitz, D. (1986) What professors actually require: academic tasks for the ESL classroom. *TESOL Quarterly*, 20(3): 445–62.

Hyland, F. (1998) The impact of teacher written feedback on individual writers. *Journal of Second Language Writing*, 7(3): 255–86.

Hyland, K. (1993) ESL computer writers: what can we do to help? *System*, 21(1): 21–30.

Hyland, K. (2002) Options of identity in academic writing. *ELT Journal*, 56(4): 351–58.

Hyland, K. (2003) *Second language writing*. New York: Cambridge University Press.

Hyland, K. (2004a) *Disciplinary discourses: social interactions in academic writing*. Ann Arbor, MI: University of Michigan Press.

Hyland, K. (2004b) Graduates' gratitude: the generic structure of dissertation acknowledgements. *English for Specific Purposes*, 23(3): 303–24.

Hyland, K. (2004c) *Genre and second language writing*. Ann Arbor, MI: University of Michigan Press.

Hyland, K. (2005) *Metadiscourse*. London: Continuum.

Hyland, K. (2008) As can be seen: lexical bundles and disciplinary variation. *English for Specific Purposes*, 27(1): 4–21.

Hyland, K. and Hyland, F. (1992) Go for gold: integrating process and product in ESP. *English for Specific Purposes*, 11: 225–42.

Hyland, K. and Hyland, F. (eds) (2006) *Feedback in second language writing: contexts and issues*. New York: Cambridge University Press.

Hyland, K. and Tse, P. (2007) Is there an 'academic vocabulary'? *TESOL Quarterly*, 41(2): 235–54.

Hyon, S. (1996) Genre in three traditions: implications for ESL. *TESOL Quarterly*, 30(4): 693–722.

Ivanic, R. (1998) *Writing and identity: the discoursal construction of identity in academic writing*. Amsterdam: John Benjamins.

Ivanic, R. and Weldon, S. (1999) Researching the writer–reader relationship. In C.N. Candlin and K. Hyland (eds), *Writing: texts, processes and practices* (pp. 168–92). Harlow: Longman.

Jarratt, S., Losh, E. and Puente, D. (2006) Transnational identifications: biliterate writers in a first-year humanities course. *Journal of Second Language Writing*, 15(1): 24–48.

Jenkins, S., Jordan, M. and Weiland, P. (1993) The role of writing in graduate engineering education. *English for Specific Purposes*, 12: 51–67.

Johns, A.M. (1997) *Text, role and context: developing academic literacies*. Cambridge: Cambridge University Press.

Johns, A.M. (ed.) (2001) *Genre and pedagogy*. Hillsdale, NJ: Erlbaum.

Johns, A.M. (ed.) (2002) *Genre and the classroom*. Mahwah, NJ: Erlbaum.

Johns, A., Bawashi, A., Coe, R., Hyland, K., Paltridge, B., Reiff, M. and Tardy, C. (2006) Crossing the boundaries of genres studies: commentaries by experts. *Journal of Second Language Writing*, 15(3): 234–49.

Jones, K. (2000) Becoming just another alphanumeric code: farmers' encounters with the literacy and discourse practices of agricultural bureaucracy at the livestock auction. In D. Barton, M. Hamilton and R. Ivanic (eds), *Situated literacies* (pp. 70–90). London: Routledge.

Jones, R.H., Garralda, A., Li, D.C.S. and Lock, G. (2006) Interactional dynamics in on-line and face-to-face peer-tutoring sessions for second language writers. *Journal of Second Language Writing* 15, 1, pp. 1–23.

Jordan, B. (1998) *English for academic purposes*. Cambridge: CUP.

Kachru, Y. (1999) Culture, context and writing. In E. Hinkel (ed.), *Culture in second language teaching and learning* (pp. 75–89). Cambridge: Cambridge University Press.

Kaplan, R. (1966) Cultural thought patterns in intercultural education. *Language Learning* 16(1): 1–20.

Killingsworth, M.J. and Gilbertson, M.K. (1992) *Signs, genres, and communication in technical communication*. Amityville, NY: Baywood.

Knapp, P. and Watkins, M. (1994) *Context, text, grammar*. Broadway, NSW: Text Productions.

Kramsch, C. (1993) *Context and culture in language teaching*. Oxford: Oxford University Press.

Kramsch, C. (1997) Rhetorical models of understanding. In T. Miller (ed.), *Functional approaches to written text: classroom applications* (pp. 50–63). Washington, DC: USIA.

Kress, G. (2003) *Literacy in the New Media age*. London: Routledge.

Kress, G. and van Leeuwen, T. (2006) *Reading images: the grammar of visual design*, 2nd edn. London: Routledge.

Krishnamurthy, S. (2005) A demonstration of the futility of using Microsoft Word's spelling and grammar check. *http://faculty.washington.edu/sandeep/check/*. Accessed 2/12/2008.

Krishnamurthy, R. and Kosem, I. (2007) Issues in creating a corpus for EAP pedagogy and research. *Journal of English for Academic Purposes*, 6(4): 356–73.

Kroll, B. (ed.) (2003) *Exploring the dynamics of second language writing*. Cambridge: Cambridge University Press.

Kubota, R. (1998) Ideologies of English in Japan. *World Englishes*, 17: 295–306.

Kuiken, F. and Vedder, I. (2008) Cognitive task complexity and written output in Italian and French as a foreign language. *Journal of Second Language Writing*, 17(1): 48–60.

Lantolf, J.P. (1999) Second culture acquisition: cognitive consideration's. In E. Hinkel (ed.), *Culture in second language teaching and learning* (pp. 28–46). Cambridge: Cambridge University Press.

Lave, J. and Wenger, E. (1991) *Situated learning: legitimate peripheral participation*. Cambridge: Cambridge University Press.

Lecercle, J.-J. (2000) *Interpretation as pragmatics*. London: Palgrave.

Lee, G. and Schallert, D. (2008) Meeting in the margins: effects of the teacher–student relationship on revision processes of EFL college students taking a composition course. *Journal of Second Language Writing*, 17(3): 165–82.

Leech, G. (1997) Teaching and language corpora: a convergence. In A. Wichmann *et al.* (eds), *Teaching and language corpora* (pp. 1–24). Harlow: Longman.

Leech, G. (1998) Preface. In S. Granger (ed.), *Learner English on computer* (pp. xiv–xx). Harlow: Longman.

Leki, I. (1997) Cross-talk: ESL issues and contrastive rhetoric. In C. Severino, J. Guerra and J. Butler (eds), *Writing in multicultural settings* (pp. 234–44). New York: Modern Languages Assn.

Lewis, M. and Wray, D. (1997) *Writing frames*. Reading: NCLL.

Liebman, J.D. (1992) Toward a new contrastive rhetoric: differences between Arabic and Japanese rhetorical instruction. *Journal of Second Language Writing*, 1(2): 141–66.

Lo, J. and Hyland, F. (2007) Enhancing students' engagement and motivation in writing: the case of primary students in Hong Kong. *Journal of Second language Writing*, 16(4): 219–37.

Louhiala-Salminen, L. (2002) The fly's perspective: discourse in the daily routine of a business manager. *English for Specific Purposes*, 21(3): 211–31.

Lundstrom, K. and Baker, W. (2009) To give is better than to receive: the benefits of peer review to the reviewer's own writing. *Journal of Second language Writing*, 18(1): 30–43.

Malinowski, W. (1949) The problem of meaning in primitive languages. In A. Ogden and C. Richards (eds), *The meaning of meaning: a study of influence of language upon thought and of the science of symbolism*. London: Routledge and Kegan Paul.

Marefat, F. (2002) The impact of diary analysis on teaching/learning writing. *RELC Journal*, 33(1): 101–21.

Martin, J.R. (1992) *English text: system and structure*. Amsterdam: John Benjamins.

Martin, J.R. (1993) Genre and literacy – modeling context in educational linguistics. In W. Grabe (ed.), *Annual review of applied linguistics*, 13 (pp. 141–72). Cambridge: Cambridge University Press.

Martin, J.R., Christie, F. and Rothery, J. (1987) Social processes in education: a reply to Sawyer and Watson (and others). In I. Reid (ed.), *The place of genre in learning: current debates* (pp. 58–82). Deakin, Australia: Deakin University Press.

McLeod, C. (1987) Some thoughts about feelings: the affective domain and the writing process. *College Composition and Communication*, 38: 426–35.

Miller, C. (1984) Genre as social action. *Quarterly Journal of Speech*, 70: 157–78.

Milton, J. (1997) Providing computerized self-access opportunities for the development of writing skills. In P. Benson, and P. Voller (eds), *Autonomy and independence in language learning* (pp. 204–14). Harlow: Longman.

Milton, J. (1999) *Wordpilot 2000* (computer program). Hong Kong: CompuLang.

Milton, J. (2006) Resource-rich web-based feedback: helping learners become independent writers. In K. Hyland and F. Hyland (eds) *Feedback in second language writing* (pp. 123–39). Cambridge: Cambridge University Press.

Moffett, J. (1982) Writing, inner speech and mediation. *College English*, 44: 231–44.

Murray, D. (1985) *A writer teaches writing*, 2nd edn. Boston, MA: Houghton Mifflin.

Myers, G. (1988) The social construction of science and the teaching of English: an example of research. In P. Robinson (ed.), *Academic writing: process and product* (pp. 143–50). Basingstoke: Modern English Publications.

Nation, I.S.P. (2001) *Learning vocabulary in another language*. New York: Cambridge University Press.

Nelson, G. and Carson, J. (1998) ESL students' perceptions of effectiveness in peer response groups. *Journal of Second Language Writing*, 7(2): 113–31.

North, S. (1987) *The making of knowledge in composition*. London: Heinemann.

Nystrand, M. (1987) The role of context in written communication. In R. Horowitz, and S.J. Samuels (eds), *Comprehending oral and written language* (pp. 197–214). San Diego, CA: Academic Press.

Nystrand, M. (1989) A social interactive model of writing. *Written Communication*, 6: 66–85.

Nystrand, M., Doyle, A. and Himley, M. (1986) A critical examination of the doctrine of autonomous texts. In M. Nystrand (ed.), *The structure of written communication* (pp. 81–107). Orlando, FL: Academic Press.

Nystrand, M., Greene, S. and Wiemelt, J. (1993) Where did composition studies come from? An intellectual history. *Written Communication*, 19: 267–333.

O'Regan, D. (2003) *Vocabulary*. http://www.bilkent.edu.tr/%7Eodavid/Vocabulary/vocabularyhome.html

Pare, A. (2000) Writing as a way into social work: genre sets, genre systems, and distributed cognition. In P. Dias and A. Pare (eds), *Transitions: writing in academic and workplace settings* (pp. 145–66). Kresskill, NJ: Hampton Press.

Park, D. (1982) The meanings of 'audience'. *College English*, 44(3): 247–57.

Partington, A. (1998) *Patterns and meanings: using corpora for English language research and teaching*. Amsterdam: John Benjamins.

Patton, M. (1990) *Qualitative Evaluation and Research Methods*, California: Sage.

Pecorari, D. (2008) *Academic writing and plagiarism*. A linguistic analysis. London: Continuum.

Phillipson, R. (1992) *Linguistic imperialism*. Oxford: Oxford University Press.

Pica, T. (1987) Second language acquisition, interaction and the classroom. *Applied Linguistics*, 8: 3–21.

Pierce, B.N. (1995) Social identity, investment, and language learning. *TESOL Quarterly*, 29(1): 9–31.

Pole, C. and Morrison, M. (2003) *Ethnography for education*. Maidenhead: Open University / McGraw Hill.

Polio, C. (1997) Measures of linguistic accuracy in second language writing research. *Language Learning*, 47: 101–43.

Polio, C. and Glew, M. (1996) ESL writing assessment prompts: how students choose. *Journal of Second Language Writing*, 5(1): 35–49.

Prior, P. (1998) *Writing/disciplinarity: a sociohistoric account of literate activity in the academy*. Hillsdale, NJ: Lawrence Erlbaum.

Purves, A.C.E., Quattrini, J. and Sullivan, C. (eds) (1995) *Creating the writing portfolio*. Lincolnwood, IL: NTC.

Raimes, A. (1987) Language proficiency, writing ability and composing strategies. *Language Learning*, 37: 439–68.

Ramanathan, V. and Atkinson, D. (1999a) Individualism, academic writing, and ESL writers. *Journal of Second Language Writing*, 8(1): 45–75.

Ramanathan, V. and Atkinson, D. (1999b) Ethnographic approaches and methods in L2 writing research: a critical guide and review. *Applied Linguistics*, 20(1): 44–70.

Reid, J. (1993) *Teaching ESL writing*. Englewood Cliffs, NJ: Prentice Hall.

Roen, D. and Willey, R. (1988) The effects of audience awareness on drafting and revising. *Research in the Teaching of English*, 22(1): 75–88.

Rohman, D.G. (1965) Pre-writing: the stage of discovery in the writing process. *College Composition and Communication*, 16: 106–12.

Rothery, J. (1986) Teaching genre in the primary school: a genre-based approach to the development of writing abilities. In *Writing project-report 1986* (pp. 3–62). Sydney: University of Sydney, Department of Linguistics.

Russell, D.R. (1997) Rethinking genre in school and society: an activity theory analysis. *Written Communication*, 14(4): 504–54.

Scardamalia, M. and Bereiter, C. (1986) Research on written composition. In M. Wittrock (ed.), *Handbook of research on teaching* (pp. 778–803). New York: Macmillan.

Schank, R. and Abelson, R. (1977) *Scripts, plans, goals and understanding*. Hillsdale, NJ: Lawrence Erlbaum.

Schmitt, D. and Schmitt, N. (2005) *Focus on vocabulary: mastering the academic word list*. London: Longman.

Schriver, K. (1992) Teaching writers to anticipate readers' needs. *Written Communication*, 9(2): 179–208.

Scollon, R. and Scollon, S. (1981) *Narrative, literacy and face in interethnic communication*. Norwood, NJ: Ablex.

Scribner, S. and Cole, M. (1981) *The psychology of literacy*. London: Harvard University Press.

Shannon, C. and Weaver, W. (1963) *Mathematical theory of communication*. Champaign, IL: University of Illinois Press.

Shaw, P. and Liu, E. (1998) What develops in the development of second-language writing? *Applied Linguistics*, 19(2): 225–54.

Shuman, A. (1993) Collaborative writing: appropriating power or reproducing authority? In B. Street (ed.), *Cross-cultural approaches to literacy* (pp. 247–71). Cambridge: Cambridge University Press.

Silva, T. (1993) Toward an understanding of the distinct nature of L2 writing: the ESL research and its implications. *TESOL Quarterly*, 27: 665–77.

Sinclair, J. (1991) *Corpus, concordance collocation*. Oxford: Oxford University Press.

Skills for life network (2008) http://www.skillsforlifenetwork.com/default.aspx

Smagorinsky, P. (ed.) (1994) *Speaking about writing: reflections on research methodology*. London: Sage.

Snyder, I. (ed.) (1998) *Page to screen: taking literacy into the electronic era*. London: Routledge.

Song, M.-J. and Suh, B.-R. (2008) The effects of output task types on noticing and learning of the English past counterfactual conditional. *System*, 36(2): 295–312.

Sperber, D. and Wilson, D. (1986) *Relevance: communication and cognition*. Oxford: Basil Blackwell.

Stake, R. (1995) *The art of case study research*. Thousand Oaks, CA: Sage.

Stapleton, P. (2003) Assessing the quality and bias of web-based sources: implications for academic writing. *Journal of English for Academic Purposes*, 2(3): 229–45.

Storch, N. (2005) Collaborative writing: product, process, and students' reflections. *Journal of Second Language Writing*, 14(3): 153–73.

Street, B. (1995) *Social literacies*. Harlow: Longman.

Street, B. and Lefstein, A. (2008) *Literacy: an advanced resource book*. London: Routledge.

Sullivan, K. and Lindgren, E. (eds) (2006) *Computer keystroke logging and writing*. London: Elsevier.

Swales, J. (1990) *Genre analysis: English in academic and research settings*. Cambridge: Cambridge University Press.

Swales, J. (1998) *Other floors, other voices: a textography of a small university building*. Hillsdale, NJ: Lawrence Erlbaum.

Swales, J. (1999) How to be brave in EAP: teaching writing in today's research world. *Proceedings of Languages for Specific Purposes Forum, 1999*.

Swales, J. and Feak, C. (2004) *Academic writing for graduate students: essential tasks and skills*, 2nd edn. Ann Arbor, MI: University of Michigan Press.

Swales, J. and Feak, C. (2000) *English in today's research world: a writing guide*. Ann Arbor, MI: University of Michigan Press.

Teo, P. (2000) Racism in the news: a critical discourse analysis of news reporting in two Australian newspapers. *Discourse and Society*, 11: 7–49.

Tottie, G. (1991) *Negation in English speech and writing*. London: Academic Press.

Truscott, J. and Hsu, A. (2008) Error correction, revision, and learning. *Journal of Second Language Writing*, 17(4): 292–305.

Tsang, W. (1996) Comparing the effects of reading and writing on writing performance. *Applied Linguistics*, 17(2): 210–33.

Tsui, A.B.M. (1996) Learning how to teach ESL writing. In D. Freeman and J.C. Richards (eds), *Teacher learning and language teaching* (pp. 97–119). Cambridge: Cambridge University Press.

Turkle, S. (1995) *Life on the screen: identity in the age of the internet*. New York: Simon and Shuster.

Tyner, K. (ed.) (1998) *Literacy in a digital world: teaching and learning in the age of information*. Hillsdale, NJ: Lawrence Erlbaum.

Van Den Bergh, H. and Rijlaarsdam, G. (2001) Changes in cognitive activities during the writing process and relationships with text quality. *Educational psychology*, 21(4): 373–85.

Van Dijk, T.A. (2008) *Discourse and context: a sociocognitive approach*. Cambridge: Cambridge University Press.

Vygotsky, L. (1962) *Thought and language*. Cambridge, MA: MIT Press.

Vygotsky, L. (1978) *Mind in society: the development of higher psychological processes* (M. Cole, V. John-Steiner, S. Scribner and E. Souberman (eds)). Cambridge, MA: Harvard University Press.

Wallace, M.J. (1998) *Action research for language teachers*. Cambridge: Cambridge University Press.

Ware, P. and Warshauer, M. (2006) Electronic feedback. In K. Hyland and F. Hyland (eds), *Feedback in second language writing* (pp. 105–22). Cambridge: Cambridge University Press.

Watson-Gegeo, K. (1988) Ethnography in ESL: defining the essentials. *TESOL Quarterly*, 22: 575–92.

Weissberg, R. (2006) *Connecting speaking and writing.* Ann Arbor, MI: University of Michigan Press.

Wertsch, J. (1991) *Voices of the mind.* Cambridge, MA: Harvard University Press.

White, A. (2007) A tool for monitoring the development of written English: T-unit analysis using the SAWL. *American Annals of the Deaf*, 152(1): 29–41.

Wichmann, A., Fligelstone, S., McEnery, T. and Knowles, G. (eds) (1997) *Teaching and language corpora.* Harlow: Longman.

Widdowson, H. (2000) The theory and practice of critical discourse analysis. *Applied Linguistics*, 19: 136–51.

Willett, J. (1995) Becoming first-graders in an L2: an ethnographic study of L2 socialization. *TESOL Quarterly*, 29(3): 473–503.

Williams, R. (1962) *Communications.* Harmondsworth: Penguin.

Winter, E.O. (1977) A clause relational approach to English texts: a study of some predictive lexical items in written discourse. *Instructional Science*, 6(1): 1–92.

Wodak, R. and Chilton, P. (eds) (2007) *A new agenda in (critical) discourse analysis*, 2nd edn. Amsterdam: Benjamins.

Wodak, R. (1996) *Disorders of discourse.* Harlow: Longman.

Wong, A.T.Y. (2005) Writers' mental representations of the intended audience and of the rhetorical purpose for writing and the strategies that they employed when they composed. *System*, 33(1): 29–47.

Wray, D. and Lewis, M. (1997) *Extending literacy: children reading and writing non-fiction.* London: Routledge.

Xue, G. and Nation, I.S.P. (1984) A university word list. *Language Learning and Communication*, 3(2): 215–99.

Yancey, K.B. (1999) Looking back as we look forward: historicizing writing assessment. *College Composition and Communication*, 50(3): 483–503.

Yang, H. (1986) A new technique for identifying scientific/technical terms and describing science texts. *Literacy and Linguistic Computing*, 1: 93–103.

Young, L. and Harrison, C. (2004) Introduction. In L. Young and C. Harrison (eds), *Systemic functional linguistics and critical discourse analysis* (pp. 1–11). London: Continuum.

Yi, Y. (2007) Engaging literacy: a biliterate student's composing practices beyond school. *Journal of Second Language Writing*, 16(1): 23–39.

Zamel, V. (1983) The composing processes of advanced ESL students: six case-studies. *TESOL Quarterly*, 17: 165–87.

Zhu, W. and Flaitz, J. (2005) Using focus group methodology to understand international students' academic language needs: a comparison of perspectives. *TESOL-EJ*, 8(4): A–3.

Author Index

Subject Index

Academic Word List (AWL), 115–18
Action research, 140–1, 162–3, 183, 202
affordances, 59, 161, 226
Assessment, 84–5, 94, 100, 104, 110, 113, 123, 128–34, 143, 233, 244, 246
audience, 8, 11, 17, 24, 30–3, 65–6, 71, 77, 79, 80, 83, 84, 88, 96–101, 107, 119, 133, 160–2, 166, 167, 172, 175–9, 189, 194, 211, 216, 217, 219, 220, 243, 245
Autonomous texts, 8–12, 18, 31, 53, 128

CARS Model, 66
Case study research, 146, 151
Check My Words, 122–5
Cognitive view of writing, 18–26, 30–3, 70, 105, 119, 141, 147, 176, 214, 234
cohesion and coherence, 34, 121, 133, 243, 244
collocation, 116, 244
Computer Mediated Communication, 39, 62, 63, 147
Computer writing, 9, 21, 47, 59, 62, 89, 104, 108–10, 116, 117, 123, 142, 147, 190, 192, 204, 220
conduit metaphor, 10
concordance, 104, 109–13, 126, 127, 192, 238, 239, 244
context, 8–15, 18, 20–2, 25–9, 32–5, 38–9, 44–50, 53, 57, 63, 68, 71–2, 78, 86, 88, 91, 95, 97, 100–3, 110, 129, 134, 141–6, 150–9, 162, 167, 169, 176, 178–9, 185, 190, 194–9, 201, 202, 205, 206, 210–15, 218–20, 224, 244–6
contrastive rhetoric, 54, 55, 57, 190, 217, 244
corpora, 9, 13, 108–16, 134, 150, 153, 185, 187, 190–3, 211, 213, 228, 238, 239, 244
Corpus analysis, 13, 109–14, 150–1, 191

Creative writing, 20, 29, 222–4, 229, 230, 234, 237, 239, 241
Critical Discourse Analysis (CDA), 38–42, 47, 212, 216, 244
Culture, 14–15, 25, 28, 35, 39, 47, 52, 54–7, 63, 71, 107, 152, 192, 201, 203, 221, 222

Daedalus writing software, 22, 239
Diary studies/ process logs, 27, 128, 145, 148, 154, 157, 180–3, 204, 225, 236
Discourse, 12–18, 31, 33, 35, 38–9, 70, 72, 86, 170, 172, 205, 211, 216–17, 222, 227, 234
Discourse community, 15, 33–8, 40, 42, 45, 49, 51–3, 63, 68–9, 71–4, 77–8, 95, 142, 145, 161, 174–5, 186, 189–90, 203, 210, 212, 237, 244–5
drafting, 21–4, 31, 79–81, 84–5, 88, 90, 119, 121, 130, 155, 170, 195, 229, 245–6

editing, 21–4, 58, 61, 81–4, 88, 100, 121, 155, 178, 222, 229, 245–6
Electronic texts, 58–63, 113, 231
English for Academic Purposes (EAP), 9, 36, 52, 57, 104–5, 114, 190, 193, 202, 223–4
English for Specific Purposes (ESP), 65–8, 92–3, 212, 223–4
ESL students, 25, 43, 56, 71, 74, 78, 134, 149, 168–9, 198, 218, 232
Ethnographic research, 27, 50, 68–9, 145, 151, 162, 199, 206, 209–10, 214, 245–6
Experimental research, 22, 140, 144, 146, 150–1, 153, 156, 161, 168–71
Expressivist view of writing 7, 18–20

feedback, 10, 24, 79–87, 91, 93, 96–7, 100, 122–31, 147–8, 151–4, 156–8, 165, 168–71, 178–82, 198–202, 212, 245

An Introduction
to Clinical
Pharmaceutics

Alexander T. Florence Emeritus Professor
The School of Pharmacy, University of London, UK

QV 785
FLORENCE

London • Chicago **Pharmaceutical Press**

Published by Pharmaceutical Press

1 Lambeth High Street, London SE1 7JN, UK
1559 St. Paul Avenue, Gurnee, IL 60031, USA

© Pharmaceutical Press 2010

(PP) is a trade mark of Pharmaceutical Press

Pharmaceutical Press is the publishing division of the Royal Pharmaceutical Society of
Great Britain

First published 2010

Typeset by Thomson Digital, Noida, India
Printed in Great Britain by TJ International, Padstow, Cornwall

ISBN 978 0 85369 691 9

A catalogue record for this book is available from the British Library.

Contents

Preface

This book has had a long period of gestation. I made a proposal for a book such as this in 1982 to Robert Campbell of Blackwell Scientific Publications Ltd. He encouraged me to write it, provided it was 'reasonably short and inexpensive.' Over the intervening years in collaboration with David Attwood, four editions of *Physicochemical Principles of Pharmacy* appeared, the latest in 2006 and the concise version, *FASTtrack: Physical Pharmacy*, in 2008. We also co wrote *Surfactant Systems* published in 1983. These and other activities took over and the present book obviously did not materialise. But it has always remained an ambition to complete it, especially as the pharmacy scene has been changing and some subjects are now under pressure of one kind and another, in spite of the four-year degree programme. A few subjects such as pharmaceutics and pharmaceutical chemistry appear to not a few students to be too far away from real practice. Well it depends on how we define practice and what practice will look like in the future.

The main premise of the book is that the subject matter of pharmaceutics is relevant far beyond the confines of the laboratory and pharmaceutical industry. Undergraduate and postgraduate lectures that I have given over the years incorporated many of the concepts espoused in this book. It was not until retirement from the Deanship of the School of Pharmacy, University of London in 2006 that there was some more time to write this book. It is not meant to be a compendium, nor is it for advanced practitioners, but more a primer that I hope will encourage readers to think about the principles of applying basic scientific facts to solving problems in medication. If it provides a single insight to any student or practitioner that enables the solution of one medication conundrum, it will have been worth it. A warning: it is not written in that linear style that has been the bane of many subjects, as it takes too long from the very first principle to get to the application or the problem. The basics are covered in AT Florence and D Attwood, *Pharmaceutical Principles of Pharmacy*, 4th edition, 2006 or D Attwood and AT Florence, *Physical Pharmacy* 2007, both published by the Pharmaceutical Press.

I thank Louise McIndoe and Charles Fry of Pharmaceutical Press for their encouragement and patience, and my wife Florence for her critiques and support.

Alexander T. Florence
Edzell Angus, UK and Nice, France
2009

Introduction

This book is designed to be an introductory text to aid the understanding of the role of basic pharmaceutics in determining or modifying clinical outcomes. Pharmaceutics is often considered by pharmacy students at least early in their academic career to be relevant only to the design and production of dosage forms. This is one of the keystones of pharmacy, of course. While it goes without saying that dosage forms are vital for the delivery of medication to the body, they are not always inactive vectors. Not only that, not all dosage forms are produced in industry, so there are clinical needs for special formulations, for example those for neonates, that call pharmaceutics knowledge to the fore. However, this is neither a formulation textbook nor a pharmaceutics textbook. What it attempts to do is to connect the concepts that are part of most pharmaceutics curricula, not only issues of formulation but also the underlying phenomena such as surface tension, rheology, solubility, crystallisation, aggregation and adsorption among others, to a wider clinical and practice base. At the same time we discuss here the ways in which formulations, dosage forms and devices as well as excipients can influence the outcome of therapy, not least their infrequent but important ability sometimes to cause adverse events.

Cases and examples from the literature are important learning aids in the book. The cases discussed are not necessarily new: there is much to learn from the lessons and mistakes of the past. The skill of the professional is not to know everything but to recognise when and where to access information and to apply it to new practice situations.

The book is aimed at undergraduate pharmacy students, those on taught Masters courses of clinical and hospital pharmacy, and new practitioners who require an updating on the relevance of the phenomena that are virtually unique to pharmacy. Examples and implications of each phenomenon are discussed with a brief reminder of the underlying pharmaceutics.

A pharmacist's deep knowledge of medicines as physical products helps the patient, the physician and the nurse tackle the increasingly complex world that is medicine today. The Princess Royal, on a visit to the School of Pharmacy as Chancellor of the University of London, when one clinical tutor suggested that we aimed to convert scientists into practitioners said perceptively 'surely it should be the other way round!' It is important for a profession such as pharmacy to have sets of knowledge different from those of other health care professionals. It must also generate its own body of knowledge if it is to remain relevant.

For one reason or another, there has developed a disjunction between the scientific basis of pharmacy, or what were the traditional divisions of the pharmaceutical sciences, and practice. Industrial pharmacy has been the most direct beneficiary of the traditional sciences taught in the traditional manner. Yet only a minority, albeit a vital minority, of graduates practise in industry, and not all do so in formulation research and development. Few schools of pharmacy now have traditional subject divisions. Nevertheless it is sometimes considered, even by those expert in pharmacy education and some students too, that subjects such as pharmaceutical chemistry and pharmaceutical technology have little place in the day-to-day practice of pharmacy. The emphasis on the patient has sometimes obscured the emphasis on the product. Clinical pharmacy as a discipline may major on therapeutics, but we must offer more, else no one will claim more than passing knowledge of the products that are central to pharmacy. Our input must be founded on the basics honed and challenged in the clinical environment of primary and secondary care. The more pharmacists know about the products they handle, the more patients will benefit: if applied to its full there emerges a discipline of clinical pharmaceutics, whence the title of this book, the application of the unique knowledge base in the subject to patients and to clinical situations. Biopharmaceutics has been a surrogate for this practical application. It is of course vital. What we try to tease out here are topics that fall between subject divisions. If we do not retain these skills and apply them more obviously – applying our knowledge of the both the nature of the materials used in formulation and their biological effects or influence – patients lose out.

This small book, then, attempts to place some of the basics of pharmaceutics into the context of clinical practice in its broadest sense: the application of pharmaceutics and some pharmaceutical chemistry to patient care. One must not repeat the mistake of working in subject silos. The administration of a medicine to a patient is the direct application of pharmaceutics, but the issue goes much deeper. We cannot utilise and apply only the knowledge that the physician or the nurse has and act only as watchdogs. Clinical pharmaceutics is not promoted here simply to maintain its academic input, but because it is centrally important, as I hope the examples in the book will demonstrate. It is easy to jettison skills that exist now because of their temporary or apparent disuse: the future of medicine is changing so rapidly that many skills will be required to successfully handle the complexities of modern therapies, not least in some specialist environments, even in the extemporaneous preparation of specialised dosage forms. Possibly the best way to

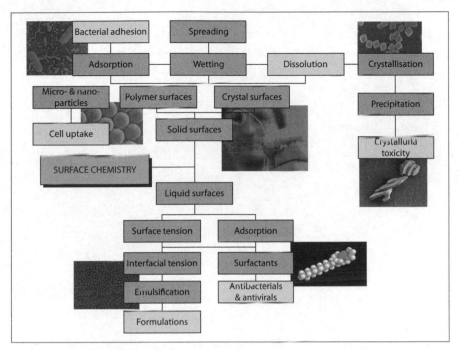

Figure I.1 The ubiquitous importance of one of the basic subjects – surface chemistry – taught in pharmaceutics and physical pharmacy. The areas involved include formulations, cell uptake, antibacterials and antivirals, bacterial adhesion, dissolution and precipitation *in vivo*. Some of these connections are explored in Chapter 1.

illustrate just some of the connections between pharmaceutics and 'real life' is given in the Figure I.1. It refers only to surface chemistry, but we could construct other such diagrams for the other basic areas too.

It is not easy to prepare for a future that is largely unknown. To learn from the experience of the past is beneficial. Whether the approach used in this book is successful remains to be seen. I would be happy to hear from readers of errors in interpretation and new and better examples to illustrate the themes.

Alexander T. Florence
Edzell Angus, UK and Nice, France
2009

Book outline

The first chapter addresses the question 'what is clinical pharmaceutics' using as many examples as possible. Chapter 2 follows with a discussion of excipients, not infrequently inadvertently bioactive substances. Chapter 3 reasserts the view that chemistry is important in the discipline, while Chapter 4 is entitled 'Looking at formulations'. This encourages us to view products in the round, as dose forms to aid in the delivery of reproducible doses but also as agents for irreproducibility on odd occasions and causes of adverse events in a minority. Chapter 5 considers adverse events caused by the dosage form or by excipients, or by the nature of the formulation and the way in which it can influence outcomes. Chapter 6 addresses some issues of medicines for the young and for the old.

Generic medicines are rightly used widely in practice after the expiry of patents on innovator products, although to varying degrees in Europe. Chapter 7 points out the differences in the evaluation of generic medicines when the drug substance is a small molecule and when it is a large biological agent. The latter are forming a larger percentage of the therapeutic arena. Here, for example, we explore the concept of biosimilarity rather than identicality.

Chapter 8 speculates about the future form of medicines and raises the question of the role of pharmaceutics in personalised medicines.

About the author

Alexander T. Florence is Emeritus Professor at The School of Pharmacy, University of London from which he retired as Dean in 2006. Previously he was JP Todd professor of Pharmacy at the University of Strathclyde. His research interests have been in physical pharmacy, pharmaceutics, surfactants and pharmaceutical nanotechnology. He continues to lecture and to write on these subjects and for a long time has sought to better integrate the basic, applied and clinical sciences in pharmacy. He is the co-author with David Attwood of *Physicochemical Principles of Pharmacy* (4th edition 2006) and *FASTtrack: Physical Pharmacy* (1st edition 2008) both published by the Pharmaceutical Press.

1

What is clinical pharmaceutics?

This chapter promotes the view that the fundamentals of pharmaceutics have a wider significance than is sometimes recognised. These fundamentals include among other things concepts of surface tension, adsorption, rheology, crystallisation and solubility. The chapter also underlines that fact that the chemical composition, physical nature and properties of dosage forms have an influence not only on bioavailability but on the quality of action of many drugs. Adverse reactions to medicines, which are a serious problem, are most often and rightly attributed to the drug substance, but they can also be caused or influenced by excipients, including dyes, flavouring agents, stabilisers, electrolytes or solvents. Even the physical form of the dose may be a factor in adverse events, as in the case of non-disintegrating slow-release tablets, which can become trapped in diverticula in the gut, or injections that precipitate on administration. Most of the topics in this introductory chapter, aimed at introducing the field in a general way, will be discussed in more detail later in the book.

Introduction

It is essential that pharmacists know more about the nature of medicines than the public and patients or indeed other health care professionals. It is clear to most practitioners that pharmacology and therapeutics are vital to practice; nonetheless, there has been a tendency to think of pharmaceutics as a subject that is necessary in the undergraduate curriculum but that has little significance to those graduates who will not work in industry or who are not involved in manufacturing in hospitals. It is not claimed here that pharmaceutics is more important than other subjects, but there are at least three aspects of pharmaceutics that should be relevant to practice, perhaps in an unexpected order:

- First, how concepts such as surface tension, crystallinity, precipitation, viscosity, adsorption and solubility are relevant in a range of clinical situations.

- Second, an understanding of the nature of the dosage form and its properties and how these can influence outcomes or modulate or even cause adverse events.
- Third, knowing intimately the nature and properties of the ingredients other than the active substance.

These examples are often important in idiosyncratic reactions to medicines, and more generally in the behaviour of many drugs *in vivo*.

Physical concepts

The last two points listed above are possibly more obvious than the first, so we begin with the topics outlined in the first point to demonstrate some instances where knowledge of these physical parameters can provide insight into medication outcomes and biological behaviour. The phenomenon of crystallisation is a good example.

Crystallisation

Figure 1.1 summarises some of the situations in which the solid state is important. Highlighted are crystalluria, gout, the precipitation of drugs before or after injection, inhalation therapy and understanding the potential toxic effects of particulates.

A case of crystalluria reported recently[1] illustrates one of the propositions put forward in this book. The case concerned a 60-year-old man infected with HIV whose medications included efavirenz, emtricitabine,

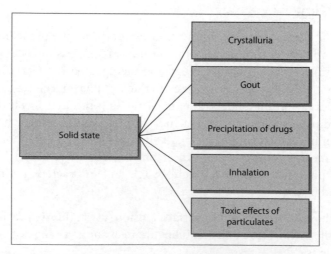

Figure 1.1 Schematic of situations in which the solid state is important.

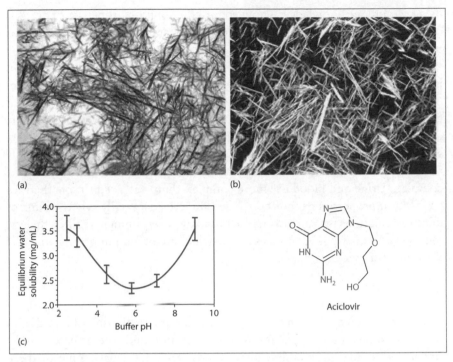

Figure 1.2   (a, b) Photomicrographs of aciclovir crystals harvested from the urine of the patient in question (a) and a pure sample (b). (From reference 1.) (c) The solubility–pH relationship for aciclovir is shown along with its chemical structure. (From reference 2.)

tenofovir and pravastatin sodium: a heady cocktail. Two hours after he had received aciclovir, his urine became cloudy and white in the proximal part of a Foley catheter. Microscopic analysis showed birefringent needle-like crystals 'consistent with the precipitation of acyclovir [aciclovir]' as shown in Figure 1.2. Additional treatment with intravenous aciclovir did not result in urinary crystallisation of the drug. Aciclovir (pK_a values: 2.27 and 9.25) has a solubility in water at 25°C of >100 mg/mL. At physiological pH, aciclovir sodium is un-ionised and has a minimum solubility in water (at 37°C) of 2.5 mg/mL (Figure 1.2b).[2] The concentration of aciclovir in human urine after *oral* administration of 200 mg reaches 7.5 µg/mL,[3] clearly not exceeding its aqueous solubility. As urine is concentrated as it passes along nephrons, urine drug concentrations increase. Determination of saturation solubilities of drugs in urine is more predictive of problems.

While crystallisation of drugs *in vivo* will be discussed later, this case illustrates that a knowledge of the solution properties of drugs and the pH at which drugs might precipitate or become saturated in body fluids and compartments is essential if we are to make contributions to patient care using our unique knowledge. Knowledge of the solution properties of drugs is of course applied directly in the formulation and delivery of intravenous mixtures of drugs or when drugs are added to infusion fluids.

Some time ago an editorial in the *Lancet*[4] discussed the topic of crystals in joints. It pointed out that it is not only in gout that crystals (of monosodium urate monohydrate, or of calcium pyrophosphate in pseudogout) appear but that calcium hydroxyapatite deposits cause apatite deposition disease. The discussion indicated that synovial fluid may contain pieces of cartilage, strands of fibrin, cholesterol crystals and, in some patients, steroid crystals remaining after intra-articular injection. Biological systems are of course complex. Urine and blood are more complex than water, so simple theories of solution properties cannot be applied directly, especially when we introduce formulations into already multicomponent environments. Nevertheless, theory and equations give clues as to what might be happening *in vivo*. Without them we only guess.

Rheology

Rheology, which deals with the flow properties or the viscosity of liquids and semi-solids, has many implications in the function and role of natural substances, such as mucus and synovial fluids. Figure 1.3 lists some of these connections.

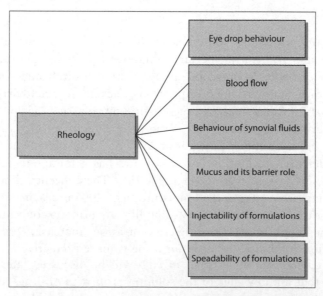

Figure 1.3   Areas in which rheology is important: the spreading and elimination of eye drops; blood flow; synovial fluid performance; mucus as a viscous protectant in the gastrointestinal tract; the injectability of formulations; and the 'spreadability' of formulations, say, on the skin.

The rheology of liquid medications can be important in determining their ease of handling. The viscosities of oily vehicles as depots for long-acting neuroleptics and steroids range from 3.9 cP to 283 cP and can determine their dispersion in muscle. Viscous liquids are retained at sites of administration.

The rheology of creams and ointments can affect patient acceptance and, of course, spreadability: very viscous systems may spread unevenly. The viscosity of ophthalmic preparations has clear implications for comfort and spreading. If the viscosity is too high then the spreading of the drops on the corneal surface is impaired; patients might experience discomfort as eyelids may adhere to the corneal surface.

Viscous solutions of sodium hyaluronate have been used to enhance the nasal absorption of vasopressin.[5] Solutions of hyaluronic acid (HA) with molecular weights greater than 3×10^5 Da have been found to be effective, while HA with a molecular weight of 5.5×10^4 Da was not as effective. The viscosity of hyaluronate solutions and many other materials can be selected according to the mean molecular weight. Viscosity increases with increasing molecular weight, larger macromolecule fractions having higher viscosities. Macromolecule concentration and added salt concentrations also affect the flow of these systems, the latter through changing the net surface charge on the molecules. Increasing concentrations of polymer increase viscosity. Increasing electrolyte concentrations can increase or decrease viscosity depending on whether the polymer is charged or not. There are biological implications of macromolecular viscosity as discussed below.

Synovial fluid acts as a lubricant between adjacent joints. The properties of synovial fluid that contribute to this biological function include its viscoelasticity (see Box 1.1). In osteoarthritis, hyaluronan in the form of sodium hyaluronate, with a molecular weight of some 10^6 Da, is injected into the synovial joint space. The product supplements the natural lubricant fluids. The molecule is highly folded in the absence of shear, but with increasing shear the molecule unfolds and has the characteristics of a pseudoplastic material (see Box 1.1). Products such as Fermathron comprise a clear solution of 1% hyaluronate in phosphate-buffered saline.

Intra-articular hyaluronic acid

Synovial fluid is rheopexic, which, as stated in Box 1.1, means that stress increases with time in steady shear. This is thought to be due to protein aggregation with time and the influence of stress. It is suggested that there is a connection between the observed rheopexy and the remarkable lubrication properties of synovial fluid;[6] one can envisage that the fluid that exists between two bony surfaces becomes more effective in 'cushioning' the contacts as its viscosity increases with the forces placed on it.

Products such as Hyalgan, Artzal, Synvisc, Suplasyn, Hyalart and Orthovisc have been developed for administration into the synovial space

> *Box 1.1 Rheological terms and descriptors*
>
> - **Newtonian** and **non-Newtonian** liquids:
>   Viscosity $\eta = $ shear stress (τ)/rate of shear (γ).
>   Shear-thinning systems are termed **pseudoplastic** while shear-thickening systems are known as **dilatant**.
> - **Thixotropic** systems show a decrease in apparent viscosity when stirred at a constant rate over a period of time. In **rheopexic** systems viscosity builds up with time on stirring at a constant shear.
> - **Viscoelasticity** is the property of materials that exhibit both *viscous* and *elastic* characteristics when undergoing *deformation*. Viscous materials, like honey, resist *shear flow* and *strain* linearly with time when a stress is applied. Elastic materials strain instantaneously when stretched and quickly return to their original state once the stress is removed. Viscoelastic materials have elements of both these properties.

of joints to enhance the activity of the natural synovial fluid. The perception that higher-molecular-weight HA is superior to lower-molecular-weight (MW) species is based on the suggestion that high-molecular-weight HA normalises synovial fluid and results in effective joint lubrication. However, it is claimed[7] that there is little evidence from a meta-analysis of clinical trials to support these ideas. Higher-molecular-weight HA are chemically cross-linked forms and are claimed to have a greater residence time in the joints.[8] *In vivo*, HA with a higher viscosity has been found to be more effective in lubricating joints.[9] There is some controversy about modes of action. It has also been suggested that viscoelasticity does not in fact form the foundation of the beneficial properties of these injections.[10] This point is added because explanations of the behaviour of complex systems are fraught with confounding factors. One must, however, speculate from a reasoned base when necessary. It is highly reasonable to conclude that one of the important properties of hyaluronan and hyaluronan solutions is their pseudoplastic behaviour. These then serve as lubricants when joint movements are slow and as shock absorbers when movements are fast.[11] In *ex vivo* experiments, HA with higher viscosity was more effective in lubricating joints.

Viscous solutions and disorders of the eye

Sodium hyaluronate, chondroitin sulfate and methylcellulose have been compared for maintaining the form of the anterior chamber of the eye.[12] The rheological characteristics of the polymers used in the anterior chamber are

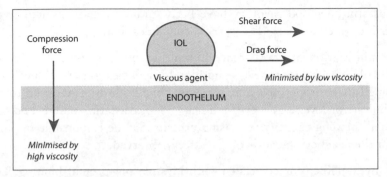

Figure 1.4 A schematic diagram of the forces on an intraocular lens (IOL). The applied force on the IOL is represented by two vectors: the compression force and the shear forces. High viscosity transmits more of the shear force to the endothelial surface. The compression force is minimised by a high viscosity (note the similarity to synovial fluid) and the drag force is minimised by low viscosity.

key. Pseudoplastic fluids are ideal for maintaining the chamber since they are more viscous at rest. Sodium hyaluronate and methylcellulose are pseudoplastic, while chondroitin sulfate displays Newtonian flow properties.

High viscosity is critical when the agent is applied in a thick layer to prevent mechanical damage to the corneal epithelium when an intraocular lens is drawn across the endothelium. Compression and shear are responsible for the damage:[12] thin layers of highly viscous HA convey the shear forces to the endothelium, whereas thick layers provide a physical barrier to compression, as can be seen in Fig. 1.4. Clearly there are analogies to synovial fluid here.

Optiflex is an ophthalmic product containing sodium hyaluronate with a molecular weight of 4×10^6 Da in a sterile isotonic vehicle. When injected through a cannula it becomes less viscous, but it regains its viscosity in the anterior chamber of the eye. It is used for lubrication and protection of cells and tissue during surgical procedures.

In the extreme, viscosity also affects drop size (though surface tension is the primary determinant of size, as we will see later). The ideal viscosity of ophthalmic solutions has been suggested to be between 15 and 30 mPa s, as this does not affect drop formation or delivery but offers better retention in the eye. More viscous systems blur vision as they can inhibit blinking. In general, solutions that possess pseudoplastic behaviour offer less resistance to the movement of the eyelids and are more comfortable than Newtonian liquids.[13]

Effect of drug lipophilicity on blood rheology

High dose intravenous (IV) immunoglobulin therapy increases blood viscosity to an extent that can impair blood flow.[14] Blood rheology is complex, affected by patient age, exercise and various pathologies. The binding of drugs to fibrinogen can increase blood viscosity. The effects of pravastatin and simvastatin on blood rheology have been studied in patients with type II hyperlipoproteinaemia.[15] This work[15] concludes that:

> administration of pravastatin sodium, but not simvastatin, reduced the plasma fibrinogen levels and blood viscosities to normal levels in type II hyperlipoproteinemic patients while both drugs reduced total cholesterol levels. The hydrophilicity of pravastatin sodium and its small binding capacity to plasma protein may be responsible in part for the beneficial hemorheologic effects observed.

Here hydrophilicity is correlated with low plasma protein binding. Lovastatin, simvastatin, atorvastatin, fluvastatin and cerivastatin are hydrophobic statins. At physiological pH (7–7.4) the relative lipophilicity of various statins currently in clinical use follows the order simvastatin ≈ cerivastatin > lovastatin ≈ fluvastatin ≈ atorvastatin >> pravastatin. Pravastatin is 70–300 times more hydrophilic than the other statins.[16]

Pravastatin

Lovastatin

Fluvastatin

The relative hydrophobicities of drug molecules cannot always be determined visually from their structures, as there are other determinants of solubility such as hydrogen bonding and the cohesion of the crystals. Lovastatin's methyl substituent instead of a pravastatin's hydroxyl is one clue; the structure of fluvastatin is quite different but contains the very hydrophobic fluorine substituent. Lipophilic and non-lipophilic statins have different metabolic pathways, the former using the CYP3A4 pathway, while the latter do not utilise the CYP pathway.

Surface tension, wetting and de-wetting

Surfaces and interfaces are ubiquitous. They may be solid, such as the surface of workbenches, or be flexible or hard plastics like catheters and giving sets. The cell membrane is an also interface. The corneal epithelium is a surface. Wherever there are surfaces, surface active molecules and many lipids will adsorb to them. Many formulations such as emulsions, suspensions and creams depend on surfactants for their formation and stability. There are surface-active drugs (including the phenothiazines, some local anaesthetics) that interact with membranes because of their amphipathic structure. Bacteriostatic and bactericidal excipients like benzalkonium chloride and similar molecules are also surface active. In eye drops these molecules not only perform their primary function but can also adsorb onto hydrogel contact lenses and at the tear film–corneal interface. Adsorption onto hydrogel contact lens polymers can lead to the slow release of these molecules and to eye damage.

Figure 1.5 summarises the ubiquity of surface tension and surface chemical effects, from formulation, surface-active drugs and excipients, through lung

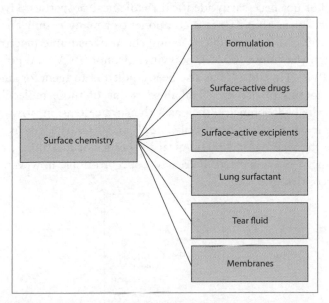

Figure 1.5 A simplified version of the diagram shown in the Introduction (p. xiii). Surface chemistry is important directly in formulation, in understanding surfactants and surface-active drugs and excipients, natural surfactants as in the lung and in tears, and the manner in which drugs and excipients interact with membranes.

surfactant and tear fluids. The next section discusses tears and tear films, the behaviour of which involves several surface effects, especially in the presence of materials such as benzalkonium chloride, mentioned above.

Tear fluid

Tears are released from the Meibomian glands in the eye. Tears are important for lubrication of the eye. When we blink the tear film is replenished and re-spread, thus compensating for evaporation of the aqueous film and preventing the drying that would otherwise occur. In some patients, the supply of tear fluid, comprising a largely aqueous solution containing protein, lipids and enzymes, is impaired. Tears spread over the surface of the cornea, which is hydrophobic. The tears contain phospholipids, which act as a surfactant, lowering the surface tension of the fluid and allowing spreading. The thin lipid layer on the surface of the tear film (like most lipid monolayers) also prevents or slows down evaporation of the aqueous medium beneath. Dry eye[17] (xerophthalmia; Sjögren's syndrome) is caused when the tear film thins to such an extent that it ruptures, exposing the corneal surface to the air. Drying out of patches on the corneal surface follows. This can be painful and must be avoided. Evaporation over 5–10 minutes can actually eliminate the tear film completely.[18]

Artificial tear fluids may replace the natural tear fluid with varying degrees of similitude. Most aim for formulations that have an appropriate viscosity, but not necessarily identical rheological properties. Hydroxypropylmethylcellulose (HPMC) is a component of many commercial replacement or 'artificial' tear products, as are the water-soluble macromolecules carboxymethylcellulose (CMC), polyvinyl alcohol (PVA) and polyvinylpyrrolidone (PVP). Trehalose[19] has also been studied as an agent for amelioration of the symptoms of dry eye. Trehalose is one of those molecules which, because of its hydrophilicity, increases the surface tension of water, but at 0.8 mol/L it has a viscosity of only ~2 cP at 30°C. The aim is usually to reproduce the wetting and rheological properties of tear fluids, but in this case wetting is not enhanced. Increased concentrations, however, will have higher viscosities.

Trehalose

The formation and rupture of tear films was explained over 30 years ago by Holly.[18] Eye drops can disrupt the natural tear film, either by the physical

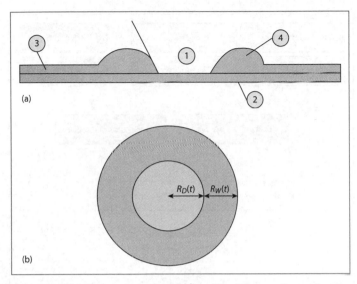

Figure 1.6 (a) Simplified diagram showing a thin liquid film (3) on a surface such as the cornea (2). When the film reaches a critical thickness, instability causes the film to rupture and surface forces pull the film away from that point, leaving an exposed surface (1). The liquid in the film is gathered in a rim (4). The contact angle between the broken film and the corneal surface will be reduced on addition of an agent that lowers surface tension. On the other hand, the adsorption of, say, benzalkonium chloride on the surface, with the onium group towards the negative cells, will render the surface in (1) more hydrophobic, exacerbating the situation. (b) Schematic diagram used to calculate the radial velocity of de-wetting. (Diagram from reference 20.)

action of the drugs they contain or through additives such as benzalkonium chloride. The latter is a component of eye drops but it can be toxic as it is a cationic surfactant (see Chapter 3), and can adsorb onto the corneal surface in dry eye syndrome, rendering the surface even more hydrophobic. The film can then de-wet the surface, thereby exposing the corneal epithelial cells to the air. The process may start at a given point on the corneal surface. A critical thickness for stability is breached and the film breaks, as shown in Figure 1.6.[20]

Dry eye encompasses a number of ophthalmological complaints shown in Figure 1.7.

Tear film formation may be compromised but not necessarily cause clinical problems unless the eyes are challenged with smoke or dust or certain drugs. Contact lenses may also of course affect tear film formation and stability.

Neonates have normal tear fluid but low rates of blinking.[21] This incomplete blinking[22] allows time for the film to evaporate, as discussed above, and to cause the dry spots that lead to exposed corneal epithelium. A low rate of tear fluid turnover is believed also to be the cause of reduced barriers to potential pathogens. The tear film in effect has a 'washing function' reducing

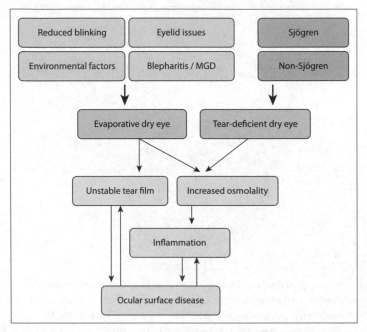

Figure 1.7 Diagram showing the causes of dry eye, through reduced blinking, problems with eye lids (evaporative dry eye) or Sjögren's tear deficiency (Tear-deficient dry eye). MGD, meibomian gland dysfunction.

the likelihood of bacterial adhesion to the corneal surface. This is similar to the case with saliva, which removes bacteria on teeth (see Xerostomia below).

Drugs and tear films

Drugs administered to the eye may affect the functioning of tear fluid. One aspect, connected with the earlier discussion on crystallisation, has been the solubility characteristics of drugs applied to the eye. Tear pH is dominated by the pH of the formulation. Immediately after instillation ciprofloxacin 0.3% has been shown to precipitate in the eye, driven by supersaturation as the pH changes.[23] In this case the pH was found to drop initially to 4.7 (the formulation has a pH of 4.5), normalising after 15 minutes to around 6.8. The solubility of ciprofloxacin is at a minimum at pH 7,[24] as can be seen from Figure 1.8.[25] Hence, drug that is in solution in the formulation will precipitate in the tear fluid. There is 100-fold reduction in ciprofloxacin solubility as the pH increases from 4.8 to 6.8.

Fleroxacin has a 10-fold greater solubility at pH 7 than ciprofloxacin, although this is not immediately obvious from comparing the structures of the two drugs. Each drug must of course be considered on the basis of its complete physical chemistry and its dose/solubility ratio. As a consequence, at equal doses one would not expect fleroxacin to precipitate to the same extent as ciprofloxacin.

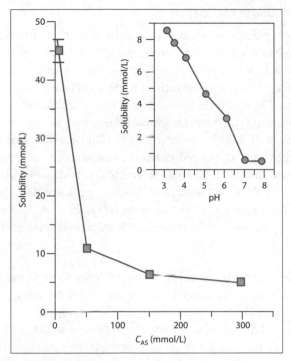

Figure 1.8 Ciprofloxacin solubility as a function of pH (inset) and as a function of the concentration of added salt (ammonium sulfate) (c_{AS}) from reference 25.

Ciprofloxacin

Fleroxacin

Eye drops and surface tension

Conventional eye dropper devices deliver drops with a volume between 25 and 70 µL. It has been argued[26] from many points of view, not least the biopharmaceutical one, that volumes of 5–15 µL should be instilled in the eye. The surface tension of the solutions to be instilled obviously has an effect on droplet size. The lower the surface tension, the smaller the drop delivered for a given expulsion pressure. Drops range from 44 µL for a solution with a surface tension of 71.9 mN/m to 25 µL for a solution with a surface tension of 32 mN/m. As has been mentioned, many drugs and some excipients are surface active, as we will discuss in Chapter 3. Tetracaine hydrochloride at a concentration of 16.6 mmol/L has a surface tension of 50.5 mN/m. Benzalkonium chloride 0.01% lowers the surface tension of water to 45 mN/m. The effect of lowering droplet size is relevant also in intravenous giving sets.

Xerostomia

Another syndrome that requires replacement or supplementation of a natural fluid with an artificial substance is xerostomia ('dry mouth'). Normal saliva function and control are compromised in this condition. Saliva is a clear, usually alkaline and somewhat viscous secretion from the parotid, submaxillary, sublingual and smaller mucous glands of the mouth.[27] In some cases xerostomia is caused by medication, especially with anticholinergics. Chemotherapeutic agents can also have a direct effect on salivary glands, reducing saliva output. Saliva consists primarily of water but contains enzymes and other proteins and electrolytes. It has a surface tension of around 58 mN/m. Saliva is essential for the normal 'feel' of the mouth and it assists lubrication, possesses antimicrobial activity and aids mucosal integrity. Saliva provides protection by constantly flushing non-adhered microbes, their toxins and nutrients from the mouth. It is also been suggested that the flow of saliva detaches adsorbed microbes from the teeth or prevents their adhesion, as shown in Figure 1.9. Saliva contains a wide spectrum of agents such as lactoferrin, lysozyme, histatins, cystatins, mucins, agglutinins, secretory leukocyte proteinase inhibitor, tissue inhibitors of proteinases, chitinase, peroxidases, and calprotectin.

Dry mouth can be treated with artificial saliva, although these solutions, as can be imagined from the list of components of natural saliva, rarely truly mimic the properties of the natural lubricant and wetting material. Designed to behave as far as possible like natural saliva, commercially available artificial salivas mostly contain agents such as carboxymethylcellulose and hydroxyethylcellulose to increase viscosity.

The rheological properties of saliva are quite complex, but these polymer additives do at least increase the residence time of the fluid. Gels that can prolong contact between the fluid and the oral mucosa are sometimes preferred.

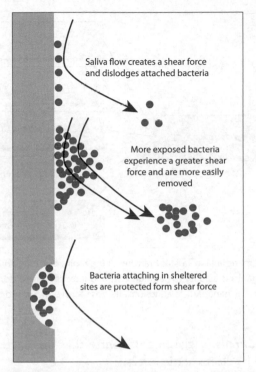

Saliva flow creates a shear force and dislodges attached bacteria

More exposed bacteria experience a greater shear force and are more easily removed

Bacteria attaching in sheltered sites are protected form shear force

Figure 1.9 Diagram of the effect of salivary flow in the normal mouth, dislodging bacteria adsorbed on teeth. Different situations are shown, with more exposed bacteria and bacteria in sheltered sites such as crevices.

Adhesion and adsorption

Adsorption usually refers to the process whereby small or large molecules attach themselves to surfaces, whereas the term adhesion is usually applied when two macrosurfaces or crystals come into close contact. Adhesion of solids and adsorption of molecules to surfaces are topics often discussed in basic pharmaceutics. Adsorption by definition involves deposition of molecules on surfaces. There are many surfaces to consider: biological surfaces or membranes, glass, plastics, teeth and so on. Figure 1.10 deals with some of the effects of adhesion ranging from the use of adsorbents to removing toxins in overdose to pathogenicity and infection. There are aspects of adhesion that are important in medication, as we will see later in relation to the unintended capture of dose forms in the oesophagus.

Bacterial adhesion to catheters can be reduced if the properties of both the organism and the plastic or other materials of the catheter are known. Box 1.2 gives the summary from a paper by Homma and colleagues.[28] One can speculate why these effects are exhibited. Surface hydrophobicity and surface charge are both important: it is interesting that the anionic heparinised catheters were free from biofilms of the negatively charged *Escherichia coli* and

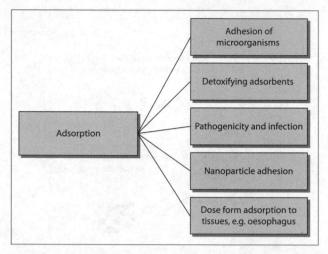

Figure 1.10 A schematic linking various branches of the topics of adsorption and adhesion, from adhesion of microorganisms leading to pathogenicity and infection, the adsorption of toxins on material such as charcoal, nanoparticle adhesion, and dose form adhesion to tissues such as the oesophagus.

Staphylococcus aureus, suggesting of course that the bacteria are repelled from the surface by electrostatic forces.

The role of hydrophobic interactions between bacteria and surfaces is important, for example, in the oral cavity, in contact lenses,[29] in surgical and dental materials, in polymers[30] for pharmaceutical and food use and in food itself. The adhesion of crystalline drugs to carrier particles such as lactose in aerosol suspensions can determine their effectiveness: too strong adhesion

---

Box 1.2 *Bacterial adhesion*

The inhibitory effects on bacterial adhesion of a new hydrophilic heparinised catheter to be used in patients with malignant obstructive jaundice, has been investigated in a randomised controlled study[28] of indwelling endoprostheses using either implantable port-connected heparinised catheters ($n = 25$) or silicone catheters ($n = 21$). Catheters withdrawn from patients were cultured for bacteria and examined for the presence of adherent organisms. Examination of the two types of catheters exposed to suspensions of *E. coli* and *Staph. aureus* showed the formation of a biofilm coated with glycocalyces in the silicone catheters, but not in the heparinised catheters. There was little bacterial adhesion to the heparinised surface, but significant formation of biofilm on the silicone surface. Anionic heparinised catheters have inhibitory effects on bacterial adhesion.

means that the drug will not free itself from the carrier. The adhesion of suspension particles to glassware is an unwanted effect, and in low-dose systems can reduce the amount of drug delivered.

Electrostatics and adhesion

Electrostatics deals with phenomena that result from stationary electric charges on non-conducting surfaces. The build-up of charge on the surface of objects after contact with other surfaces is important pharmaceutically. In powder handling on the large scale, accumulation of charge can lead to sudden discharge and explosions. On the smaller scale, electrostatics is important particularly when plastic surfaces are involved. Plastic (e.g. polycarbonate) spacers used with pressurised inhalers can acquire charges and attract aerosol particles to their surface. This can reduce drug availability by up to 50%.[31] The simple expedient of washing the spacer, such as a Volumatic (see Figure 1.11), with a detergent (surfactant) solution can reduce electrostatic charge and, as a consequence, improve performance.

The effect of the surfactant is to change the nature of the surface, so that the particle 'sees' the surfactant rather than the polymer. The nature of the induced charge on polymers depends on the nature of the polymer. Such interactions between drug and spacer are probably more important with steroids, but with beta-agonists the dosage is less critical and adsorption might not have significant clinical effects that can be measured.

When lactose is used as a carrier for the drug in aerosol formulations, lactose–drug interactions can occur and lead to the drug being released less readily from the lactose.

Charcoal, calcium carbonate and sevelamer

Highly adsorbent charcoal is used to reduce free toxin in the case of orally administered overdoses, deliberate or accidental. Patients who have to undergo haemodialysis are prone to hyperphosphataemia as the excretion of phosphate by dialysis is poor and renal function is impaired. Calcium as its carbonate or acetate is a phosphate-binding agent that is administered orally

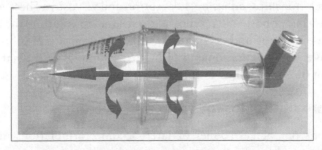

Figure 1.11 Volumatic spacer showing hypothetical trajectories of particles attracted electrostatically to the plastic internal surface of the device.

to reduce phosphate ion levels. A polymeric ion exchange resin, sevelamer (see structure) is also used. It is a copolymer of 2-(chloromethyl)oxirane (epichlorohydrin) and prop-2-en-1-amine. The marketed form is a partial hydrochloride salt, being present as ~40% amine·HCl and 60% sevelamer base. The amine groups of sevelamer become partially protonated in the intestine and interact with phosphorus molecules through ionic and hydrogen bonding.

The structure shows the exposed binding site for phosphates – the repeating and adjacent NH_2 groups. The dose both of calcium salts and of sevelamer is high, being 1.25 g for Calcichew tablets and 800 mg for the sevelamer, and patients who are already on several medications have reported problems with compliance.[32] The sevelamer tablets are large and one patient reports 'the tablets are so disgusting, their consistency is so disgusting – so disgusting that you don't want to take [them]'. Here the concept is good with the agents used, but they are insufficiently powerful adsorbents or ion exchangers to allow dosage reduction. Tablets not taken are a negation of therapeutics.

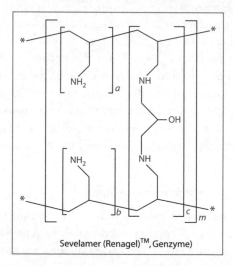

Sevelamer (Renagel)™, Genzyme)

So far, the selected examples have touched on the importance in a range of circumstances of surface tension, wetting, de-wetting, precipitation, pH–solubility relationships, adhesion, adsorption and viscosity. These were related variously to xerophthalmia, synovial fluid supplementation, the behaviour of drugs in eye drops and crystalluria. Other examples will follow in later chapters. We now discuss some introductory examples of the nature of the formulation (dose form) and events and outcomes in the clinic.

The nature of the dosage form and outcomes

Formulations on shelves sooner or later become formulations in patients, unless, as referred to above with phosphate-binding agents, patients forget or refuse to take their medication. Many changes in products can occur as a

result of the sudden change of environment when the medicine is administered. Drugs precipitate from injection solutions after administration; infusion pumps become blocked when the proteins they are delivering aggregate;
some oral dose forms adhere to oesophageal membranes; the ghosts of insoluble matrix tablets can accumulate in gut diverticula; and eye drops can not
only irritate but may deliver lethal doses in the very young.

It is clear from knowledge of biopharmaceutics that dosage forms can
considerably influence medication outcomes.[33] The development of controlled-release dosage forms is a good example of that influence, where the
properties of the dosage form have been adjusted to ensure an optimal release
of active to reduce the frequency of administration by prolonging the therapeutic levels of drug, and to reduce peak plasma levels that contribute to toxic
effects.

The era of personalised medicines will bring great challenges for the
development of products for groups of patients identified by their physiological, pathological and even genetic status, rather than as now when, apart
from dosage adjustments, all patients may receive the same product that has
been designed for the average patient. Aspects of personalised medicines are
discussed in Chapter 8.

Quality of effect

The quality of the clinical effect of medicines is often a pharmaceutical concern. As one example shows, considerable advances have been made with
ciclosporin formulations to reduce the inter- and intra-patient variability in
plasma levels. This is vital because appropriate levels are crucial in the sup-
pression of rejection following transplantation. Comparison of the former
product Sandimmune with Neoral (microemulsion) demonstrates (Figure
1.12) improvements in the consistency of plasma levels with the latter,
although there is still considerable patient-to-patient variability in both
C_{max} and t_{max}. But the point is clear: formulation can influence outcomes.

The variability of many non-disintegrating controlled-release formulations taken orally is the result not of differences in the nature of the dosage
form but of variability in their gastrointestinal transit times in different
patients or in the same patient at different times. However, such effects are
felt mainly with non-disintegrating dosage forms such as oral osmotic pumps
and matrix tablets. Transit times vary considerably and the challenge for the
future is to take these differences into account in the design of formulations. It
is clear that if mouth-to-anus transit times are of the order of 2 hours in one
individual and 12 hours in another, then a product that releases its content
over 8 hours will not perform well in the former patient. Ideally we need to
have available dose forms that accommodate the extremes for the future when
personalised medicine is more accepted and catered for.

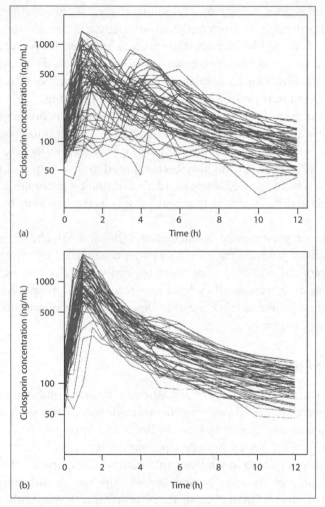

Figure 1.12 Plasma levels of ciclosporin after administration of Sandimmune (a) and Neoral (b), showing the reduction (but not elimination) of patient-to-patient variability. The logarithmic scales conceal to an extent the very considerable variability even with the improved formulation. Variability of ciclosporin and other immunosuppressives has an extremely important effect on outcomes following transplants. Neoral is a concentrate which on dilution produces a microemulsion.

Transdermal products *in situ* enjoy a more static environment. But variability of performance of transdermal patches has been demonstrated many times. Patches do of course modulate the intra-individual differences in absorption, but only to an extent that is determined by the transport properties of the drug through the polymer membrane separating the reservoir from the skin surface. Patches do not generally control the onward movement of drug. An example in Figure 1.13 makes this point, showing the variability in plasma levels attained from fentanyl patches from a commercial system.[34]

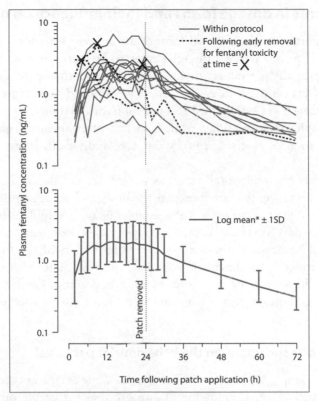

Figure 1.13 Plasma levels of fentanyl administered via a Cygnus transdermal device. This shows clearly the wide variability of levels. (From reference 34.)

Modes of injection and formulation

An editorial in the *British Medical Journal*[35] pointed out the importance of injecting vaccines into muscle in the deltoid or the anterolateral aspect of the thigh. As the article indicates, 'injecting a vaccine into the layer of subcutaneous fat, where poor vascularity may result in slow mobilisation and processing of antigen is a cause of vaccine failure for example in hepatitis B, rabies and influenza vaccines.' The use of a standard size of needle will not guarantee successful intramuscular injection in all patients; hence thought must be given to choice of needle length and bore. It is in such apparently minor details that success or failure can reside, or at least on which less favourable or more favourable outcomes depend. Some years ago, the dispersion of diazepam after intramuscular injection was found to depend on whether a doctor or a nurse administered the dose; plasma levels varied more and mean levels less when the nurse carried out the injection, because of the variation in the site and mode of injection. The sex of the patient can affect responses to antibiotic injections owing to differences in the distribution of fatty tissues in men and women, since women have greater lipidic deposits in the gluteal region.

Ingredients in dosage forms and their influence on outcomes

Just as important as the physical form of the delivery system are its ingredients, the excipients, which although chosen to be inert, are not always so.[36] This is principally the subject of Chapter 2. Transdermal patches can cause adverse effects on the skin as the adhesive employed may cause irritation. Solubilisers such as Cremophor EL in injection formulations of paclitaxel can initiate anaphylactic reactions, while a battery of excipients, from dyes and stabilisers to preservatives, can in sensitive individuals cause unwanted effects.[37]

Excipients are rarely totally inert as we will see in Chapter 2. Most excipients are substances that are foreign to the body and hence can elicit adverse effects. These may occur even if the excipients are insoluble. The effect of inhaled powders that can cause a cough reflex may be one example. Paradoxical bronchoconstriction has been described in inhaler formulations for the treatment of asthma, for example. The precipitation of drugs from injection vehicles can be the cause of pain and thrombophlebitis. Hence dosage forms must be chosen with care. They must also be used with care.

Influence of a surfactant on the behaviour of paclitaxel

A specific example is given here of the effects of one excipient type, namely a non-ionic surfactant, Cremophor EL, an ethoxylated castor oil used as a solubiliser in many formulations. Cremophor EL, a component of Taxol (paclitaxel) injections, not only solubilises the drug, but also inhibits the metabolism of the drug to the 6α-hydroxypaclitaxel by cytochrome P45 (CYP) 2C8. This is the major route of detoxification of paclitaxel.[38] This surfactant has also been found to decrease the accumulation of the hydroxyl derivative in cells and decrease the ratio of 6α-hydroxypaclitaxel to paclitaxel. To complicate matters, it also contributes to the non-linear kinetics of the drug.

Clearly, Cremophor EL is more than a substance that simply increases the solubility of the drug. When observing the effect of a drug on adverse events we need always to consider the question: does the formulation itself or ingredients in the formulation play a part in the behaviour of the medicine or indeed other medicines given concomitantly?

In the following chapters we will elaborate on some of these issues, using cases that have been reported as the starting point to refresh collective memories of the pharmaceutics involved. The examples can only be selected cases. What should be developed is a sense of asking questions about the nature of medication that may (or may not) have affected an outcome, or caused an adverse event, or have suited one patient more than another. Pharmacists can only play a useful independent clinical role if they bring to the ward, the bedside and the community interface the additional knowledge that is embodied in subjects with which physicians and nurses are less well versed. It goes without saying that pharmaceutics must of course be coupled with a through knowledge of pharmacology and therapeutics and key pharmaco-chemical facts.

Conclusion

To conclude this introduction to clinical pharmaceutics, we can use Figure 1.14 to illustrate the case when considering adverse events. It emphasises the need for a comprehensive synthesis of the disciplines of pharmacy to interpret complex events intelligently. Here the cause may be the drug, excipients or the nature of the dosage form itself. If it is the drug, we ask: Is it a class effect or is it compound specific? Is it a chemical or physical problem, arising from precipitation, lipophilicity or complexation? Does the chemical structure or reactivity of the drug result in hapten formation or cross-reactivity with other drugs? Excipient effects may be due to surfactants, dyes, preservatives or antioxidants. The dosage form may affect drug distribution or precipitation, and the nature of the dosage form itself (size, adhesivity) may cause problems in the oesophagus or intestine. Even tonicity, viscosity and density may in some rare cases cause problems with drug administration.

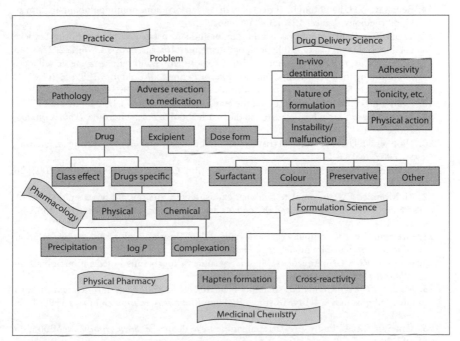

Figure 1.14 Scheme showing the relationship between a problem in practice – in this example an adverse event or reaction – and the physical, pharmacological and chemical sciences. Adverse reactions to formulations are discussed in Chapter 5.

References

1. Mason WJ, Nickols HH. Crystalluria from acyclovir use. *N Engl J Med* 2008; 358: e14.
2. Shojaei AH *et al*. Transbuccal delivery of acyclovir: I. *In vitro* determination of routes of buccal transport. *Pharm Res* 1998; 15: 1181–1188.
3. Testerecí H *et al*. The determination of acyclovir in sheep serum, human serum, saliva and urine by HPLC. *East J Med* 1998; 3: 62–66.
4. Editorial. Crystals in joints. *Lancet* 1980 May 10; 1(8176): 1006–1007.
5. Moriomto K *et al*. Effects of viscous hyaluronate sodium solutions on the nasal absorption of vasopressin and an analogue. *Pharm Res* 1991; 8: 471–474.
6. Oates KMN *et al*. Rheopexy of synovial fluid and protein aggregation. *Interface* 2006; 3: 164–174.
7. Lo GH *et al*. Intra-articular hyaluronic acid in treatment of knee osteoarthritis. *JAMA* 2003; 290: 3315–3121.
8. Aviad AD, Houpt JB. The molecular weight of therapeutic hyaluronan (sodium hyaluronate): how significant is it? *J Rheumatol* 1994; 21: 297–301.
9. Mori S *et al*. Highly viscous sodium hyaluronate and joint lubrication. *Int Orthop* 2004; 26: 116–121.
10. Allard S, O'Regan M. The role of elastoviscosity in the efficacy of viscosupplementation for osteoarthritis of the knee: a comparison of Hylan G-F 20 and a lower molecular weight hyaluronan. *Clin Ther* 2000; 22: 792–795.
11. Biomet Inc. Technical literature: Fermathron™. fr.biomet.be/befr-medical/befr-biomaterials/befr-fermathron (accessed 17 September 2009).
12. Hammer ME, Burch TG. Viscous corneal protection by sodium hyaluronate, chondroitin sulfate and methylcellulose. *Invest Ophthalmol Vis Sci* 1984; 25: 1329–1332.
13. Dudinski O *et al*. Acceptability of thickened eye drops to human subjects. *Curr Ther Res* 1983; 33: 322–328.
14. Reunhart WH, Berchtold PE. Effect of high dose intravenous immunoglobulin therapy on blood rheology. *Lancet* 1992; 339: 662–663.
15. Tsuda Y *et al*. Effects of pravastatin sodium and simvastatin on plasma fibrinogen level and blood rheology in type II hyperlipoproteinemia. *Atherosclerosis* 1996; 122: 225–233.
16. Joshi HN *et al*. Differentiation of 3-hydroxy-3-methylglutaryl-coenzyme A reductase inhibitors by their relative lipophilicity. *Pharm Pharmacol Commun* 1999; 5: 269–271.
17. Tabbara KF, Sharara N. Dry eye syndrome. *Drugs Today* 1998; 34: 447.
18. Holly FJ. Formation and rupture of the tear film. *Exp Eye Res* 1973; 15: 515–525.
19. Matsuo T *et al*. Trehalose eye drops in the treatment of dry eye syndrome. *Ophthalmology* 2002; 109: 2024–2029.
20. Njobuenwu DO. Spreading of trisiloxanes on thin water film: dry spot profile. *Leonardo J Sci* 2007; 6: 165–178.
21. Lawrenson JG, Murphy PJ. The neonatal tear film. *Contact Lens Anterior Eye* 2003; 26: 197–202.
22. McMonnies CW. Incomplete blinking: exposure keratopathy, lid wiper epitheliopathy, dry eye, refractive surgery and dry contact lenses. *Contact Lens Anterior Eye* 2007; 30: 37–51.
23. Firestone BA *et al*. Solubility characteristics of three fluoroquinolone ophthalmic solutions in an *in vitro* tear film model. *Int J Pharm* 1998; 164: 119–128.
24. Ross DL, Riley CM. Aqueous solubilities of some variously substituted antimicrobials. *Int J Pharm* 1990; 63: 237–250.
25. Maurer N *et al*. Anomalous solubility behavior of the antibiotic ciprofloxacin encapsulated in liposomes: a ^{1}H-NMR study. *Biochim Biophys Acta Biomembranes* 1998; 1374: 9–20.
26. Van Santvliet L, Ludwig A. Determinants of eye drop size. *Surv Ophthalmol* 2004; 49: 197–213.
27. McKee CD *et al*. Drug-induced photosensitivity reactions. *Drug Store News* 1998 July 20: CP 39-CP 43. www.DrugStoreNews.com.

28. Homma H *et al.* Bacterial adhesion on hydrophilic heparinized catheters, with compared with adhesion on silicone catheters, in patients with malignant obstructive jaundice. *J Gastroenterol* 1996; 31: 836–843.
29. Miller MJ, Ahearn DG. Adherence of *Pseudomonas aeruginosa* to hydrophilic contact lenses and other substrata. *J Clin Microbiol* 1987; 25: 1392–1397.
30. Van Pelt A *et al.* Adhesion of *Streptococcus sanguis* CH3 to polymers with different surface free energies. *Appl Environ Microbiol* 1985; 49: 1270–1275.
31. Windhaber JH *et al.* Reducing electrostatic charge in spacer devices and bronchodilator response. *Br J Pharmacol* 2000; 50: 277–280.
32. Lindberg M, Lindberg P. Overcoming obstacles for adherence to phosphate binding medication in dialysis patients: a qualitative study. *Pharm World Sci* 2008; 30: 571–576.
33. Florence AT, Jani PU. Novel oral drug formulations. Their potential in modulating adverse effects. *Drug Saf* 1994; 10: 232–266.
34. Fiset P *et al.* Biopharmaceutics of a new transdermal fentanyl device. *Anesthesiology* 1995; 83: 459–469.
35. Zuckerman JN. The importance of injecting vaccines into muscle. *Br Med J* 2000; 321: 1237–1238.
36. American Academy of Pediatrics. 'Inactive' ingredients in pharmaceutical products: update. *Pediatrics* 1997; 99: 268–278.
37. Uchegbu IF, Florence AT. Adverse drug events related to dosage forms and delivery systems. *Drug Saf* 1996; 14: 39–67.
38. Shord SS, Camp JR. Intravenous administration of paclitaxel in Sprague–Dawley rats: what is a safe dose? *Biopharm Drug Dispos* 2006; 27: 191–196.

2

Excipients: Not always inert

Introduction

Excipients are components of formulations other than the drug or other active ingredient. Their functions are many, variously to aid processing, to aid dissolution of solid dose forms or conversely to retard release of the drug, to stabilise the formulation or to protect the drug from adverse environments both *in vitro* and *in vivo*. Excipients are the dominant material in many tablet and capsule formulations as sometimes their main role is to provide sufficient bulk for a low-dose drug to be administered safely. This chapter deals with the potential for excipients to influence outcomes of medication. Excipients are not always the inert substances that we presume. Some cases and reports of the adverse action of excipients are discussed here. While labelling requirements insist on the listing of ingredients in some products, the plethora of trade names (e.g. for surfactants, polymers, lipids and other excipients) can make accurate identification of materials a difficult task. (The European Commission guidelines requires that all excipients need to be declared on the labelling if the product is an injectable, or a topical (for skin, for inhalation, delivery to the vaginal, nasal or rectal mucosae) or an eye preparation.) Batch-to-batch variation of many excipient raw materials adds another layer of complexity in tracking down and comparing case histories. One problem we face is that products available in one national market may have different formulations from those marketed in another. Papers do not always detail the formulations or brands used in clinical studies.

Usually but not always inert

Excipients are intended to be inert, but they are not always so in all patients.[1] In a review on the safety of pharmaceutical excipients, Figure 2.1 was used.[2] This summarised the main requirements of excipients: to be of high quality, to be safe and to have a high degree of functionality, that is, fitness for use.

Fitness for use in one application may not mean fitness for use in another, for example by another route of administration. Even though adverse reactions to excipients might be relatively rare, it is for this reason that the

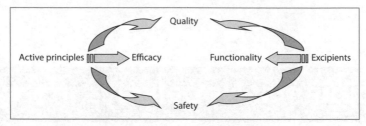

Figure 2.1 The main requirements of excipients: high quality, safety and functionality, the property of being in effect fit for purpose. (From reference 2.)

possibility that an excipient might be the cause of any adverse event should be kept in mind. Fillers like lactose bulk out a low dose (milligrams or micrograms) so that the resulting tablet or capsule can be manufactured and is of a sufficient size to be handled. Lactose is also used in dry powder inhaler formulations as a carrier for the drug. There may be lubricants such as magnesium stearate to aid the flow of powders and their subsequent tabletting or filling into capsules.

Preservatives and dyes are listed in Tables 2.1 and 2.2, the result of surveys of these ingredients and their frequency of use,[3] albeit not in the UK. These figures are used here to give an impression of the excipients most likely to be encountered.

Relatively simple molecules are used as excipients in formulations, from substances such as lactose or magnesium stearate through surfactants, preservatives, colours and flavours to macromolecules. Macromolecules (polymers) may be soluble, swellable or insoluble. With small molecules,

Table 2.1 Preservatives found in liquid pharmaceutical formulations (*n* = 73)

Preservatives	% of formulations
Methylparaben	45.2
Propylparaben	35.6
Sodium benzoate	32.8
Sodium metabisulfite	11
Benzoic acid	8
Hydroxyparabenzoate	4
Potasssium sorbate	2
Hydroxyparabenzoic acid	1
No preservatives	2

From reference 3.

Table 2.2 Dyes found in pharmaceutical formulations ($n = 73$)

Dyes	% of formulations
Dusk Yellow (FD&C #6)	15
Tartrazine Yellow (FD&C #5)	9.5
Erythrosine	6.8
Ponceau 4R Red	5.4
Caramel	4.1
Red #40	4.1
Food Red	4.1
Bordeaux S Red	2.7
Quinoline Yellow	2.7
Yellow #10	2.7
Blue #1	1.3
Red #10	1.3
Iron oxide	1.3

From Reference 3.

such as the *para*-aminobenzoic acid esters (parabens), we can know whether the compound is pure, and know exactly what we are dealing with. It is not possible to generalise about the effects of excipients with all their structural diversity and uses. With polymers and other macromolecules one needs to know their molecular weight, or more likely their molecular weight distribution, or about the presence of impurities, such as catalysts and peroxides, the latter in polysorbate 80 for example. Cremophor EL, which is used in paclitaxel formulations is 'cleaned' rather than pure. Unpurified material causes some instability in the paclitaxel, possibly due to the presence of carboxylate anions.[4] Excipients are rarely produced to the extremely high standards of purity that apply to drug substances. Hence the presence of impurities rather than the material itself might be the cause of any adverse event, perhaps by inducing degradation of the drug. There may be batch differences or brand differences in excipients, which are confusing. A mutein is a protein with its amino acid sequence altered usually sufficiently to alter its properties. Oxidised IL-2 mutein forms in the presence of a high-peroxide-value polysorbate sample to a greater extent than with a low-peroxide-value sample.[5] Some polymeric materials are complex, not only because of the existence in any one sample of a range of molecular weights, but also because many contain plasticisers to adjust their physical properties or agents to aid production. Plasticisers such as diethyl phthalate leach out from plastic giving sets into infusions, particularly those that have ingredients (such as surfactants) that might aid the solubilisation of the phthalate. Dioctyl phthalate and dioctyl adipate have been found in some silicone tubing.

Problems with excipients to which the American Academy of Pediatrics have drawn attention are shown in Table 2.3. Note that the route of administration and sometimes the mode of administration (for example, a particular device such as a nebuliser) and the concentration will affect the appearance or severity of many adverse effects.

Table 2.3 Excipients that have caused problems in paediatric and adult medicines

Excipient or class	Selected observed reactions
Sulfites	Wheezing, dyspnoea, anaphylactoid reactions
Benzalkonium chloride	Paradoxical bronchoconstriction, reduced forced expiry volume
Aspartame	Headache, hypersensitivity
Saccharin[a]	Dermatological reactions; avoid in children with sulfa allergies
Benzyl alcohol	In high concentrations can cause neonatal death
Various dyes	Reactions to tartrazine[b] similar to aspirin intolerance; patients with the 'classic aspirin triad' reaction (asthma, urticaria, rhinitis) may develop similar reactions from other dyes such as amaranth, erthyrosin, indigo, carmine, Ponceau, Sunset Yellow, Brilliant Blue
Lactose	Problem in lactose-sensitive patients (lactase deficiency)
Propylene glycol	Localised contact dermatitis topically; lactic acidosis after absorption

[a] Saccharin is an o-toluene sulfonamide: [b] Tartrazine:

E-numbers

From Table 2.2 it is clear that there are many ways of referring to additives. A classification system has been developed that codifies additives both in food and in pharmaceuticals in terms of E-numbers. Box 2.1 gives the general numbering system for several classes of ingredients found in food. It is useful when trying to detect cross-reactivity and sensitivities to know the E-numbers of colours, preservatives, and other ingredients. Each additive has a number within the classifications shown in Box 2.1.

Further deconstruction of E-numbers might be useful in identifying possible causes of adverse events. E100–109 are yellow dyes; for example, tartrazine (F&DC Yellow 5) is E102. E140-149 are green dyes. E430–439 are polyoxyethylene derivatives such as polysorbate, 80 which is E433. E210–219 are benzoates. E230–239 are phenols and methanoates. E220–220 are sulfites (e.g. sodium metabisulfite has an E number of 223).

One case report[6] reads as follows:

> During the 1999/2000 influenza outbreak, a 53-year-old man consulted because of a persistent productive cough that followed flu-like illness. The patient was examined and prescribed erythromycin (Erymax™, Elan). He made it clear that he had a previous history of aspirin allergy and was reassured that there was no known cross-sensitivity between erythromycin and aspirin. Two days later, the patient's wife came into the surgery; she was angry and upset because shortly after taking the erythromycin capsules, her husband had developed some tingling and swelling of his fingers and feet similar to the symptoms he had previously experienced with aspirin. They were both disturbed to find the following warning in the patient information leaflet: 'Capsules contain the colouring agent E110. This can cause allergic-like reactions including asthma. You are more likely to have a reaction if you are also allergic to aspirin'.

This case raised many issues. Was the patient allergic to E110 (Sunset Yellow FCF, Orange Yellow S, FD&C Yellow 6), or was the patient allergic to

---

Box 2.1 General system of E-numbers

E100–E199 (colours)
E200–E299 (preservatives)
E300–E399 (antioxidants, acidity regulators)
E400–E499 (thickeners, stabilisers, emulsifiers)
E500–E599 (acidity regulators, anti-caking agents)
E600–E699 (flavour enhancers)

erythromycin itself? The physician concerned was unaware both of the presence of E110 in the formulation and of the apparent cross-reactivity between aspirin and this colouring agent, there being no mention of either in the physician's BNF or in the Pharmaceutical Data Sheet Compendium. To be able to foresee such interactions requires that the structures of the molecules concerned be known and this is a tall order. However, understanding after the event is a reasonable goal for avoiding future occurrences. The structures of some of these dyes are quite complex, as can be seen in Table 2.4, and perhaps

Table 2.4 Adverse effects of dyes and colouring agents

Compound	Structure	Adverse effects
Sunset Yellow		Urticaria exacerbation
Indigo carmine		Urticaria exacerbation
Tartrazine		Headache, gastrointestinal disturbance, exacerbation of asthma, dangerous in aspirin-intolerant individuals
Amaranth		Potential carcinogenicity (banned)
Brilliant Blue		Hypersensitivity reactions

From reference 2.

not surprisingly, some do have pharmacological effects, which are listed in Table 2.4.

Another report[7] discussed patients with reactions to E102 (tartrazine (F&DC Yellow 5)) in oxytetracycline tablets and to E131(Patent Blue V) in a doxycycline formulation.

Azo dyes (those with the –N=N– linkage) account for 60–70% of dyes used in food and textile manufacture. Their acute toxicity is low but some azo dyes have been banned from foods because of the toxicity of dye breakdown products rather than the dye itself. The mechanisms by which tartrazine causes allergic reactions is not fully understood.

Cross-reactivity

Cross-reactivity can be defined as a reaction to different compounds which may or may not have some structural similarity. Often the immune system is involved. Cross-reactions between different azo dyes and *para*-amino compounds have been studied[8] in azo-dye-sensitive subjects, in the clinical aspects of azo dye dermatitis, and to attempt to relate the pattern of cross-sensitisations to the chemical structure of the different dyes. Out of 6203 consecutively tested patients, 236 were sensitised to at least 1 of 6 azo compounds employed as textile dyes. One hundred and seven subjects reacted to Disperse Orange 3 (DO3), 104 to Disperse Blue 124 (DB124), 76 to *para*-aminoazobenzene (PAAB), 67 to Disperse Red 1 (DR1), 42 to Disperse Yellow 3 (DY3), and 31 to *p*-dimethylaminoazobenzene (PDAAB). Co-sensitisations to *para*-phenylenediamine were present in most subjects sensitised to DO3 (66%) and PAAB (75%), in 27% and 36% of DR1 and DY3-sensitive subjects, and in only 16% of subjects sensitised to DB124. After the hands and the face, the neck and the axillae were the most frequently involved skin sites. Cross-sensitisations between azo dyes and *para*-amino compounds can partially be explained on the basis of structural affinities.

Dyes used in lymph node identification

Dyes are used for lymphatic mapping and sentinel lymph node biopsy in patients with breast cancer and other malignant tumors.[9] Some are shown in Figure 2.2.[10] Reports of anaphylactic reactions have become more frequent, although mechanisms remain unclear. Blue dyes administered by a variety of routes can results in the skin of patients turning blue.[11]

Non-ionic surfactants

Non-ionic surfactants are widely used in formulations as wetting agents and solubilising agents. As discussed in Chapter 3, because surfactants are by structure and nature surface active they will accumulate at interfaces, the

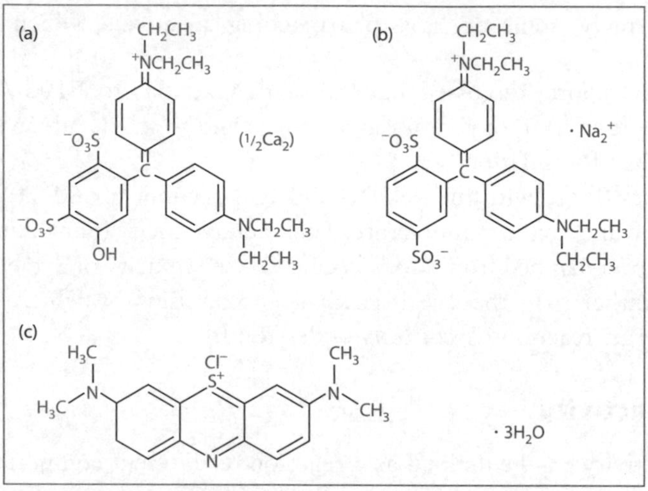

Figure 2.2 Structural formulae of dyes commonly used for sentinel lymph node localisation: (a) Patent Blue V; (b) Isosulfan Blue; (c) Methylene Blue. (Used with permission from reference 10.)

air–water interface and the oil–water interface as well as the membrane–water interface. At membranes they can influence the fluidity of the membrane, and at higher concentrations, generally above their critical micelle concentrations (CMCs), they can cause membrane damage because they can solubilise structural lipids and phospholipids. While non-ionic surfactants allow poorly water-soluble drugs to be formulated as injectables, some have side-effects that are by now well known. The two most commonly used, and therefore cited as causing adverse events, are polysorbate 80 (Tween 80; E433) and a polyoxyethylated castor oil (Cremophor EL). Anaphylactic reactions are the most frequently cited, although they occur in a minority of patients. Hence it is useful, should such reactions to injections occur in new or experimental formulations, that their presence be recognised. Some products that contain Cremophor EL include teniposide, ciclosporin and paclitaxel formulations; docetaxel contains polysorbate 80, as does etoposide. The pharmacological effects of formulation vehicles have been discussed in detail elsewhere.[12] Different formulations of these drugs exist in different countries, hence the true composition must be ascertained in assessing outcomes.

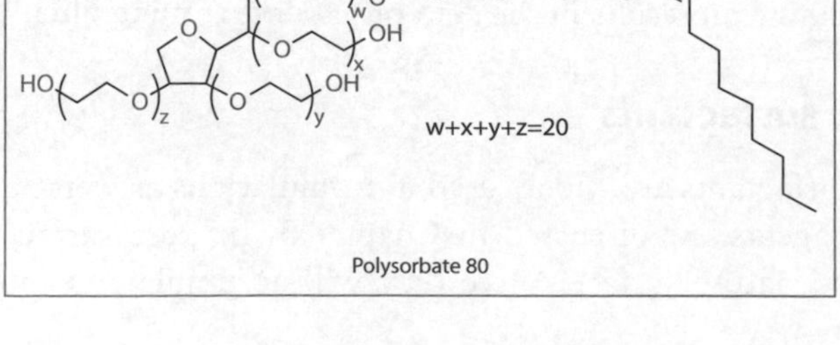

Polysorbate 80

Polyoxyethylene glycols (PEGs)

Polyoxyethylene glycols (PEGs) (macrogols) when used as suppository bases are not surface-active as they are completely hydrophilic with no hydrophobic domains, but they exert an adverse effect through being hygroscopic. They absorb water from the rectal tissues and cause irritation, but this can be minimised by first moistening the PEG base before insertion. This affinity for water is the result of the interaction of water molecules with the oxygen of the repeating $-CH_2CH_2O-$ units; a macrogol of molecular weight 44 500 has approximately 1000 such ethylene oxide units, each interacting with up to four H_2O molecules. Macrogols 4000 and 3350 are used to sequester water in the bowels (Idrolax (Ipsen) or Laxido (Galen). As the BNF states, 'giving fluids with macrogols may reduce the dehydrating effect sometimes seen with osmotic laxatives.'

Paediatric powder formulations of PEGs are available for faecal impaction and constipation (Movicol Paediatric, Norgine) with a dose of 6.563 g of Macrogol 3350. Sodium dodecyl (lauryl) sulfate is also an ingredient of an osmotic laxative, Relaxit Micro-enema. Usually it is found as a wetting agent in pharmaceuticals. Its presence in laxative formulations is most likely to aid the penetration of water into the faecal mass.

Adjuvants as therapeutic substances

Nonoxynol-9 is similar to many non-ionic surfactants used as excipients to increase wetting and entry of water into dosage forms as well as solubilisers. It is used as a spermicide because, being membrane active, it interacts with spermatozoa and reduces their mobility. It has also some activity against HIV. However it also is suspected to increase HIV access through the vaginal wall as it can damage biomembranes. It also increases rectal infection by the herpes simplex virus. The microscopic evidence is clear that the compound damages the epithelial wall as shown in Figure 2.3 in the case of rectal tissue.[13]

Nonoxynol-9

Poloxamers are ABA block copolymer surfactants; in designating them, A is the hydrophilic polyoxyethylene chain and B is the hydrophobic polyoxypropylene chain. The properties of the poloxamers depend of the length of each chain. ABA block copolymer surfactants such as poloxamer 199 have many pharmaceutical uses, as wetting, solubilising and emulsifying agents,

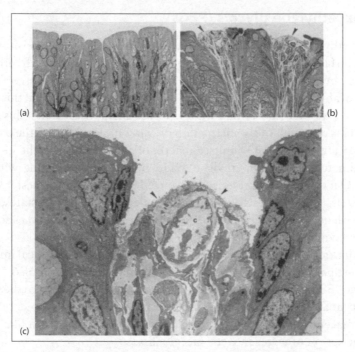

Figure 2.3 Light micrographs of the rectal epithelium and lamina propria of mice treated for 10 min with phosphate buffered saline (PBS) (a) and nonoxynol-9. (b). Control (PBS-treated) tissue is characterised by a continuous epithelium of columnar and goblet cells. In tissue treated with nonoxynol-9, epithelial cells appear necrotic. In some areas the epithelium is missing and connective tissue is directly exposed to the rectal lumen (arrows). In the transmission electron micrograph shown in (c), connective tissue (arrows) appears to be exposed to the rectal lumen. Epithelial cells are missing microvilli. A capillary is shown in (c). (From reference 13 by permission of Elsevier.)

but some like poloxamer 188 (Pluronic F68) have interesting pharmacology. Poloxamer 118 has some haemorheological, antithrombotic and neutrophil-inhibiting properties, although studies in a canine model have not proved exciting.[14] However, it improves microvascular blood flow by reducing blood viscosity, particularly in low-shear conditions. Its mechanism of action is not clear, but it is suggested that the surfactant binds to cells hydrophobically leaving the polyoxyethylene chains to provide a hydrated barrier reducing cell–cell, cell–protein and protein-protein interactions in the blood.[15]

Poloxamer 188 has also been studied as a cell repair agent or membrane sealant (Figure 2.4).[16] Researchers are investigating whether poloxamer 188 can help keep muscle cells intact in muscular dystrophy. It can have a protective effect on damaged heart muscle cells. Purified poloxamer 188 also has a beneficial effect on the treatment of sickle cell disease,[17] perhaps because of decreased adhesion of sickle cells to the microvasculature.

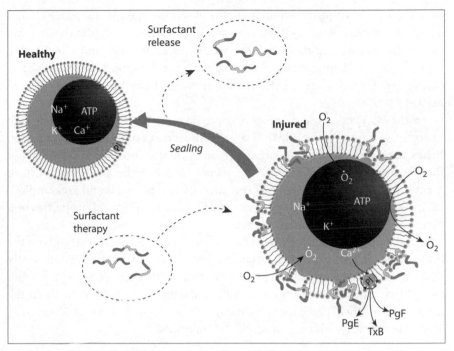

Figure 2.4 Suggested mechanism of action of poloxamer 188 operating at a cell membrane, acting as a sealant. The surfactant shown with its hydrophobic portion in light grey and hydrophilic part in blue interacts with the injured cell 'sealing' the membrane and returning it to normal. ATP, adenosine triphosphate; PgE, PgF, prostaglandin E and F, respectively; T × B, thrombozane B. (From reference 16.)

Talc as therapeutic agent and excipient

Talc is hydrated magnesium silicate; there are variable amounts of calcium, magnesium and iron present in different samples of talc. Its particle size can vary considerably. Humble talc is used not only in baby care but also as a lubricant in the manufacture of tablets and also as a lubricant for surgical gloves.

There is one less well known use of talc, which is as a therapeutic agent rather than as an excipient. This is in the procedure of pleurodesis, when the membranes around the lung adhere. Talc prevents the build-up of fluid between the membranes. An irritant such as bleomycin, tetracycline or talc powder is instilled inside the pleural cavity to instigate an inflammatory response that 'tacks the two pieces together'.[18] Talc is one of the most effective agents to achieve the desired outcome, but there have been concerns about side-effects, especially acute respiratory distress syndrome (ARDS), assumed to be related to both the particle size and perhaps the shape of the talc particles.[19] Particle size has been found to be key in determining the distribution of talc in the body.[20] Marchi *et al.* point out that absorption of pleural fluid and particles from the pleural space occurs 'through stomas described on the parietal pleura of animals (in rats the medium cross section area of the stomas is $12.9 \pm 10.3\,\mu m^3$, suggesting the possibility of migration of talc through the lymphatics).' When 85% of the talc particles are greater than $10\,\mu m$, talc has been seen in several organs.[21]

In the USA, talc used in this procedure has a smaller particle size than in European samples, and it is in the USA that most cases of ARDS seem to occur. It has been shown[22] in comparing two sizes of talc (normal and large) that they both elicit the same benefit in pleurodesis but the smaller sizes have greater pulmonary and systemic deposition of talc particles and greater pleural inflammation. This is another example where the physical properties of a material influence its biological effect.

Small particles, once they gain entry, can in fact translocate throughout the body, depending on their size and surface properties, an issue discussed briefly in Chapter 8 in the section on pharmaceutical nanotechnology. The smaller the particles, the farther they can travel; hence there is real concern about the migration of such particles whether inhaled, swallowed or inadvertently placed in contact with open wounds, for example.

Freedom from talc on medical gloves

The FDA guidance on surgical and other gloves that come into contact with patients includes the following:[23]

> Donning lubricants such as cornstarch and silicone may make it easier to put on medical gloves. Powdered lubricants are also called *donning powders* or *dusting powders*. Powder from medical gloves directly contacts wounds, body cavities, and skin and can contaminate both the patient's and the user's environment. FDA believes it is important to minimize the amount of powder on finished gloves.
>
> **Examination Gloves.** Cornstarch that meets the specification for absorbable donning or dusting powder in the United States Pharmacopeia (U.S.P.) is a commonly used lubricant for examination gloves. Any powder used for lubricating examination gloves should meet the U.S.P. monograph for absorbable dusting powder or be equivalent in terms of safety and effectiveness. The type, specifications, and source of powder or other donning lubricant used on the gloves [should be specified]. You should not use talc, cotton flock, and other non-absorbable materials as a lubricating, dusting, or donning powder. Recognized consensus standards specify that the inside and outside surface of medical gloves be free of talc.

Active excipients in multiple therapies

When an excipient in one formulation affects, say, P-glycoproteins (P-gp), and is administered along with another product whose absorption is P-gp-dependent, then interpretation of interactions can be obscured if the excipients in both products are not taken into account. Examples might include paclitaxel formulations with Cremophor EL and polysorbate 80 when used along with other formulations. Several non-ionic surfactants have been found to inhibit P-gp-mediated transport *in vitro*;[24] in one system the descending order of effect was Tocopheryl Polyethylene Glycol 1000 Succinate (TPGS) > Pluronic PE8100 > Cremophor EL > Pluronic PE6100 ≈ Tween 80. These surfactants had no effect on MRP2 (multiple drug resistance protein 2) function, suggesting specificity.

The well-known effects of surfactants on absorption enhancement have in the past been thought to be mainly due to direct interactions of the surfactant with biomembranes, at low concentrations causing increased fluidity and transport and at high concentrations causing solubilisation of key membrane components. Sometimes surfactants affect absorption in multiple ways, by interacting with the barrier membrane, by forming a microemulsion and thus aiding dispersal of lipophilic drugs or by affecting intestinal secretory transit.[25]

Conclusions

From these few examples it can be seen that excipients are not always just bystanders in formulations. The field is made more complex by the use of many trade names for dyes and surfactants, so identifying causative agents of adverse events, or positive events such as absorption enhancement, is not always straightforward. Batch-to-batch variation in excipients may be a problem: different amounts of certain impurities such as catalysts may be present depending on the batch and mode of manufacture.

More examples of how excipients contribute to the properties of the finished dose form are discussed in Chapter 6.

References

1. Uchegbu IF, Florence AT. Adverse drug events related to dosage forms and delivery systems. *Drug Saf* 1996; 14: 39–67.
2. Pifferi G, Restani P. The safety of pharmaceutical excipients. *Il Farmaco* 2003; 58: 541–550.
3. Balbani APS *et al*. Pharmaceutical excipients and the information on drug labels. *Rev Bras Otorinolaringol* 2006; 72: 400–406.
4. Gogate US *et al*. Effect of unpurified Cremophor El on the solution stability of paclitaxel. *Pharm Dev Technol* 2009; 14: 1–8.

5. Ha E *et al*. Peroxide formation in polysorbate 80 and protein stability. *J Pharm Sci* 2002; 91: 2252–2264.
6. Millar JS. Pitfalls of 'inert' ingredients. *Br J Gen Pract* 2001; 51: 570.
7. Cubitt GT. Pitfalls of 'inert' ingredients. *Br J Gen Pract* 2001; 51: 756.
8. Seidenari S *et al*. Cross-sensitisations between azo dyes and *para*-amino compound: a study of 236 azo-dye-sensitive subjects. *Contact Dermatitis* 1997; 36: 91–96.
9. Mertes PM *et al*. Anaphylaxis to dyes during the perioperative period: reports of 14 clinical cases. *J Allergy Clin Immunol* 2008; 122: 348–352.
10. Scherer K *et al*. Blue dyes in medicine – a confusing terminology. *Contact Dermatitis* 2006; 54: 231–232.
11. Yusim Y *et al*. Blue dyes, blue people: the system effects of blue dyes when administered via different routes. *J Clin Anesth* 2007; 19: 315–3321.
12. ten Tije AJ *et al*. Pharmacological effects of formulation vehicles: implications in cancer chemotherapy. *Clin Pharmacokinet* 2003; 42: 665–685.
13. Phillips DM, Zacharopoulous VR. Nonoxynol-9 enhances rectal infection by herpes simplex virus in mice. *Contraception* 1998; 57(5): 341–348.
14. Kelly RF *et al*. Effect of poloxamer 188 collateral blood flow, myocardial infarct size and left ventricular function in a canine model or prolonged coronary occlusion and reperfusion. *J Thromb Thrombolysis* 2004; 5: 239–247.
15. See for example: Smith CM *et al*. Pluronic F-68 reduces the endothelial adherence and improves the rheology of liganded sickle erythrocytes. *Blood* 1987; 69: 1631–1636.
16. Lee R. Pipe Dream or Paradigm Shift? *University of Chicago Magazine* 2006 February; 98(3). Available at magazine.uchicago.edu/0602/features.
17. Orringer EP *et al*. Purified poloxamer 188 for treatment of acute vaso-occlusive crisis of sickle cell disease. *JAMA* 2001; 286: 2099–2106.
18. Medicine.net.com. Pleurisy. http://www.medicinenet.com/pleurisy/article.htm (accessed 20 September 2009).
19. Aelony Y. Talc pleurodesis and acute respiratory distress syndrome. *Lancet* 2007; 369: (9572), 1494–1496.
20. Marchi E *et al*. Talc for pleurodesis. Hero or villain? *Chest* 2003; 124: 416–417.
21. Werebe ED *et al*. Systemic distribution of talc after interpleural administration in rats. *Chest* 1999; 115: 190–193.
22. Ferrar J *et al*. Influence of particle size on extrapleural talc dissemination after talc slurry pleurodesis. *Chest* 2002; 122: 1018–1027.
23. US Food and Drug Administration. Centre for Devices and Radiological Health. Device Advice: Device Regulation and Guidance. http://www.fda.gov/MedicalDevices/DeviceRegulationandGuidance/default.htm.
24. Bogman K *et al*. The role of surfactants in the reversal of active transport mediated by multidrug resistance proteins. *J Pharm Sci* 2003; 92: 1250–1261.
25. Hu Z *et al*. A novel emulsifier, Labrasol enhances gastrointestinal absorption of gentamicin. *Life Sci* 2001; 69: 2899–2810.

3

Thinking chemically

In this chapter we consider the value of remembering more about the chemistry of drugs, that is, both their organic and their physical chemistry. Chemistry has a large part to play in applying pharmaceutics. There is no pharmaceutics proper without a consideration of the issues in this chapter. However, in the context of this book we cannot go far into the field of medicinal chemistry as such.

Introduction

The representation of a drug molecule by a structural formula, especially a space-filling model, should convey several important messages about the molecule, about its size, shape and nature, frequently determined by the reactive groups and side-chains. Structures often show clearly the relationship to other drugs. Equations used in physical chemistry should convey a meaning also, but when one is faced with both formulae and equations the relevance does not always shine through. One cannot retain in one's memory the structures of all drugs and excipients one has come across. There are particular problems with the structures of proteins and oligopeptides, which do not lend themselves to detailed representation in the same way as for smaller molecules. Nonetheless, there are things to be learned from a knowledge of the primary, secondary and tertiary structures of proteins and other macromolecules and constructs. Even the comprehension of the size and molecular volume of these molecules can be valuable, especially in relation to their absorption.

It is not so much the knowledge of one particular compound that is of utmost importance, but the recognition of similarities between molecules and between classes of molecules; for example, to allow prediction of whether or not a new drug is likely to have similar pharmacological effects and side-effects to an established one with similar structure.

The chemistry of drugs and clinical pharmaceutics

Pharmaceutics would not exist without taking into account the chemistry of drugs and other therapeutic agents. Although chemistry is part and parcel of each pharmacy course, the clinical practice of pharmacy is hampered by the neglect of structural knowledge. For all the chemistry that is taught, sometimes the knowledge of drug properties and especially structure that remains in the memory at the end of a course is wanting. Yet the chemistry of a drug tells us much more than the manner of its synthesis and manufacture, important as these are, or about its mode of analysis; it hints at its stability, its methods of detection *in vivo*, its metabolism and its potential to form toxic, long-lasting or even active metabolites. Does drug X form adducts with proteins to cause adverse reactions? Are there indeed structural similarities between drug A and drug B. If so, this might allow us to define similarities in primary activity and also in side-effects. It is in these situations that a knowledge of chemistry allows pharmacists to be more scientific in their evaluation of drugs, drug actions and side-effects.

Remembering chemistry

Some feel that chemical formulae are really not important. Of course if one has never been convinced of their importance, chemical knowledge such as this fades and clearly will not be used in practice: this is a vicious cycle. In interviews I have had with a range of final-year students over three years, too many had difficulty showing that they were at ease with the chemistry of drugs, even at a superficial level. Getting them to recognise the generic structure of a given tricyclic compound (Figure 3.1a) (that is, that it was a tricyclic compound) or a tetracyclic compound (b) (that is, that it was a tetracycle) or a steroid (c) was sometimes painful. The question was not 'What is the INN (International Non-proprietary Name) of this compound whose structure is shown here?', but 'Can you comment on what you see?'. The structures are shown in Figure 3.1.

There were also problems in differentiating macromolecules and smaller organic molecules. A feeling for the order of magnitude of the molecular weight of, say, insulin was far from universal. Some believed that this was around 600, perhaps in line with the expressed belief that steroids are macromolecules. Knowing the INN or chemical names of drugs, but not having a feeling for their structures or properties tells only part of the story. If one can remember the pharmacological action or therapeutic use of a drug but can convey little of what the compound is like chemically, the opportunities to contribute over and above the common knowledge of other health care providers will be lost. This is especially true when we are discussing comparisons between drugs in the same pharmacological class with different chemistries, or those that are in different classes but which have similar chemistry.

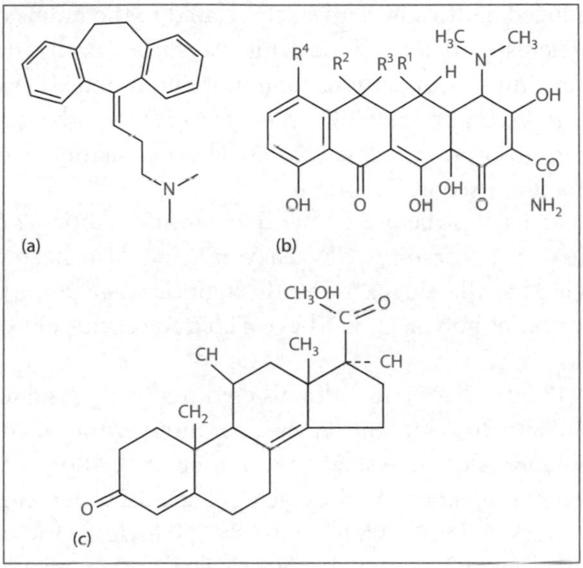

Figure 3.1 (a) A tricyclic compound; (b) a tetracyclic compound; (c) a steroid used in questions.

Some peptides

Having said this, the structure of most oligopeptides and proteins and drugs such as vancomycin (see Figure 3.2) could never be memorized, so other strategies have to be adopted when dealing with these: knowledge of molecular size is important. Molecular size is key in relation to absorption and diffusion. The larger the molecule, all other things being equal, the lower is the

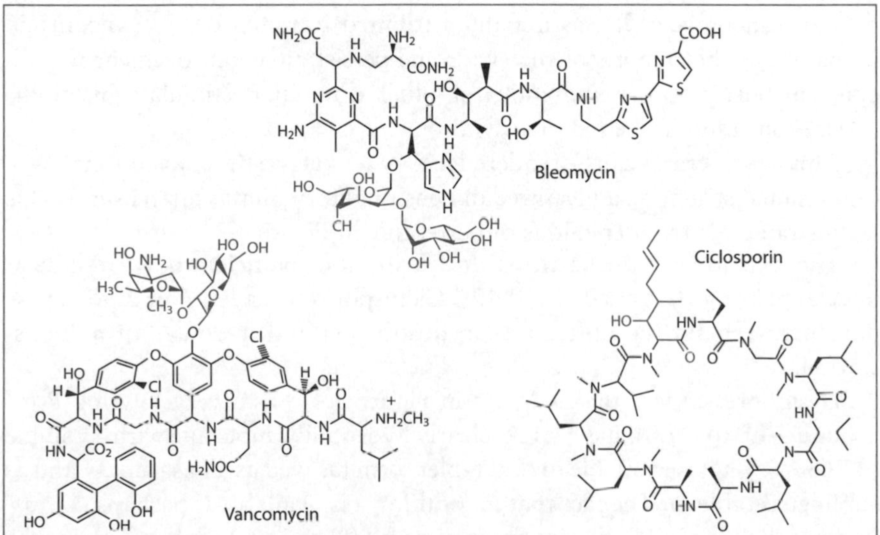

Figure 3.2 Bleomycin, vancomycin and ciclosporin structures.

absorption reduced. Diffusion is inversely related to the radius of a molecule or a particle. Ciclosporin is a peptide yet it is absorbed orally to the extent of around 15% in simple formulations (and more in optimised systems). It is a cyclic peptide and it is also lipophilic: these features contribute to its stability in the gut and its absorption characteristics. The formulation of ciclosporin in lipid vehicles is discussed in Chapter 4.

Knowing the basic structure of the β-lactam antibiotics, one will recall why penicillin can be destroyed by enzymes, but also how impurities in penicillin can lead to allergic reactions, through cleavage of the β-lactam ring and the formation of polymers that have a characteristic peptide linkage (as we will discuss).

Bleomycin (Figure 3.2) is not administered orally; its systemic absorption ranges from 40% to 80% after intrapleural or intraperitoneal administration. The pharmacokinetics of large single intramuscular (IM) or intravenous (IV) injections are almost identical. Vancomycin (Figure 3.2) is a complex molecule with six pK_a values: 7.75 (the NH_2) and 8.89 (NH-Me) (basic) and 2.18 (the carboxyl), 9.59, 10.4 and 12 (the phenolic OH groups) (acidic).[1] Vancomycin is given both intravenously and orally. Because of its size and relative hydrophilicity it is poorly absorbed after oral administration, but as it is used to treat colitis its effect is local and not systemic. Nonetheless, significant absorption has been reported in a patient with bowel inflammation caused by *Clostridium difficile*.[2] The permeability of the epithelium is enhanced in a variety of inflammatory bowel conditions. A 23-month-old child has also been reported to have experienced 'red man syndrome' after oral vancomycin for *C. difficile* colitis, usually experienced after high parenteral doses.[3] Red man syndrome (flushing of the upper body) is often associated with rapid infusion of the first dose of vancomycin. It was initially attributed to impurities in vancomycin preparations, but reports of the syndrome persist after improvement in vancomycin purity. Other antibiotics or other drugs that stimulate histamine release can result in the red man syndrome.

Peptide structures can be rendered in different ways: the conventional two-dimensional structure, and a three-dimensional form that is often useful. This is illustrated for two depictions of octreotide in Figure 3.3.

The logarithm of the partition or distribution coefficient of octreotide at neutral pH (log P) is cited as -0.49.[4] Ciclosporin has a log P of 2.96. These data may explain the differences in absorption and in routes of administration.

Desmopressin (see the structure in Figure 3.4) has a very low log P (of around -4.0 to -5.0). It is a large, clearly hydrophilic molecule with a volume of 768 Å^3, yet it is available in oral tablet form (as well as a nasal spray and as sublingual tablets). The fact that an oral form is available is perhaps confusing, but the bioavailability (in the range of 0.08–0.16%) must be one of the lowest that has been accepted for oral administration.

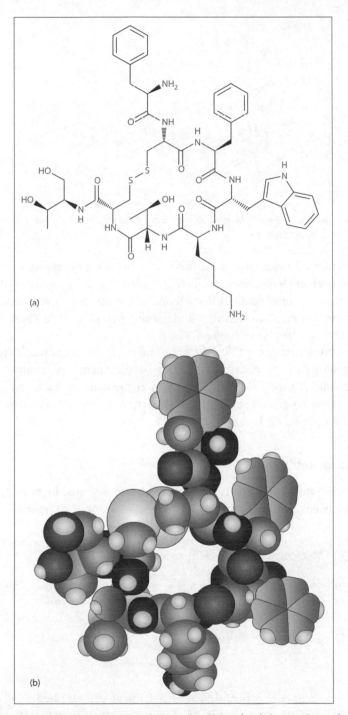

(a)

(b)

Figure 3.3 Octreotide structure in 2D and 3D modes. The molecule has a volume of 751.35 Å^3.

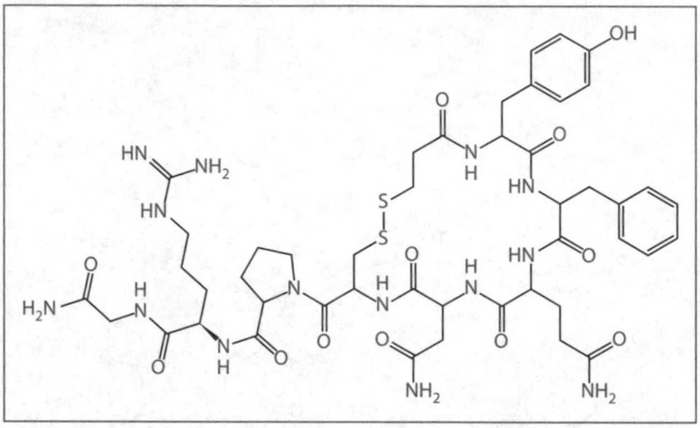

Figure 3.4 Desmopressin: its hydrophilic character can be readily seen in this structural diagram. It is used as the acetate trihydrate.

Molecular size is related to diffusion in tissues, and also to absorption across biological membranes (see Box 3.1). With generic versions of recombinant proteins, some detailed knowledge of the effect of amino acid substitution is important if we wish to understand potential differences between so-called biosimilars (see Chapter 7).

The formulation of peptides, proteins and other macromolecules to a large extent determines the pharmacokinetics of the agent. An example would be octreotide as Sandostatin LAR, in which the drug is dispersed in 30 μm poly(D,L-lactic-co-glycolic acid) (PLGA) particles; these release drug into the body over a period of 4 weeks.

Monoclonal antibodies

Monoclonal antibodies are large structures whose introduction into medicine has been a slow process. To give an example of complexity, the

---

Box 3.1 Molecular size and diffusion

For spherical molecules and particles the Stokes–Einstein equation applies. The diffusion coefficient, D, is related to the radius (r) of the system diffusing by this equation, where η is the viscosity of the liquid in which the molecule diffuses:

$$D = kT/6\pi\eta r$$

For asymmetric molecules, whether linear or branched or planar, the radius is the so-called hydrodynamic radius, which reflects the effective radius of the molecule in tumbling motion.

molecular weight of infliximab (which binds to the soluble and transmem-branous forms of TNFα) is 144 190 Da and its atomic composition is $C_{6428}H_{9912}N_{1694}O_{1987}S_{46}$, which reveals little apart from its sheer size. However, its size perhaps explains both the time to reach a maximum serum concentration (some 7 days[5] after subcutaneous (SC) administration) and its plasma half-life of 9.5 days. The crystalline form of infliximab used in the study was developed for SC administration and shows an extended serum pharmacokinetic profile and high bioavailability compared with the soluble form delivered intravenously.[6]

Chemical nomenclature

The INN names chosen for drugs naturally indicate something about their structure and therapeutic class. Excipients are classified in a less forma-lised way. If we consider for discussion a compound that is not a drug but is an active formulation component, benzalkonium chloride (see Figure 3.5), it is clear from its name alone that it has a benzyl group, an alkyl group (hydrophobic) and an 'onium' group (hydrophilic). The space-filling model clearly exhibits the form of a surface-active agent. Even if it can be sketched out only roughly, it will be evident that it is a molecule with a hydrophobic portion and hydrophilic entity. It is in fact a cationic surfactant.

Benzalkonium chloride is often found as a mixture of alkyl derivatives of different chain lengths, but it is shown in Figure 3.5 as dodecyl dimethyl

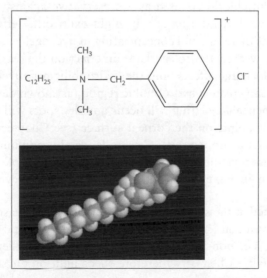

Figure 3.5 Benzalkonium chloride: conventional representation above and space-filling representation below.

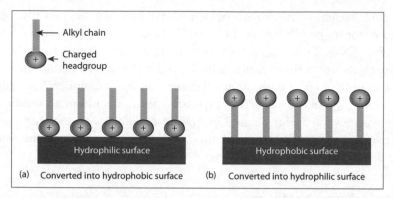

Figure 3.6 Diagrammatic representation of the effects of the adsorption at low concentrations of a cationic surfactant or bactericide (a) by charge–charge interactions with a polar hydrophilic surface and (b) by hydrophobic interactions with a non-polar surface.

benzyl ammonium chloride: conventional representation above and space-filling diagram below). The compound is often a mixture of alkyl chain lengths. The fact that the substance is known as a benzyl-alkyl compound – rather than say a benzyl-dodecyl compound – reflects the fact that it contains a mixture of alkyl derivatives.

Apart from its antibacterial properties, not unrelated to its surface activity, it will adsorb onto all surfaces including biological membranes, contact lenses and glassware; it will lower surface tension, and will change hydrophobic surfaces into hydrophilic surfaces and hydrophilic surfaces into hydrophobic surfaces (Figure 3.6).

Benzalkonium chloride is used as a preservative against microbial contamination in eye drops during use. It might exert other effects: adsorbing onto contact lens material, and concentrating in hydrogel lenses, it can cause irritation to the wearer. It also can have an effect on the tear film itself: if it adsorbs through charge effects onto the hydrophilic negatively charged corneal surface, it can create a hydrophobic region (as shown diagrammatically in Figure 3.6); hence de-wetting will occur and dry spots will give rise to dry eye syndrome at points on the corneal surface (see Chapter 1). Other cationic surfactants are antibacterial. Cetrimide (cetylpyridinium chloride) and CTAC (cetyltrimethylammonium chloride) are two examples, whose structures are shown in Figure 3.7. All those discussed are cytotoxic at high concentrations.

Having looked at the surface-active bactericides, it is reasonable perhaps to expect that even non-ionic surfactants may have biological activity, which indeed they do. The non-ionic nonoxynol has both anaesthetic activity and spermicidal activity. Chemistry therefore sheds light on physical properties, and common properties such as amphipathic structures can lead to intelligent speculation about a compound's behaviour.

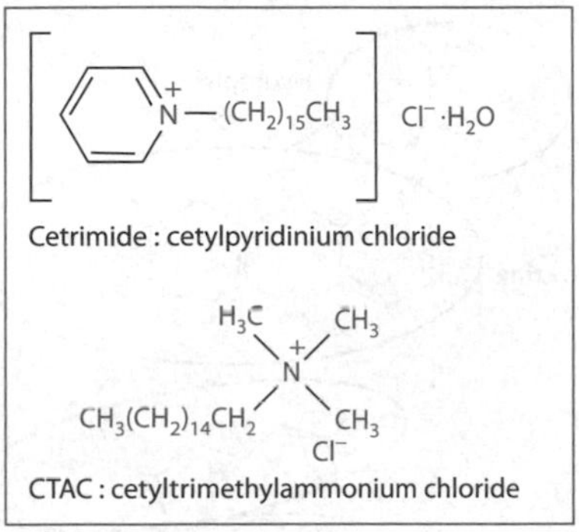

Cetrimide : cetylpyridinium chloride

CTAC : cetyltrimethylammonium chloride

Figure 3.7　Cetrimide (cetylpyridinium chloride) and CTAC (cetyltrimethylammonium chloride).

Surface-active drugs

Many drugs have properties of surfactant molecules[7], possessing in their structure both clearly differentiated hydrophobic and hydrophilic groups. Examples include chlorpromazine, tetracaine, oxprenolol, sodium fusidate, nortriptyline and amphotericin B. The structures of some of these are given in Figure 3.8 to demonstrate the individual structural features necessary for surface activity.

Does surface activity really matter? Given the wide range of actions of surfactant molecules, the possession of this characteristic implies membrane-activity in the case of drug molecules. Critical micellar concentrations of most surface-active drugs are higher than the concentrations they attain *in vivo*, so micellar properties are unlikely to be an issue except in concentrates. The abilities of molecules in dilute solution to decrease surface tension, cause haemolysis, adsorb onto glassware or interact with membranes are all properties of surface-active agents.

Acids and bases

Knowledge of the acidic and basic, zwitterionic or non-ionic properties of drugs allows us to approach answers to questions such as:

1　Is absorption of drug A affected by H_2-blockers, antacids or achlorhydria?
2　Will an increase in pH of the drug solution cause an increase or decrease in the solubility of the drug?
3　Will the drug precipitate when mixed with this fluid?
4　Will alkalinisation of the urine increase or decrease tubular reabsorption?

and so on.

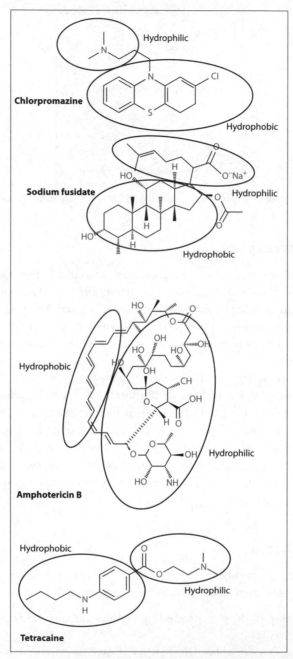

Figure 3.8 Chlorpromazine, sodium fusidate, amphotericin B and tetracaine, showing the hydrophilic and hydrophobic moieties that confer surface-active properties to the molecules.

We cannot really opt for omitting fundamental pieces of pharmaceutical knowledge. We cannot predict under what circumstances, or when, these stored pieces of information will become vital, even if only once in a lifetime. They may save someone's life.

Solubility of acidic and basic drugs

One of the most important relationships in pharmacy, and one that has many ramifications in practice, is that linking pH, pK_a and solubility for acids and bases (see Box 3.2). This is mostly relevant in predicting precipitation of drugs or the outcome of mixing drugs in IV fluids and giving sets. Even in very complex molecules one can look for the appropriate chemical groups, which are those that ionise, confer solubility in aqueous or lipid environments, or lead to breakdown or metabolism. It has to be admitted that in some cases, for example vancomycin, which we have seen has six ionisable groups, it is not simple to predict solubility at different pH values. But solubility experiments are quite straightforward to carry out to determine whether precipitation occurs, for example.

From the equations in Box 3.2, the solubility, S, can be calculated if S_0 is known and the pK_a of the drug is known. One unit change in pH causes a 10-fold change in solubility. Many solutions used in IV therapy, such as dextrose, have pH specifications that vary over at least this range.

Examples of unwanted precipitation of drugs are discussed in Chapter 1. Precipitation can occur when the equilibrium solubility of a compound in solution is exceeded, when the pH of the medium changes either because of addition of buffers or addition of an acidic or basic drug, or owing to electrostatic interactions between an acidic and a basic drug where both are in the ionised state.

Box 3.2 pH, pK_a and solubility

The equation relating pH, pK_a and solubility of acidic drugs, where S is the solubility at any given pH and S_0 is the solubility of the undissociated form of the drug takes the following forms.

For *acidic* drugs:

$$pH - pK_a = \log \left[(S - S_0)/S_0 \right]$$

For *basic* drugs:

$$pH - pK_a = \log \left[S_0/(S - S_0) \right]$$

In the first case the equation can be used in the form

$$S = S_0 [\text{antilog} (pH - pK_a) + 1]$$

and the analogous expression in the second case.

(For further details, see AT Florence and D Attwood, *Physicochemical Principles of Pharmacy*, 4th edn, Pharmaceutical Press, London, 2006, pp. 150–155 and D Attwood and AT Florence, *Physical Pharmacy*, Pharmaceutical Press, London, 2008, pp. 14–19.)

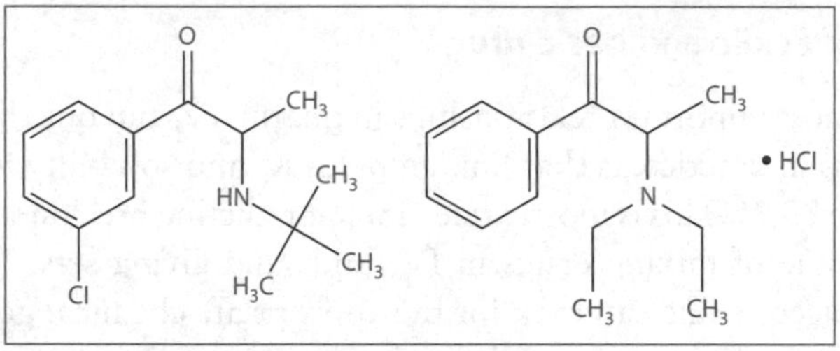

Figure 3.9 Bupropion (left) and diethylpropion·HCl (right).

Structural similarities between drugs

Bupropion and diethylpropion

It has been suggested that the structure of bupropion – a drug with antide-pressant properties used primarily as an aid in smoking cessation – is 'almost identical to' that of the controlled drug diethylpropion. The question that this raised is why the two are treated differently in their legal classification. The structures of the drugs are shown in Figure 3.9. Is there indeed the pharmacological effect that one would expect from such analogues? Diethylpropion (Tenuate) is used in the pharmacotherapy of obesity; bupropion (Zyban) has also been studied as an aid to weight loss. One report[8] states that 'there is a serious risk of incorrectly identifying bupropion as only a therapy for nicotine withdrawal without taking the precaution of exploring possible psychiatric co-morbidity.' Diethylpropion also can induce psychotic episodes, but rarely does so at normal doses.

Cross-reactivity

Cross-reactivity relates to the observation of similar pharmacological, immu-nological or adverse effects of a drug that has structural similarities to another causative agent. The topic of cross-reactivity (generally in the adverse event sense) is a good example of how we need a chemical basis to understand this aspect of medicine. Shenfield and Jackal[9] discuss the possibility of the cross-reactivity between sulfonamides and structurally related drugs such as the sulfonylureas. They refer to a suggestion that sulfonylureas were not recom-mended in patients with a history of adverse drug reactions (ADRs) to sulfonamides was unwarranted. They provide some evidence that this is true. Why indeed should there be such suggestions in the first place? Some struc-tures of sulfonamides and sulfonylureas given in Figure 3.10 and Table 3.1 suggest why.

Cross-reactivity of sulfonamides

Understanding cross-reactivity is a powerful aid to prediction and explana-tion of adverse events. As we can see from Figure 3.10, the structural feature

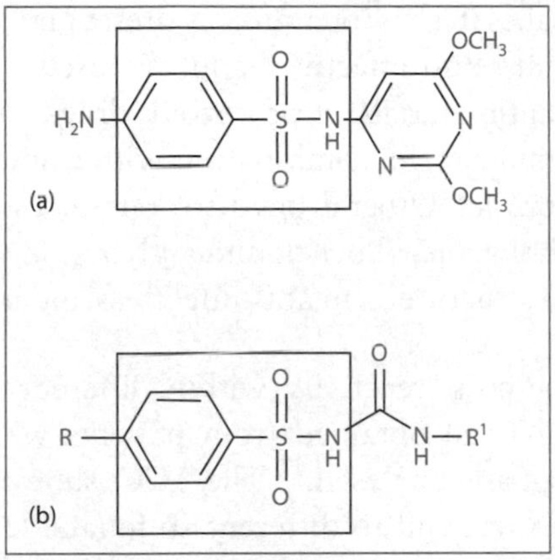

Figure 3.10 Structures of sulfonamides and sulfonylureas. (a) and (b) show the overlapping structures in sulfonamides (a) and sulfonylureas (b).

Table 3.1 The structures of some common sulfonylureas

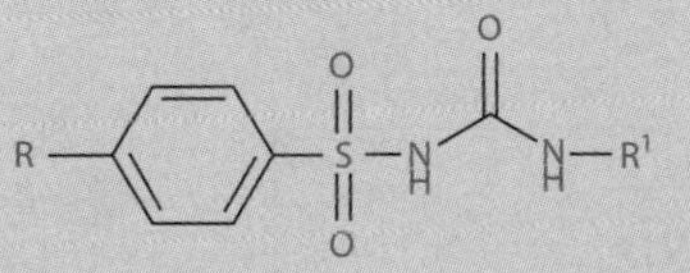

Name	R	R¹
Tolbutamide	–CH₃	–CH₂CH₂CH₂CH₃
Chlorpropamide	–Cl	–CH₂CH₂CH₃
Tolazamide	–CH₃	(azepane ring)
Acetohexamide	(CH₃C=O)	(cyclohexyl)
Glibenclamide	(Cl, OMe substituted benzamide, –NHCH₂CH₂–)	(cyclohexyl)
Glipizide	(methylpyrazine carboxamide, –NHCH₂CH₂–)	(cyclohexyl)
Glimepiride	(pyrroline derivative, –NHCH₂CH₂–)	(4-methylcyclohexyl)

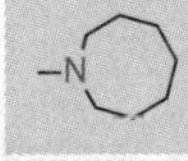

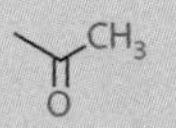

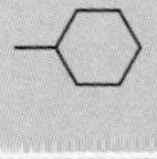

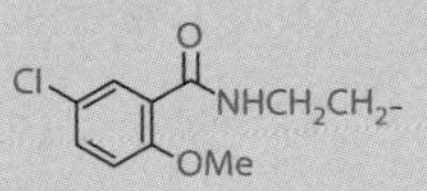

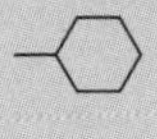

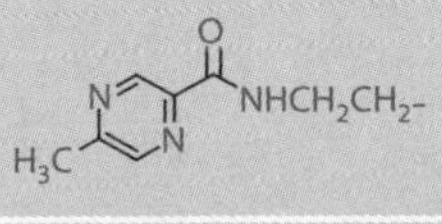

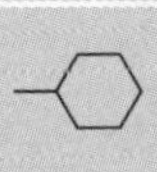

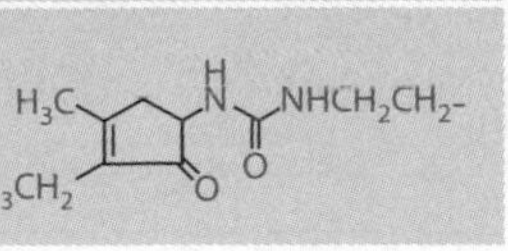

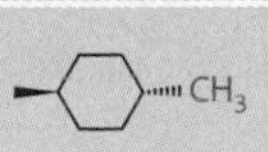

within a drug that makes it a 'sulfonamide' is present in many different drugs. Some sulfonamides are anti-infectives and are used in combination with pyrimethamine as antimalarial/antiprotozoal drugs, as anti-infectives in eye-drops (sulfacetamide), or in combination with trimethoprim (sulfamethoxazole in co-trimoxazole). Other drugs also contain a sulfonamide structure (celecoxib, sulfamethoxazole, glibenclamide (glyburide); see Figure 3.11) but not the sulfanilamide structure as in anti-infectives and have no anti-infective capacity.

To investigate the cross-reactivity within different sulfonamide derivatives, T-cell clones (TCCs) obtained from patients with sulfamethoxazole allergy were generated and analysed.[10] The TCCs showed a quite high diversity in their ability to respond to different sulfonamide derivatives. On the one hand, one-half of the clones were highly specific and could be stimulated by sulfamethoxazole only. On the other hand, several clones showed a broad cross-reactivity, responding to up to nine different compounds sharing only a small structural similarity of the side-chain.[10] But all cross-reactive compounds had the sulfanilamide-core structure in common.

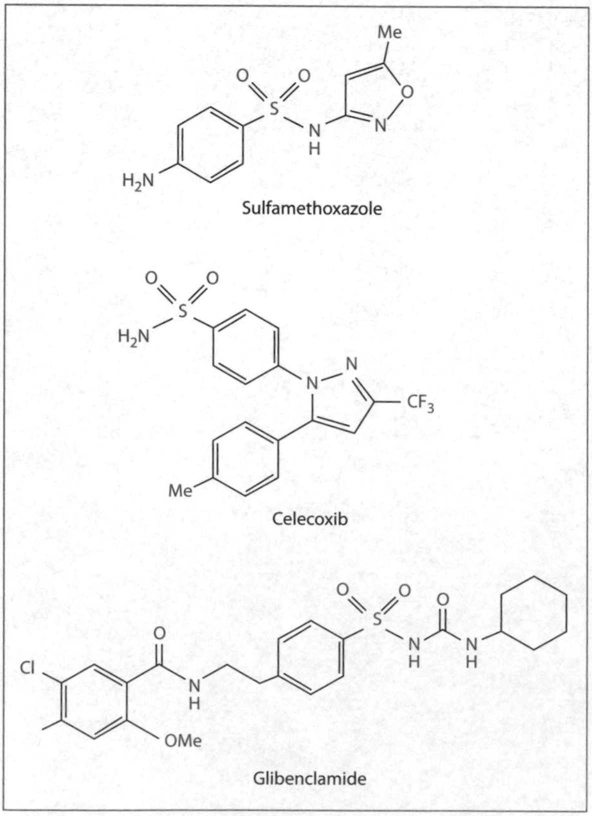

Figure 3.11 Sulfamethoxazole, celecoxib and glibenclamide.

Table 3.2 Classification of allergy due to topical corticosteroids	
Group	**Agent**
A	Hydrocortisone (see structure in Figure 3.12a), hydrocortisone acetate, cortisone acetate, tixocortol pivalate (see structure in Figure 3.12a), prednisolone, meprednisone
B	Triamcinolone acetonide, triamcinolone alcohol, amcinomide, budenoside, desonide, fluocinonide, flucinolone acetonide (see structure in Figure 3.12b), halcinonide
C	Betamethasone, betamethasone sodium phosphate, dexamethasone, dexamethasone sodium phosphate, fluocortolone
D	Hydrocortisone 17-butyrate, hydrocortisone 17-valerate, alclometasone dipropionate, betamethasone valerate, betamethasone dipropionate, prednicarbate, clobetasol 17-butyrate, clobetasol 17-propionate, fluocortolone caproate, fluocortolone pivalate, fluprenidene acetate

Cross-reactivity of topical steroids

Contact dermatitis and testing for topical reactivity are discussed in Chapter 5. Here we refer to the observed cross-reactivity in allergies to topically applied corticosteroids. A classification of allergy due to steroids[11] is given in Table 3.2, but it is not easy to understand from a simple structural point of view (see Figure 3.12)! The table is included here to demonstrate that not all explanations have a straightforward chemical basis.

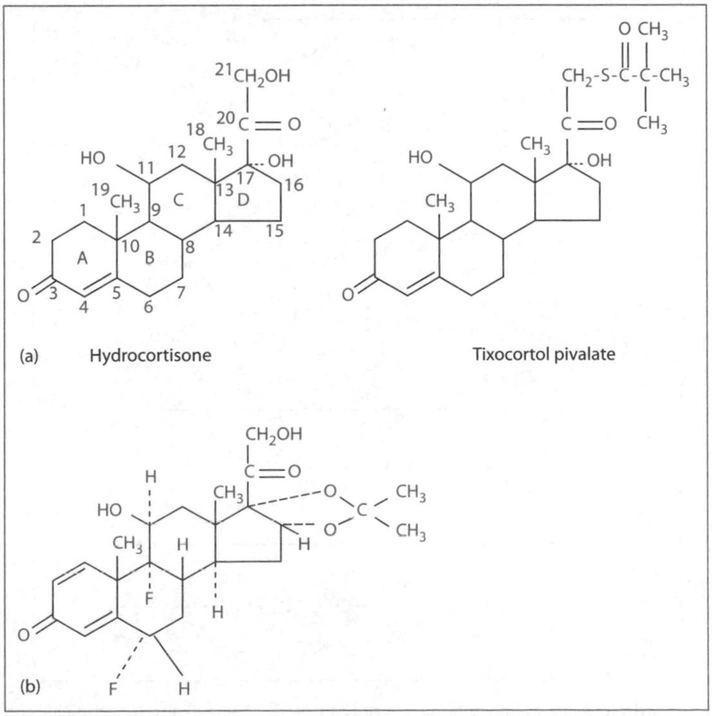

Figure 3.12 (a) Hydrocortisone and tixocortol pivalate, two compounds from Group A steroids. (b) Fluocinonide acetonide: a steroid from Group B. (See Table 3.2)

All these structures of the steroids would need examination along with their physical properties to begin to appreciate their activity. This is the dilemma. However, a neglect of structure will not aid the process and the table will remain a list to be memorised without a solid basis.

Beta-lactam antibiotics and the formation of oligomers

It is clear from the basic structure of the β-lactam antibiotics (see Figure 3.13[12]) how these compounds can be degraded through cleavage of the β-lactam ring and form polymers that have a characteristic peptide linkage. This is what causes these oligomers, dimers, trimers, etc. to have allergic potential.

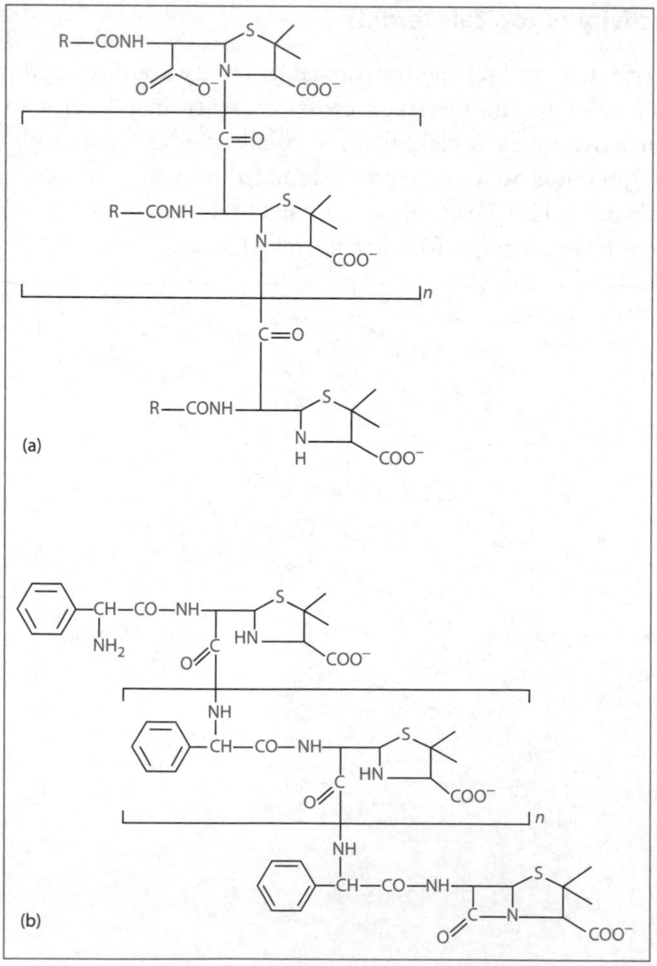

Figure 3.13 Structures of (a) benzylpenicillin polymers (R = benzyl) and (b) ampicillin polymers. In the latter the terminal β-lactam ring may be intact or open. (From reference 12.)

The bisphosphonates

The bisphosphonates are used in osteoporosis to inhibit the resorption of bone by osteoclasts. Their structure gives them a high affinity for bone. They are structurally similar to pyrophosphoric acid and their structural features important to activity are shown in Table 3.3.[13] The binding to hydroxyapatite and the biological action of bisphosphonates depends on the P–C–P group and the structure of the R^1 and R^2 side-chains As one might imagine from their hydrophilic properties, in spite of various modifications to the R^1 and R^2 side-chains, they are generally very poorly absorbed after oral administration. They are administered as their sodium salts, and have bioavailabilities as

Table 3.3 Bisphosphonate structures.

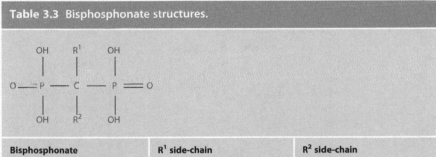

Bisphosphonate	R^1 side-chain	R^2 side-chain
Etidronate[a]	OH	CH_3
Clodronate[b]	Cl	Cl
Pamidronate[b]	OH	$CH_2CH_2NH_2$
Alendronate[a]	OH	$(CH_2)_3NH_2$
Risedronate[a]	OH	CH_2-3-pyridine
Tiludronate[a]	H	CH_2-S-phenyl-Cl
Ibandronate[b]	OH	$CH_2CH_2N(CH_3)$(pentyl)
Zoledronate[b]	OH	CH_2-imidazole
YH 529	OH	CH_2-2-imidazo-pyridinyl
Incadronate	H	N-(cylclo-heptyl)
Olpadronate	OH	$CH_2CH_2N(CH_3)_2$
Neridronate	OH	$(CH_2)_5NH_2$
EB-1053	OH	CH_2-1-pyrrolidinyl

[a] Bisphosphonates approved for use in non-malignant conditions.
[b] Bisphosphonates approved for use in malignancy for one or more indications.
Other agents are only available for experimental purposes.
(Modified from reference 13 and other sources.)

low as 1%. The instructions for use by patients are to take the products with copious water because the bisphosphonates are irritant to the oesophageal tissues and one must avoid oesophageal capture which results in oesophageal pain and dysphagia.[14] For further examples of this, see Chapter 5 on adverse reactions to formulations.

Hydrophobic and hydrophilic statins

Statins lower blood cholesterol and are prescribed for patients with hypercholesterolaemia or hyperlipidaemia. There are two main types of statins, classified on the basis of their physical properties.[15] These are the hydrophobic statins such as simvastatin or atorvastatin, and hydrophilic statins such as pravastatin (Figure 3.14). The pharmacokinetics of individual statins are

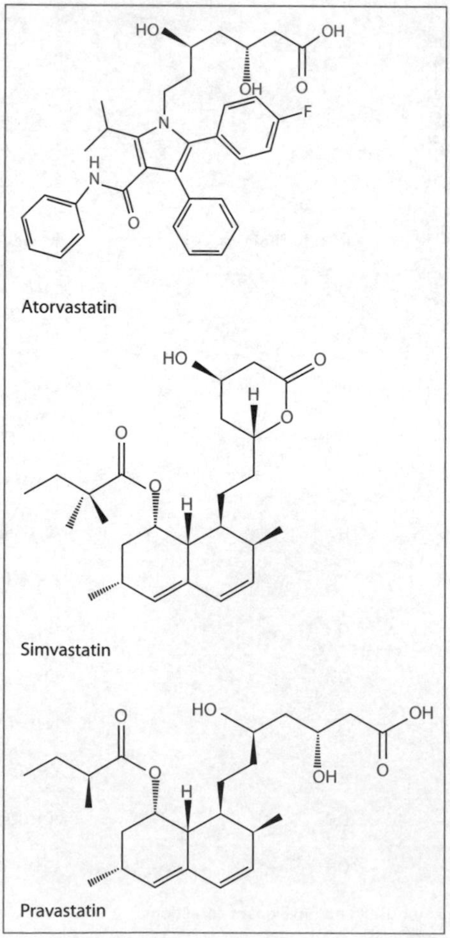

Figure 3.14   Atorvastatin, simvastatin and pravastatin.

influenced by their hydrophobicity. The hydrophobic compounds are transported by passive diffusion and are better substrates for both the P450 (CYP) family of enzymes and transporters involved in biliary excretion. The more hydrophilic pravastatin requires active transport into the liver, is less metabolised by the cytochrome CYP family, and exhibits more pronounced active renal excretion.

Hydrophobic statins can enter extrahepatic and hepatic cells by passive diffusion. Hydrophilic statins are distributed more selectively in hepatic cells. It has been suggested that the former inhibit not only cholesterol synthesis but also the production of essential substances in many extrahepatic tissues and hence cause additional side-effects.

Statins act by inhibiting 3-hydroxy-3-methylglutaryl-coenzyme A (HMG-CoA) reductase, thereby reducing cholesterol synthesis (see structures in Figure 3.15). Differences in statin structure and binding characteristics contribute to differences in potency of HMG-CoA reductase inhibition and other pharmacological properties.

X-ray crystallographic studies[16] show that the HMG-like moiety built into statin molecules occupies the HMG binding site of the enzyme. Hydrophobic groups of the statins occupy a binding site exposed by movement of flexible helices in the enzyme catalytic domain. In addition to bonds formed by the HMG-like moiety, statins exhibit different binding interactions in association with their structural differences. Type 1 statins (e.g. simvastatin) exhibit binding via a decalin ring structure, and type 2 statins (e.g., rosuvastatin, atorvastatin, fluvastatin) exhibit additional binding via their fluorophenyl group. Rosuvastatin and atorvastatin exhibit hydrogen bonds absent from other type 2 statins; rosuvastatin forms a unique bond through its electronegative sulfone group (see Figure 3.15).

Photochemical reactions and photoinduced reactions

First, it is essential to define a variety of light-induced effects. These include:

- *Photoallergy*: an acquired immunological reactivity dependent on antibody- or cell-mediated hypersensitivity.
- *Photosensitivity*: a broad term used to describe an adverse reaction to light after drug administration, which may be photoallergic or phototoxic in nature.
- *Phototoxicity*: the conversion of an otherwise non-toxic chemical or drug to one that is toxic to tissues after absorption of electromagnetic radiation.
- *Photodynamic effects*: photoinduced damage requiring the presence of light, photosensitiser and molecular oxygen.

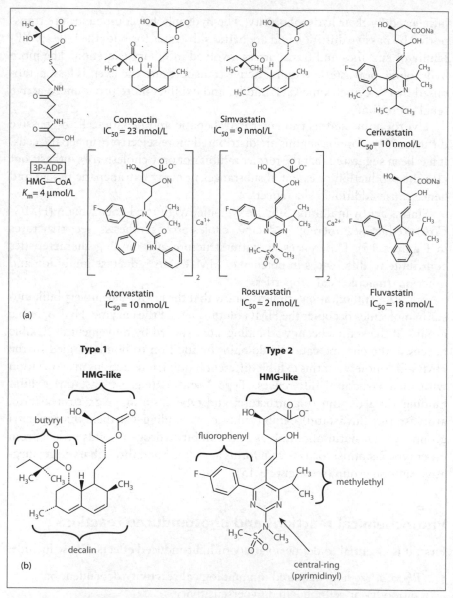

(a)

(b)

Figure 3.15 (a) The structure of HMG-CoA is shown at the left side of the diagram. Type 1 statins including compactin and simvastatin, and type 2 statins including atorvastatin and fluvastatin are shown. (b) The diagrams of the two types show some of the chemical differences between the them. The similarities between the HMG-like portions of the molecules are clear. The hydrophobic sites are indicated. (From reference 16.)

- *Photodynamic therapy (PDT)*: therapy in which photoactive drugs inactive in the unexcited state are administered and activated at particular sites in the body.

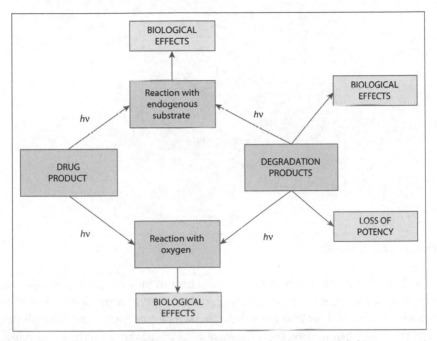

Figure 3.16 The consequences for a light-sensitive drug of interaction with light energy, causing biological effects and loss of potency depending on the compounds involved. (Redrawn from reference 17.)

Many drugs decompose *in vitro* after exposure to light, but the consequences depend on the nature of the breakdown products (Figure 3.16)[17]. Some derivatives of nifedipine have a very short photochemical half-life, sometimes of the order of a few minutes, while others decompose only after several weeks' exposure. A drug may not decompose after exposure to light, but may be the source of free radicals or of phototoxic metabolites *in vivo*. Adverse reactions occur when the drug or metabolites are exposed to light and the absorption spectrum of the drug coincides with the wavelength of light to which it is exposed. (The wavelengths of UV-A are 320–400 nm; of UV-B 280–320 nm; and of UV-C 200–290 nm.) To behave as a photoallergen, a drug or chemical must be able to absorb light energy present in sunlight and on absorption of the light generate a chemical species capable of binding to proteins in the skin, either directly or after metabolism.[18]

How do photosensitisers work?

In photodynamic therapy, drugs that may be activated by light are administered intravenously. The drug remains inactive until exposed to light with a wavelength that can penetrate the skin but is not completely attenuated by the

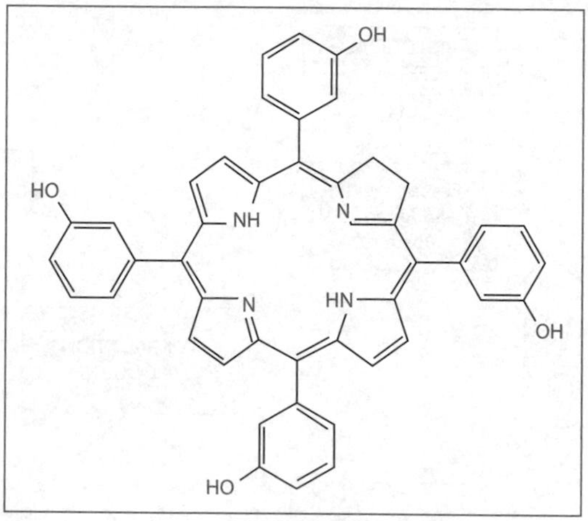

Figure 3.17 Temoporfin.

blood. Most photosensitive drugs respond best to blue or green light *in vitro*, but these wavelengths can pass through only a thin layer of human skin. Red blood cells absorb blue and green light, making it impossible for most photosensitisers to work in deep or bloody places. Texaphyrins, on the other hand, respond best to a specific red light that passes through blood. Light energy is directed to the required site through a fibre-optic device. When activated, the drug – usually a porphyrin derivative – creates oxygen radicals that destroy tissue in its vicinity. Principal side-effects of drugs like Photofrin are a skin sensitivity to light for up to 6 weeks as the drug is available systemically and partitions into lipid layers.

Other drugs cause light sensitivity; these are those that deposit in the skin and either interact with light or degrade to form coloured complexes. Coloration is not always sign of pathological change.

Temoporfin (Foscan; see Figure 3.17) and porfimer sodium (Photofrin) are used in PDT of various tumours. Activated by laser light they produce a cytotoxic effect in the tissues in which they accumulate. Temoporfin is licensed in the UK for the therapy of advanced head and neck cancers, while porfimer sodium is used in the PDT of non-small-cell lung cancer and oesophageal cancer. The cautions given in the BNF for porfimer are to 'avoid exposure of the skin to direct sunlight or bright indoor light for at least 30 days', and for temoporfin 'for at least 15 days' but to avoid prolonged exposure of the injection site to direct sunlight for 6 months after administration.

Chemical photosensitivity

In chemical photosensitivity, patients develop redness, inflammation, and sometimes brown or blue discoloration in areas of skin that have been

Table 3.4 Some substances that sensitise skin to sunlight	
Type	**Examples**
Anxiolytics	Alprazolam, chordiazepoxide
Antibiotics	Quinolones, sulfonamides, tetracyclines, trimethoprim
Antidepressants	Tricyclics
Antifungals (oral)	Griseofulvin
Antihypertensives	Sulfonylureas
Antimalarials	Chloroquine, quinine
Antipsychotics	Phenothiazines
Diuretics	Furosemide, thiazides
Chemotherapeutics	Dacarbazine, fluorouracil, methotrexate, vinblastine
Anti-acne drugs (oral)	Isotretinoin
Cardiovascular drugs	Amiodarone, quinidine
Skin preparations	Chlorhexidine, hexachlorophene, coal tar, fragrances, sunscreens

exposed to sunlight for a brief period. This reaction occurs after ingestion of drugs, such as tetracycline, or the application of compounds topically in consumer products such as perfumes or aftershaves. These substances (Table 3.4) may make some skin more sensitive to the effects of ultraviolet (UV) light. Some develop hives with itching, which indicates a type of drug allergy triggered by sunlight.

Burns after photodynamic therapy

Problems have been reported during a clinical trial with Foscan. This contains temoporfin as its active ingredient. In the trial it was alleged that a high proportion of patients suffered burns.[19] The manufacturer of the product complained that the results were at odds with more extensive trials of the product.[20] It subsequently emerged that in the trials the formulation of the product was different from that of the marketed product. It was claimed that a new solvent had been added so that the drug would be more soluble and less painful to administer. Here was the scenario: trial data are disputed, there is some confusion or inadequate reporting of the formulation used (there are many instances of this including the problems that arise with the different formulations of amphotericin) and an underlying effect of the active substance, a porphyrin. Later, two of the physicians involved in the trial[21] admitted that there may have been a connection between the leakage and the effect of the solvent as the active agent had spread from the point of administration. The adverse events were not due to extravasation injury itself as they occurred only after photoactivation.[22] This is a good example of the interlocking effects of drug, formulation and the nature of clinical trials, where the influence of the formulation was underestimated or neglected.

Chelation and tetracyclines

It is well known that tetracyclines chelate with divalent or trivalent ions, forming coloured compounds. The tetracyclines also chelate with growing teeth, so that children who have been prescribed tetracyclines can develop discoloured dentition. The colour of the complex depends on the tetracycline concerned. A tetracycline can be chosen that chelates only poorly or that does not form a strongly coloured product. The three potential chelation sites of doxycycline are shown in Figure 3.18. Chelation can also reduce the absorption of the tetracycline as the complexes formed have twice the molecular weight of the single drug molecule, as seen in see Figure 3.18b.

Sugammedex: a cyclodextrin derivative

Sugammedex (Figure 3.19) is an example of a modified excipient that is used therapeutically. It is a γ-cyclodextrin derivative which, when administered intravenously, complexes with rocuronium and other neuromuscular blocking agents (Figure 3.20) and thus reduces the levels of the anaesthetic, acting as an antagonist.[23] The complex is excreted mainly in the urine. The concept has been described as the 'doughnut and the hole' approach.[24]

The negative charge on the sugammedex (it is used as the sodium salt) attracts the positive charge of the rocuronium. Clearly sugammedex has affinities with other similar anaesthetic molecules such as vecuronium, but not atracurium which, as can be seen in Figure 3.20, has bulky benzylisoquinolinium groups that cannot be accommodated into the cavity of the cyclodextrin. Hence, levels of atracurium will not be changed by administration of sugammedex, but vecuronium levels are reduced. Although its affinity for the sugammedex is weaker, it is itself seven times more potent than rocuronium, so that fewer molecules are present. Vecuronium blockage can thus be successfully achieved. The possibilities of forming complexes with other steroidal molecules such as aldosterone and glucocorticoids have been found to be insignificant.

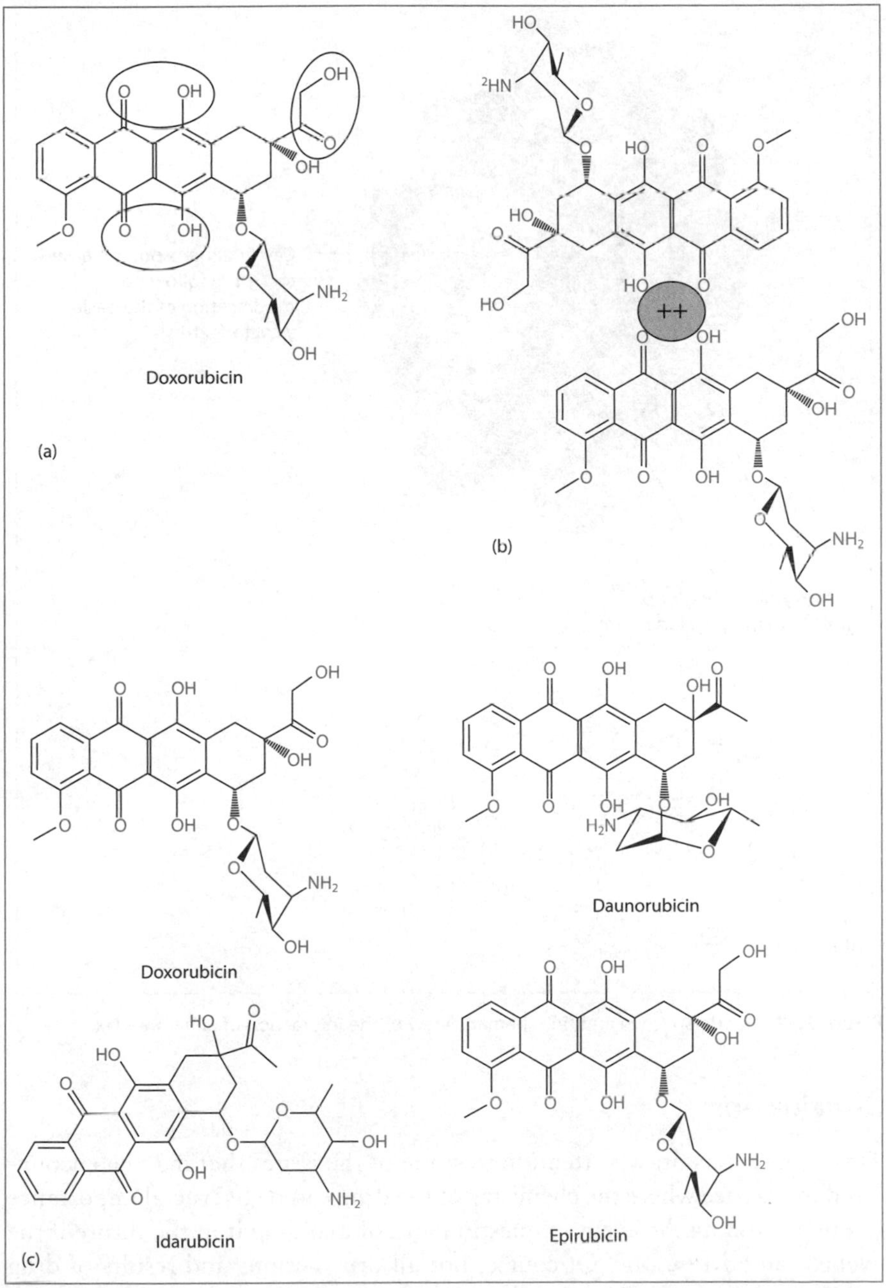

Figure 3.18 (a) Doxorubicin. (b) A 2:1 complex of doxycycline with a divalent ion, e.g. calcium. (c) Tetracycline derivatives: doxorubicin, daunorubicin, idarubicin and epirubicin do not all have the same ability to chelate with divalent or trivalent ions.

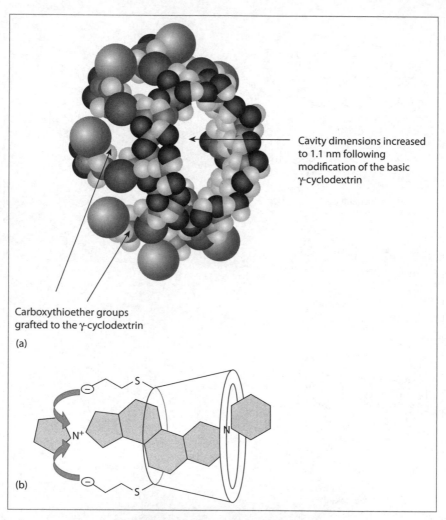

Cavity dimensions increased to 1.1 nm following modification of the basic γ-cyclodextrin

Carboxythioether groups grafted to the γ-cyclodextrin

(a)

(b)

Figure 3.19 (a) Perspective and (b) schematic view of the interaction of sugammedex.

Conclusions

This chapter has drawn attention to some of the issues that may be encountered in practice where the chemistry of the drug can be of crucial importance in understanding the event in question and of avoiding it in the future if the event is an adverse one. Of course, not all drug actions and results of drug intake can be explained by chemistry alone. One also has always to remember that the metabolite or metabolites of a drug, or its degradation products, may be the molecule or molecules to be concerned with. Thinking chemically gives an added dimension to the knowledge that pharmacists can bring to patient care. It does not require us to know every drug structure by heart, but it does require practice to think of a therapeutic agent as a molecule in a product – a

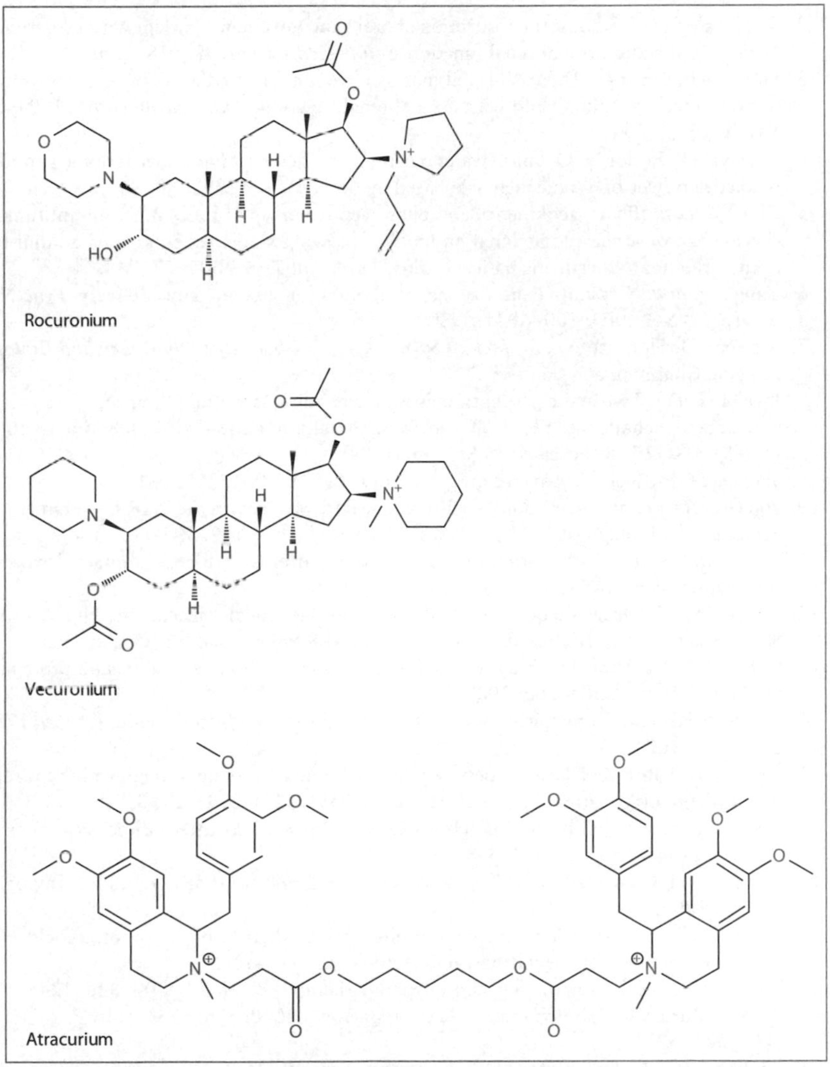

Figure 3.20 Neuromuscular blocking agents: rocuronium, vecuronium and atracurium.

molecule that degrades, that may photosensitise, that may complex with proteins, that may precipitate, and all the other possibilities dealt with in this short chapter. This forces us to look at drug structures and, where this is difficult, as with biological products, nevertheless to think of issues of overall size and charge and stability. In short, when faced with a problem concerning therapy, it is worth asking 'could it be the drug structure that holds the clue?'

References

1. Takács-Novák K *et al*. Acid–base properties and proton-speciation of vancomycin. *Int J Pharm* 1993; 89: 261–263.

2. Aradhyala S *et al*. Significant absorption of oral vancomycin in a patient with *Clostridium difficile* colitis and normal renal function. *South Med J* 2006; 99: 518–520.

3. Bergeron L, Boucher FD. Possible red-man syndrome associated with systemic absorption of oral vancomycin in a child with normal renal function. *Ann Pharmacother* 1994; 28: 581–584.

4. Buchwald P, Bodor N. Octanol–water partition coefficients of non-zwitterionic peptides: predictive power of a molecular size-based model. *Proteins* 1998; 30: 86–99.

5. Zhu YW *et al*. Pharmacokinetics and pharmacodynamics of infliximab, an antitumour necrosis factor-alpha monoclonal antibody, following single subcutaneous administrations in rheumatoid arthritis patients. *Clin Pharmacol Ther* 2005; 77: P43.

6. Yang MX *et al*. Crystalline monoclonal antibodies for subcutaneous delivery. *Proc Natl Acad Sci U S A* 2003; 100: 6934–6939.

7. Attwood D, Florence AT. *Surfactant Systems, Their Chemistry, Pharmacy and Biology*. London: Chapman and Hall, 1983.

8. Javelot H *et al*. Two acute psychotic episodes after administration of bupropion: a case of involuntary rechallenge. *Pharm World Science* 2009; 31: 238–240 (2008; doi 10.1007/s11096-008-9272-x, accessed 14 September 2009).

9. Shenfield GM, Jacka J. Adverse drug reactions. *Lancet* 2001; 357: 561.

10. von Greyerz S *et al*. Interaction of sulfonamide derivatives with the TCR of sulfamethoxazole-specific Human αβ+ T cell clones. *J Immunol* 1999; 162: 595–602.

11. Coopman S *et al*. Identification of cross-reaction patterns in allergic contact dermatitis from topical corticosteroids. *Br J Dermatol* 1989; 121: 27–34.

12. Bundgaard H. Drug allergy: chemical and pharmaceutical aspects. In: Florence AT, Salole EG, eds. *Formulation Factors in Adverse Reactions*. London: Wright, 1990.

13. Catterall JB, Cawston TE. Drugs in development: bisphosphonates and metalloproteinase inhibitors. *Arthritis Res Ther* 2002; 5: 12–24.

14. de Groen PC *et al*. Esophagitis associated with the use of alendronate. *N Engl J Med* 1996; 335: 1016–1021.

15. Ichihara K, Satoh K. Disparity between angiographic regression and clinical event rates with hydrophobic statins. *Lancet* 2002 Jun 22; 359(9324): 2195–2198.

16. Istvan E. Statin inhibition of HMG-CoA reductase: a three dimensional view. *Atheroscleroisis Supp* 2003; 4: 3–8.

17. Tønnesen HH, ed. *Photostability of Drugs and Drug Solutions*. London: Taylor & Francis, 1996.

18. Barratt MD. Structure–activity relationships and prediction of the phototoxicity and phototoxic potential of new drugs. *ATLA* 2004; 32: 511–524.

19. Hettiaratchy S *et al*. Burns after photodynamic therapy. *Br Med J* 2000; 320: 1245.

20. Bryce R. Burns after photodynamic therapy. *Br Med J* 2000; 320: 1731. Dow R. *Br Med J* 2000; 321, 53.

21. Täubel J, Besa C. Burns after photodynamic therapy. *Br Med J* 2000; 320: 1732.

22. Hettiaratchy S, Clarke J. Burns after photodynamic therapy. *Br Med J* 2000; 320: 1731.

23. Hemmerling TM, Geldner G. Sugammedex: good drugs do not replace good clinical practice. *Anesth Analg* 2007; 105: 1506.

24. Hunter JM, Flockton EA. The doughnut and the hole: a new pharmacological concept for anaesthetists. *Br J Anaesth* 2006; 97: 123–126.

4

Looking at formulations

Introduction

In this chapter some formulations are examined to explore the variety of ways devised to deliver drugs by a variety of routes. Some techniques have solved problems of delivery of 'difficult' drugs, that is, drugs which are insoluble or unstable or are macromolecules which are unstable *in vivo*. Some formulations utilise newer technologies to achieve improved pharmacokinetics and ultimately enhanced patient benefit. Formulation is, of course, still carried out by pharmacists, not only in industry but also in 'specials' laboratories and in many hospital settings. Modern technologies might also allow its return to community pharmacy in the promised era of personalised medicines.

A selection of systems, both as types or as specific formulations, is described here, but it is by no means exhaustive. The purpose is to alert us to recognise issues that might arise with their administration, their admixture, their use and their activity. Some of the effects that are influenced by the nature of the formulation or its ingredients are indeed subtle. One instance that reminds us of this fact is given by the case we discuss later of propofol (Diprivan) injections and the role of lidocaine addition to the formulation. This results in a marked reduction in the pain of injection. It might be expected that a local anaesthetic would act in this way but, as discussed later, it is not so straightforward and this is at least in part due to the effect of the additive on the pH of the preparation.

A general caution is that the formulations of some branded products differ depending on the country of source. We cannot assume that a European formulation is the same as that available in the USA (although most are). This, coupled with the fact that many clinical papers are not specific about the formulation of drugs used, makes the interpretation of the literature somewhat difficult.

Of new drug types, apart from those that are poorly soluble, small ('conventional') organic molecules (molecules up to about 600 Da), proteins and other fragile, poorly absorbed molecules are increasingly part of the pharmaceutical armamentarium. We begin by considering some general aspects of protein formulations.

Protein drugs and formulations

The complexity of proteins as drugs is well known. Peptides and proteins are subject to a variety of chemical and physical instabilities in aqueous solution and at interfaces, and can also suffer during the stresses of some manufacturing processes.

Issues with protein generics

Now that the protein therapeutic market has matured, generic versions of protein drugs are becoming available (see Chapter 7). The source and mode of production of the protein therapeutic is an important issue. With the so-called 'follow-on' protein drugs,[1] compound or product identicality cannot always be demonstrated as it can with conventional molecules. Even with the latter there are often small regulated amounts of impurities, such as dimers, breakdown products and products of side-reactions. The impurities in proteins are often very similar to the parent compound and, although present in low concentrations, may be pharmacologically or immunologically active. Small changes in manufacturing processes may lead to final products that are not identical to the originator's product. Aggregation, protein folding and glycosylation may be affected, any of which can lead to differences in pharmacokinetics, immunogenicity or indeed efficacy. The formulation may or may not influence outcomes. One example has been seen with recombinant human erythropoietin (Eprex). A change of stabiliser from albumin to sorbitol caused the formation of anti-erythropoietin antibodies revealed in pure red cell aplasia.[2]

Pegylated therapeutic proteins

For many years now, proteins have been modified by the covalent addition of polyoxyethylene (PEG, polyethylene glycol) chains to their structures (the process of PEGylation or pegylation). While the intrinsic activity of the protein is generally unaffected, other parameters change so that a pegylated protein must be considered to be a new chemical entity. Pegylation of therapeutic proteins changes their pharmacokinetics and dynamics. It improves the performance of therapeutic proteins, providing them with a longer circulation time *in vivo*, and a reduction in immune responses. There is often also enhanced solubility of the peptide or protein (as might be expected from the addition of these very hydrophilic chains) or improved stability. Increased circulation time decreases the dose of protein necessary for biological action. Reduced antigenicity, immunogenicity and proteolysis are some of the benefits claimed for pegylated over non-pegylated forms of proteins and peptides.

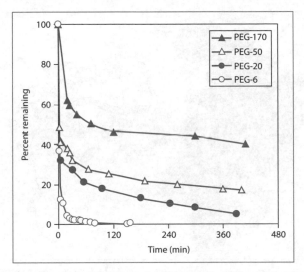

Figure 4.1 The percentage of polyethylene glycols remaining in the circulation as a function of their size (molecular weight: 6 = 6 kDa, 20 = 20 kDa etc.). (From reference 3.)

Why is this? The barrier produced by the PEG chains is both a physical and a thermodynamic one. The polyoxyethylene molecules shield the protein, reducing uptake and loss by the reticuloendothelial system. The resulting larger size of the molecule may, however, confer slower diffusional characteristics on the molecules. The addition of these water-soluble entities not only increases solubility but can also decrease the pH-dependency of protein solubility. Above all, the PEG layer shields the protein from opsonisation *in vivo* and thus the molecules are not scavenged by the reticuloendothelial system (RES) and hence circulation times are enhanced. As might be anticipated, the length of the PEG chain is important: the longer the chain, the longer the circulation time. Figure 4.1 shows the kinetics of unattached PEG molecules as a function of molecular size.[3]

Pegfilgastim is a pegylated recombinant methionyl human granulocyte-stimulating factor indicated in the reduction of the duration of neutropenia and incidence of febrile neutropenia during cancer chemotherapy. It is administered by intramuscular (IM) injection.

PEG-Intron (Peginterferon alfa) (see Figure 4.2) is a covalent conjugate of recombinant interferon alfa-2b with monomethoxy polyethylene glycol. Compared to standard interferon alfa, this modified molecule has a longer half-life after injection, allowing once-weekly injections and superior antiviral efficacy in the treatment of hepatitis C when used in combination with ribavirin. A case of a local blistering reaction developing in a patient receiving pegylated interferon alfa-2b has been reported.[4] Dalmau *et al.*[5] state that although injection site pain is infrequent (2–3%), site inflammation

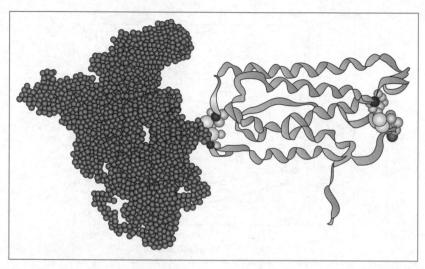

Figure 4.2 Pegylated interferon (Mire Zloh, The School of Pharmacy, University of London). The right-hand portion of the molecule represents the interferon while the left-hand part represents the polyoxyethylene chains.

and skin reactions (e.g. bruises, itchiness, irritation) occur at approximately twice the incidence with pegylated interferon alfa-2b treatment (in up to 75% of patients) compared with ordinary recombinant interferon alfa-2b. Dalmau and co-workers suggest that 'because pegylated interferon alfa-2b has almost completely replaced interferon for its most frequent indications, increased awareness of the possibility of cutaneous necrosis is necessary for early diagnosis to prevent continuation of pegylated interferon alfa-2b injections at the involved area.' There are hints that the pegylated interferon is more toxic at the site of injection than the unpegylated form. This might be due to its higher molecular weight and slower diffusion from the site.

Methoxy polyethylene glycol-epoetin beta (pegzerepoetin alfa; Mircera) is given by subcutaneous injection or intravenous infusion. Its half-life is extended over other forms of epoetin alfa or epoetin beta, as shown in Figure 4.3.

Pegvisomat (Somavert), a pegylated analogue of human growth hormone (hGH) structurally altered to act as a growth hormone (GH) receptor antagonist, comprises 191 amino acids with an average of 4–6 PEG molecules covalently bound to lysine residues and one bound to the terminal phenylalanine. It acts by binding to GH receptors on cell surfaces. The molecular weight of the protein is 21 998 Da and the molecular weight of each PEG chain is 5000 Da; hence there are three predominant molecular sizes in the product with molecular weights of 42 000, 47 000 and 52 000 Da. Thus it is not a homogeneous product, but it should be a *consistent* product in terms of the ratios of the

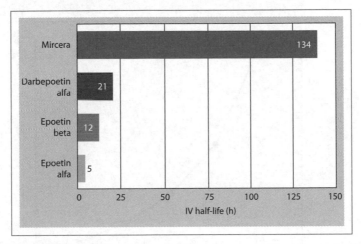

Figure 4.3 The half-life of pegzerepoetin alfa (Mircera) compared with darbepoetin alfa, epoetin alfa and epoetin beta.

predominant species. Clearly, when generic versions become available, information on the molecular weight species will be an important parameter. Peak concentrations after subcutaneous (SC) administration are achieved 33–77 hours after administration, a result likely to be due to its high molecular weight.

Monoclonal antibodies (MAbs)

There are now many monoclonal antibody products available for clinical use. They are most often given by the intravenous (IV) route, but when larger and more frequent doses are required the SC route is preferred. The MAb products, Rituxan (rituximab) and Herceptin (trastuzumab) are administered by the IV route. Treatments with high doses of antibody (>1 mg/kg or 100 mg per dose) require solution formulations at concentrations above 100 mg/mL, given the small volume (around 1.5 mL) that can be administered subcutaneously.[6] Proteins have a tendency to aggregate at high concentrations and there are as well limits to solubility. Aggregation of proteins can affect activity, pharmacokinetic behaviour and immunology. Not least, the viscosity of formulations can increase through aggregation. As the viscosity increases, the force required for injection increases. Even without aggregation there can be a marked temperature dependence of viscosity of MAbs, as shown in Figure 4.4.[7] The appearance of solutions may be indicative of excessive aggregation; opacity usually means that aggregation has occurred.

While proteins (and also RNA and DNA, which can be used therapeutically) require special formulations and handling, there is a range of drugs that have provided challenges and require more or less complex techniques for their delivery. Some of these are discussed here.

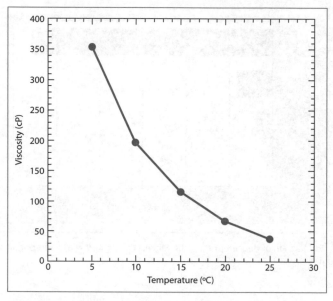

Figure 4.4   The temperature dependence of the viscosity of a solution of a monoclonal antibody in clinical development. The refrigerated product had a very high viscosity which falls markedly on warming. (From reference 7.)

Amphotericin B formulations

Amphotericin B is used in the treatment of severe systemic fungal infections. It is poorly soluble in water and hence a variety of lipid-based and non-lipid formulations have been developed to deliver the drug. Because of the range of types of formulation and trade names, confusion of the nature of the formulation can occur.

A news item in the *British Medical Journal* of 8 September 2007[8] reported on the National Patient Safety Agency's warning about the risk of dosing error following the death of two cancer patients receiving amphotericin. Confusion

Table 4.1 Pharmacokinetic properties of amphotericin B formulations

Formulation	Dose (mg/ kg per day)	Maximum concentration (μg/mL)	Area under the curve (μg × h/mL)	Volume of distribution (L/kg)	Clearance (mL/h per kg)
AMB desoxycholate	1	2.9	36	1.1	28
Abelcet	5	1.7	14	131	436
Amphotec	5	3.1	43	4.3	121
AmBisome	5	83	555	0.1	11

From reference 9.

between the lipid and non-lipid formulations, it stated, can lead to a dose that is too high or a dose that is too low. The item stated (*in error*) that the patients died after being prescribed the non-lipid form of amphotericin, stated to be AmBisome, but were treated with Fungizone, described as the lipid formulation.

Of course, as will be seen below, Fungizone is the non-lipid formulation while AmBisome is a lipid (liposomal) formulation, which is less toxic than the former. The formulations are described below. This report demonstrated (1) that formulation matters, not least because of differences in the doses of the products but also because of their different pharmacokinetics; (2) that knowledge of formulation matters; and (3) that confusion can arise when there are several formulations of the same drug available that are not bioequivalent.

The various formulations have different doses, clearance rates and bio-availabilities even by the IV route (see Table 4.1 [9]). If the drug is sequestered in lipidic systems such as liposomes, then it is clear that the pharmacokinetics of the drug will be affected. Micellar systems (such as Fungizone) tend not to change significantly the pharmacokinetics of the drug they contain, as micelles have a shorter existence than liposomes and complexed systems.

Fungizone

Fungizone is the original clinical formulation of amphotericin B. It employs sodium desoxycholate (see below) as a micelle-forming bile salt, to solubilise the drug. The formulation is termed the 'conventional' amphotericin B in Martindale (35th edition, page 473). Each vial contains a sterile lyophilised cake or powder containing 50 mg amphotericin B and 41 mg sodium desoxycholate with 20.2 mg sodium phosphate as buffer. It forms a clear colloidal solution, which is then further diluted before administration with 5% dextrose injection with a pH above 4.2. The use of any diluent other than those recommended, or the presence of bacteriostatic compounds such as benzyl alcohol in any such diluent, may cause the precipitation of the amphotericin B. The side-effects of Fungizone have resulted in the development of the lipid-based systems.

Sodium desoxycholate

Abelcet

This formulation, introduced by the Liposome Company in 1995, is an amphotericin B–lipid complex, the lipids being dimyristoyl phosphatidylcholine and dimyristoyl phosphatidylglycerol. These complexes, illustrated in Figure 4.5, are described as ribbon-like and have dimensions of 500–5000 nm.

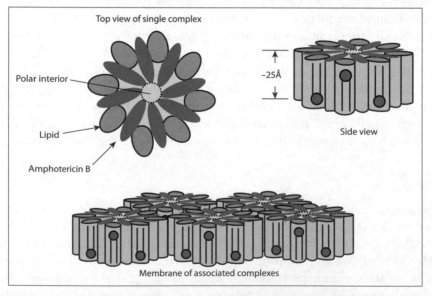

Figure 4.5 The structures of Abelcet in diagrammatic form showing the amphotericin lipid complex from the top and from the side. The lower diagram shows the membrane-associated complexes. (The Liposome Co.)

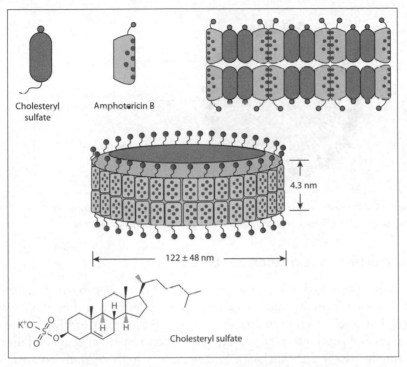

Figure 4.6 Cartoon illustration of the nature of the amphotericin B–cholesteryl sulfate complex and its dimensions, 122 ± 48 nm by 4.3 nm. (Sequus Pharmaceuticals Inc.)

Amphotec

Amphotec was introduced by Sequus Pharmaceuticals in the USA in 1996. It is a sodium cholesteryl sulfate complex, forming disc-like aggregates with a mean diameter of 125 nm (Figure 4.6).

Amphocil (UK)

This is another formulation of amphotericin B as a sodium cholesteryl sulfate complex.

AmBisome

A liposomal formulation of amphotericin B was first marketed by Fujisawa USA and NeXstar Pharmaceuticals in 1997. The liposomes are unilamellar, spherical vesicles with a mean diameter of 90 nm. The liposomes comprise soy phosphatidylcholine, cholesterol and distearoyl phosphatidylglycerol.

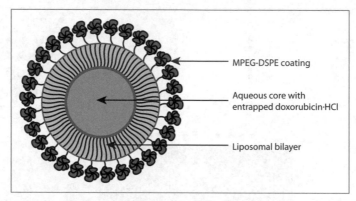

MPEG-DSPE coating

Aqueous core with entrapped doxorubicin·HCl

Liposomal bilayer

Figure 4.7 Representation of a cross-section of a doxorubicin Stealth™ liposome. MPEG-DSPE, methylpolyethylene glycol conjugate of distearoyl phosphatidyl ethanolamine.

A doxorubicin formulation: Doxil

Doxil is a formulation containing so-called Stealth liposomes encapsulating doxorubicin hydrochloride (see Figure 4.7). Surface-grafted PEG chains allow longer circulation *in vivo* (analogous to the effect of PEG chains on proteins and peptides). Hence there is a greater statistical chance of uptake by tumour tissues. Doxil has a longer plasma half-life than doxorubicin at an equivalent dose; it is less cardiotoxic, myelotoxic and nephrotoxic than doxorubicin (Adriamycin) because of its changed biodistribution patterns.[10]

Nonetheless, generic stealth liposomes differ from conventional liposomes and clearly the formulation differs from simple doxorubicin injections. Hypersensitivity reactions occur in about 45% of patients. Complement activation may play a part,[11] but the mechanism has not yet been elucidated. The long circulation times are related to another often significant problem that is exhibited by pegylated liposomal doxorubicin, that of plantar–palmar erythrodysaesthesia (hand–foot syndrome).[12] Its occurrence is related to prolonged exposure to the drug, in this case because of the prolonged half-life, for example in the sweat glands of the hands. Local cooling reduces the problem, possibly due to vasoconstriction leading to lower extravasation into surrounding tissues.[13]

A propofol formulation: Diprivan

Diprivan is a brand of propofol (2,6-diisopropylphenol; its structure is shown in Figure 4.8) formulated as an oil-in-water emulsion. There are also other branded and generic formulations. There have been some changes to the formulation in the USA, with the addition of EDTA and sulfite to prevent bacterial contamination.

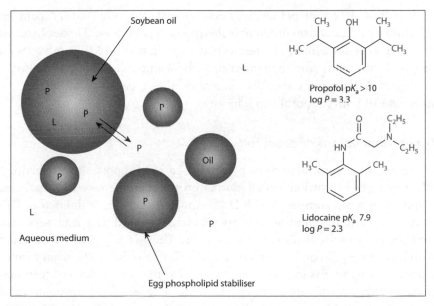

Figure 4.8 Representation of the emulsion formulation of propofol (P) with added lidocaine (L) and the structures of both propopol and lidocaine and their pK_a and log P values.

Pain on injection

Propofol has the disadvantage of causing pain on injection. Not unexpectedly lidocaine (lignocaine) reduces this pain. However, it is not a straightforward effect. In one study[14] the conclusions were as follows:

> When propofol partitions into the aqueous phase of the preparation there is a higher incidence of pain on injection. The addition of 1% lignocaine to propofol reduces pain. The low concentration of this local anaesthetic and the rapid pain relief observed indicates that mechanisms other than local anaesthesia are involved... A clinical study was performed to investigate the influence of lignocaine and pH on pain during injection of 1% Diprivan. Ten parts of 1% Diprivan were mixed with one part of saline, 1% lignocaine or hydrochloric acid to achieve the same pH as that after addition of lignocaine. Diprivan 1% mixed with 1% lignocaine and with hydrochloric acid gave mean pain ratings (1–10) of 0.32 (SD 0.75) ($n = 25$) and 0.88 (1.30) ($n = 24$), respectively. These ratings were significantly lower than ratings after injection of a saline-Diprivan mixture (2.18 (2.06), $n = 22$). The pH of the 1% Diprivan formulation decreased after mixing with 1% lignocaine. The concentration of propofol in the aqueous phase was lower when 1% Diprivan was mixed with 1% lignocaine (0.376 g litre^{-1}) or HCl (0.392 g litre^{-1}) compared with 1% Diprivan and saline (0.476 g litre^{-1}) mixed in the same proportion.

It is thus clear that pH changes may modify propofol-induced pain on injection by a mechanism different from the effects of the local anaesthetic on the vascular endothelium. The results may explain why lidocaine mixed with propofol causes less pain than injection of lidocaine followed by propofol.

Figure 4.8 diagrammatically illustrates the situation and shows the structures of both propofol and lidocaine.

Other formulations of propofol

There are other formulations of propofol:[15] a brief report [16] described the effect of a 'new' emulsion formulation of propofol on the severity of pain on IV injection when compared with Diprivan (AstraZeneca, Wilmington, DE, USA). A generic formulation of propofol containing a different preservative (sodium metabisulfite) (Baxter, Chicago, IL, USA) is apparently associated with less severe pain on injection than an EDTA-containing Diprivan formulation.[17] So again it is important to ensure that the components of formulations described in the literature are the same as those in the formulation of interest.

Long-acting depot injections

Long-acting oily neuroleptic formulations

Long-acting depot injections of drugs such as fluphenazine decanoate (Modecate) or flupentixol decanoate (Depixol) function because the long-chain ester (e.g. decanoate) is very hydrophobic and soluble almost exclusively in the oil phase (e.g. sesame oil). Table 4.2 [18] lists some of the oil phases used in such preparations. The oil has some affinity for water and thus allows penetration of water; the ester is hydrolysed at the surface of the

Table 4.2 Vehicles in depot antipsychotic formulations

Preparation	Group	Vehicle	$t_{1/2}$
Fluphenazine decanoate	Phenothiazine	Sesame oil	14 days
Flupentixol decanoate	Thioxanthene	Viscoleo[a]	17 days
Zuclopentixol decanoate	Thioxanthene	Viscoleo	19 days
Pipothiazine palmitate	Phenothiazine	Coconut oil	15–16 days
Haloperidol decanoate	Butyrophenone	Sesame oil	21 days
Fluspirilene	Phenylbutyl-piperidine	Aqueous suspension	>72 hours

From reference 18.
[a] Viscoleo is a fractionated coconut oil.

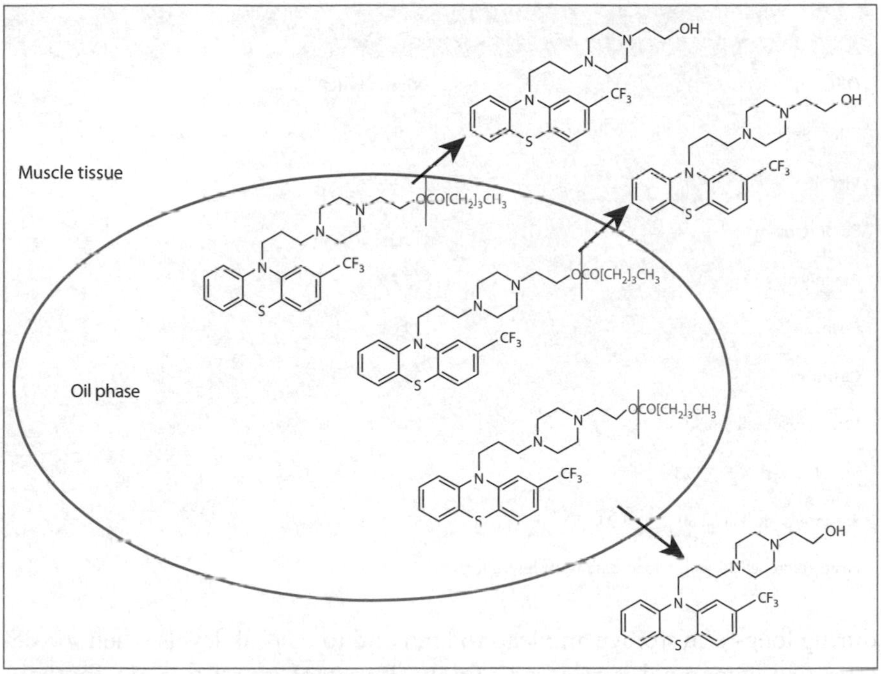

Figure 4.9 Diagrammatic representation of the release of fluphenazine from oily depots of long-chain esters in muscle tissue. Hydrolysis occurs at or near the oil–tissue interface.

droplet. Figure 4.9 is a diagrammatic scheme of the formulation and its action. The total surface area of the droplet can influence the release rate and hence affect the pharmacokinetics of the drug. Depot droplet dimensions and total surface area be influenced by (a) the force of injection, (b) the viscosity and surface tension (interfacial tension) of the oil phase, and (c) the size of the needles and the environment in which the injection finds itself. As several oils are used in these formulations, it is useful to consider the viscosity of some as given in Table 4.3.[19] Oils can be mixed with other oils to reduce the viscosity and so ease administration. The oils disappear from the injection site slowly over a period of a month. In one study[20] the more viscous arachis oil (35.2 cP) had a half-life of 27 days after subcutaneous injection compared with 9 days for ethyl oleate (3.9 cP). There is apparently little difference between the half-life of the oil after IM or SC injection. Note that there will be differences between the half-life of therapeutic substances at the site of injection and the half-life of the oily depots.

Fluphenazine itself in its un-ionised state is quite lipophilic. The log P value of the drug between sesame oil and water is 2.58 and between isopropyl myristate and water is 2.80. Contrast these values for fluphenazine enanthate with values at pH 7.4, of 6.3 and 6.5, respectively.[21] The rate of hydrolysis is not thought to be rate determining,[22] but hydrolysis of the drug can occur

Table 4.3 Viscosity of oils used in depot injections

Oil	Viscosity (cP)
Ethyl oleate	3.9
Viscoleo	12
Sesame oil	33
Arachis oil	35.2
Peanut oil	38
Castor oil	283
Viscoleo/sesame 50:50	23
Viscoleo/castor oil 75:25	27
Sesame/castor oil 50:50	55

From reference 19 with added data from reference 20.

during long-term storage and lead to high and toxic peak levels when the de-esterified compound is released rapidly. Bursts of exercise, as in football-playing patients, have been known to raise plasma levels, most probably by increasing the surface area of the droplets.

Other long-chain antipsychotic drugs include formulations of haloperidol decanoate (Haldol) (see structures of haloperidol and its decanoate below), pipothiazine palmitate (Piportil Depot) and zuclopenthixol decanoate

Haloperidol long chain (decanoate) ester as in Haldol decanoate [TM]

(Clopixol). When administered by deep intramuscular injection, all of these provide therapeutic cover over periods of 2–4 weeks which is thus the interval between injections.

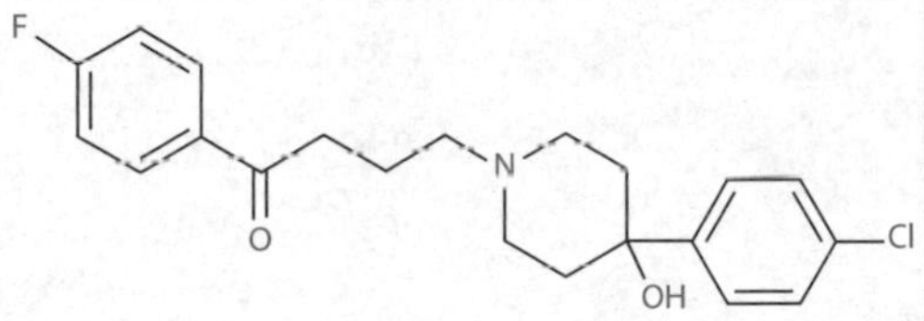

Haloperidol

Long-acting depot steroid injections

A number of steroids are formulated in the same manner as the neuroleptics, as oil-soluble esters dispersed in oils such as sesame oil or arachis oil. For example, nandrolone decanoate (Deca-Durabolin) is a long-acting anabolic steroid formulation. This formulation also contains benzyl alcohol (which acts as a solvent and an analgesic).

Testosterone enanthate, testosterone propionate (Sustanon 100 and 250) and the undecanoate (Nebido) and the cypionate (the 3-cyclopentyl-1-oxopropoxyl ester) are available for intramuscular injection. Depo-Testosterone contains testosterone cypionate, benzyl benzoate (as a solubilisation aid), cottonseed oil (the main carrier) and benzyl alcohol as a preservative, as shown below:

Depo-Testosterone formula (10 mg/mL product)	
Testosterone cypionate	100 mg
Benzyl benzoate	0.1 mL
Cottonseed oil	736 mg
Benzyl alcohol	9.45 mg

Soft capsules of testosterone undecanoate (Restandol) in an oil are used in the treatment of androgen deficiency by oral administration.

Raft-producing oral formulations

Gaviscon and related products Algicon, Gastrocote, Gaviscon Advance, Mylanta, Peptac and Rennie Duo are antacid formulations used in the treatment of gastric oesophageal reflux disease (GORD). The formulations have

Table 4.4 Alginate raft resilience measurements

Product	Raft resilience (range) (min)
Algicon	0–0
Gastrocote	2–10
Gaviscon Advance	60–60
Gaviscon Liquid	10–30
Gaviscon Regular Strength[a]	0–0
Gaviscon Extra Strength[a]	0–0
Mylanta Heartburn Relief	2–5
Peptac	2–10
Rennie Duo	0–2

[a] US products.

the ability to form a buoyant alginate raft to prevent oesophageal reflux of acidic gut contents. A variety of techniques including gamma-scintigraphy, radiography and MRI scanning have shown that alginates do form physical rafts on the stomach contents after ingestion. Techniques have been developed to measure raft strength,[23] including their 'resilience', a measure used to compare a variety of raft-forming products in terms of speed of raft formation, flotation potential and coherence. Table 4.4 shows some of the resilience data. The higher the value the stronger the raft.

Etoposide (Vepesid, VP 16 and etoposide phosphate)

Etoposide is a widely used cytotoxic drug with poor water solubility. It thus requires solubilisers to prevent its precipitation at clinical concentrations of the IV formulation. Etoposide concentrate for IV infusion (Vepesid) contains polysorbate 80, ethanol and benzyl alcohol. This is diluted for intravenous use.

Note that polysorbate 80, like other micelle-forming non-ionic surfactants in other formulations, may enhance the leaching of plasticizers such as DEHP (di-(2-ethylhexyl) phthalate) from PVC bags and tubing.[24] Thus non-PVC tubing and sets are recommended.

An alternative product, Etophos uses etoposide phosphate, a water-soluble prodrug of etoposide, as a powder for reconstitution.

A product containing etoposide, polysorbate 80 and polyethylene glycol has been compared with etoposide phosphate and found to be pharmacokinetically virtually equivalent, although the phosphate provides slightly higher

Etoposide

Etoposide phosphate

peak levels.[25] Surfactants present in formulations in solubilising drugs can sometimes lead to a slightly slower release of drug *in vivo*, although the influence of agents such as polysorbate 80 and Cremophor EL are complex, as was discussed in Chapter 2.

Data on the stability of diluted concentrates of etoposide can be contradictory. Before the literature can be useful, it is essential that the formulation and brand of the product in source literature and that in the pharmacy are identical, as minor formulation differences can influence outcomes.

Paclitaxel

Paclitaxel

Paclitaxel and its close relative docetaxel are poorly water-soluble anticancer drugs. Paclitixel has been formulated both as a generic preparation and as the branded Taxol as a concentrate containing high concentrations of Cremophor EL for addition to infusion fluids such as 5% glucose or 0.9% sodium chloride. The solvent for the concentrate (6 mg/mL paclitaxel) is a 50:50 mixture of Cremophor EL and ethanol. The surfactant alone would be too viscous for manipulation and would disperse only slowly on addition to aqueous infusion fluids. The ethanol reduces the viscosity and aids the dispersal of the concentrate in an infusion fluid. This is best done in stages, however, to prevent gel formation. On dilution of the concentrate to final paclitaxel concentrations of 0.3–1.2 mg/mL, the micellar solution formed solubilises the paclitaxel sufficiently to prevent the precipitation of the drug. Other taxanes are similarly formulated in polysorbate 80–ethanol mixtures. Taxotere is a 40 mg/mL concentrate of docetaxel and uses polysorbate 80 in its formulation. Some claim that Cremophor EL induces more adverse events than does polysorbate

Docetaxel

80, but both surfactants in fact can induce adverse reactions (see Chapters 2 and 5). Whichever surfactant is used, the infusion, which is given over 3 hours, should not be administered via PVC sets, as the surfactant can solubilise plasticisers from the giving sets.

Eutectic mixtures of local anaesthetics

EMLA is a eutectic mixture of the local anaesthetics lidocaine and prilocaine in a 1:1 mixture (2.5%, 2.5%). It can be used, for example, to prevent the pain of injection or catheter insertion. Lidocaine and prilocaine bases are two structurally related solids with respective melting points of 66–69°C and 36–30°C. The combination of the two compounds forms a eutectic mixture. A eutectic is a mixture of often similar materials whose melting point is below that of either individual component; in this case it is lowered to 16°C. The result is an oil that can be formulated as an oil-in-water emulsion where the disperse phase is the anaesthetic mixture; or it can be incorporated into a cream or formulated as a patch. A 5% EMLA cream when applied to the oral mucosa achieves maximum concentrations of 418 ng/mL for lidocaine and 223 ng/mL for prilocaine.[26] Patents exist for eutectic mixtures of other drugs.

Ciclosporin (cyclosporin)

Ciclosporin is an immunosuppressant cyclic peptide that has an oral bioavailability of around 15% in its amorphous and unformulated form. This is in contrast to the majority of (non-cyclic) peptides, which have little or no oral availability. Ciclosporin, being poorly water-soluble, is difficult to formulate as an oral product. It has been available in several innovative forms: an emulsion-forming (Sandimmun) and a microemulsion-forming product (Neoral).[27] Figure 4.10 shows the variability of absorption after oral administration of Sandimmun and also with the improved microemulsion system Neoral. The latter is less variable, that is, it improves the quality of effect. Reproducibility of effect is extremely important in transplantation patients to avoid under-dosing and transplant rejection. In transplantation patients, initial treatment is by way of intravenous dosing and later maintenance through the oral route.

It is logical to assume that the absorption of the drug would be improved by its formulation in a microemulsion form, where the lipid droplets are in the nanometre rather than micrometre size range. A simple surface area effect would operate – the smaller droplets, having a larger surface area per unit weight, present a greater surface from which the ciclosporin can diffuse directly into intestinal absorbing tissue. It has been suggested that with the microemulsion, inhibition of metabolism in the gut wall leads to higher availability. Several formulations of ciclosporin are available. The BNF 55

Different representations of the structure of ciclosporin (Commons.Wikimedia.org/wiki/File/ciclosporin.svg)

(page 476) states that 'because of differences in bioavailability, the brand of oral ciclosporin to be dispensed should be specified by the prescriber.'

Ingredients:[28] Neoral oral solution contains in addition to ciclosporin, DL-α-tocopherol, ethanol, polyoxyethylated 40, hydrogenated castor oil, maize oil (corn oil mono-, di-, tri-glycerides) and propylene glycol. (The listing in one document (Novartis, Canada) does not mention polyoxyethylated hydrogenated castor oil.) The oral solution should be diluted in orange juice or apple juice to improve its taste, or with water immediately before dosing. The concentrate forms a microemulsion. Neoral soft gelatin capsules also contain the above excipients and this also forms a microemulsion *in vivo*.

Sandimmun IV concentrate for solution for infusion contains ciclosporin 50 mg/mL, ethanol 278 mg/mL and [sic] castor oil 650 mg/mL (the Novartis information states 'polyoxyethylated castor oil'). The variety of formulations

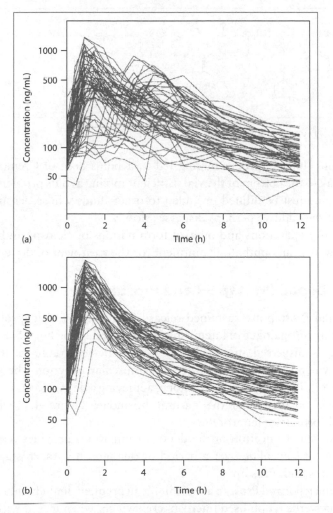

Figure 4.10 Plasma concentrations of ciclosporin after (a) Sandimmune and (b) Neoral, showing the improvement in average performance of the latter.

now available from other manufacturers makes the elucidation of pharmacokinetics, bioavailability, dosing and adverse reactions complex. Not all the preparations are available in all countries, hence literature reports have to be scanned carefully to determine which formulation has been used.

Inadequate mixing of ciclosporin formulations

One report[29] in 1995 referred to anaphylactoid reactions during a Phase I/II clinical trial of high-dose IV preparations of ciclosporin in children. The problem was ascribed to the presence of Cremophor EL. However, it was exacerbated by the inadequacy of mixing of the formulation with the

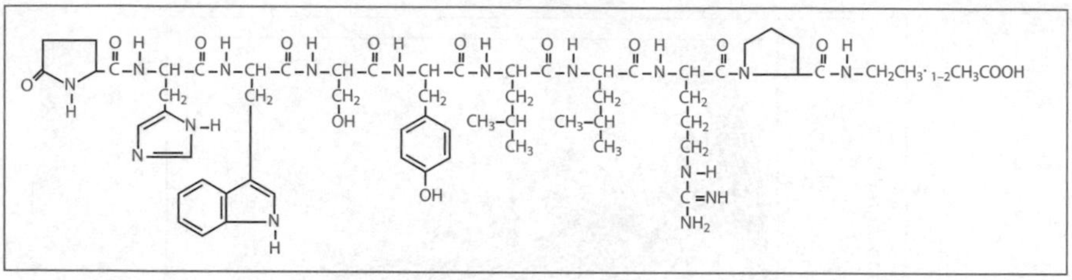

Figure 4.11 Leuprorelin structure.

intravenous fluid. Improper mixing led to a bolus dose of Cremophor EL, which sank to the bottom of the vial. Efficient mixing avoids problems when a formulation must be diluted or added to other fluids whose densities differ and when the additive perhaps disperses slowly.

Topical preparations and inhaled formulations of ciclosporin have been used, as well as an ophthalmic ointment for the treatment of dry eye.

Lupron Depot, Prostap SR and Prostap 3

Lupron and Prostap are sustained-release formulations of leuprolide (INN leuprorelin), an analogue of luteinising hormone-releasing hormone (LHRH). The drug is dispersed in PLGA (poly(D,L-lactic-co-glycolic acid)) microspheres, which slowly degrade after intramuscular injection (the peptide is not active orally) to release the hormone, achieving a depot effect. Leuprorelin has greater potency than the natural hormone. Figure 4.11 shows the structural formula of leuprorelin.

Intramuscular injection of the depot formulations provides plasma concentrations of leuprolide over a period of one month with Prostap SR, and three months with Prostap 3.

Lupron Depot and Prostap are available in prefilled dual-chamber syringes containing sterile lyophilised microspheres which, when mixed with diluent, form a suspension. The first chamber of the 3.75 mg product contains leuprolide acetate (3.75 mg), purified gelatin (0.65 mg), PLGA (33.1 mg), and D-mannitol (6.6 mg). The second chamber with the diluent contains carboxymethylcellulose sodium (5 mg), D-mannitol (50 mg), polysorbate 80 (1 mg), water for injection, and glacial acetic acid to control pH.

Zoladex

Zoladex is an injectable implant containing goserelin acetate, the nonapeptide luteinising hormone-releasing hormone analogue (LHRHa).[30] It prevents the production of testosterone and oestrogen. It is used to treat hormone-sensitive cancers of the prostate and breast (in pre- or peri-menopausal women) and some benign gynaecological disorders. Zoladex is available in a 28-day form and a long-acting 3-month formulation. The product is administered using the Zoladex SafeSystem (Figure 4.12) designed to protect from the risk of

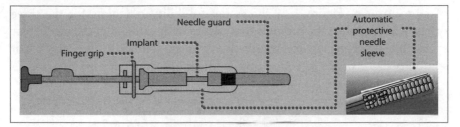

Figure 4.12 Zoladex SafeSystem. (From www.prostateinfo.com.)

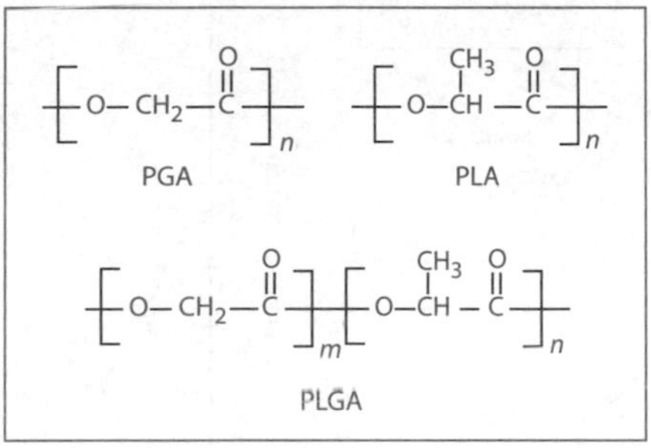

Figure 4.13 Chemical structures of poly(glycolic acid) (PGA), poly(lactic acid) (PLA) and poly(lactic-co-glycolic acid) (PLGA).

needle-stick injury. Both depots are used for the treatment of prostate cancer, endometriosis and uterine fibroids but only the 28-day depot is approved for breast cancer, endometrial thinning and assisted reproduction. Zoladex was first launched in 1987;[31] Zoladex SafeSystem was launched in 2003. The design of the formulation was discussed in 1990 by scientists[32] involved in the work at the then ICI Pharmaceuticals (now Astra-Zeneca), Macclesfield, UK. Controlled release of the goserelin is dependent on the molecular weight of the PLGA and the ratio of the lactic acid and glycolic acid monomers in the polymer (see structures of the monomers and polymers in Figure 4.13). Particle size, and hence the surface area of the particles, is optimised. The higher the molecular weight of the PLGA the slower the release, facilitated by degradation of the polymer chains and by entry of water into the system.

Fluoroquinolone eye drops

How do different fluoroquinolones behave in tears? In one study, three fluoroquinolone solutions were evaluated:[33] ciprofloxacin 0.3% (Ciloxan), norfloxacin (Chibroxin) and ofloxacin 0.3% (Ocuflox). The pH of the tear film for the first 15 minutes after instillation of each of the drugs is determined by the pH of its formulation. Rapid precipitation of ciprofloxacin was seen in a model system 8 minutes after dosing of ciprofloxacin owing to the supersaturation of the drug in tears, while the tear concentration of ofloxacin and norfloxacin remained below saturation solubility at all pH values studied. These findings may explain the reports of pre-corneal deposits following use of ciprofloxacin. Figure 4.14 shows the solubility–pH plots for the three drugs, which explain the problem that occurs with Ciloxan in the model tear system when drug tear concentrations exceed drug solubility. One can see that solubility line crosses the concentration line in the diagram for Ciloxan).

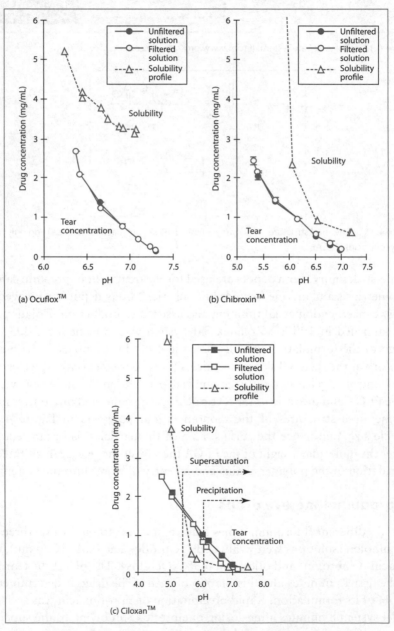

Figure 4.14 Relationship between the drug concentration in a tear turnover model and drug solubility (dashed lines). (From reference 33.)

The pH–solubility profiles of the fluoroquinolones up to pH 7.2 are typical of a base. Solubility decreases with increasing pH, with a minimum in solubility around pH 7. If the pH were to increase above 7.5, solubility would increase again as the compound possesses a carboxyl group. The pH of tear fluids is just over 6.8. When the solubility curve falls below the concentration curve, precipitation can be anticipated, a quick way of predicting the occurrence of precipitation.

Ionsys: Iontophoretic transdermal device for fentanyl

Ionsys is an iontophoretic device comprising an electronic controller and two hydrogel reservoirs, one of which contains 40 mg fentanyl hydrochloride in a gel formulation for on-demand delivery.[34] It is used for the management of acute moderate to severe postoperative pain in hospital settings only – a potentially dangerous amount of fentanyl remains in the Ionsys system after use. Figure 4.15 shows some pharmacokinetic data comparing fentanyl levels from the Ionsys product and an IV injection.

The many ingredients of the system should not be of consequence in intact systems. For interest and to emphasise the complexity, they comprise the following: in the housing assembly, glycol-modified polyethylene terephthalate; in the anode hydrogel, purified water, sodium hydroxide, polacrilin and polyvinyl alcohol; in the cathode hydrogel, sodium citrate, polyvinyl alcohol, anhydrous citric acid, cetylpyridinium chloride, purified water and sodium chloride. The skin adhesive contains polybutene resin ester.

Parenterals

The administration of many formulations parenterally leads to the possibility of drug precipitation in the blood because of the dilution of the solvent systems that solubilise the drug in the vial. The effect of this on pain and on the fate of the precipitated particles can be discussed. Above all, the issue of solubility and its pH dependence has to be revisited[35] (see Chapter 3). Many of the problems with parenterals occur before administration and result from the addition of one product to intravenous fluids such as dextrose and physiological saline and subsequent precipitation of the active due to pH changes or to interaction with a second drug.

Solubility considerations

A query raised by a nurse on Levaquin (levofloxacin) and Lasix (furosemide):[36]

> The patient was on Levaquin i.v. and was prescribed a Lasix i.v. push.
> I stopped the Levaquin, ran the saline line at 100 for 25–30. Then I
> proceeded to push the Lasix. I drew back and the *syringe* contents

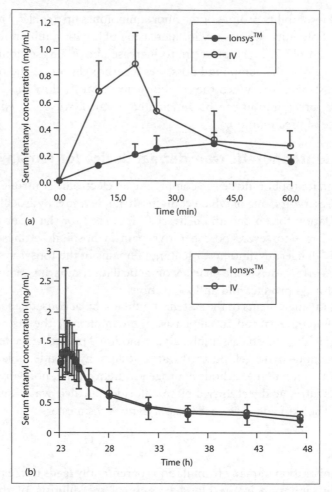

Figure 4.15 Pharmacokinetic data comparing fentanyl levels from the Ionsys product and an IV injection. (a) First hour of a representative treatment. (b) Last hour and upon termination of a representative treatment. The treatments were: *Ionsys*, 40 μg, two sequential doses over 20 minutes every hour for 23 hours 20 minutes. *IV*, 80 μg dose over 20 minutes every hour for 23 hours 20 minutes. (Source: FDA, http://www.accessdata.fda.gov/drugsatfda_docs/label/2006/021338lbl. pdf.)

looked a little cloudy. I had never seen a drug precipitate (I thought it would have crystallized immediately). I started to push it but then second guessed myself and stopped. I turned off the pump immediately and took the line off the patient. Only then did I see the crystallization. Did I need to flush for longer or should I have gotten a new saline bag and pushed it through a new line? I worry that some of the [sic] contaminated fluid entered the patient.

This shows that not everyone is clear about the nature of precipitates and crystallisation. We should remember that not all interactions lead to visible crystals, and we should be aware of changes in the appearance of fluids. From the structures given below can you identify the reasons for the precipitation referred to by the nurse in question?

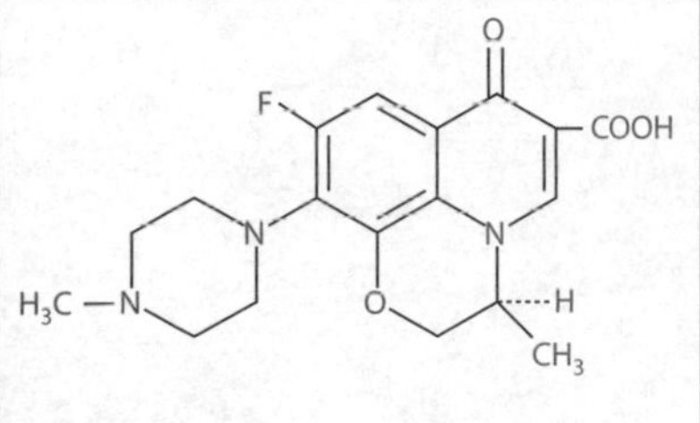

Levofloxacin

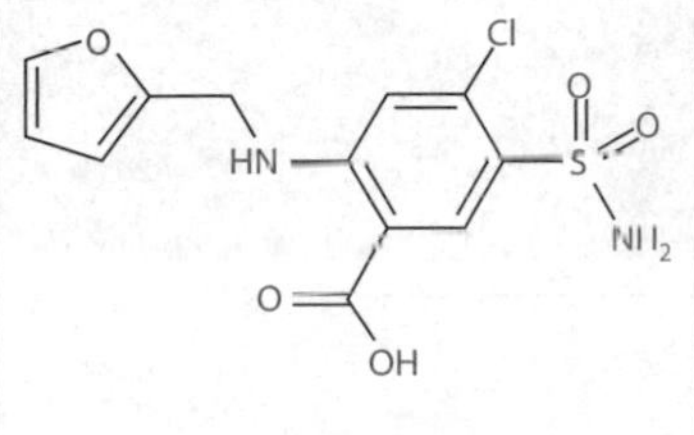

Furosemide

Chloramphenicol

Chloramphenicol is available as 250 mg capsules or as a liquid (125 mg/ 5 mL). In some countries, chloramphenicol is sold as chloramphenicol palmitate ester. Chloramphenicol palmitate ester is inactive, and is hydrolysed to active chloramphenicol in the small intestine. There is no difference in bioavailability between chloramphenicol and chloramphenicol palmitate. The IV preparation of chloramphenicol is the succinate ester, because chloramphenicol itself does not dissolve in water. This creates a problem: chloramphenicol succinate ester is an inactive prodrug and must first be hydrolysed to chloramphenicol. The hydrolysis process is incomplete and 30% of the dose is lost unchanged in the urine; therefore, serum concentrations of chloramphenicol are only 70% of those achieved when chloramphenicol is given orally. For this reason, the chloramphenicol dose needs to be increased to 75 mg/kg per day when administered intravenously in order to achieve levels equivalent to the oral dose. The oral route is therefore preferred to the intravenous route.

Materials used in drug delivery

Plasticised PVC Bags

(The information in this section was derived from a web page by Inga Rustamova, PSIV, University of California, San Francisco.[37])

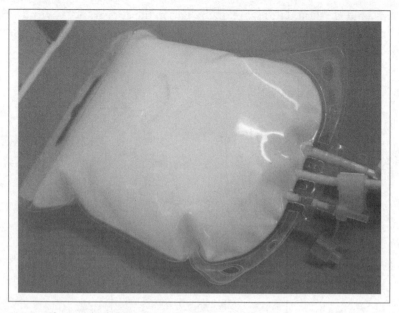

Figure 4.16   Plasticised PVC bag.

Plasticised polyvinyl chloride (PVC) is one of the most widely used polymeric materials in medical and related fields. In the medical field, flexible PVC is used for blood storage bags, tubing used during haemodialysis, endotracheal tubes, intravenous solution dispensing sets, as well as for drug product storage and packaging (Figure 4.16). PVC is a rigid polymer, so plasticisers are added to increase its flexibility. Phthalic acid esters, mainly di-(2-ethylhexyl) phthalate (DEHP), are the preferred plasticisers used in the medical field. Since these additives are not covalently bound to the polymer, there is a possibility for migration of the plasticiser from the matrix. The migration of DEHP (structure below) from PVC bags into the solution has been a major concern for many years. The toxicity of DEHP and PVC has raised serious questions about their use[38].

Diethylhexyl phthalate (DEHP)

Plasticised bags allow evaporation of water and sorption and loss of drug. Kowaluk *et al.* examined interactions between 46 injectable drug products and Viaflex (PVC) infusion bags. Study results showed that: (a) sorption increases as drug concentration increases; (b) loss is negligible for ionised or polar drugs (apparent octanol–water partition coefficient < 5). Migration of drug into plastic may lead to subtherapeutic drug concentrations of, for example, insulin, vitamin A acetate, diazepam and nitroglycerin.[39] Influencing factors include (a) pH, (b) temperature, (c) structure of the plastic, (d) the volume/surface area ratio, (e) storage time. Formulations may alter the properties of plastic, for example, fat emulsions and the presence of surfactants like polysorbate and Cremophor as we have discussed. The benefits of DEHP include (a) increased flexibility of PVC, and (b) increased survival time of platelets. Indeed no specific toxicity in humans has been reported.

Leakage of plasticisers into the solution is influenced by (1) shaking, although it has been found[40] that agitation had no effect on rate or the amount of DEHP leached into D5 injection, ethanol 25 %, and polysorbate 80 1% solutions; (2) storage time and temperature; (3) pH; (4) drug concentration; (5) manufacturing processes that involve, for example, thermal exposure; (6) formulations with surfactants (DEHP is leached by polysorbate 80, polyoxyethylated castor oil and formulations which normally contain surfactants, such as ciclosporin, miconazole, teniposide, and etoposide). In total parenteral nutrition (TPN) mixtures[41] 0–3 mg DEHP/mL (depending on lipid concentration and storage condition) was found in products administered 24 to 36 hours after admixture. Total DEHP exposure range was 0–9 mg.

It has been suggested that decreasing plasticiser migration by coating PVC bags with hydrophilic polymers, using polymeric plasticisers or grafting molecules such as polyethylene glycol, improves blood compatibility. Other plasticisers include tri-(2-ethylhexyl)trimellitate (TOTM). Specific toxicity from exposure to DEHP has not been well established in humans.[42] Most toxicity studies were carried out in rats, making extrapolation of toxicity data to human toxicity unreliable. There is not enough scientific data to completely or partially ban use of DEHP and PVC in medical or related fields. The balance of opinion is to suspend use of PVC administration sets and containers with formulations that are known to leach DEHP. This would limit the potential DEHP exposure as much as possible until further studies establish DEHP toxicity.

Conclusions

Only a selection of formulations has been covered in this chapter. Each example has been chosen to display some facet of formulation and how it might impinge on the performance of the medicine in question. Other formulations will be dealt with in other chapters according to other themes. The object has been not only to draw attention to the ingenuity of formulators, but also to heighten awareness of what to look for in formulations, especially when problems arise before or after their administration, or when formulations behave in a manner other than anticipated. It is not always simple to determine compositions of formulations, and this hampers fuller understanding of their properties. However, there are key questions to be posed when considering the influence of formulations.

First ask whether the product contains:

- A surfactant
- A surface-active bactericide
- Dyes that might cause allergic reactions
- Stabilisers
- Flavours
- Viscosity-enhancing agents
- Benzyl alcohol
- Solvents such as ethanol
- Another additive?

Then one must consider whether or not any observed event may be caused by one of these ingredients or whether the whole formulation has changed because of precipitation or the other phenomena discussed.

The next chapter deals with adverse events associated with formulations, where we examine more closely some of the activities of materials used in formulations, following on from Chapter 2. These of course can include synergistic effects.

References

1. Dudzinski DM, Kusselheim AS. Scientific and legal viability of follow-on protein drugs. *N Engl J Med* 2008; 358: 843–849.
2. Louëts S. Lessons from Eprex for biogeneric firms. *Nat Biotechnol* 2003; 21: 956–957.
3. Mehrar R. Modulation of the pharmacokinetics and pharmacodynamics of proteins by polyoxyethylene glycol conjugation. *J Pharm Pharm Sci* 2000; 3: 125–136.
4. Gallina K *et al.* Local blistering reaction complicating subcutaneous injection of pegylated interferon in a patient with hepatitis C. *J Drugs Dermatol* 2003; 2: 63–67.
5. Dalmau J *et al.* Cutaneous necrosis after injection of polyethylene glycol-modified interferon alfa. *J Am Acad Dermatol* 2005; 53: 62–66.
6. Shire SS *et al.* Challenges in the development of high protein concentration formulations. *J Pharm Sci* 2004; 93: 1390–1402.
7. Cromwell MEM *et al.* Protein aggregation and processing. *AAPS J* 2006; 8(3): E572–579.
8. Hawkes N. Agency warns about dosing error for amphotericin after patients with cancer die. *BMJ* 2007; 335: 467.
9. Quilitz R. The use of lipid formulations in cancer patients. Moffitt Cancer Centre. http://www.moffitt.org/moffittapps/ccj/v5n5/department3.html.
10. Working PK *et al.* Pharmacokinetics, biodistribution and therapeutic efficacy of doxorubicin encapsulated in Stealth liposomes (Doxil). *Liposome Res* 1994; 4: 667–687.

11. Chanan-Khan A *et al.* Complement activation following first exposure to pegylated liposomal doxorubicin. *Ann Oncol* 2003; 14: 1430–1437.
12. Lorusso D *et al.* Pegylated liposomal doxorubicin palmar-plantar erythrodsysesthesia (hand–foot syndrome). *Ann Oncol* 2007; 18: 1159–1164.
13. Molpus KL *et al.* The effect of regional cooling on toxicity associated with intravenous infusion of pegylated liposomal doxorubicin in recurrent ovarian carcinoma. *Gynecol Oncol* 2004; 93: 513–516.
14. Eriksson M *et al.* Effect of lignocaine and pH on propofol-induced pain. *Br J Anaesth* 1997; 78: 502–506.
15. White PF. Propofol formulation and pain on injection. *Anesth Analg* 2002; 94: 1042 [Letter].
16. Rau J *et al.* Propofol in an emulsion of long- and medium-chain triglycerides: the effect on pain. *Anesth Analg* 2001; 93: 382–384.
17. Shao X *et al.* Bisulfite-containing propofol: is it a cost-effective alternative to Diprivan for induction of anesthesia? *Anesth Analg* 2000; 91: 871–875.
18. Kane JM *et al.* Guidelines for depot psychiatric treatment in schizophrenia. *Eur Neuropharmacol* 1998; 8: 55–66.
19. Fridhout K *et al.* Modification of *in vitro* drug release rate from oily parenteral depots using a formulation approach. *Eur J Pharm Sci* 2000; 11: 231–237.
20. Howard JR, Hadgraft J. The clearance of oily vehicles following intramuscular and subcutaneous injection in rabbits. *Int J Pharm* 1983; 16: 31–39.
21. Vezin WR, Florence AT. The determination of dissociation constants and partition coefficients of phenothiazine derivatives. *Int J Pharm* 1979; 3: 213–237.
22. Dreyfuss J *et al.* Release and elimination of ^{14}C-fluphenazine enanthate and decanoate esters administered in sesame oil to dogs. *J Pharm Sci* 1976; 65: 502–507.
23. Hampson FC *et al.* Alginate rafts and their characterisation. *Int J Pharm* 2005; 294: 137–147.
24. de Lemos ML *et al.* Leaching of diethylhexyl phthalate from polyvinylchloride materials into etoposide intravenous preparations. *J Oncol Pharm Pract* 2005; 11: 155–157. See also: Demoré B *et al.* Leaching of diethylhexyl phthalate from polyvinyl chloride bags into intravenous etoposide solution. *J Clin Pharm Ther* 2002; 27: 139–142.
25. Dorr RT *et al.* Comparative pharmacokinetic study of high dose etoposide and etoposide phosphate in patients with lymphoid malignancy receiving autologous stem cell transplantation. *Bone Marrow Transplant* 2003; 31: 643–649.
26. Vickers ER *et al.* Pharmacokinetics of EMLA cream 5% application to oral mucosa. *Anesth Progress* 1997; 44: 32–37.
27. Trull AK *et al.* Absorption of cyclosporin from conventional and new microemulsion formulations in liver transplant recipients with external biliary diversion. *Br J Clin Pharmacol* 1995; 39: 627–631.
28. Novartis Information sheets: *Neoral* and *Sandimmune I.V.*, 26 October 2007.
29. Thela JG *et al.* Anaphylactoid reactions in children receiving high dose intravenous cyclosporine for reversal of tumor resistance: the causative role of improper dissolution of Cremophor EL. *J Clin Oncol* 1995; 13: 2508–2516.
30. Astra-Zeneca International Web page on Zoladex. www.prostateinfo.com.
31. Hutchinson FG. Continuous release pharmaceutical compositions. *European Patent Application* 58 481. 25 August 1982.
32. Hutchinson FG, Furr BJA. Biodegradable polymer systems for the sustained release of polypeptides. *J Control Release* 1990; 13: 279–294.
33. Firestone BA *et al.* Solubility characteristics of three fluoroquinolone ophthalmic solutions in an *in vitro* tear model. *Int J Pharm* 1998; 164: 119–128.
34. *electronic Medicines Compendium.* Janssen-Cilag Ltd, 2008. www.janssen-cilag.co.uk.
35. Florence AT, Attwood D. *Physicochemical Principles of Pharmacy*, 4th edn. London: Pharmaceutical Press, 2006. Attwood D, Florence AT. *Physical Pharmacy.* London: Pharmaceutical Press, 2008.
36. allnurses.com

37. Inga Rustamova. PSIV. University of California, San Francisco, January 2000. web.ucsf. edu/dpsl/pvc.html.
38. Lakshimi S, Jayakrishnan A. Migration resistant, blood-compatible plasticized PVC for medical and related applications. *Artif Organs* 1998; 22(3): 222–229.
39. Kowaluk EA *et al*. Interactions between drugs and polyvinyl chloride infusion bags. *Am J Hosp Pharm* 1981; 38: 1308–1314.
40. Pearson SD, Trissel LA. Leaching of DEHP from PVC containers by selected drugs and formulation components. *Am J Hosp Pharm* 1993; 50: 1405–1409.
41. Mazur HI *et al*. Extraction of DEHP from total nutrient solution-containing polyvinyl chloride bags. *J Parenter Enteral Nutr* 1989; 13: 59–62.
42. Rubin RJ, Schiffer CA. Fate in humans of the plasticizer DEHP arising from transfusion of platelets stored in vinyl plastic bags. *Transfusion* 1976; 16: 330–335.

5

Adverse events and formulations and devices

Introduction

It is generally assumed when an adverse reaction or adverse event occurs (see Box 5.1) that the drug is the causative agent. So what is the connection between pharmaceutics and adverse reactions to medications? It is generally the case that the drug is the culprit, but there are instances when formulation factors come into play. Sometimes, as we discussed in Chapter 2, excipients have their own biological effect; sometimes the way in which the product is constructed and behaves may cause the drug to have enhanced toxicity.

This chapter summarises the potential for formulations, their form or the ingredients that they contain, to precipitate adverse reactions or events. Figure 5.1 shows both product and patient factors in the causation of adverse events. Errors of choice of product or drug aside, when the correct drug and formulation has been administered, there are still many opportunities for matters to go awry. These include effects which are the result of:

- Abnormal bioavailability (both large and small) caused by a product or manufacturing defect
- Sensitivities to formulation ingredients (discussed in Chapter 2)
- Reactions to impurities and breakdown products
- Aggregation of protein drugs in devices
- Device failure, for example with medicated stents or infusion pumps
- The nature of the formulation, for example adhesive tablets lodging in the oesophagus or drug precipitation from injections.

Figure 5.1[1] elaborates on these cases, dividing adverse events into those dependent on patient factors and those related to medicinal formulations and devices. Adverse events include allergic reactions, local toxicities, systemic effects or idiosyncratic reactions. It is not the place here to recount

> **Box 5.1** *Adverse events and adverse drug reactions*
>
> Adverse reactions following administration of a medicine or use of a device can be discussed in terms of adverse events (where the causality is not known) or adverse drug reactions (where the causative factor is the drug itself).
>
> When both drug and formulation are involved, or when an excipient is implicated, the term adverse event is possibly the more accurate.

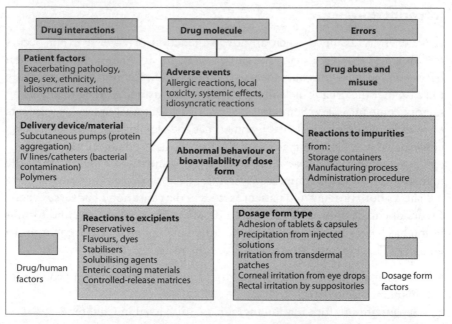

Figure 5.1 Drug/human factors and dosage form factors in adverse events following medication administration. (Modified from reference 1.)

patient-related factors in detail, although there are of course dose form–patient interactions that make these of interest. Changed physiology in the postnatal growth period, in childhood and in the elderly can mean that dose forms may behave differently in certain patient groups (see Chapter 6). Some factors include exacerbating pathology, age, sex and ethnicity. The following sections deal with some product-related adverse effects.

The variety of adverse events that have occurred in the recent past is illustrated in Table 5.1.

Table 5.1 Some 'classic' adverse events as a result of use of formulations

Dosage form	Trade name	Adverse event
Indometacin osmotic minipump tablets	Osmosin	Intestinal perforation
Fluspirilene IM injection	Redeptin	Tissue necrosis at site of injection
Epidural injection of prednisolone injection containing benzyl alcohol as preservative	Depo Medrol	Mild paralysis
Inhalation of nebulised ipratropium bromide solution containing benzalkonium chloride as preservative	Atrovent	Bronchoconstriction
Vaginal application of povidone iodine solution		Anaphylactoid reaction
Application of timolol eye drops	Timoptic	Bronchoconstriction
Fentanyl transdermal patch	Duragesic	Respiratory depression and death

From reference 1.

Dosage form type

Adhesion and trapping of tablets

Oesophageal damage caused by tablets is discussed later, but it is worth considering here a recent and graphic case that has been described[2] in a patient (a 57-year-old woman) with oesophageal dysmotility. A tablet of pantoprazole (Protonix) was seen 'perched' (Figure 5.2a) in the oesophagus of this patient with diffuse bronchiolar disease that required hospitalisation. The photograph in Figure 5.2b shows an enteric-coated aspirin tablet, its coating

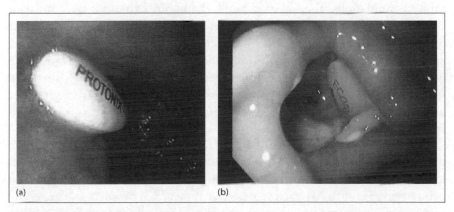

(a)   (b)

Figure 5.2 Tablets adhering to the oesophageal mucosa. (a) Pantoprazole (Protonix™). (From reference 2.) (b) An enteric-coated aspirin tablet with coating still intact within an ulcer of the gastric antrum of a 76-year-old woman. (From reference 3.)

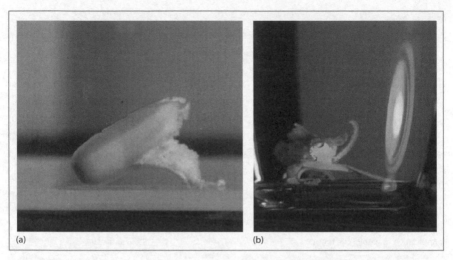

(a)   (b)

Figure 5.3 Two tablets disintegrating in an aqueous medium at room temperature. Both show the splitting of the coating layer on the tablets, but (b) shows a now-discontinued dose form of emepromium bromide (Cetiprin) that is unravelling to expose the core of pure drug, irritant to the oesophageal lining. (From reference 4.)

still intact, in an ulcer in the gastric antrum of another patient.[3] Thus, adhesion or simply entrapment in diverticula may be an issue.

In these cases a combination of pathology and dose form conspired to cause a problem. Adverse events are rarely simple. The manner in which dose forms behave in the presence of small or larger amounts of aqueous media, which may be found respectively in the oesophagus or later in the stomach, are varied. Simple *in vitro* studies can be illuminating, as Figure 5.3 illustrates.[4] This shows the unusual disintegration properties of two tablet formulations, the lower example being an extreme case typical of emepromium bromide tablets once marketed as Cetiprin for the treatment of nocturnal enuresis. The Cetiprin tablet is seen to break apart, exposing a core of pure drug, which has surfactant properties. If this occurred in the oesophagus, pain and damage would result and this indeed was the case. Given its indication, many patients took the tablets with insufficient water and many cases of dysphagia were reported. The product was withdrawn from the market.

In this case the combination of adherence and the presence of a potentially irritant drug is the problem. Close connection between epithelia and product leads to high concentrations of drug and to damage. The oesophagus is a primary site for such adverse events, since tablets and capsules will generally not have disintegrated during their oesophageal transit and retain their bulk. Small uncoated tablets may also cause problems in the oesophagus because they can adhere firmly to the mucosal surface. A range of drugs have been reported to cause oesophageal injury (Table 5.2).

Table 5.2 Some drugs that cause oesophageal injury

- Alendronate
- Alprenolol
- Aspirin
- Clindamycin
- Doxycycline
- Emepromium bromide
- Ferrous salts
- Indometacin
- Potassium chloride
- Risendronate
- Tetracycline
- Thioridazine

We may ask what, if any, are the common features of the drugs listed in this table? What might be the main reason or reasons for each to cause injury? These include the acidity of the concentrated solutions of some of the drugs (aspirin, alendronate and risendronate); the proximity of high concentrations of drugs such as doxycycline which chelate calcium and hence disrupt the epithelial lining; the surface activity of agents such as emepromium bromide; or high electrolyte concentrations from the inorganic drugs. If these agents are in dose forms that are swallowed with sufficient water and do not lodge in the oesophagus, damage will not be caused.

Dose forms have other effects and influences in modulating or causing adverse events. Precipitation of drugs from injection solutions is one prime example which was discussed in Chapter 1. Figure 5.1 reminds us of others: irritation from the adhesives of transdermal patches, corneal irritation from eye drops and rectal irritation from the use of suppository bases (such as the polyoxyethylene glycols, PEGs) that extract water from the mucosa.

Reactions to impurities

Reactions to impurities generally refer to the effect of breakdown products of the drug, which may be initiated by interactions with moisture or acidity or with excipients or materials from containers and packaging. The manufacturing process may contribute some impurities, although these will be limited by the marketing authorisation, but the validity of these requirements and limitations will depend on the same route of synthesis and production being adhered to.

Heparin

In January 2008, Baxter Healthcare Corporation withdrew batches of nine lots of heparin sodium in the USA[5] because around 700 acute allergic-type adverse reactions had been reported after their use. The number of deaths was 19. The source of the active ingredient for this product was the Scientific Protein Laboratories (SPL) in Changhzou, China. The FDA found that the heparin batches associated with the reactions contained 5–20% of a heparin-like compound as a contaminant. It was later identified as over-sulfated chondroitin sulfate (OSCS) (see Figure 5.4). More than 80 adverse reactions were also reported in Germany with products where the heparin was again sourced from China, although from another company in Changzhou. Methods were developed rapidly to determine the quantities of OSCS in heparin preparations.[6]

This example illustrates that the name of a respected manufacturer does not always guarantee the safety of products if the raw material has been sourced from another company. In-house testing of the incoming material should have detected that there was a problem, given the high percentage of the impurities, but it is difficult to cater for previously unknown impurities. Another case is illustrated by the recent reports of melamine-contaminated milk powder products in China (levels ranged from 0.1 to

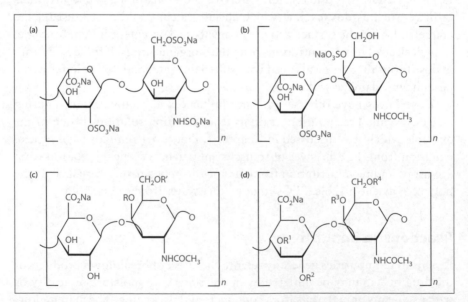

Figure 5.4 Structural formulae of heparin (a), dermatan sulfate (b), chondroitin sulfate A and C (c), and oversulfated chondroitin sulfate (OSCS) (d). For chondroitin sulfate A, group R represents the sulfated moiety, as for chondroitin sulfate C the residual group R' is sulfated. For OSCS, R^1–R^4 label possibly sulfated moieties. The dermatan in heparin preparations is a signal of poor purification methods. (From reference 6.)

2500 ppm).[7] The melamine was added criminally to increase the measured but not actual protein content. Children consuming the product developed nephrolithiasis.[8]

A detailed discussion of the outbreak of adverse reactions as a result of the use of contaminated heparin is provided by Blossom et al.[9]

Hyaluronic acid

The use of hyaluronic acid (HA) in osteoarthritis as a synovial fluid supplement was discussed in Chapter 1. It has also been used in ophthalmic surgery. In vivo metabolic degradation of HA by hyaluronidase is one of the determinants of its biological half-life. HA can be sourced from bacteria, from rooster combs or from human umbilical cord, and the resulting HA products contain different impurities.[10] Several commercially available products in one study did not degrade on digestion with hyaluronidase, clearly indicating that biological half-life will not be the same. Vigilance is necessary and, where problems arise, the provenance of biological products must be determined. Sources might vary from batch to batch as discussed in Chapter 4. Source matters, processing matters, purification matters and, of course, proving this by the application of the highest-quality analytical technology is essential. Finding out about such problems before damage is done or suspected is certainly difficult. We must be prepared to ask the obvious questions of suppliers when problems are suspected. It is not always possible to wait for final proof.

Oligomeric impurities in penicillins

Acute sensitivity to penicillins occurs in a minority of patients, but the reaction is well known in practice. Nevertheless, the source of at least some of the adverse reactions is not always appreciated. Impurities in penicillins have been blamed for sensitivities and allergies to this class of drug. The number of impurities found in samples of amoxicillin is quite remarkable.[11] Amoxicillin's structure is shown in Figure 5.5.

Impurities in amoxicillin samples can include 2-hydroxy-3-(4-hydroxy-phenyl)pyrazine, 4-hydroxyphenylglycine, 4-hydroxyphenylglyclamoxicillin,

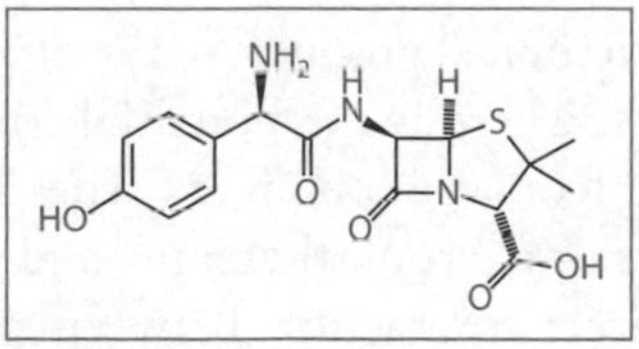

Figure 5.5 Structure of amoxicillin.

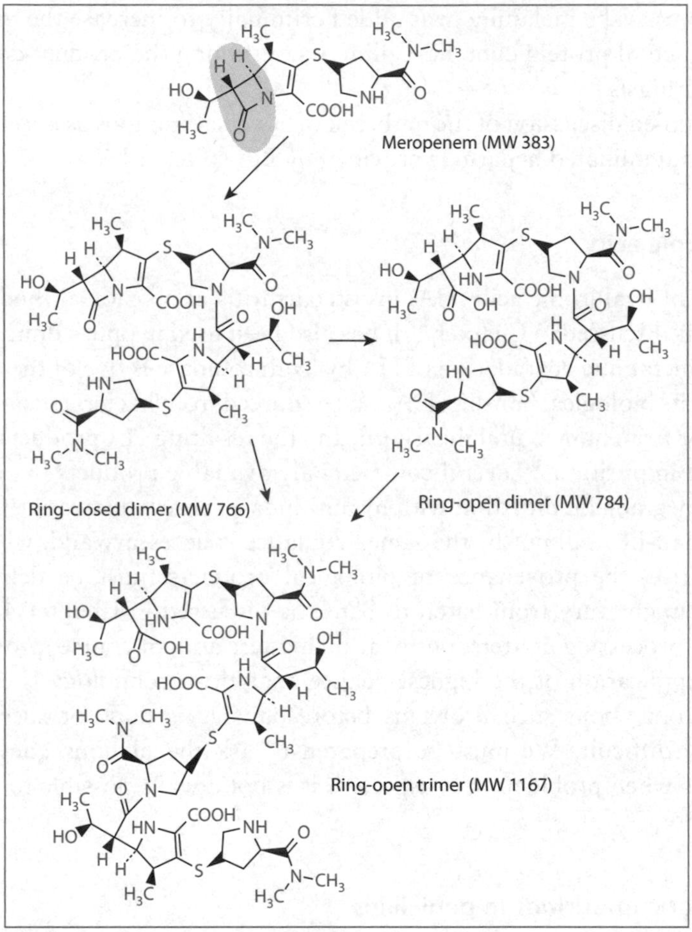

Figure 5.6 Ring-opened and ring-closed dimers and a ring-open trimer. The ring in question, the β-lactam ring, is highlighted.

6-aminopenicillanic acid, amoxicilloic acid and seven others not including the dimer and the trimer (see Figure 5.6) These and other oligomers are possibly prime culprits in penicillin allergies as they are formed with peptide bonds and resemble peptides.

Contamination of products from containers

Sensitisation of the skin to topical products may not always be the result of the drug or of the excipients. There is the potential for contamination by substances that have leached from the containers. The aluminium tube is still the most widely used container for topical creams and ointments; the tubes are lacquered to prevent direct interaction between product and aluminium. Epoxy resins are used as the protective layer in most cases, particularly bisphenyl A diglycidyl ether (BADGE)-based resins. Leaching of BADGE and its congeners depends to an extent on the formulation and the mechanical stresses applied to the tubes.[12] Adverse effects due to these leachables have not been assessed but they are a potential cause, for example, of contact dermatitis.

Delivery devices and materials

There is an increasing number of devices and biomaterials that are used to deliver drugs, genes and vaccines. Issues can arise with the materials used in such devices, which include syringes and giving sets, or with the manner in which the device as a whole behaves (system plus active material). There might also be technical failure of a pump or reservoir, or conditions in the device that destabilise the drug, especially if it is a protein.

Insulin pumps

A good example of problems that arise through system–drug interactions is the phenomenon of protein aggregation in insulin pumps.[13] Insulin aggregation is accompanied by a significant loss of biological activity. Various problems have been encountered with insulin pumps: obstruction in the infusion set or leakage at the infusion set connection or from the infusion site. Insulin aggregation (when insulin fibrils form after heating) can also occur owing to agitation of the pump during wear and to temperature fluctuations. The stability is influenced by the type of insulin, the solvent and the concentration.[14] Metal ion contamination has also been implicated and the use of EDTA has been recommended to sequester ions.[15] Insulin aggregates will at times block delivery channels.

Figure 5.7 illustrates the different deposition patterns of insulin in solution following administration by pen injector, a jet injector and an external insulin pump. The diffusion of insulin from sites of administration is important for its activity; retention of insulin and its degradation at the site of deposition might reduce biological activity. Pharmacokinetic differences between these modes of administration might also be found.

In one study of bovine zinc-insulin, aggregation occurred only when agitation and hydrophobic surfaces were present.[16] Other proteins also degrade physically in pumps; interleukin 2 can lose 90% of its activity over a 24-hour period of infusion. Adsorption, which is a precursor of aggregate formation in some insulin systems, does not occur with interleukin 2, but irreversible structural changes can occur.[17] Methods of maintaining the physical stability of protein solutions are discussed by Lougheed et al.[18]

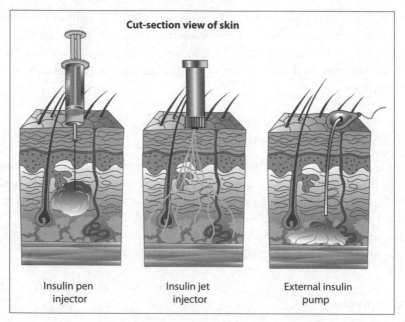

Figure 5.7 Different distribution patterns after administration of insulin by injector pen, jet injector and external insulin pump. (From http://adam.about.com/care/diabetes.)

Adsorption of proteins onto solid surfaces is a well-known phenomenon. Insulin adsorbs to glass, so that in low concentrations drug can be lost. Figure 5.8 shows the rate at which Asp^{B25} insulin adsorbs onto a silanated silica wafer surface.[19] At the higher concentrations adsorption is rapid, as one

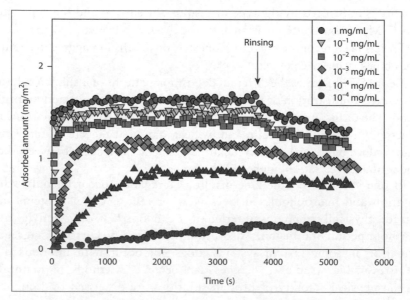

Figure 5.8 Adsorption onto silanised silica surfaces of Asp^{B25} insulin, showing the influence of concentration, (From reference 19.)

might expect from diffusion-controlled kinetics. One technique to avoid loss of insulin by adsorption is to add small amounts of albumin to the infusion; the albumin adsorbs first and inhibits further adsorption of the active.

Stents

Drug-eluting stents have made an impact in the therapy of restenosis but there have been many reports of adverse events ranging to death due to early and late stent thrombosis.[20] It has been suggested that many of the problems have been due to the polymer used in the stent coating.[21] Many variants have been studied: changing the polymer[22] and including the use of biodegradable polymers[23] and also designs with non-polymeric systems. Figure 5.9 shows a stent in place in a coronary artery close to plaque; the figure to the right (b) represents the release of drug from a polymer coating on the stent structure.

The components of a drug-eluting stent comprise a platform (the stent), a carrier (usually a polymer) and an agent (a drug).[24] Stents allow the local delivery of the active agent to the area of vascular injury, averting the need to deliver high doses systemically. The device must have mechanical resistance to abrasion during implantation, resist sterilisation, control drug release, and not damage the vessel wall and tissue. Various coatings have been developed, including phosphorylcholine; biocompatible non-erodible, biodegradable, or bioabsorbable polymers, as well as ceramic layers. Polymers are the most commonly used carriers. Clinical trials of safety and efficacy are required for each device.

Problems that have arisen with drug-eluting stents have been reviewed from an FDA perspective.[25] Some relate to the reports of subacute thrombosis and 60 associated deaths (up to 2004). While it was not possible to determine whether the adverse events are more common in drug-eluting or bare metal

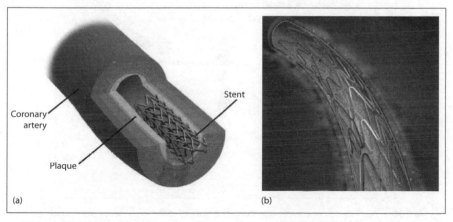

(a) (b)

Figure 5.9 (a) A cartoon of a stent in a coronary artery (www.csmc.edu/images). (b) The release of active agent from the polymer coating on the stent (Boston Scientific Corporation).

stents, some are related to problems with failure of the stent to deflate after deployment (Taxus Express). This problem has been ascribed to issues in the manufacturing process that could have led to a weakening of the outer lumen of the delivery catheter. The resistance of the stent to withdrawal has been ascribed to 'stickiness'. One suggestion was that it was due to the friction between the stent delivery balloon and the drug–polymer coating on the stent.

Catheters

Intravascular catheter-related infections can be an important source of blood-stream infections in patients who are critically ill.[26] It is said that more than 250 000 vascular catheter-related bacterial or fungal infections occur each year in the USA, with mortalities in critical ill patients of up to 25%. Bacteria can adhere to and form biofilms on catheter surfaces. Preventive stratagems include cutaneous antisepsis, use of sterile barriers during insertion, application of chlorhexidine-impregnated sponges and the use of antimicrobial, antibiotic-coated or silver-impregnated catheters. Urinary catheters also suffer from bacterial film formation, and there are several points of entry of bacteria in such systems, as seen in Figure 5.10. This is clearly an area of great importance, but some of the issues are outside the scope of this book. What is clear is that antibiotic-coated catheters are drug delivery devices and that bacterial biofilms that form on catheters are the result of an adhesion process, two areas that are outwith our scope (although we should never be concerned in practice about such boundaries).

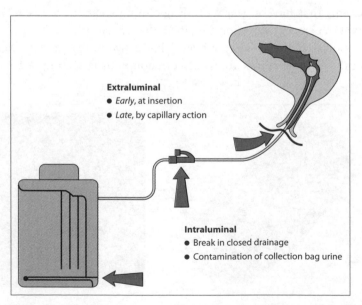

Figure 5.10 A schematic of the arrangement of a urinary catheter. Sources of infection are indicated by arrows.

Table 5.3 Contact angles of different *Pseudomonas* spp.

Strain number and name	Contact angle (°)
Pseudomonas fluorescens	21.2
Pseudomonas aeruginosa	25.7
Pseudomonas putida	38.5
Pseudomonas sp strain 26-3	20.1
Pseudomonas sp strain 52	19.0
Pseudomonas sp. strain 80	29.5

Values for other organisms can range up to 60° for an *Arthrobacter* sp. strain 177 and 70° for a *Corynebacter* sp. strain 125.

Bacteria adhere to solid surfaces. Bacterial hydrophobicity can be correlated with the adhesion of bacteria to experimental surfaces such as negatively charged polystyrene. Different bacteria have different hydrophobic properties; the contact angles of water with bacterial surfaces correlate with hydrophobicity. The higher the contact angle, the higher the hydrophobicity and the greater the adsorption.[27] Different strains of bacteria, e.g. of pseudomonads, behave differently as can be seen in Table 5.3. However, it is generally unlikely that only one parameter correlates with bacterial adsorption onto a wide range of surfaces, which are not always smooth as in experimental systems. Nonetheless, knowing the surface properties of bacteria and of the catheter material can be valuable in understanding problems.

Transdermal patches as devices?

Transdermal patches can be considered devices. Problems that have arisen with these include adverse reactions to the adhesive used to adhere the patch to the skin. Allergic contact dermatitis from hydroxymethylcellulose has been reported with an estradiol patch.[28] Mishaps related to use of transdermal patches include many involving patches falling off under a variety of conditions, including subsequent adhesion to another person! Other events include swelling and itching at the application site; too strong adhesion, leading to pain on removal; excessive adhesion of the plastic backing to the adhesive layer, leading to tearing of the patch; inflexible patches that do not flex with the skin; and cases of drug crystals being seen on patches.[29] Cases of burning have been reported when medicated patches containing even small amounts of aluminium are worn during magnetic resonance imaging, as a result of overheating in the area of the patch.[30]

Abnormal bioavailability, high or low

Classical examples where the bioavailability has changed after a period when patients have been stabilised and physicians are accustomed to responses from a particular dose form or brand include digoxin (Lanoxin). In the 1970s a change in the manufacturing process led to a marked difference in bioavailability through an increase in particle size. A change in the main excipient from calcium carbonate to lactose in a brand of phenytoin sodium led to a marked increase in bioavailability and overdosing. The calcium was clearly forming a calcium salt of the drug, decreasing its solubility and rate of dissolution. Its removal led to faster absorption and toxic effects in titrated patients.

Testing for adverse effects

Can pharmacists become more involved in searching for the causes of adverse effects? One example might be our own experience in the University of Strathclyde working with the Contact Dermatitis Unit at Belvidere Hospital Glasgow some years ago, where we explored modes of measurement of skin reactions to substances applied to the skin. The aim was to replace more subjective clinical scoring when pharmacists had an opportunity to assess reactions scientifically. Contact dermatitis is a term for a skin reaction resulting from exposure to allergens (allergic contact dermatitis) or irritants (irritant contact dermatitis). Phototoxic dermatitis occurs when the allergen or irritant is activated by sunlight. Contact dermatitis can occur from contact with jewellery but also from drugs and devices (e.g. transdermal patch adhesives).

Contact dermatitis testing

Suspected contact dermatitis is usually tested for by application of a series of patches containing putative causative agents. The formulation of these materials has often been fairly crude (for example by dispersing nickel sulfate in a paraffin base) and this might affect the outcome. Poor attention to pharmaceutical principles of release, poor choice of vehicle and lack of consideration of particle size all contribute to imprecision.[31] Proprietary patch formulations are available. Test results are often evaluated against a control or controls by clinical scoring of reactions from severe (+++), through (++), (+), 0 and equivocal (<+). Skin reflectance measurements were evaluated as a measure of skin haemoglobin content and correlated well with clinical scoring.[32] The following is an example of a study conducted some time ago.[31]

> A group of 43 patients with a clinical history of nickel allergy who exhibited an equivocal or no allergic reaction to a patch test at 48 h were further challenged using several different formulations of nickel

sulphate. This experimental test battery comprised aqueous, dimethyl sulphoxide (DMSO) and propylene glycol (PG) solutions of nickel sulphate, and nickel sulphate incorporated into Cetomacrogol cream and yellow soft paraffin (PMF). Although some of these vehicles were irritant, a formulation-dependent test response was observed, such that in terms of the number of responses per unit weight of nickel sulphate applied to the skin, the vehicles could be ranked: DMSO greater than PG greater than aqueous solution greater than Cetomacrogol cream greater than PMF preparations. This ranking could be correlated with the relative ease with which nickel sulphate could be dialysed from each vehicle in vitro. This study demonstrates that for nickel sulphate, the vehicle can influence the outcome of patch testing apparently by modifying the quantity of nickel released into the skin for elicitation of the allergic response.

(Cetomacrogol is a non-ionic surfactant with a C_{16} hydrocarbon chain and an average 24-unit polyoxyethylene oxide hydrophilic chain.)

Release of nickel sulfate from the test preparations varied considerably, as shown in Figure 5.11. The correlation between skin blood flow (plotted in Figure 5.12 as the Hb (haemoglobin index) and clinical scoring is good. The response is often a weal which reflects increased blood flow and, of

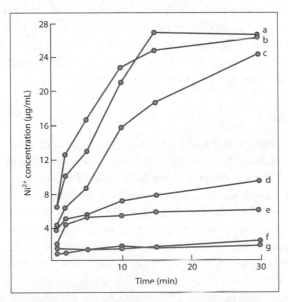

Figure 5.11 *In vitro* release of nickel sulfate from various vehicles at 37°C using a dialysis technique. Curve a, an aqueous solution of nickel sulfate ($NiSO_4$); curve b, propylene glycol solution; curve c, dimethyl sulfoxide (DMSO) solution; curve d, Cetomacrogol cream; curve e, 2.5% $NiSO_4$ in yellow soft paraffin (proprietary formulation); curve f, yellow soft paraffin; curve g, 5% $NiSO_4$ in yellow soft paraffin (proprietary formulation). (From reference 31.)

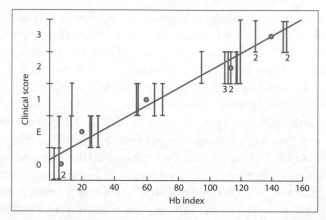

Figure 5.12 Correlation between clinical scores of patient responses to a variety of proprietary test patches and the haemoglobin (Hb) index derived from a skin reflectance technique. The individual test patches contained separately nickel, chromium, colophony fragrances, thiomersal, benzoic acid, parabens, neomycin and a range of other materials implicated in contact dermatitis. (From reference 32.)

course, heat output. Infra-red thermography has also been used.[33] This is a convenient non-invasive technique that employs an infra-red (IR) camera and can be used to discriminate between irritant and allergic responses and to quantify the latter.

Figure 5.13 shows some results after application of the contact dermatitis test patches, both the appearance of the reactions to different formulations and the results when assessed using the IR camera. The IR thermograms, which detect the increased blood flow and heat profiles, show not only the intensity but also the spread of the reaction on the skin.

Nanosystems

The next few years will see the advent in medicine and pharmacy of many particulate systems. There are several reasons why we should be concerned and observant about potential toxicity. The first is that nanosystems, although they have been around in pharmacy since the mid 1970s, have not been widely used. The second is that their small size allows them to translocate in the body and end up in higher concentrations in organs such as the liver and spleen that larger particles cannot access. Lastly, their small size leads to large surface areas per unit weight and this can bring its own problems with regard to interaction with blood components and with tissues. Figure 5.14 illustrates some of the nanosystems now available experimentally from polymer particles, fullerenes, dendrimers and gold sols, and also their potential for interactions *in vivo*: interactions with blood components, interaction with and effects on immune cells, accumulation in the reticuloendothelial system and immunogenicity.[34]

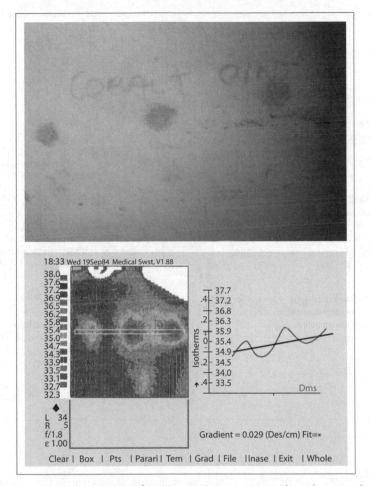

Figure 5.13 (a) Typical appearance of positive reactions to contact with patch tests on the back of a subject. (b) An infrared thermogram of the back of a (different) patient who has been assessed for contact dermatitis to nickel with three formulations of nickel sulfate. The image shows not only differences in intensity but also difference in the spread of the response. These thermograms are more informative than physicians' scoring systems.

Undoubtedly new adverse effects will arise from the use of nanosytems after their widespread use. Inhaled systems will reach sensitive lung tissue, but like other inhaled medicines, material swallowed will end up in the gut and it is known that small quantities of nanoparticles can be absorbed intact through the M-cells of the gut-associated lymphoid tissue (GALT) and also through enterocytes.[14] Much has still to be learned about the potential down sides of nanomedicines and assurances on the safety of the materials from which they are made is not always sufficient to instil confidence in the safety of the nanoparticles. Because of the vast array of possible systems, it is impossible to generalise. Each system will have to be examined and tested on its merits.

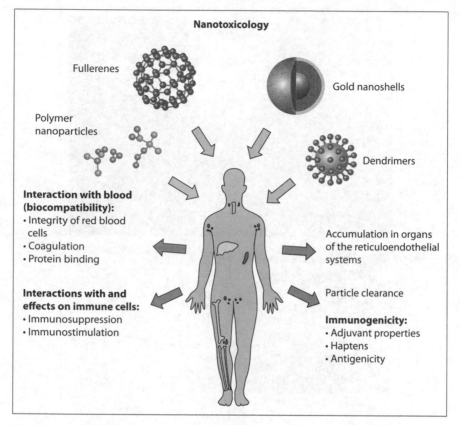

Figure 5.14 Mechanisms of toxicity of nanosystems.

Conclusions

Detecting the causes of adverse events is not an easy task, especially when drugs or drug products are novel. It is essential that we look for analogies, reports on closely related drugs, and similar formulations, perhaps identical excipients.

Potential mechanisms should be proposed and the following questions asked:

- Is the event due to the drug?
- Is it an excipient effect?
- Is it a result of the dosage form?

and of course:

- Is it unrelated to the medication?

This requires a breadth of knowledge of similar events recorded in the literature or from experience. The few examples noted in this chapter may assist in

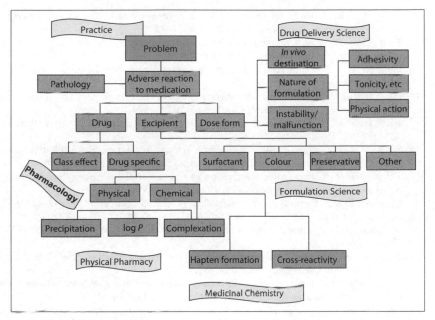

Figure 5.15 Charting the causes of adverse reactions to medications. The many causes are shown in relation to drug, excipient, nature of formulation, the dosage form or device and whether there are physical or chemical causes.

asking the right questions. The concluding illustration (Figure 5.15) summarises how one might approach the issues. A fuller record of adverse events and the involvement of delivery systems (up to 1996) can be read:[1] the older literature should not be discarded as there may be clues there which might have relevance to new medicines and treatments.

References

1. Uchegbu IF, Florence AT. Adverse events related to dose forms and delivery systems. *Drug Saf* 1996; 14: 36–97.
2. Singh MK *et al.* Another reason to dislike medication. *Lancet* 2008; 371: 1388.
3. Levy DJ. An aspirin tablet and a gastric ulcer. *N Engl J Med* 2000; 343: 863.
4. Florence AT, Salole EG, eds. *Formulation Factors in Adverse Reactions.* London: Wright, 1990.
5. *WHO Drug Information* 2008; 22(2): 84–85.
6. Beyer T *et al.* Quality assessment of unfractionated heparin using ^{1}H nuclear magnetic resonance spectroscopy. *J Pharm Biomed Anal* 2008; 48: 13–19.
7. Guan N *et al.* Melamine-contaminated powdered formula and urolithiasis in young children. *N Engl J Med* 2009; 360: 1067–1074.
8. Langman CB, Melamine, powdered milk and nephrolithiasis in Chinese infants. *N Engl J Med* 2009; 360: 1139–1141.
9. Blossom DB *et al.* Outbreak of adverse reactions associated with contaminated heparin. *N Engl J Med* 2008; 359: 2674–2684.
10. Matsuno Y K *et al.* Electrophoresis studies on the contaminating glycosaminoglycan in commercially available hyaluronic acid products. *Electrophoresis* 2008; 29: 3628–3635.

11. Jouyban A, Kenndler E. Impurity analysis of pharmaceuticals using capillary electromigration methods. *Electrophoresis* 2008; 9: 3531–3551.
12. Haverkamp JB *et al.* Contamination of semi-solid dosage forms by leachables from aluminium tubes. *Eur J Pharm Biopharm* 2008; 70: 921–928.
13. Guilhem I *et al.* Technical risks with subcutaneous insulin infusion. *Diabetes Metab* 2006; 32: 279–284.
14. Hirsh IB *et al.* Catheter obstruction with continuous subcutaneous insulin infusion. Effect of insulin concentration. *Diabetes Care* 1992; 15: 593–594.
15. James DE *et al.* Insulin precipitation in artificial infusion devices. *Diabetologia* 1981; 21: 554–557.
16. Sluzky V *et al.* Kinetics of insulin aggregation in aqueous solutions upon agitation in the presence of hydrophobic surfaces. *Proc Natl Acad Sci U S A* 1991; 88: 9377–9381.
17. Tzannis ST *et al.* Irreversible inactivation of interleukin 2 in a pump-based delivery environment. *Proc Natl Acad Sci U S A* 1996; 93: 5460–5465.
18. Lougheed W *et al.* Physical stability of insulin formulations. *Diabetes* 1983; 32: 424–432.
19. Mollman SH *et al.* *J Colloid Interface Sci* 2005; 286: 28–35.
20. Waksman R. Drug-eluting stents: is new necessarily better? *Lancet* 2008; 372: (9644), 1126–1128.
21. Joner M *et al.* Endothelial cell recovery between comparator polymer-based drug-eluting stents. *J Am Coll Cardiol* 2008; 52: 333–342.
22. Stone GW *et al.* Comparison of an everolimus-eluting stent and a paclitaxel-eluting stent in patients with coronary artery disease. *JAMA* 2008; 299: 1903–1913.
23. Grube E, Buellesfeld L. BioMatrix biolimus A9-euting coronary-stent: a next generation drug-eluting stent for coronary artery disease. *Expert Rev Med Devices* 2006; 3: 731–741.
24. Serruys PW *et al.* Coronary artery stents. *N Engl J Med* 2006; 354: 483–495.
25. Muni NI, Gross TP. Problems with drug-eluting coronary stents-the FDA perspective. *N Engl J Med* 2004; 351: 1593–1596.
26. Raad I *et al.* Intravascular catheter-related infections: advances diagnosis, prevention and management. *Lancet Infection* 2007; 7: 645–657.
27. vanLoosdrecht MCM *et al.* The role of the bacterial cell wall hydrophobicity in adhesion. *Appl Environ Microbiol* 1987; 53: 1893–1897.
28. Schwartz BK, Glendinning WE. *Contact Dermatitis* 2006; 18: 106–107.
29. Wokovich AM *et al.* Transdermal drug delivery systems (TDDS) adhesion as a critical safety, efficacy and quality attribute. *Eur J Pharm Biopharm* 2006; 64: 1–8.
30. Lowry F. Medicated patch can cause burns during MRI, FDA warns. *Medscape Medical News* 2009. www.fda.gov/NewsEvents/Newsroom/PressAnnouncements/ucm149537.htm (accessed 14 May 2009).
31. Mendelow AY *et al.* Patch testing for nickel allergy. The influence of the vehicle on the response rate to topical nickel sulphate. *Contact Dermatitis* 1985; 13: 29–33.
32. Mendelow AY *et al.* Skin reflectance measurements of patch test responses. *Contact Dermatitis* 1986; 15: 73–78.
33. Baillie AJ *et al.* Thermo graphic assessment of patch-test responses. *Br J Dermatology* 1990; 122: 351–360.
34. Florence AT. Oral absorption of micro- and nanoparticles: neither exceptional nor unusual. *Pharmaceutical Research* 1997; 14: 613–617.

6

Paediatric, geriatric and special formulations

This chapter covers some aspects of formulation in paediatric and geriatric practice, a branch of pharmacy in which personalised medication comes into its own. We deal with the need for special formulations for individual cases and some of the more general needs of the population at the different ends of the age spectrum. This has been termed 'age-specific' medicine. We will deal also with medication and enteral delivery by feeding tubes, in both children and the elderly.

Introduction

If there was ever a case of continued emphasis on pharmaceutics it is the need to design patient-specific medicines both nationally, in specialist units in hospitals and, one would hope, in community pharmacies in the future. The possibility of errors in medication increases with the number of manipulations and calculations required; hence even simple technologies that provide dosing systems to avoid the large dilutions that are frequently necessary in paediatric care would be of benefit. In the 1950s and 1960s, extemporaneous formulations were the norm even if the drugs and ingredients they contained were inferior to today's. We now have a wider range of excipients and active agents available and also a much broader range of methods of formulation and modes of delivery of drugs. We can now also characterise and manipulate materials in a superior way. Unfortunately, many formulations for children are perforce prepared from products designed for adults; the same applies for the elderly, who may have difficulties in swallowing or have problems that demand modified approaches to medication. We do not deal here with the differences in the pharmacokinetic and pharmacodynamic or metabolic aspects of drugs in the different categories of patients. These often necessitate the use of sustained-release (SR) or modified-release (MR) formulations or individualised therapies, but are covered in detail in other texts. However, formulations are not chosen in isolation. There are age-related developmental changes in the pharmacokinetics[1,2] and pharmacodynamics[3] of drugs. Changes occur in gastric acidity, drug clearance and receptor expression, as discussed in an article by Kearns *et al.*[4] Many of these changes are relevant to drug absorption. Neonatal stomachs are achlorhydric soon after birth, so the absorption of, for example, acid-labile drugs may be increased. The rate of gastric emptying falls as infants get older, being faster in the neonate than in adults, but slower in infants and children than in adults. This has consequences with some formulations. Because the liver takes up a relatively large percentage of body volume in infants, clearance rates often exceed those in adults. It is clear then that extrapolation of data from adult data sets in terms of absorption or the behaviour of both drugs and dose forms is hazardous. Many of these issues are discussed in more detail in a review on the topic of developing paediatric medicines.[5] One problem with assessing the literature on the use of medicines in children is that journals 'permit inadequate formulation information in pediatric drug trials ... impairing their validity and reliability'.[6] Full formulation information should be provided in all paediatric clinical trial reports and in other publications.

Extemporaneous formulations

Extemporaneous formulation would not be so daunting were it not for the reluctance of manufacturers to provide pure drug samples for human administration. Hence, formulations are frequently prepared from tablets, capsules and injections to produce medicines suitable for an individual child or for groups of children. This should be considered unacceptable in the twenty-first century, as much as the need for the elderly to have to cut tablets in half. Nonetheless, it is pharmacy's role to provide appropriate medicine for individuals.

Figure 6.1 illustrates some of the basic approaches used when converting existing formulations of tablets, capsules and injections into alternative forms. It may be that the contents of an injection can be incorporated directly into a suitable vehicle. The same may be true of soft-gelatin capsules, whose contents may be amenable to emulsification depending on their nature. In a survey of extemporaneously prepared dosage forms in NHS trusts in Yorkshire, NE England, and in London, it was found that 66% were aqueous suspensions, 22% solutions, 4% powders, 1.2% oils and 0.2% capsules.[7] Most were for use in paediatric patients, and included drugs such as midazolam, vancomycin, clonidine hydrochloride, diazoxide, clobazam and warfarin. Yet in this study it was found that 28% of extemporaneously prepared products had neither chemical nor microbiological supporting data and close to 8% had their formulae and expiry dates taken from the literature. Much of the data was not on file.

Often the issue is dose reduction, but it is also frequently to provide a dosage form that aids swallowing in both the young and the elderly. The

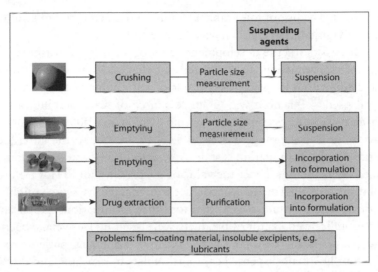

Figure 6.1 Stratagems applied when there is a necessity to convert existing adult dosage forms (tablets, hard- and soft-gelatin capsules and injections) for use in children or the elderly. Drug substance may also be sourced from chemical manufacturers, but must undergo strict quality control before use.

pharmacokinetic and metabolic differences in patients are clearly also among the drivers of formulation choice, as outlined in Figure 6.2.

The problem in the extemporaneous formulation of medicines 'that children can take', as Nunn[8] has put it, is that many products used have inadequate data on stability and shelf-life, let alone bioavailability, and have an unpleasant taste. He calls for a national standard for extemporaneously dispensed medicines. Solid dosage forms are usually more stable than liquid

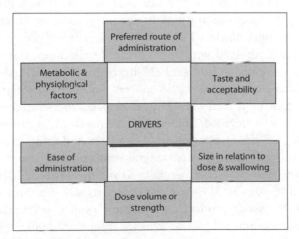

Figure 6.2 The matrix of drivers for special formulations.

formulations. The use of mini-tablets, 3 mm in diameter, to aid swallowing has been investigated in children aged from 2 to 6 years.[9]

In a discussion of the development of an oral captopril formulation for paediatric patients it has been pointed out that the stability of the liquid products was variable, partly as a result of variability of the purity of the captopril used.[10] But even with a single source of drug, stability after one month at room temperature ranged from 71.5% to 100%, although with storage at $5 \pm 3°C$ the range was from 82% to 99.7%. At the latter storage temperatures, the formulation is stable for two years. Captopril oxidation is catalysed by metal ions, hence the value of the presence of EDTA for a stable formulation and the avoidance of contact with metal ions, which might come from use of drug substances extracted for other formulations. Apparently, a variety of unlicensed captopril products were used in 13 tertiary paediatric cardiac centres in the UK and 13 large hospitals referring patients to these centres: four hospitals dispensed captopril tablets by crushing and dissolving in water before administration, and the other 22 used nine different liquid formulations. As the authors conclude,[11] this degree of inconsistency raises 'issues about optimal captopril dosing and potential toxicity, such that its use may influence paediatric cardiac surgical and interventional outcomes'. This is an indictment of modern pharmacy.

Effect of formulation and presentation: a case from the literature

Isoniazid absorption in two young children

The abstract of a paper by Notterman *et al.* reads in full:[12]

> In an 8-month-old infant with tuberculosis meningitis treatment with isoniazid was unsuccessful and was associated with lower than expected plasma concentrations of isoniazid (measured concentration 0.1 microgram/mL). The infant had received isoniazid as a crushed tablet admixed with apple sauce. Oral administration of the parenteral solution of isoniazid (Nydrazid, Squibb) mixed in apple juice produced a higher isoniazid concentration (2.9 micrograms/mL) and the child improved clinically. Pharmacokinetic studies in two subjects were performed following intramuscular injection of isoniazid and oral administration of (1) an isoniazid tablet crushed and mixed with apple sauce, (2) parenteral isoniazid solution mixed with apple juice, and (3) a commercially available syrup containing isoniazid and pyridoxine (P-I-N Forte, Lannett). Of the three oral preparations, the syrup produced the highest peak concentrations (8.3 and 6.9 micrograms/mL). The crushed tablet in apple sauce produced the lowest peak concentrations (1.4 and 2.4 micrograms/mL).

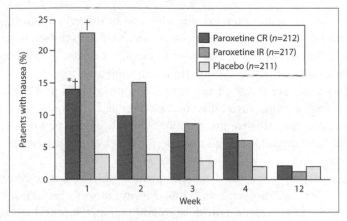

Figure 6.3 The number of patients with nausea as a function of the nature of the dosage form versus placebo. CR, controlled-release; IR, immediate-release. * $p \leq 0.05$ vs paroxetine IR; † $p \leq 0.05$ vs placebo. (From reference 13.)

Administration of crushed isoniazid tablets with food may be associated with impaired gastrointestinal absorption, lower than expected isoniazid concentrations, and treatment failure.

There are issues of the particle size or granule size in the case of the crushed tablets and of the effect of the apple sauce, as suggested, on gastrointestinal (GI) absorption. One of the key issues when using crushed tablets or the contents of capsules is the determination of particle size distributions so that different batches at least consist of the same size as far as possible.

Formulation of paroxetine and reduction of nausea

Controlled-release formulations have long been used not only to prolong the effectiveness of drugs, but also to reduce side-effects. As one example, Figure 6.3 [13] shows the effectiveness of controlled-release formulations versus immediate-release formulations in reducing the incidence of nausea after paroxetine administration. There is an interesting time-dependence of the effect.

Developing paediatric medicines: liquid or solid oral forms?

Children are far from being a homogeneous group. As patients they may range from pre-term newborn infants (premature) with an average weight of less than 3.4 kg, through full-term infants (neonates) (0–27 days), infants and toddlers (28 days to 23 months) with weights of 3.4–12.4 kg, children from 2 to11 years (12.4–39 kg) and adolescents from 12 to 16/18 years weighing on average 39–72 kg for males and 60 kg for females.

In devising formulations for this variable group, note has to be taken of the issue of excipient biological activity, discussed in Chapter 2 and Chapter 5.

Liquid formulations are often favoured because of the ease of administration and acceptability to the child. Some researchers have actually studied methods of teaching children as young as 6 years to swallow tablets.[14] Taste masking is more of an issue with liquid formulations, but solid dose forms can be difficult to swallow and may lodge in the young oesophagus. Liquid formulations suffer somewhat from variability of measurement of dose, although oral injectors can reduce this frequent domestic error. The teaspoon is far from a standard measure, delivering in use between 2.5 and 9 mL according to a 1975 study.

The conversion from liquid to solid formulations of antiretrovirals is of interest.[15] There are problems with liquid formulations other than measurement of dose in practice: the daily dose volumes for a 20 kg child are 40 mL for stavudine, 22 mL for zidovudine 16 mL for abacavir and 12 mL for didanosine, for example,[8] and there are other practical issues in terms of bulk drug. Stavudine is available as a powder for reconstitution. In a single month, 18 packs would be required, needing as many reconstitutions. Three boxes of capsules hold equivalent treatments to the injection.

Itraconazole

Itraconazole is used in children with invasive fungal infections following chemotherapy. The drug is highly lipophilic and capsules have been reported to have variable absorption; a liquid itraconazole formulation employing a cyclodextrin as a solubilising agent has a bioavailability 60% higher than that of the capsules.[16]

Extemporaneous formulations and performance

If tablets are crushed to provide drug for extemporaneous formulations (avoiding of course the crushing of sustained-release forms), the process must be standardised as far as possible and the particle size distribution must be evaluated as minimal quality procedures.

There are commercial devices on sale for crushing tablets. Frequently these do not instruct patients or carers not to crush controlled-release tablets. Even if they did so, patients and carers would not be able to tell which were and which were not controlled-release systems.

The elderly and their medication

There are many reasons why medicines are required for use in the elderly patient. There are changes with ageing of the oral cavity and oesophagus, gastric and intestinal changes, let alone the problems of co-morbidity and polypharmacy that complicate their pharmaceutical care.[17] Prescribing appropriately for the elderly is discussed in some detail elsewhere.[18] Xerostomia (see also Chapter 1) and delayed oesophageal emptying may have relevance for the use of certain oral medications, such as fast-dissolving dosage forms or buccal and sublingual forms. Here paucity of fluid intake may slow the release of drug in the oral cavity. The relationship between dose forms and oesophageal damage is dealt with in Chapter 5. The elderly are more susceptible to the lodging of tablets and capsules in the oesophagus than are younger patients. This is not necessarily the fault of the dose form, but can be the result of taking the tablet with no or too little water. The variability of water intake in 108 female subject in a trial of a film-coated placebo tablet when they were free to use whatever volume they wished is shown in Figure 6.4.[19]

The incidence of achlorhydria is found to be up to 20% in elderly patients and hypochlorhydria in 20% of patients over 70 years of age. Around 11% of the elderly have a median fasting gastric pH of above 5.[20] Intestinal transit may be slowed in the elderly. The effects of these many changes may be self-cancelling or may be significant. Much will depend on the drug and it is difficult to predict largely because the individual patients data are not available. More prosaic problems such as difficulty of patients in opening child-proof containers are well known.

Difficulties in swallowing are a problem not only in the young but also in the elderly[21] with dysphagia and those in particular with dementia. Patients

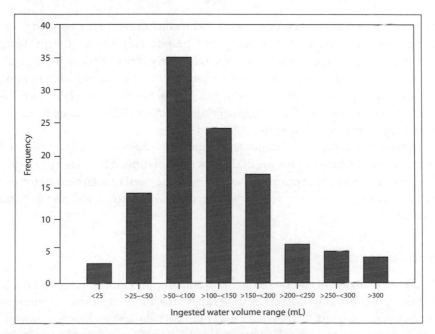

Figure 6.4 Distribution of volume of water ingested by participants swallowing a film-coated placebo tablet in a study of oesophageal transit (From reference 19 with permission.)

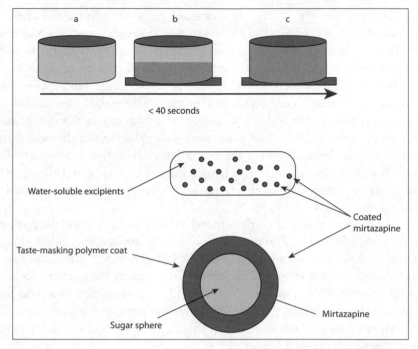

Figure 6.5 Top: the process of dissolution of mirtazapine SolTab in the saliva of the oral cavity: the penetration of water (stages a, b c) takes less than 40 seconds. Bottom: the structure of these fast-dissolving systems. (From reference 22 with permission.)

may simply refuse to take their oral solid medications. Fast-dissolving formulations administered sublingually can be one solution to the problem (see Figure 6.5); such formulations are frequently bioequivalent to the conventional oral forms. The problems of xerostomia, mentioned above, may, however, compromise outcomes somewhat. The benefits have been emphasised of having available for administration a range of different drug formulations, not least in psychopharmacology.[22]

Alternative routes of administration may be employed. The transdermal route has been promoted for use in the older population. There are apparently few differences in the permeability of the skin: the need to adapt doses for use in the elderly relate more to changes in cardiovascular, renal and hepatic change.[23]

Enteral feeding

While the main use of enteral feeding is to enhance nutrition in patients unable to take food normally, enteral feeding tubes also allow the administration of drugs to such patients.[24] This poses many pharmaceutical problems, however. Different feeding tubes have different destinations (Figure 6.6) and hence it is important to choose the correct site for the administration of the drug,

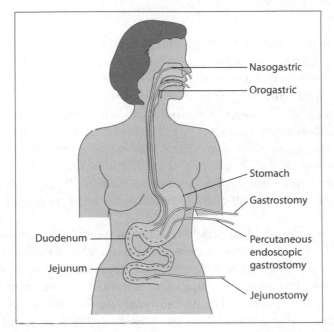

Figure 6.6 Different types of feeding tubes leading to the stomach. Nasoduodenal, nasojejunal and percutaneous jejunostomy tubes extend to the small intestine.

depending on the characteristics of the medication. Even though drugs may be absorbed maximally in the intestine, bypassing the stomach may result in poor absorption as the drug will not have the opportunity to dissolve in the acidic environment of the stomach.

Liquid formulations and solid dosage forms can be administered this way, and with caution several medications can be given at the same time. Nevertheless, drug–nutrient interactions can take place, there can be problems with the osmolality of the liquids administered, and there can be blockage of the tubes (see Table 6.1).

Table 6.1 Some liquid medications that are physically incompatible with most enteral fluids

- Brompheniramine (Dimetane Elixir, Wyeth, USA)
- Calcium gluconate (Rugby, USA)
- Ferrous sulfate (Feosol Elixir, GSK, UK)
- Guaifenesin (Robitussin Liquid, Wyeth, USA)
- Lithium citrate (Cibalith-S syrup, CIBA, USA)
- Potassium chloride liquid (Wyeth, USA)
- Pseudoephedrine hydrochloride (Sudafed Syrup, Pfizer, USA)

Osmolality

The osmolality of enteral feeding formulae is important because of its influence on the GI tract. Osmolality is expressed in mOsm/kg,[25] and is affected by the concentration of amino acids, carbohydrates and electrolytes. If quantities of a liquid with a higher osmolality than the gut contents are administered, water is drawn into the intestine; such a process leads to diarrhoea, nausea and distension. The osmolality of normal body fluids is 300 mOsm/kg and isotonic formulations have values close to this. Table 6.2 taken from Dickerson and Malnik[26] lists liquid medications that have osmolalities greater than 300 mOsm/kg. The exact osmolalites will vary with the exact formulations used and will often differ between various brands of a formulation.

There are some liquid preparations that are not suitable for administration by enteral feeding tubes. Some may be too viscous and may occlude the tubes. Syrups with pH values below 4 often produce incompatibility with the enteral nutrition (EN) formulations, which may result in clumping, increase in viscosity and clogging of the tubes. Not all syrups produce this effect.

Solid conventional-release dose forms can be crushed for administration with EN fluids. The finely ground tablet is added as a suspension in water (15–30 mL). The contents of liquid gelatin capsules are often viscous and it is not easy to remove all of the contents from a single capsule. Delayed-release pancreatic enzyme capsules that contain enteric-coated beads[27] can be mixed with apple sauce or juice for administration via feeding tube. It has been suggested that the soft-gelatin capsule can be dissolved in hot water and the whole contents administered. Extended-release tablets and capsules have to be treated as special cases: the contents of capsules containing coated pellets

---

Table 6.2 Some liquid medications with osmolalities greater than 300 mOsm/kg[a]

- Acetominophen (paracetamol) elixir, 65 mg/mL
- Amantadine HCl solution, 10 mg/mL
- Chloral hydrate syrup, 50 mg/mL
- Cimetidine solution, 60 mg/mL
- Docusate sodium syrup, 3.3 mg/mL
- Lactulose syrup, 0.67 mg/mL
- Metoclopramide HCl syrup, 1 mg/mL
- Promethazine HCl syrup, 1.25 mg/mL

From reference 26.
[a] The exact osmolalities will vary with the exact formulations used and will often differ between various brands of a formulation.

can be mixed with EN fluids, but there can be a tendency for these to clump and block narrow-bore feeding tubes.

Drug interactions with nutrient formulations

Certain drugs have been found to interact with nutrient solutions. It is not surprising, given the nature of these solutions, that drugs may bind to proteins or be affected by electrolytes. Phenytoin, carbamazepine, warfarin and some fluoroquinolones have been reported to have lowered bioavailability because of various interactions. Phenytoin absorption has been reported to be reduced by up to 70% on co-administration with enteral feeds.[28,29]

Conclusions

This chapter has covered many of the areas in which drug formulation is important clinically. Special formulations for paediatric and geriatric patients form a group of products that are key to optimising therapy in these vulnerable age groups. Some wider issues are also discussed, including enteral feeding, interactions of drugs with nutritional fluids and the osmolalities of liquid formulations. These are only snapshots but further searching of the literature should provide many more examples of special formulations.

References

1. Johnson TN. The development of drug metabolising enzymes and their influence on the susceptibility to adverse drug reactions in children. *Toxicology* 2003; 192: 37–48.
2. Strassburg CP *et al.* Developmental aspects of human hepatic drug glucoronidation in young children and adults. *Gut* 2002; 50: 259–265.
3. Hamalainen ML *et al.* Sumatriptan for migraine attacks in children: a randomized placebo-controlled study. Do children with migraine respond to oral sumatriptan differently to adults? *Neurology* 1997; 48: 1100–1103.
4. Kearns GL *et al.* Developmental pharmacology-drug disposition, action, therapy in infants and children. *N Engl J Med* 2003; 349: 1157–1167.
5. Ernest TB *et al.* Developing paediatric medicines: identifying the needs and recognizing the challenges. *J Pharm Pharmacol* 2007; 59: 1043–1055.
6. Standing JF *et al.* Poor formulation information in published pediatric drug trials. *Pediatrics* 2005; 116: e559–e562.
7. Lowey AR, Jackson MN. A survey of extemporaneous preparation in NHS trusts in Yorkshire, the North East and London. *Hosp Pharm* 2008; 15: 217–219.
8. Nunn AJ. Making medicines that children can take. *Arch Dis Child* 2003; 88: 369–371.
9. Thomson SA *et al. Paediatrics* 2009; 123: e235–e238.
10. Berger-Gryllaki M *et al.* The development of a stable oral solution of captopril for paediatric patients. *Eur J Hosp Pharm Sci* 2007; 13: 67–72.
11. Mulla H *et al.* Variations in captopril formulations used to treat children with heart failure: a survey in the United Kingdom. *Arch Dis Child* 2007; 92: 409–411.
12. Notterman DA *et al.* Effect of dose formulation on isoniazid absorption in two young children. *Pediatrics* 1986; 77: 850–852.
13. Golden RN *et al.* Efficacy and tolerability of controlled-release and immediate-release paroxetine in the treatment of depression. *J Clin Psychiatry* 2002; 63: 577–584.

14. Dalquist LM, Blount RL. Teaching a six-year old girl to swallow pills. *J Behav Ther Exp Psychiatry* 1984; 15: 171–173. Blount RL *et al.* A brief, effective method for teaching children to swallow pills. *Behav Ther* 1984; 15: 381–387.
15. Yueng VW, Wong ICK. When do children convert from liquid antiretroviral to solid formulations? *Pharm World Sci* 2005; 27: 399–402.
16. Barone JA *et al.* enhanced bioavailability of itraconazole in hydroxypropyl β-cyclodextrin solution versus capsules in healthy volunteers. *Antimicrob Agents Chemother* 1998; 42: 1862–1865.
17. Gidal BE. Drug absorption in the elderly: biopharmaceutical considerations for the anti-epileptic drugs. *Epilepsy Res* 2006; 68S: S65–S69.
18. Spinewine A *et al.* Appropriate prescribing in elderly people: how well can it be measured and optimised? *Lancet* 2007; 370: 173–184. Mallet L *et al.* The challenge of managing drug interactions in elderly people. *Lancet* 2007; 370: 185–191.
19. Perkins AC *et al.* The use of scintigraphy to demonstrate the rapid esophageal transit of the oval film-coated placebo risedronate tablet compared to a round uncoated placebo tablet when administered with minimal volumes of water. *Int J Pharm* 2001; 222: 295–239.
20. Russell TL *et al.* Upper gastrointestinal pH in seventy-nine healthy, elderly, North American men and women. *Pharm Res* 1993; 10: 187–196.
21. Schindler JS, Kelly JH. Swallowing disorders in the elderly. *Laryngoscope* 2002; 112: 589–602.
22. Frijlink HW. Benefits of different drug formulations in psychopharmacology. *Eur Neuropsychopharmacol* 2003; 13: S77–S84.
23. Kaestli L-Z *et al.* The use of transdermal formulations in the elderly. *Drugs Ageing* 2008; 25: 269–280.
24. Williams NT. Medication administration through enteral feeding tubes. *Am J Health-Syst Pharm* 2009; 65: 2347–2357.
25. Florence AT, Attwood D. *Physicochemical Principles of Pharmacy*, 4th edn. London: Pharmaceutical Press, 2006.
26. Dickerson RN, Melnik G. Osmolality of oral drug solutions and suspension. *Am J Hosp Pharm* 1988; 45: 832–834.
27. Ferrone M *et al.* Pancreatic enzyme pharmacotherapy. *Pharmacotherapy* 2007; 27: 910–922.
28. Gilbert S *et al.* How to minimise interaction between phenytoin and enteral feedings. Two approaches. *Nutr Clin Pract* 1996; 11: 28–31.
29. Doak KK *et al.* Bioavailability of phenytoin acid and phenytoin sodium with enteral feedings. *Pharmacotherapy* 1998; 18: 637–645.

7

Generic medicines: Conventional drugs and biologicals

Introduction

Generic forms of conventional (i.e. small-molecule) medicines contain the same drug as the original brand leader, although the details of the formulation may be different. The issue of generic equivalence and performance thus certainly lies within the domain of pharmaceutics. It is too simple to say that, as the drug is the same, only the formulation may differ, because as we will discuss in this chapter there can be differences in the purity of a drug even when it is within pharmacopoeial limits. The formulation and manufacturing process may indeed influence the stability of the drug and perhaps its physical form. Generic drugs are subject to strict guidelines for licensing so that, within the limits possible with modern analytical techniques and the variability of subjects, they will be bioequivalent, again with certain limits. One problem is that a generic product will be tested against the brand leader and there is no requirement to test generic versus generic. This is where there problems can arise, as we will see.

We distinguish here between so-called conventional, small-molecule drugs and those proteins and other macromolecules that are more complex. Generic forms of biologicals, especially of recombinant proteins, present other issues as the active molecule may contain, say, subtle differences in amino acid sequence due to often inevitable differences in the mode of production and processing. The term 'biosimilars' has evolved for generic forms of such biologicals; alternative terms include follow-on biologics (FOBs) or biogenerics. We deal first with small-molecule chemical medicines and issues related to branded and generic versions of a medicine. It should be noted that many generic products carry brand names, so in fact the discussion is centred around the orginator's branded product and those products that follow from expiry of patents, and the issue of substitution of a generic for a branded product or one generic for another.

A 2007 survey of recent (Australian) pharmacy graduates' knowledge of generic medicines[1] found that more than 80% believed generic medicines to be inferior, to be less effective and to produce more side-effects when compared with branded medicines. When one considers that many generic medicines are manufactured by companies such as Pfizer, Sandoz, GSK and Merck, whose primary occupation is the development of branded innovative products, one wonders where this perception comes from. There are of course differences in formulation between many generics and their branded equivalents and sometimes, as we have discussed in Chapters 2 and 5, these differences can be important for patients, but for the majority of conventional (normal) release products of most drugs there are few problems. There are some therapeutic categories where one might choose to continue with a product on which the patient has been stabilised, as with antiepileptic drugs; clearly, this is where professional intelligence has to be applied.

Regulatory statements on generic products[2]

A generic drug should be identical or bioequivalent to a brand-name drug in dosage form, safety, strength, route of administration, quality, performance characteristics and intended use. The US and European authorities adopt similar approaches. To gain approval, a generic drug must:

- Contain the same active ingredients as the innovator drug (inactive ingredients may vary).
- Be identical in strength, dosage form, and route of administration.
- Have the same use indications.
- Be bioequivalent.
- Meet the same batch requirements for identity, strength, purity, and quality.
- Be manufactured under the same strict standards of good manufacturing practice (GMP) regulations required for innovator products.

The question of bioavailability has to be looked at in several ways (Figure 7.1). Products can be bioequivalent yet not therapeutically equivalent, perhaps because the rate of absorption of the drug differs in the first 30 minutes or so. If bioavailability is measured by the area under the plasma concentration–time curve (AUC) over 24 or 48 hours, then these measures of bioavailability might not show up subtle differences.

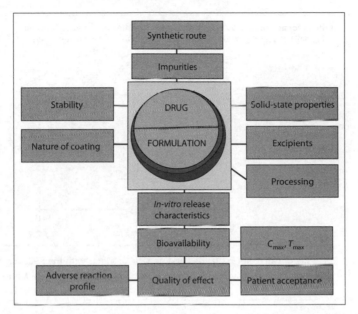

Figure 7.1   The range of issues in determining the equivalence or essential similarity of formulations.

Generics: A question of quality

Equivalence between medicinal products can be thought of at two levels, namely:

1   *Chemical equivalence*, which refers to dosage forms containing the same amount of the same drug in similar dose forms.
2   *Therapeutic equivalence*, which refers to medicines having not only the same bioavailability (as measured by the AUC), but the same clinical effects.

Figures 7.2 and 7.3 demonstrate the limits of bioequivalence and non-bioequivalence. Figure 7.3 shows how, while two generic products may be equivalent to the first brand product, the two generics may not be equivalent to each other, which may pose problems in practice.

Essential similarity of dose forms of the same drug focuses on the essential similar of purity of the drug substance as well as similarity of release rates. Chemical equivalence is ensured by pharmaceutical processes and quality assurance and is one prerequisite for therapeutic equivalence. Limits are set for drug substance; for example, tetracycline hydrochloride contains not less than 96% and not more than 102.0% of the drug. As far as therapeutic equivalence is concerned, the product should have essentially the same safety profile as the comparator product. Regulations do not speak of *identicality* between products, but *essential similarity*. One reason is that drug substances

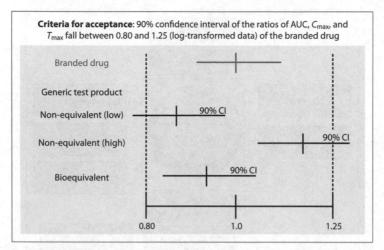

Figure 7.2 The issue of variability in branded and generic products with their 90% confidence limits and the definition of non-equivalence and equivalence in visual form. (From Medscape.)

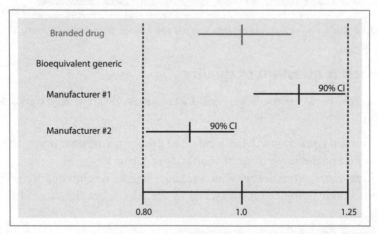

Figure 7.3 Visual demonstration of bioequivalence between generics and branded drugs, which demonstrates clearly that while generic 1 can be equivalent to the brand, generic 2 may not be equivalent to generic 1.

can vary in purity within pharmacopoeial guidelines, and there are variations in the amount of drug within each unit of product, again within limits. On top of this there are interpatient and intrapatient variability. This does not excuse differences and indeed sometimes exacerbates differences. Many drugs are absorbed readily and raise no concerns when generic versions become available. It is with drugs that have proven bioavailability problems or that require special formulation techniques that the issue of similarity becomes real. Drugs with a narrow therapeutic index have to be considered with care. On the other hand, solutions and syrups do not need such scrutiny. Simple formulations of soluble drugs for injection are unlikely to cause concern. The only concern

Table 7.1 Relative potential of oral medicines to display bioavailability problems		
High	**Intermediate**	**Low**
Enteric-coated tablets	Suspensions	Solutions
Sustained-release tablets	Chewable tablets	
Complex formulations	Capsules	
Slowly disintegrating tablets		

might be with drug purity. Pharmacopoeias of course provide limits on undesirable impurities in the drug substance. Toxic 4-epi-anhydrotetracycline is limited in tetracycline products. Even if the limit is very low (say 0.005%), there may be three products (or the same product in different batches) with levels of such an impurity at 0.0048%, 0.004% and 0.002%. Are these identical? Much depends on the nature and activity of the impurity.

For conventional tablets, solutions, simple injections and suspensions, generic versions can be used without qualms. However, once we enter the field of formulation modification, as with sustained-release products, the picture becomes more complex. One knows that towards the end of the patent life of conventional products, modified-release forms (or sometimes new polymorphs of the drug substance) are introduced to delay the introduction of generics and to retain brand loyalty. The relative potential of oral dosage forms to exhibit bioavailability problems are listed in Table 7.1. It is obvious that the more complex formulations can rarely be identical in originators and branded preparations. Among the 'complex' formulations, one might include liposomes and microparticle and nanoparticulate systems.

There are generic versions of some sustained-release formulations, but within a given class of sustained-release product of a given drug, such as theophylline, there will be a spectrum of release rates. The proliferation of sustained- and modified-release forms of branded products at the end of the patent life of a product results not necessarily from the prospect of improved clinical outcomes but for the very reason that generic versions are difficult to produce. Generic modified-release products themselves are therefore usually branded. Having said this, the benefit of having a range of formulations is recognised.[3]

Specific conditions and generics

There is just the chance that in the treatment of some conditions differences in the performance of products are relevant. There are also some conditions where particular care has to be taken in titrating patients and maintaining therapeutic levels closely throughout treatment. Such is the case with antiepileptic drugs. While generic medicines have been an issue at least since the 1970s, problems with antiepileptic drugs are still current,[4,5] as we discuss below. There are reports on the re-emergence of psychotic symptoms after conversion (a study with $n = 7$) from a brand-name clozapine to a generic formulation.[6] However, the problem with such reports is that they are often specific to a country; the results will depend on which brand and which generic are being studied. Papers do not always give full pharmaceutical information and hence their value is diminished. The difficulty in extrapolating results across borders is exhibited by clozapine. It has been found that generic preparations of the drug licensed in the UK are bioequivalent with the branded Clozaril: as the author[7] states: 'There was no evidence of clinical deterioration or the need to higher use higher doses. Generic clozapine is not inferior to Clozaril.' Some US reports suggest that there are problems in substituting the originators' product with a generic. But another study in the USA of a generic clozapine (Mylan) and Clozaril. (Novartis)[8] concluded that they were therapeutically equivalent.

Antiepileptic drugs: Clinical experience and the literature

There is, however, a relative shortage of literature comparing generic substitutions for antiepileptic drugs (AEDs). Most of the case reports, letters to the editor and some papers deal with three drugs, carbamazepine, phenytoin and valproate. These reports document breakthrough seizures or adverse events when switching from a branded antiepileptic drug to a generic version. Of around 300 US neurologists, 56% reported adverse events, and 68% reported breakthrough seizures in at least *one* patient when medication was switched from a branded to a generic AED. Burkhardt *et al.*[9] identified eight adult patients whose seizures worsened after switching from branded phenytoin to generic phenytoin. The few blinded, controlled studies reported in the literature have evaluated relative pharmacokinetics of a brand versus generic formulations. Sometimes only one generic version was studied (note Figure 7.2). No controlled studies have mirrored practice by evaluating safety, efficacy, and compliance with the therapeutic regimen when multiple generic versions are used in succession.

The American Academy of Neurology (AAN) has produced a number of recommendations regarding generic substitution for AEDs:[10,11]

- Such substitutions can be approved only if the safety and efficacy of treatment is not compromised.
- Specific pharmacokinetic information about each AED generic should be made available to physicians, who should avoid switching between formulations of AEDs.

- Labelling should identify specific manufacturers.
- Pharmacists should be required to inform patients and physicians when switching a product between manufacturers.
- Organisations that encourage or mandate substitution of AEDs should evaluate their responsibility for any problems arising from their policies.

Because changing from one formulation of an AED to another can usually be accomplished, and risks minimised, if physicians and patients monitor blood levels, seizures and toxicity, it is maintained in the USA that the individual and physician should be notified and should give their consent before a switch in medications is made, whether it involves either generic substitution for brand name products, or generic-to-generic substitutions.

Reading and deconstructing the literature on bioequivalence

If pharmacokinetic data are available, one needs to ask whether the analytical methodology was up to the task. Was the study sound? The literature can be biased because studies supported by manufacturers of products under study (both generic and branded)[8] might not be published if the results, say, show inequivalence in the former case or equivalence in the latter. In one case, with levothyroxine, it was estimated that analytical techniques commonly used were not sufficiently precise to ascertain equivalence. Figure 7.4 shows data on the levels of thyroxine in plasma after administration of doses from 400 to 600 µg, without taking into account baseline thyroxine concentrations.[12] Such a method would not be able to distinguish between generics if it cannot distinguish between the doses over the range given. The lower figure shows the data taking baseline levels into account. The latter method would be adequate.

The other issue is whether active and active metabolites are being measured, as with risperidone whose active metabolite, 9-hydroxy-risperidone has a much longer half-life than the parent drug.

Antiretroviral drugs

It is always difficult to generalise from single studies on generic equivalence or non-equivalence. Comparisons of generic and branded anti-HIV products containing the three drugs stavudine, lamivudine and nevirapine have been made in HIV-infected adults.[13] Stavudine levels were found to be significantly lower using the generic formulation. A similar but larger study, also in infected adults, found that generic fixed-dose combinations of these drugs were efficacious and safe.[14] Two generic fixed-dose combinations of these

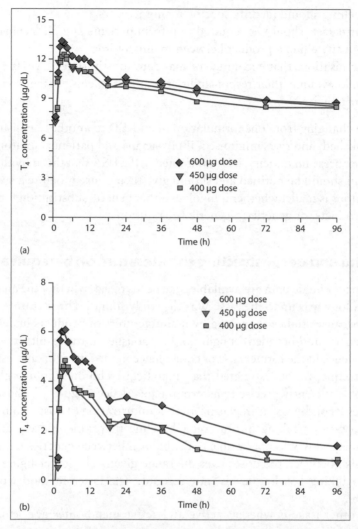

Figure 7.4 Thyroxine levels in plasma as a function of time. (a) Mean levothyroxine concentration time profiles on study day 1 following a single-dose administration of levothyroxine sodium, uncorrected for baseline levothyroxine concentrations. (b) Figures corrected for baseline levothyroxine concentrations. (From reference 12.)

drugs for children (Pedimune Baby and Pedimune Junior, Cipla Pharmaceuticals) have been found to be similar to the branded products when tested in healthy adults.[15] As with many products, the true measure of quality is not minor differences in peak plasma levels or AUCs but therapeutic outcome. Never more so than in developing countries. The stark facts are that after the introduction of cheaper antiretroviral therapies in Southern India, the numbers using these products increased and death rates decreased from 25 to 5 deaths per 100 persons between 1997 and 2003.[16]

Bioequivalence of ophthalmic products

It is difficult to assess the bioequivalence of ophthalmic products. There have been issues, however,[17] one being high rates of precipitation in a generic prednisone formulation. Some products will employ different excipients, which might lead to subtle differences in behaviour of the preparation; a generic timolol gel-forming product possessed a different 'feel' from the branded product. This also apparently gave the impression that the generic formulation was less efficacious.

The case of sevoflurane

The apparent simplicity of molecule of the anaesthetic sevoflurane masks differences in synthetic methods and degradation that may be significant in deciding between products.

Sevoflurane

Sevoflurane is available in the USA from two manufacturers as Ultane (Abbott Laboratories, Inc.) and a generic product, Sevoflurane Inhalation Anesthetic (Sevoness) (Baxter Healthcare Corp.). These products are rated therapeutically equivalent by the Food and Drug Administration, but there are some differences. Ultane is made in a single-step synthetic process and generic sevoflurane is manufactured using a three-step process, as described by Baker.[18] In the UK sevoflurane is a non-proprietary product. As there is only one UK product, the question of differences will arise only if there are several manufacturers. In the USA, as Baker points out, Ultane contains >300 ppm water and generic sevoflurane contains ≤130 ppm water. Ultane is supplied in a plastic poly(ethylene naphthalate) polymer bottle, while generic sevoflurane is supplied in lacquer-lined aluminium bottles. Here then is an example that typifies some generics issues. The products have different manufacturing processes (see Figure 7.5) and hence different impurities, have different containers, and have potential differences in the rate or extent of sevoflurane degradation.

The significance of the containers has been discussed[18] and relates to the discovery that sevoflurane can be unstable in glass bottles in which the anaesthetic was originally supplied. Reports of a cloudy product with an strong odour appeared. Such batches were found to contain HF in concentrations up to 863 ppm as well as a pH below unity. This was linked to Lewis-acid defluorination of the drug. (Lewis acids are usually metal–containing

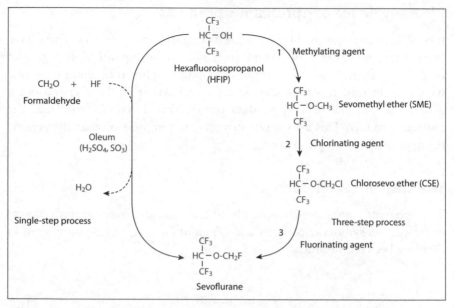

Figure 7.5 Pathways for the single-step and three-step syntheses of sevoflurane from the starting compound hexafluoroisopropanol. The potential impurity from the single-step method is formaldehyde, and from the three step process is sevomethyl ether (SME) and chlorosevo ether (CSE). (From reference 18.)

compounds that accept electrons from Lewis bases and result in Lewis base degradation. There are many Lewis acids such as metal halides and metal oxides including Al_2O_3). The Lewis acid in this case was identified as rust (iron oxide) on a valve on a bulk shipping container. The drug is especially susceptible to degradation because of the monofluoroalkyl ether group. The whole story can be read in Baker's paper.[18]

The base-catalysed conversion of sevoflurane to 'compound A' is as shown in Figure 7.6. Figure 7.7 shows a range of degradation pathways for the anaesthetic.[19]

Carbon dioxide absorption enables the use of low-flow anaesthesia, and a decreased consumption of medical gases and halogenated anaesthetics, as well as reduced pollution. Chemical absorbents (soda lime and barium hydroxide lime (Baralyme) may produce toxic compounds: carbon monoxide with all halogenated anaesthetics and 'compound A' with sevoflurane

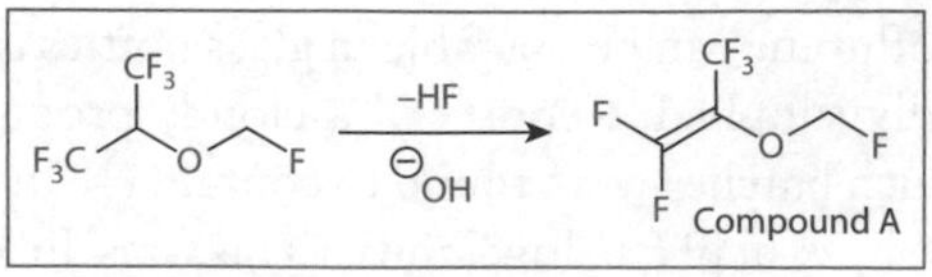

Figure 7.6 Base-catalysed conversion of sevoflurane to so-called compound A.

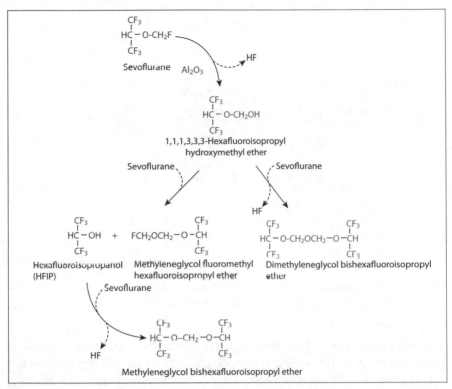

Figure 7.7 Potential pathways of degradation and the products of degradation of sevoflurane on reaction with alumina (Al_2O_3). The degradation products are detected at very low concentrations in low-flow, long-duration anaesthesia. (From reference 19.)

(see Figure 7.6). Simple measures against desiccation of the lime prevent carbon monoxide production. The toxicity of compound A, shown in the rat, has not been demonstrated in clinical anaesthesia. Recent improvements in manufacturing processes have decreased the powdering of lime. Moreover, filters inserted between the anaesthesia circuit and the patient abolish the risk for powder inhalation.

A Japanese product is marketed as Sevofrane (Maruishi Pharmaceutical Co, Osaka, Japan)[20] and is available there along with Sevoness. Both products studied contain over 99.998% sevoflurane and fluoride concentrations were the same at around 0.43 ppm. The formation and toxicity of anaesthetic degradation products can be an issue.[21] Soon after its introduction in 1935 there were reports of neuropathies following trichloroethylene anaesthesia. These were attributable to the formation of dichloroacetylene through base-catalysed elimination of HCl from the compound.

The common cause of their formation is the reaction of the anaesthetic with the bases in adsorbents in the circuit. (These include sodium hydroxide (soda lime) barium hydroxide lime, KOH-free soda lime, calcium hydroxide

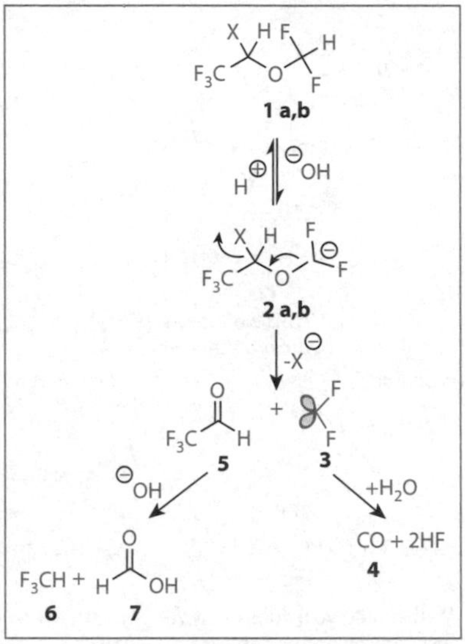

Figure 7.8 Base-catalysed conversion of desflurane and isoflurane (**1a** and **1b**) to CO (**4**). Note also trifluroacetaldehyde (**5**) and trifluoromethane (**6**) and formic acid (**7**).

and non-caustic lime. These have different reactivities: sodium hydroxide > soda lime > KOH-free soda lime > calcium hydroxide.) Understanding the nature of these reactions that affect trichloroethylene, desflurane (Figure 7.8), norflurane and enflurane has helped towards the safe use of these agents.

Although these examples are of a specialised use of these agents, nevertheless the potential formation of very low concentrations of degradants by whatever means can lead to adverse events or certainly to differences in the behaviour of products.

Generic biologicals (biologics)

A generic is, as stated above, a product that has been shown to be 'essentially similar' to the originator's product. However, biological products (biologics, biologicals, biopharmaceuticals) are more complicated than drugs that are small or relatively small organic molecules. Because of their labile nature and the fact that the products may be dependent on the mode of manufacture, it is important to remember that it is has been stated that a process 'cannot be exactly duplicated by another manufacturer'.[22] Methods used to show that small-molecule therapeutics are nearly identical to each other are clearly not sufficient for biologicals. Bioequivalence is usually defined in terms of areas under the curve (AUCs), but this is only part of the story with biological products. The nature of impurities is different. These might be analogues with a single amino acid difference, yet be potent. If the impurity is potent, this can lead to clinical problems. Impurities might be more difficult to detect in biological products if they are analogues of the main agent, so there is the risk of immunological and other side-effects. It is also possible, as we recounted in Chapter 4, that the formulation may cause there to be differences in protein products as with recombinant human erythropoietin (Eprex). A change of stabiliser from albumin to sorbitol resulted in the formation of anti-erythropoietin antibodies and hence pure red cell aplasia.[23]

Figure 7.9 summarises the issues that must be considered when dealing with biological generics.[24] The most appropriate description for generic biologicals is that they are 'biosimilar'.

The European Medicines Agency (EMEA) has stated that the generic route is not appropriate for biologics, and the FDA stated in September 2006 that it 'has not determined how interchangeability can be established for complex proteins'. Note, however, that for biologics such as insulin the transfer of patients from one product to another of the same insulin type is commonplace, though carried out with circumspection.

Why do these products have such specific problems? The molecules are large and often prepared in cell-based systems; they have complex tertiary and quaternary structures related to their activity; and they may be glycosylated. They are very sensitive to stresses such as temperature and even to shear forces

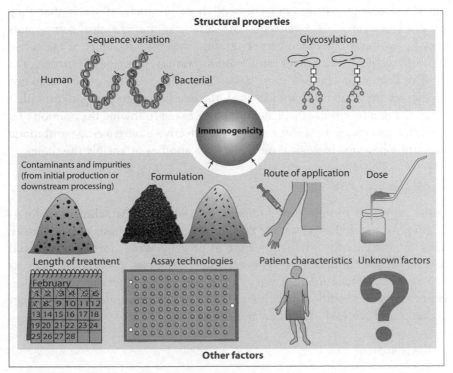

Figure 7.9 Areas of importance in determining the bioequivalence and the immunogenicity of biopharmaceuticals. (From reference 24.)

that might be used in their production. DNA, for example, suffers from degradation due to shear forces. A practical pharmacy aspect is the use of International Non-propriety Names (INNs) for such products. With conventional drugs an identical INN means a bioequivalent product and the same drug substance within pharmacopoeial or other limits. There are dangers if INNs are used for biogenerics that are subtly different.

Regulatory views on biosimilar biologicals

The FDA acknowledges that 'biosimilars have not been demonstrated to be interchangeable through any scientific process'. A different naming scheme for these products might involve utilising a different level of granularity, which may be more detailed or less detailed. If the outcome of assigning the same INN to two products with highly similar ingredient(s) creates the implication that the two products are pharmacologically interchangeable *and* there were no scientific data to support that finding, then the FDA would have serious concerns about such an outcome, especially with more complicated proteins. At present, the FDA has not determined how interchangeability can be established for complex proteins.

This initiative reinforces the EMEA communication on biosimilar medicines and recognises the uniqueness of these products. It states that they cannot be classified as 'generics' in the same way that chemical compounds may be, owing to the differences stemming from the variability of the active biotechnological substances and manufacturing processes. Further, the EMEA document clarifies that 'since biosimilar and biological reference medicines are similar but not identical, the decision to treat a patient with a reference or a biosimilar medicine should be taken following the opinion of a qualified healthcare professional'. This is effective advice against automatic substitution of one biological medicine over another ostensibly the same.

Pegylated proteins

Some pegylated proteins are discussed in Chapter 5. Attachment of long-chain polyoxyethylene glycols (PEGs) to proteins is the basis of pegylation. This can increase the circulation time of proteins with short half-lives and can reduce immunogenicity; however, there are cases[25] where the process can reduce the functional activity of the protein by blocking access to receptors. These modified proteins are clearly not biosimilar to the parent proteins and are essentially new molecules.

Conclusions

For many medicinal products the initial brand and the subsequent generic products are therapeutically equivalent. There are of course effects of differences such as the colour of capsules and tablets or the appearance of liquids, which can prejudice patients. There are drugs that have a narrow therapeutic index and that are perhaps poorly soluble, which perhaps suggests that they might not be used interchangeably, but these are few in number; experts are not agreed even with drugs such as the antiepileptic agents. There is a greater practical problem in that while biostudies might have shown generic 1 to be bioequivalent to the brand leader, and generic 2 is also bioequivalent, as we have discussed, generic 1 is not necessarily equivalent to generic 2. Pharmacists have thus to be aware of the source of generics.

With generic versions of biologicals or biosimilars the issues are somewhat more complex. Development in analytical methods and other tests might assist in elucidating the similarity or otherwise of this growing array of drugs in the future. With both conventional drugs and biological drugs, wherever a formulation has been devised to alter the rate of release or delivery of the active agent, it is not automatic that generic versions will produce identical results. Table 7.2 lists some of the diverse classes of recombinant proteins that have been approved for clinical use.[26] To be able to make informed decisions, pharmacists and drugs and therapeutics committees need access to the facts about such products and in particular their biopharmaceutical profiles in patients or volunteers.

Table 7.2 Classes of approved recombinant protein drugs	
Class	Examples
Hormones	Insulin (e.g. Humulin), glucagon (e.g. Glucagen), human growth hormone (e.g. Humatrope), erythropoietin (e.g. Epogen)
Cytokines	Interferon alfa (e.g. Roferon-A)
Clotting factors	Factor VII (NovoSeven)
Monoclonal antibodies	Antibodies to vascular endothelial growth factor (bevacizumab [Avastin]), epidermal growth factor receptor (cetuximab [Erbitux]). TNF-α (e.g. infliximab [Remicade])
Vaccines	Hepatitis B surface antigen (e.g. Recombivax HB)
Enzymes	Glucocerebrosidase (Cerezyme), DNase (Pulmozyme), thrombolytics (e.g. alteplase [Activase])
Synthetic proteins	Fusion proteins, e.g. soluble TNF receptor linked to IgG Fc
Conjugates	Pegylated proteins: interferon such as peginterferon alfa 2a (Pegasys), granulocyte colony-stimulating factor (pegfilgrastin [Neulastal]). Covalently attached metal chelators (ibritomab)

From reference 26.

References

1. Hassali MA et al. Knowledge and perceptions of recent pharmacy graduates about generic medicines. Pharm Ed 2007; 7: 89–95.
2. US Food and Drug Administration, Centre for Drug Evaluation and Research, Office for Generic Drugs. http://www.fda.gov/Drugs/ResourcesForYou/Consumers/BuyingUsing MedicineSafely/UnderstandingGenericDrugs/ucm144456.htm (updated 2009; accessed 23 September 2009).
3. Frijlink HW. Benefits of different drug formulations in psychopharmacology. Eur Neuropsychopharmacol 2003; 13: S77–S84.
4. Wilner AN. Therapeutic equivalence of generic antiepileptic drugs: results of a survey. Epilepsy Behav 2004; 5: 995–998.
5. Crawford P et al. Are there potential problems with generic substitution of antiepileptic drugs? A review of issues. Seizure 2006; 15: 165–176.
6. Mofsen R, Balter J. Case reports of the re-emergence of psychotic symptoms after conversion from brand name clozapine to a generic formulation. Clin Ther 2001; 23: 1720–1731.
7. Paton C. Generic clozapine: outcomes after switching formulations. Br J Psychiatry 2006; 189: 184–185.
8. Healy DJ et al. Clinical equivalence of generic clozapine. Community Ment Health J 2005; 41: 393–398.
9. Burkhardt RT et al. Lower phenytoin serum levels in persons switched from brand to generic phenytoin. Neurology 2004; 63: 1494–1496.
10. Assessment: generic substitution for antiepileptic medication. Report of the Therapeutics and Technology Assessment Sub-committee of the American Academy of Neurology. Neurology 1990; 40: 1641–1643.
11. Liouw K et al. Position statement on the coverage of anticonvulsant drugs for the treatment of epilepsy. Neurology 2007; 68: 1249–1250.
12. Blakesley VA. Current methodology to assess bioequivalence of levothyroxine sodium products are inadequate. AAPS J 2005; 7(1): E42–46.
13. Byakika-Kibwika P et al. Steady-state pharmacokinetic comparison of generic and branded formulations of stavudine, lamivudine and nevirapine in HIV-infected Ugandan adults. J Antimicrob Chemother 2008; 62: 1113–1117.
14. Laurent C et al. Effectiveness and safety of a generic fixed dose combination of nevipanine, stavudine and lamivudine in HIV-1 infected adults in Cameroon: open label multicentre trial. Lancet 2004; 364: 29–34.
15. L'homme RFA et al. Pharmacokinetics of two generic fixed dose combinations for HIV infected children (Pedimune Baby and Pedimune Junior) are similar to the branded products in healthy adults. J Antimicrob Chemother 2007; 59: 92–96.
16. Kumarasamy N et al. The changing natural history of HIV disease: before and after the introduction of generic antiretroviral therapy in Southern India. Clin Infect Dis 2005; 41: 1525–1528.
17. Cantor LB. Generic ophthalmic medications: as good as Xerox? Medscape Ophthalmology 2008 26 Nov. http://cme.medscape.com/viewarticle/583866 (accessed 23 September 2009.
18. Baker MT. Sevoflurane: are there differences in products. Anesth Analg 2007; 104: 1447–1451.
19. Bito H, Ikeda K. Long-duration, low-flow sevoflurane anesthesia using two carbon dioxide absorbents. Quantification of degradation products in the circuit. Anesthesiology 1994; 81: 340–345.
20. Yamakage M et al. Analysis of the composition or 'original' and generic sevoflurane in routine use. Br J Anaesth 2007; 99: 819–823.
21. Anders MW. Formation and toxicity of anesthetic degradation products. Annu Rev Pharmacol Toxicol 2005; 45: 147–176.

22. Bio. Biotechnology Industry Organization. *BIO Principles on Follow-On Biologics.* Web presentation on follow-on biologics (FOBs). 2007 March. http://www.bio.org/healthcare/followonbkg/Principles.asp (accessed 23 September 2009).
23. Louëts S. Lessons from Eprex for biogeneric firms. *Nat Biotechnol* 2003; 21: 956–957.
24. Schellekens H. Bioequivalence and the immunogenicity of biopharmaceuticals. *Nat Rev Drug Discov* 2002; 1: 457–462.
25. Kubetzko S *et al.* Protein PEGylation decreases observed target association rates via a dual blocking mechanism. *Mol Pharmacol* 2005; 68: 1439–1454.
26. Dudzinski DM, Kusselheim AS. Scientific and legal viability of follow-on protein drugs. *N Engl J Med* 2008; 358: 843–849.

8

The future: Delivery systems for modern therapeutics

Introduction

The nature of therapeutic interventions will undoubtedly change in the next decade. Already there are many additions to the medicinal armamentarium, with many biological molecules, including recombinant proteins, nucleic acids (both DNA and RNA), monoclonal antibodies and cell-based therapies. The question that must be addressed is: What will be the role of pharmacy in relation to these products, particularly those related to cell therapy? When in the future some of these therapies become more commonplace, will they be distributed, dispensed and monitored through pharmacy channels in the way in which conventional drugs are, or will they be deemed too 'technical'? The topic of delivery systems for modern therapeutics is certainly in the domain of clinical pharmaceutics, as the nature of the delivery systems used will be an important component of therapy. We need to think more imaginatively of pharmacy's role in the future. Pharmaceutical precepts of safety, quality and efficacy must be emphasised in experimental clinical procedures, as this did not always occur with early clinical studies of, say, liposomes. In particular, the consistency of the drug and the formulation, and their freedom from impurities, must be ensured. The concept of impurities in cell therapy is likely to be different from our current experience.

Personalised medicine and medicines

While tablets and capsules might remain the most popular and most used dosage forms in the future, there must be changes in the way we deliver drugs and the facility to alter doses in perhaps a continuous (e.g. 1–10 mg) rather than multiple (e.g. 2.5, 5.0, 10 mg) manner in the future. That is, dosing must change. No human population can be classified with regard to the important parameters of drug distribution (body weight, body fat, creatinine clearance), in a stepwise fashion, so why should doses? For practicality of manufacturing only, according to current paradigms. Hence the need to explore newer means of fashioning delivery systems. The core of personalised medicine is that patients will receive medications tailored for them rather than receiving the same drug at the same dose, which is the norm for most products prescribed and dispensed today. It could be argued that for many agents, such as a number of antibiotics, precision dosing is not necessary. In spite of increased specificity of many new drugs, such an approach is surely counterintuitive. The post-genomic era has promised much through a better understanding of pharmacogenetics. Through genetic profiling of patients involved in clinical trials, more valuable data will be obtained for the treatment of individual groups likely to respond well (e.g. to Herceptin (trastuzumab)) or to suffer adverse reactions. But there are other issues to contend with apart from the drug, matters we explore now.

Drug delivery and personalised medicines

The focus in discussions on personalised medicine has been on the drug itself, rather than on the mode of delivery. A report on personalised medicines emanating from the Royal Society[1] neglects to mention delivery systems. This is perhaps understandable because the emphasis has been on the drug and its suitability for a given group or subgroups of patients. There is of course a question of delivery systems: pharmaceutics (as well as pharmaco-kinetic analysis) has a large part to play in ensuring that appropriate formulations are available for appropriate drugs.

The MHRA[2] has recognised the need for a multiplicity of dosage form:

> Personalised medicine can occur on the basis of dose adjustment for side effects, dose adjustment for efficacy, dose adjustment for con-comitant medication, metabolising rate and renal excretion, drug choice due to allergic potential, drug choice due to resistance profile of the infecting organism, drug choice due to biological target, and drug choice according to the personal wishes of a patient.

> Increasingly accurate and specific medical information on each individual patient is becoming available to provide prescribers with more and more information from increasingly sensitive physical methods and the wider application of biomarkers (for instance to identify drug metabolising characteristics of each individual patient). This will result in future medicines needing to be available to provide a greater range of doses for prescribers; there will be fewer numbers of patients in the target indication at the time of product registration due to better use of inclusion and exclusion criteria; medicines will be safer, more effective and have fewer side effects as the dose will be adjusted to ensure that the most appropriate dose is prescribed to each patient.

A comprehensive report, *Priority Medicines for Europe and the World*[3] published by the World Health Organization in 2004, highlights many of the issues in the war against relatively neglected diseases such as malaria. For such, insufficient research and development efforts worldwide have led and still lead to loss of life on an unthinkable scale. There is a reminder in the report of the importance of drug delivery. The authors conclude that 'there is a wide range of existing evidence-based, very often off-patent technologies that are heavily under-utilised. Such technologies could be used to improve the 'patient-friendly' performance of a number of existing medicines'. These one might claim to be the neglected technologies, invented but discarded because funding bodies or the market will not pay for them, or because a worthy application has not been found.

In all parts of the world, there are at least two identifiable and disparate patient groups for whom there is a need for personalised medicines or personalised formulations. The latter will sound strangely familiar to pharmacists of an older generation used to preparing medicines extemporaneously for individual patients. Children and the elderly, neither of whom comprise homogeneous sets, could be considered to be neglected patients. As we have discussed in Chapter 6, children exhibit rapid changes in metabolism and physiological functions in their progression from the neonatal state through infancy and early and late childhood. The elderly also experience changes in body fat distribution, renal clearance and gastrointestinal function, and treatment is often because of concomitant pathologies.

Figure 8.1 illustrates the categories of patients for whom personalised medicines will be designed. One might include everyone if the true meaning of the phrase is considered, but this is unrealistic. The divisions are not mutually exclusive categories of age-related, disease-related and genetically determined maladies.

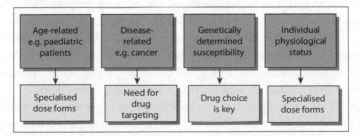

Figure 8.1 An attempt to categorise patients in terms of personalised medicine in its broadest sense. These are not exclusive categories. In the case of genetically determined susceptibility to drugs, drug choice is the key; but in the other categories drug delivery systems are likely to play a prominent part in optimising treatment.

Paediatric cardiovascular medications have been discussed elsewhere[4] and general paediatric formulations in practice are reviewed[5] in the textbook, *Paediatric Drug Handling*.[6] Paediatric medicine provision, as discussed in Chapter 6, is not necessarily a question of high-technology solutions. One of the most distressing consequences of the use of adult dosage forms in paediatric practice is the necessity for large dilutions and thus the enhanced opportunity for error. Errors of 10-fold excess or under-dosing are often the root cause of serious outcomes. It should not be beyond our wit to devise foolproof devices that make such errors difficult to commit. An alternative might be to have access to more appropriate formulations that contain doses relevant for the patient group in question.

It could be argued that individualised medicine is available now through specialised dose forms for the very young, although in many cases this is not so.[7] Genetics aside, we have not been able as a community to devise and market systems suitable for children and the elderly. We certainly have not solved the issue of the safety of dosing in these cases. Tuleu[8] states that in addition to legislative and formulary developments, innovations in pharmaceutical formulations should improve the ease in which children can access medicines. Innovative modified-release preparations represent one need. The following areas, Tuleu suggests, are also ripe for future developments and research:

- New routes of administration such as oral–transmucosal (buccal strips), intranasal and transdermal products(for neonates mainly).
- More research into alternative safe excipients for children, such as natural polymers (e.g. cyclodextrins to mask the taste of drugs, to improve solubility or to protect drugs/patient).
- Children's ability to swallow and their preferences. This will direct future formulation research towards mini-tablets, chewable tablets, dispersible tablets or more oral liquids.

Although new and innovative formulations are urgently needed, work on extemporaneous formulation should not be disregarded.

The provision of flexible dose products is key. In the twenty-first century, splitting tablets hardly seems a reasonable approach, but mini-tablets that can be administered in multiples can have a role. Self-regulating and pulsatile delivery systems, and means of delivering doses flexibly, are some of the possibilities discussed here. An important development might be the re-introduction of pharmacy-based product manufacture. Extemporaneous dispensing is not dead. In the USA, pharmaceutical compounding in community pharmacies is a thriving if controversial activity. Discussed below are several potential technological solutions for the preparation and presentation of new dose forms as well as a brief outline of pharmaceutical nanotechnology.

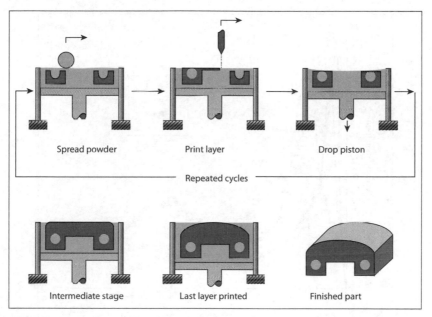

Figure 8.2 The process of three-dimensional printing (3DP) demonstrated with a ceramic process. Deposition of material, e.g. drug or coating materials, is controlled by the control of droplet size as in a bubble-jet printer.

Technologies

Three-dimensional printing

With the invention of three-dimensional printing (3DP) techniques the possibility probably now exists for the individual and batch production of either implants[9] or oral dose forms.[10] The basis of the technique of 3DP as shown in Figure 8.2 is that the finished product design is elaborated on a computer. Much depends on the particle size of active, the nature of the binder such as its viscosity, and also the potential for diffusion of drug between layers and subsets of the structure. In effect, the release rate and pattern of the active(s) can be predetermined by the possibility of placing the active in different regions of the structure. Figure 8.3 shows data demonstrating the control of release profiles of levofloxacin from a variety of implants with different geometries. A proposed 'breakaway' tablet prepared by 3DP (Figure 8.4) that breaks into two parts after the dissolution of the fixative joining the parts together is only one example of the possibilities.

Low-dose and flexible-dose products

Products with readily variable dose levels are required. Methods for depositing drugs in solution onto biosoluble and biodegradable matrices also offer the possibility of ready fabrication in hospital and community pharmacies. A

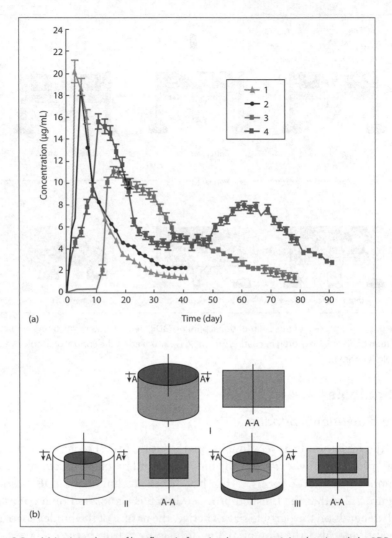

(a)

(b)

Figure 8.3 (a) *In vitro* release of levofloxacin from implants: curve 1, implant I made by 3DP; curve 2, implant I made by a conventional process; curve 3, implant II made by 3DP; and curve 4, implant III made by 3DP. (b) The design of the three implant systems I, II and III. (From reference 9.)

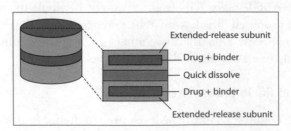

Figure 8.4 Cartoon of a conjoined tablet containing fast-release and slow-release elements, which allows two drugs to be administered at two different rates.

matrix platform for such products is required. Developments in bubble-jet devices exemplified by Hamamatsu micro-droplet technology suggest the possibility of the adsorption of the smallest doses onto suitable matrices for delivery, say, to neonates by oral or buccal routes. Microfabricated electrokinetic pumps can be used to deliver water, polar organic solvents, and biomacromolecules.[11] A new delivery system for inner-ear infections involves a microcatheter delivering gentamicin driven by an electronic micropump.[12]

Flexible dosage systems

Liquid formulations are possibly the form that most easily allow continuous increments in dosing, but they sometimes suffer from instability or simply from the fact that the drug might not be soluble in a suitable solvent. The Chinese once used rice paper impregnated with drugs as a delivery system. It is possible with modern technology to dose matrices of a variety of dimensions with accurate amounts of drug in solution, in suspension and in micro- or nanoparticulate form. Ink-jet technology has much to teach. Figure 8.5 is a simple cartoon of the possibility of dosing of a matrix for drug delivery.

Suspensions are more difficult to formulate than solutions because of the possibility of particle agglomeration, sticking and blocking of needles, but there are solutions: the SonicSyringe (Sono-Tek Corporation, USA), for example, uses ultrasonic energy to accurately and uniformly coat nanoparticles onto a surface. Hence there is no excuse for not having at our disposal a more flexible system of dosing the patient population from birth to extreme old age. Various pumps can of course provide graded dosing, often on command. Many systems (e.g. the Medtronic Synchromed infuser) are too large for implantation. Smaller devices (e.g. the Duros osmotic pump, and Gliadel implantable wafers) often do not have the flexibility to allow variable dosing.

A variety of micromachined delivery systems now exist using micropumps. Microneedles for transdermal delivery are represented in Figure 8.6. Drug is released into the epidermis and dermis through 150 microneedles from a chip 25 mm in length; the short length of the microneedles avoids the pain receptors of the skin.

Microfluidic systems

Microfluidic devices are increasingly used in analytical procedures when small quantities of materials have to be mixed and analysed. Figure 8.7 illustrates such a device. It can be envisioned either that two drugs could be mixed by proper routing of the channels or that drugs could be administered in small quantities, say in a pulsatile manner, if the droplets in the diagram represent a drug and the fluid carrier is an inactive excipient.

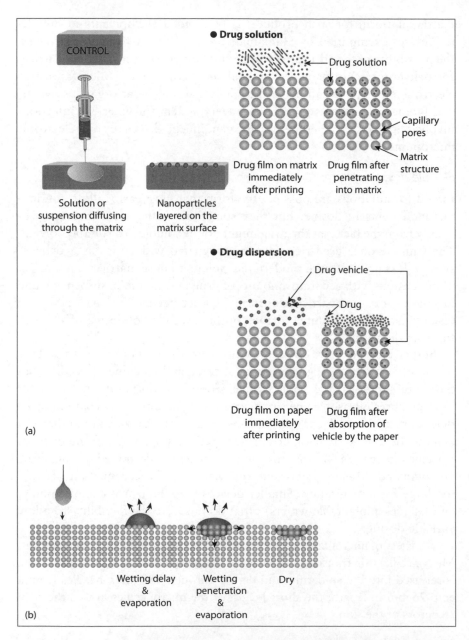

Figure 8.5   (a) A simplified set-up for dosing a matrix for drug delivery. The distribution of the drug within the matrix will depend on the nature of the matrix, the drug and its solution or suspension state. Also shown to the right is the possibility of deposition of nanoparticles of drug or polymer–drug mixtures to provide a very accurate and low-dose product. (b) Modes of penetration into a paper matrix and deposition patterns that might result from changes in the state of the applied droplets.

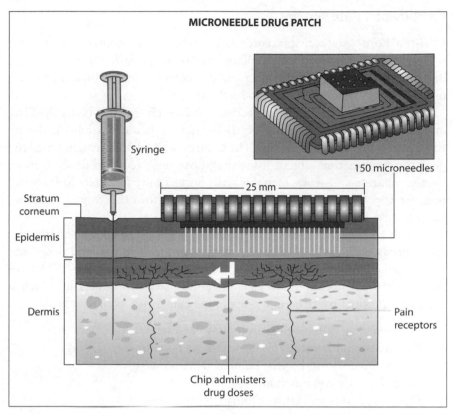

Figure 8.6 Microneedle-based drug patch for transdermal use. Drug output is controlled by the chip.

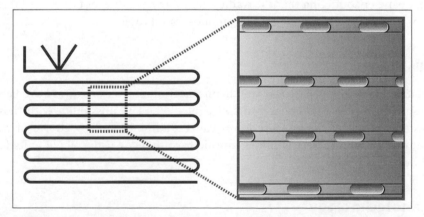

Figure 8.7 A microfluidic device with multiple channels showing droplets (or microspheres or nanosuspensions) of drug. The channels can be fabricated in any pattern and materials can be driven through the narrow capillaries into the body to provide pulsatile release. Different drugs and carriers can be mixed to provide versatile delivery systems.

Combination dose systems

Christine Ford[13] states that 'according to the FDA, a combination product is one composed of two or more regulated components – any combination of a drug and device; biological product and device; drug and biological product; or drug, device, and biological product'.

For many years combination products have been frowned on by the FDA and other regulatory authorities largely because of their inflexibility in dosing fixed ratios of two or more drugs. The treatment of AIDS has highlighted the need for combination tablets. If the drug/dose ratio required depends more than on pharmacogenetics, then this is the opportunity for three-dimensional printing approaches exemplified in Figure 8.4 or for other ways of making flexible dose forms to be adopted.

The FDA's definition is quite inclusive, encompassing drug-coated devices, drugs packaged with delivery devices in medical kits, and drugs and devices packaged separately but intended to be used together. The FDA have developed a categorisation scheme for combination products in which a product a product is placed into one of nine categories, which include:

- Prefilled drug or biologic delivery device/system
- Device, coated/impregnated or otherwise combined with drug
- Device, coated or otherwise combined with biologic
- Drug–biologic combination
- Other type of combination product.

It is interesting after the widespread use of tablets and capsules in the past that the difficulty in making combination products has been acknowledged.[14] It is, in a way, encouraging that the traditional pharmaceutics of tablet manufacture was considered in 2006 to be an underrated topic.

Mini-tablets

Matrix mini-tablets based on starch–microcellulose wax mixtures have been described by De Brabander and colleagues.[15,16] The possibility with these systems is that different dose levels can be administered by choice of the number of mini-tablets within a capsule for adults or using single units for children.

Nanotechnology

Nanotechnology is the science that deals with particles or constructs that have dimensions ranging from several nanometres to around 100–150 nm (Figure 8.8[17]), although more commonly the upper limit is stretched to 200 nm. It is not possible here to cover the whole gamut of nanotechnology or even

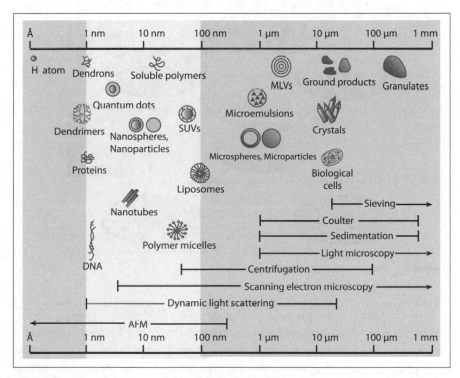

Figure 8.8 The size spectrum of nanoparticles and other nanosystems in the context of microparticulates and macrosystems. SUV, small unilamellar vesicle; MLV, multilamellar vesicle; AFM, atomic force microscopy. (Diagram from reference 17.)

pharmaceutical aspects of the subject in all its manifestations. As a discipline, nanotechnology has already spawned several journals dealing with the physics, the biology, the toxicology, the engineering and the pharmaceutical applications, as well as many books,[18,19,20,21] chapters and reviews and a rapidly growing number of papers and consensus papers.[22,23]

Figure 8.8 illustrates the size spectrum of different systems from the macroscopic, through microscopic to the nanoscopic and the modes of measurement of particle size distribution. It can be seen that dendrimers, small spherical or quasi-spherical synthetic polymers, are at the particle–molecule interface and represent irreducibly small delivery agents. Quantum dots are a form of nanocrystal made from semiconductor materials (e.g. zinc sulfide, cadmium selenide) that have applications in sensors and tracking (imaging) at the nanoscale.

Figure 8.9 illustrates the domains of nanomedicine, which can be considered to cover nanodevices, nanocarriers, nature's own nanovehicles such as low-density lipoprotein (LDL) particles[24,25] (as carriers of cholesterol), viruses (as carriers of DNA) and transmitter vesicles (as carriers of neurotransmitters). Diagnostic devices and techniques employing nanoparticles are

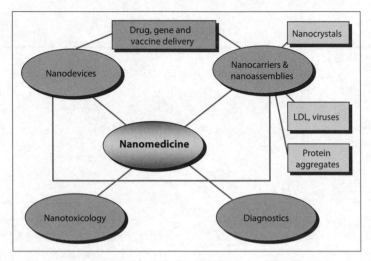

Figure 8.9   The domains of nanomedicine.

part of the scene. Nanopharmacy or pharmaceutical nanotechnology comprises, but is not limited to, the topics shown in Figure 8.10. These encompass the manipulation and processing of nanosystems in the 2–150 nm size range, their physicochemical characterisation, applications and biological evaluation. One warning: it is dangerous to try to generalise about nanosystems or nanotoxicology as so much depends not only on particle size and surface characteristics but also on physical form.

Typical pharmaceutical carrier systems in the domain of nanotechnology include nanoparticles, nanosuspensions, nano- (micro-) emulsions, nanocrystals, dendrimers and dendriplexes and carbon nanotubes as well as the smallest liposomes. Figure 8.10 suggests the main areas of focus in pharmaceutical nanotechnology and summarises the wide range of means of characterising nanosystems through investigation of their drug loading rate and capacity, release rate, chemical and physical stability of both drug and carrier, particle size and size distribution, surface charge and character (hydrophilic, hydrophobic), nanoparticle diffusion and rheology. Biological evaluation of nanosystems involves a knowledge of the absorption of the drug and the carrier with its encapsulated or adsorbed drug, distribution of both carrier and drug, as well as component excretion and metabolism.

The whole topic, however, is determined by the size and size range of the systems concerned. Small size brings with it certain advantages and disadvantages. Advantages include the ability to diffuse farther into biological tissues and to be taken up more readily by cells than microparticles. The disadvantages include the greater ability to aggregate because of their large surface area.

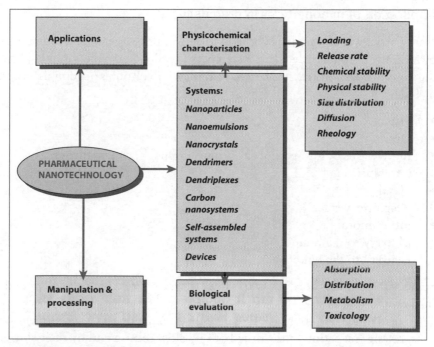

Figure 8.10 Pharmaceutical nanotechnology's main areas of focus: applications, manipulation and processing, the physicochemical characterisation of a variety of systems, their biological evaluation, particularly an understanding of the interaction between the physicochemical properties of these systems and biological barriers and environments. Absorption, distribution, metabolism and toxicology refer to both the drug once released from the delivery system and the delivery system itself, while being aware of possible synergistic effects between the two.

Nanoparticles in pharmacy

The main use of nanoparticles in pharmacy so far has been as carriers of drugs, DNA and vaccines. The nanoparticles serve several functions: (1) protecting the actives from hostile environments, (2) determining the fate of agents that are still encapsulated; and (3) acting as potential targeting moieties when the particles are decorated with ligands for appropriate proteins and receptors.

Although the descriptor *nanotechnology* came to the fore in the late 1980s, it has a somewhat longer pedigree in pharmacy, since, in fact, Professor Peter Speiser and his colleagues in Zurich prepared and investigated 'nanoparts' and 'nanocapsules' in the 1970s, as discussed in an historical perspective.[26] Surfactant micelles[27] which have diameters of some 1–3 nm, have also been studied for many decades as solubilisers of poorly water-soluble drugs,[28,29] for example, and would be considered in today's parlance to be nanosystems. Microemulsions, a descriptor coined by Schulman in 1959, have in fact droplets in the nanoscale, as produced by dilution of Neoral (see Chapter 4). It is claimed that the first commercial microemulsion was introduced in 1928.

Application of nanoparticles in drug delivery

Nanoparticles can in principle be used to deliver drugs, genes and radiolabels by a variety of routes listed here. References to individual papers that apply to the route in question are cited here as examples only. Routes of administration include:

- Ocular[30]
- Oral[31]
- Intravenous[32], intraperitoneal[33], intraluminal[34], subcutaneous[35] or intramuscular[36]
- Nasal[37]
- Respiratory tract[38]
- Intratumoral[39]
- Delivery to the brain[40]
- Delivery to the lymphatics.[41]

Some of these routes are discussed below, but the references to all will provide further information.

In ocular delivery to the cul-de-sac of the eye, nanoparticles in suspension can prolong the action of the drug both by slow release and by their slower escape by way of the punctae compared with a solution, and perhaps also the adhesive qualities of some nanosystems[42] will assist.

Oral delivery is a potential means to deliver vaccines, to provide slow release of drugs, or through bioadhesive nanoparticles to achieve uptake for systemic activity, although to date the evidence for significant uptake is limited.[43] Bioadhesive nanoparticles have been advocated to assist adhesion of the carriers to the mucosa and thus increase the probability of arrest, as well as to provide time for the transfer of drug from the carriers or the particles themselves into the gut wall. The importance of the lymphoid tissue in the gut, the gut-associated lymphoid tissue (GALT), is crucial to the understanding of some of these possibilities. The M-cells and lymphoid tissues of other anatomical regions can be important in particle delivery; for example the nasal lymphoid tissue (NALT), the bronchial tissue (BALT) and other sites (omentum, OALT) provide the possibility of access of particles in small quantities. Such small quantities may be sufficient for immunisation with oral vaccines.

Intravenous delivery allows the particles to enter the circulation immediately, but the fate of the particles so administered is not necessarily simple, as the flow properties of the particles and their interactions with blood components can be complex. Figure 8.11, much simplified, lists some of the factors that determine the success or otherwise of drug targeting using nanosystems. The idea of targeting drugs to the extent of 100% of the dose is a far-off hope.

As particle size is key in the delivery of particulates to the lung, there are possibilities for using nanoparticles, although the sizes lie below those derived

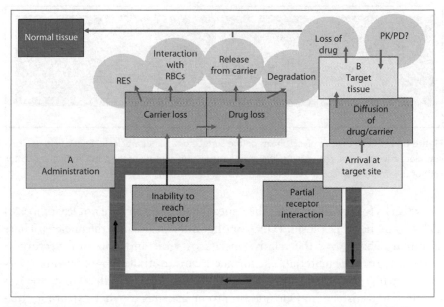

Figure 8.11 A much-simplified diagram pointing out the reasons for less-than-quantitative targeting of drugs and genes to particular sites within the body. Carrier can be lost in the reticuloendothelial system (RES), or by interaction with erythrocytes; drug can be lost through premature release from the carrier, or by degradation. Drug freed from the carrier will reach normal tissues. Interactions with receptors is a statistical process; particles that do interact then have to be taken up and diffuse through multiple cells in the tissue concerned. PK, pharmacokinetics; PD, pharmacodynamics; RBC, red blood cell.

for particulates for optimal deposition in the bronchial tree. Deposition of nanoparticles of C_{60} fullerene has been found to be 50% greater than that of microparticles.[44]

Pegylation of carriers

Surface modification of proteins to prolong their circulation was introduced after the finding that covering the surface of hydrophobic nanoparticles could change their biodistribution. The diagram in Figure 8.12[45] nicely illustrates the transformation of the surface and why the surface would inhibit the adsorption of opsonins, thus preventing extensive uptake by the reticuloendothelial system and prolonging particle circulation, enhancing the opportunity for targeting.

Cell-based therapies

After the biological 'revolution' in therapeutics has come the exploration of cell-based therapy and, of much longer provenance, gene therapy. Cell-based interventions include stem cell therapy and the use of dendritic cells and

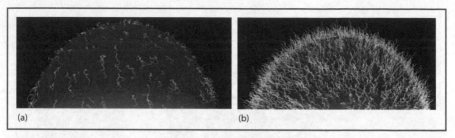

Figure 8.12 Polyethylene glycol chains on the surface of a nanoparticle: (a) light coverage; (b) complete coverage. The chains in (b) limit opsonisation and capture of the particles by the Kupffer cells of the liver and spleen (From reference 45 with permission.)

neural cells for parkinsonism. The issues in gene therapy are not least those of delivery of the labile plasmid DNA or oligonucleotides into the nucleus. There is much debate over the relative merits of viral and non-viral vectors as carriers for genetic material. The former are more efficient but there are safety issues, while the latter suffer fewer potential adverse effects but are less efficient in transfection. One question to be asked is to what extent pharmacists are to be involved with either. There are many links to pharmaceutics in the delivery of cell therapy, not only in the design of matrices for some cells but also because cells *in vivo* behave like colloidal systems, chief of which pharmaceutically would be fine dispersions or suspensions of microspheres, for example. Stem cells have been used themselves as vehicles for targeted delivery to lung metastases in the treatment of breast carcinoma.[46]

The pharmaceutics of cell delivery

There are certainly traditional pharmaceutical concepts involved in the administration of cell-based therapies: the definition of dose, the quality control of the cells, their 'purity', and their mode of delivery and their fate in the body. Conceptually the main issues are the same as with conventional therapies, but the products are somewhat more fragile and complex.

How is the dose of a cell type defined? How do we ensure purity and absence of viral load? How do we deliver cells to the right locus and avoid their deposition in unwanted sites? One study[47] on the delivery of mesenchymal stem cells showed that after intravenous administration (to rats) much of the dose of donor cells was trapped in the lungs. Within 4 hours only 1% of the cells had migrated to the myocardial epithelium.

Rosen has rightly asked[48] 'Are stem cells drugs?' Referring to stem cell therapy of cardiovascular disease, it is suggested that progress has not been fast. Questions include 'Can we really expect that after we inject stem cells into a region of the heart directly intramyocardially or via a coronary artery, they will stay in place without a subset migrating to other sites in the body?' The other key question reflects the problems with a naive approach to drug targeting which suggests that because nanoparticles or other constructs have surface ligands that bind to epithelial receptors, they somehow 'home' to their target. Rosen also asks 'When stem cells are injected into a peripheral vein and expected to follow a 'homing signal' to regions of the heart in need, will they faithfully cluster at such a site?' While many cells do remain at the site, others, in his words, 'either die or wander off.'

The administration of cells to the body should draw on the experience of the administration of microspheres and nanoparticles: intravenously administered microsystems will accumulate rapidly in the lung, indeed within seconds. Hence there is a low efficiency in delivering cells to the heart after IV infusion and cells find themselves other than at the target sites. Aggregation of cells will occur under some conditions during intracoronary infusion, and this can of course cause problems: microvascular obstruction can be caused by cell 'sludging' and this may lead to microinfarctions.[49]

Routes of administration of cells in cardiology

As might be anticipated, a variety of points of entry and delivery of cells in cardiovascular disease have been studied (Figure 8.13[50]).

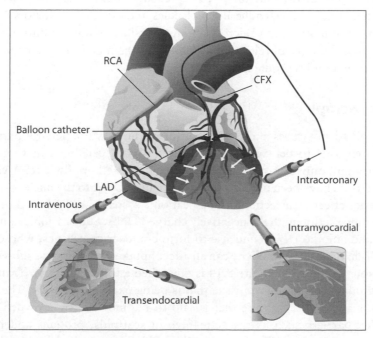

Figure 8.13 Routes of injection of cells in cardiovascular disease. CFX, circumflex artery; LAD, left anterior descending coronary artery; RCA, right coronary artery. (From reference 50.)

Cardiovascular treatment may involve[51]

- Systemic delivery, which may not be optimal for the reasons stated above.
- Local delivery, which can be achieved by direct injection at time of surgery or by percutaneous catheter-guided intracoronary infusion.
- Surgical delivery for intramyocardial injection to infarct borders.
- Catheter delivery involving a range of percutaneous catheter techniques for delivery to the myocardium.

Studies suggest that at best only 30–40% of particulates are retained in the myocardium after successful endomyocardial injections.[52]

Cell delivery for cartilage and bone regeneration

When skeletal tissue is being engineered using autologous cells, delivery is effected by polymeric bioresorbable scaffolds. These maintain the three-dimensional shape required and allow nutrient supply by diffusion.[53] Cells are usually mixed with polymers, which subsequently gel. The materials used are well known in pharmacy: materials such as collagen, hyaluronates, agarose, alginates and chitosan. There is a desire for delivery systems that can be used with minimally invasive procedures. Thermoreversible materials that gel *in vivo* (*in situ*) have been explored. Polymer-based systems have been used for the delivery of growth factors in tissue regeneration.[54] Cell scaffolds often contain a mixture of cell adhesion molecules and other tissue factors. This is mixture formulation in a microcosm and possibly requires future work to ensure that the rates of release and stability of the materials in combination are sufficient and reproducible.

Gene therapy

Although adenoviruses and other viral forms (even synthetic viral particles) have been used to deliver DNA into the nuclei of cells to achieve genetic modification, only non-viral vectors will be discussed briefly here. A variety of constructs have been used in attempt to deliver DNA to the nucleus of cells and hence effect transfection. Mainly cationic systems are preferred because of their interaction with the negatively charged DNA. Such cationic nanoparticles and anionic DNA condense to form compact complexes, whose size, overall charge and lipophilicity can all affect uptake into cells, and subsequent behaviour in the cells. Figure 8.14 is one scheme for the process. Transport through the cytoplasm is an issue that is being explored actively. The cytoplasm is a complex mixture that is said to be 'molecularly crowded' with complex barriers such as the actin–myosin scaffolds, proteins and highly concentrated macromolecules, a hostile environment for ready diffusion of even the smallest constructs.

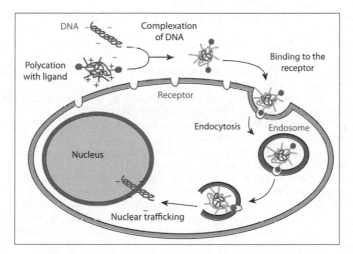

Figure 8.14 Schematic representation of complexation of DNA with a polycation (which could be a cationic dendrimer, a polycationic polymer, liposome or nanoparticle): complexation, binding to receptors, endocytotic uptake into endosomes and nuclear trafficking by way of the nuclear pore membrane. (From www.nano-lifesciences.com.)

Conclusions

With so many new materials and new means of transforming them into novel structures of a variety of shapes and sizes and surface characteristics, there is much scope for finding new means of delivering new and complex drugs in this post-genomic period. On the other hand, simple technologies may provide the answer to many of the problems of dosing individual patients. There are many opportunities for pharmacists to be involved in ensuring that the systems used in the clinic are well characterised, stable and reproducible so that we do not repeat the errors of the past. It is a dangerous exercise to attempt to predict the future, but one thing is guaranteed: if we probe the body even with new therapeutic agents based on endogenous species and transport them to sites where they are not naturally found, there will be unusual side-effects to look out for and to explain on the basis of the nature of the materials themselves, their biodistribution, and their biodegradation. There are exciting prospects.

References

1. Report. *Personalised Medicines: Hopes and Realities*. London: The Royal Society, 2005.
2. The Medicines and Healthcare products Regulatory Agency (MHRA). *The potential regulatory challenges of personalised medicine*. www.mhra.gov.uk.
3. Kaplan W, Laing R. *Priority Medicines for Europe and the World*, WHO: Geneva, 2004.
4. Standing JF, Tuleu C. Paediatric formulations: getting to the heart of the problem. *Int J Pharm* 2005; 300: 56–66.
5. Tuleu C. Paediatric formulations in practice. In: Costello I *et al.*, eds. *Paediatric Drug Handling*, ULLA Postgraduate Series. London: Pharmaceutical Press, 2007.

6. Costello I *et al. Paediatric Drug Handling*, ULLA Postgraduate Series. London: Pharmaceutical Press, 2007.

7. Florence AT. Neglected diseases, neglected devices, neglected patients? *Int J Pharm* 2008; 350: 1–2.

8. Standing JF, Tuleu C. Paediatric formulations: getting to the heart of the problem. *Int J Pharm* 2005; 300: 56–66.

9. Huang W *et al.* Levofloxacin implants with predetermined microstructure fabricated by three dimensional printing. *I J Pharm* 2007; 339: 33–38.

10. Rowe CW *et al.* Multimechanism oral dosage forms fabricated by three dimensional printing. *J Control Release* 2000; 66: 11–17.

11. Chen L *et al.* The microfabricated electrokinetic pump: a potential promising drug delivery technique. *Expert Opin Drug Deliv* 2007; 4: 119–129.

12. Thomsen J *et al.* Preliminary results of a new delivery system for gentamicin to the inner ear in patients with Menière's disease. *Eur Arch Otorhinolaryngol* 2000; 257: 362–365.

13. Ford C. Overcoming challenges on the path to combination product development. Pharmaceutical International. http://www.pharmaceutical-int.com/categories/combination-product-development/overcoming-challenges-combination-product-development.asp (accessed 20 September 2009).

14. Franz S. The trouble with making combination drugs. *Nat Rev Drug Discov* 2006; 5: 881–882.

15. DeBrabander C *et al.* Matrix minitablets based on starch/microcellulose wax mixtures. *Int J Pharm* 2000; 199: 195–203.

16. DeBrabander C *et al.* Development and evaluation of sustained release mini-matrices by hot melt extrusion. *J Control Release* 2003; 89: 235–244.

17. Pakatip Ruenraroengsak. Studies of diffusion in cells using a self-fluorescent dendrimer. London: University of London, The School of Pharmacy, 2007(PhD thesis).

18. Thassu D *et al.*, eds. *Nanoparticulate Drug Delivery Systems*. New York: Informa Healthcare, 2007.

19. Torchilin VP, ed. *Nanoparticulates as Drug Carriers*. London: Imperial College Press, 2006.

20. Ozin GA, Arsenault AC. *Nanochemistry: A Chemical Approach to Nanotechnology*. Cambridge: Royal Society of Chemistry, 2005.

21. Drexler KE. *Nanosystems. Molecular Machinery, Manufacturing and Computation.* New York: Wiley, 1992.

22. *Nanomedicine. Nanotechnology for Health.* European Technology Platform: Strategic Agenda for Nanomedicine. November 2006.

23. Roco MC. Nanotechnology: convergence with modern biology and medicine. *Curr Opin Biotechnol* 2003; 14: 337–346.

24. Florence AT, Halbert GW. Lipoproteins and microemulsions as carriers of therapeutic and chemical agents. In: Shaw JM ed. *Lipoproteins as Carriers of Pharmacological Agents.* London: Taylor & Francis/CRC Press, 1991.

25. Corbin IR *et al.* Low-density lipoprotein nanoparticles as magnetic resonance imaging contrast agents. *Neoplasia* 2006; 8: 488–498.

26. Kreuter J. Nanoparticles – a historical perspective. *Int J Pharm* 2007; 331: 1–10.

27. Hartley GS. *Aqueous Solutions of Paraffin-chain Salts. A study in micelle formation.* Paris: Hermann & Cie, 1936.

28. McBain MEL, Hutchinson E. *Solubilization and Related Phenomena.* New York: Academic Press, 1955.

29. Elworthy PH *et al. Solubilization by Surface Active Agents*. London: Chapman and Hall, 1968.

30. Sanchez A, Alonso MJ. Nanoparticulate carriers for ocular drug delivery. In: Torchilin VP, ed. *Nanoparticles as Drug Carriers*. London: Imperial College Press, 2006: 649–673.

31. Jung T *et al.* Biodegradable nanoparticles for oral delivery of peptides: is there a role for polymers to affect mucosal uptake? *Eur J Pharm Biopharm* 2000; 50: 147–160.

32. Lu W *et al.* Cationic albumin-conjugated pegylated nanoparticles allow gene delivery into brain tumors via intravenous administration. *Cancer Res* 2006; 66: 11878–11887.
33. Maincent P *et al.* Lymphatic targeting of polymeric nanoparticles after intraperitoneal administration in rats. *Pharm Res* 1992; 9: 1534–1539.
34. Guzman LA *et al.* Local intraluminal infusion of biodegradable polymeric nanoparticles. *Circulation* 1996; 94: 1441–1448.
35. Pandey R, Khuller GK. Subcutaneous nanoparticle-based antitubercular chemotherapy in an experimental model. *J Antimicrob Chemother* 2004; 54: 266–268.
36. Zhou X *et al.* The effect of conjugation to gold particles on the ability of low molecular weight chitosan to transfer DNA vaccine. *Biomaterials* 2007; 29: 111–117.
37. Allemann E *et al.* Distribution, kinetics and elimination of radioactivity after intravenous and intramuscular injection of ^{14}C savoxepine loaded poly(d,l-lactic acid) nanospheres in rats. *J Control Release* 1994; 29: 97–104.
38. Sham JO-H *et al.* Formulation and characterization of spray-dried powders containing nanoparticles for aerosol delivery to the lung. *Int J Pharm* 2004; 269: 457–467.
39. Oyewumi MO *et al.* Comparison of cell uptake, biodistribution and tumor retention of folate-coated and PEG-coated gadolinium nanoparticles in tumor-bearing mice. *J Control Release* 2004; 95: 613–626.
40. Kreuter J. Nanoparticulate carriers for drug delivery to the brain. In: Torchilin VP, ed. *Nanoparticles as Drug Carriers*. London: Imperial College Press, 2006: 527–547.
41. Phillips W. Nanoparticles for targeting lymphatics. In: Torchilin VP, ed. *Nanoparticles as Drug Carriers*. London: Imperial College Press, 2006: 598–608.
42. De TK *et al.* Polycarboxylic acid nanoparticles for ophthalmic drug delivery: an *ex vivo* evaluation with human cornea. *J Microencapsul* 2004; 21: 841–855.
43. Florence AT. Nanoparticle uptake by the oral route: fulfilling its potential? *Drug Discov Technol* 2005; 2: 75–81.
44. Baker GL *et al.* Inhalation toxicity and lung toxicities of C_{60} fullerene nanoparticles and microparticles. *Toxicol Sci* 2008; 101: 122–131.
45. Owens DE, Peppas NA. Opsonization, biodistribution, and pharmacokinetics of polymeric nanoparticles. *Int J Pharm* 2006; 307: 93–102.
46. Stoff-Khalili MA *et al.* Mesenchymal stem cells as a vehicle for targeted delivery of CRSds to lung metastases of breast carcinoma. *Breast Cancer Res Treat* 2007; 105: 156–167.
47. Barbash IM *et al.* Systemic delivery of bone marrow-derived mesenchymal stem cells to the infracted myocardium. *Circulation* 2003; 108: 863–868.
48. Rosen MR. Are stem cells drugs? The regulation of stem cell research and development *Circulation* 2006; 114: 1992–2000.
49. Heldman AW, Hare JM. Cell therapy for myocardial infarction: special delivery. *J Mol Cell Cardiol* 2008; 44: 473–476.
50. Strauer BE, Kornowski R. Stem cell therapy in perspective. *Circulation* 2003; 107: 929–934.
51. de Silva R, Lederman RJ. Delivery and tracking of therapeutic cell preparations for clinical cardiovascular applications. *Cytotherapy* 2004; 6: 608–614.
52. Grossman PM *et al.* Incomplete retention after direct myocardial injection. *Catheter Cardiovasc Interv* 2002; 55: 392–397.
53. Sittinger M *et al.* Current strategies for cell delivery in cartilage and bone regeneration. *Curr Opin Biotechnol* 2004; 15: 411–418.
54. Richardson TP *et al.* Polymeric system for dual growth factor delivery. *Nat Biotechnol* 2001; 19: 1029–1034.

Index